Sassy Mamas
and Other Plays

Wittliff Collections Literary Series

Steven L. Davis, General Editor

Sassy Mamas
and Other Plays

~~~~~~

Celeste Bedford Walker

Foreword by Eileen J. Morris

With an Introduction by Sandra M. Mayo

TEXAS A&M UNIVERSITY PRESS
College Station

This paper meets the requirements of ANSI/NISO Z39.48-1992
(Permanence of Paper).
Binding materials have been chosen for durability.

Library of Congress Control Number: 2022947626
Identifiers: LCCN: 2022947626 | ISBN 9781648431203 (cloth) |
ISBN 9781648431210 (paperback) | ISBN 9781648431227 (ebook)
LC record available at https://lccn.loc.gov/2022947626

Contents

Foreword

Reflections on Celeste Bedford Walker
from the Ensemble Theatre

Eileen J. Morris

There will always be a place for you at the Ensemble Theatre, Celeste.

> —George Hawkins, Founder,
> the Ensemble Theatre,
> Houston, Texas

Celeste Bedford Walker is a dramatist whose award-winning plays have been produced in New York, regional, and international theaters. While the *New York Times* has praised her work as "forceful, well-crafted," and "vigorous social satire," our audiences are proud to claim this master storyteller as one of our own.

In the 1980s, at the start of my career, George Hawkins, founder of the Ensemble Theatre, hired me to work at the Ensemble both as an actor and as the theater's first managing director. It was in that capacity that I was introduced to Houston playwright Celeste Bedford Walker. When I think of Celeste, the words *historian, collaborator, embodiment of character, nuance,* and *authenticity* come to mind. When we first met, I stood in awe of this petite woman with a quiet presence who packed her scripts with love and a joyful heart. I have always admired Celeste's ability to craft and present stories from a place of truth that captures, reflects, and deeply resonates within the Black communities that we serve. Celeste is the type of playwright that writes what she knows, and she knows *a lot* because of her research. She has a beautiful way of incorporating the actor's vision and thoughts into what she has on the written page, yet she is not uncomfortable with editing to serve the needs of the character or the overall story. When I think of community, everything about Celeste comes to mind. That is why her relationship with the Ensemble Theatre has been so long-standing.

The Ensemble has produced over ten of her plays in our history, and I have had the honor of directing two productions and acting in one. Celeste has a thirty-nine-year history with the Ensemble Theatre, from the early days, in which two of her plays were presented at the old location (1010 Tuam). The majority of her work was commissioned and produced at the current location (3535 Main Street). Our audiences were introduced to plays such as *Over Forty*, a musical journey of song and dialogue; *Distant Voices*, the commissioned play in which voices from the grave were resurrected, hunting for a location to call home; and *Brothers, Sisters, Husbands and Wives*, the commissioned comedic story of siblings and their mates.

In the early 2000s, the Ensemble Theatre produced her plays *Praise the Lord, and Raise the Roof!* and *Harlem after Hours*, cowritten with Audrey H. Lawson. *I, Barbara Jordan*, one of the Ensemble Theatre's signature touring education plays, tells the story of Texas congresswoman Barbara Jordan and her journey from childhood to adulthood. *Where My Girls At?* was produced with high school students. The hilarious play *Sassy Mamas*, produced by the Ensemble Theatre, made every mature woman feel important, sexy, and needed—with a little help from the male species. And pre-COVID, we commissioned her holiday musical, *More Than Christmas*. Over the years, we have produced staged readings, both virtual and in-person, of Celeste's plays, among them *Greenwood: An American Dream Destroyed* and *Black Spurs*; both plays have educational and informative content as well as awareness of our community.

When asked to write about Celeste and her partnership with the Ensemble Theatre, I decided to ask other artists who have worked with Celeste over the years as actors, directors, and producers to reflect their thoughts. Wayne DeHart (appeared in *The Wreckin' Ball* and *Camp Logan*): "Celeste is the type of writer that writes about people in the neighborhood and is open to their total experience." Shirley Whitmore (actress and historian for *Distant Voices*): "Celeste understands the language of Black people and how to shape their stories. And that the people are real with historical content speaking in many varied voices." Alex Morris (actor, director, and producer of Celeste's plays *Once in a Wifetime*, *Camp Logan*, and *Sassy Mamas*): "Celeste's attention to detail and her ability to highlight the heroism of her characters are essential factors in her success."

Peter Webster (creative concept and director of *Distant Voices*): "In all of her plays, in each individual voice, all of her characters speak in many languages—what they wished they had said, what they said, what we heard them say, what we know they meant. Truth laid bare."

From such foremothers as Alice Childress, Adrienne Kennedy, Lorraine Hansberry, and Pearl Cleage, Black women playwrights have shared a unique vision of the American experience. So it is with Celeste Bedford Walker, whose work has been lauded by the *Washington Post* as a "textbook example of how to simultaneously entertain and educate an audience." Her body of work is prolific, and her call to service, Texas roots, and abiding love for Black people are as strong as a hurricane. The words that George Hawkins said to Celeste in the early 1980s ring true to this day: "Celeste, we have an artistic home for you at the Ensemble Theatre—now and always."

Introduction

Sandra M. Mayo

With authentic dialogue and captivating storytelling filled with humor and pathos, Celeste Bedford Walker's dazzling plays bring to life the rich history and experiences of African Americans in Texas and beyond. She's written of the tragedy of Black soldiers caught in a World War I riot in Houston as well as the shocking 1921 rampage in Tulsa that killed over three hundred people. She's also penned a lively murder mystery set around a class reunion, an ensemble historical pageant filled with music, and a witty feminist comedy that reshapes our thinking about Black women's lives. Along the way, Walker has earned scores of prestigious awards and made dozens of notable productions around the country.

Walker, a veteran of the Houston theater scene, born and raised in Houston, attended Jack Yates Senior High and Texas Southern University, both historically Black institutions. After studying English and journalism at Texas Southern, Walker worked as a data processor. Admiration of Toni Morrison briefly led her to consider writing novels until she discovered she was more interested in dialogue. The thoughtful examination of the Black experience in the plays of Lorraine Hansberry (e.g., *A Raisin in the Sun* [1958]) and the romantic comedies of Neil Simon (e.g., *Barefoot in the Park* [1963]) sparked and shaped her theatrical style. Her love of literature and the arts soon led her to seek out creative activity in her community at the Black Arts Center in Houston's Fifth Ward. At the center, she immersed herself in the Black pride and assertiveness of the Black Arts movement of the sixties and seventies. She helped organize the Writers Clinic Inc. with a group of artists who helped launch her first play, *Sister, Sister*, in 1978 (renamed *Once in a Wifetime*), directed by Alma Y. Carriere and produced by Shirley "Sage" Edwards, with Operation Breadbasket. Thus began a lifelong passion for developing and sharing African American cultural stories for the stage, often juxtaposing the serious with the comic and returning frequently to African American women's issues.

Celeste Bedford Walker's extensive canon includes over twenty-five produced stage plays. Her honors include the National Black Theatre's August Wilson playwriting award for significant contributions to Black and American theater, the Beverly Hills / Hollywood NAACP Theatre Awards for best playwright and best play, and the Lifetime Achievement Award from the Texas Institute of Letters, one of the highest literary honors in Texas.

Walker is perhaps best known for her celebrated historical drama *Camp Logan* (1987), which has been performed at major venues across the country, including the Kennedy Center. *Camp Logan* is also featured in the anthology *Acting Up and Getting Down* (University of Texas Press, 2014). Her other plays featured in this collection have also garnered wide acclaim. The romantic comedy *Sassy Mamas* (2007) has received numerous production recognitions: BroadwayWorld.com Houston, best play, 2017; AUDELCO award, outstanding ensemble, H.A.D.L.E.Y. Players, Black Spectrum Theatre, 2020; NAACP Image Awards, Sparkling City Entertainment, 2016. Her historical pageant *Distant Voices* (1998) was selected as a finalist for the international Susan Smith Blackburn Prize for outstanding work by a female playwright in English-speaking theater. Her drama *Greenwood: An American Dream Destroyed* (2021) was produced in Tulsa as part of the one hundredth anniversary commemoration of the notorious riot.

From *Once in a Wifetime* and *Over Forty* to *Sassy Mamas*

Like many Black feminist playwrights, Walker creates an authentic voice for Black women on the stage, clarifying their status in a moment in history and dumping stereotypes.* Her significant feminist journey began with her early play *Once in a Wifetime* (originally *Sister, Sister* [1978]). It continued with *Over Forty* (1989) and culminated in her hit *Sassy Mamas* (2007), which has been produced all over the nation.

In *Once in a Wifetime*, set in the 1970s, married to Irma, mild-mannered middle-class Black husband Willie, under the influence of a Pan-African organization, attempts to practice polygamy by bringing home a second wife. Irma, with the assistance of her feisty liberated mother, "flips the

*Lisa M. Anderson, *Black Feminism in Contemporary Drama* (Urbana: University of Illinois Press, 2008), 115.

switch" on Willie by employing a handsome French West Indian hunk for herself in a plot that brings Willie back to monogamy.

A decade later, with *Over Forty*, set in the 1980s, Walker presents a group of professional Black women who remember the vigor and joy of their youth (often with popular songs) as well as the challenges along the way. The ladies—an investment banker, a judge, a community and church organizer, and a recently divorced mother—defy societal definitions of older women by declaring that they are still productive, vital, and vibrant over forty.

With *Sassy Mamas*, Walker returns her audacious ladies to the stage, shaping the course of their lives. These mature women have decided to reverse the paradigm of older men with younger women, thereby opening themselves to the possibility of finding companionship with younger men. The comedy unfolds with sassy, sophisticated Black women who exemplify self-confidence, verve, financial security, career success, and agency, set in a triad of beauty—luxury apartments in DC, elegant clothing, and attractive physical form (both females and their male lovers). Laughs abound in this romantic comedy filled with witty banter and comic business, though not without serious self-reflection and growth. Walker juxtaposes serious, heartrending moments (as in the narration of the pain of loss by the widow [Jo Billie] and betrayal of the wife [Mary]) with joyous dancing to the characters' favorite rhythm and blues recordings and kinky sex scenes (titillating but not pornographic). Jo Billie, Mary, and Wilhelmina mirror the lives of their privileged counterparts in the real world. Hospital administrator (a job once held by former first lady Michelle Obama) Jo Billie is recently widowed. World traveler, organizer, and women's club member Mary brings to mind many well-educated wives of successful Black men. Never-married, career-driven national security adviser Wilhelmina seems inspired by former secretary of state and national security advisor Condoleezza Rice.

While many writers have explored the Black female struggling underclass in relation to race, sex, and gender, Walker has consistently expressed the challenges and triumphs of the more privileged Black women—educated, spirited, empowered middle-class women bonding as they set the table of their lives.

The Historical Plays:
Camp Logan, Distant Voices, and
Greenwood: An American Dream Destroyed

Walker's celebrated historical works recover and remember significant moments in African American history, presenting the stories in a creative medium that makes them more accessible. Her plays are part of the American canon of over two hundred historical dramas written by African American playwrights since the late 1800s. Walker began her journey reimagining Black history for the stage with *Camp Logan*, first directed and produced by Lindi Yeni, with Kuumba House Theatre in 1987. In 1990, with a grant from San Antonio's Carver Cultural Community Center, she formed Mountaintop Productions to tour the play.

Growing up in Houston, Walker heard references to the Camp Logan riot and had the opportunity to interview Houstonians whose relatives had been caught up in the event. Though she studied the archives in the Texas Southern University library, the Black history section of the downtown Houston library, and Robert Haynes's *Night of Violence*, she found the oral history an especially rich source for the emotional and personal stories of the soldiers.

Camp Logan is a two-act tragedy in eight scenes bookended with a prologue and epilogue. It is a faithful retelling of the 1917 Houston, Texas, military riot, with the events leading up to the riot, the carnage, and the sentences meted out to the Black soldiers. The action revolves around six Black soldiers who are a composite of the group immersed in the tumultuous event along with their White captain. Walker frames and imbues the work with the facts of the event but creatively reimagines the dialogue of the soldiers in the barracks. Walker's re-creation of the language of her male military characters is especially notable, since she is a female with no military experience. She brings the soldiers' humanity to life through their camaraderie in the barracks; they discuss stories of home, women, brushes with discrimination, and hatred. "There must be something worth fighting and dying for" rises to the top as the salient trope. In saluting courage under fire, Walker's *Camp Logan* evokes memories of the celebrated movies *Glory* (1989) and *Tuskegee Airmen* (1995).

With *Distant Voices* (1998), Walker chronicles the history of the Houston metro area, one of the largest Black populations in Texas. Outside of New York's Harlem, very few cities with significant Black populations have received cultural attention in the theater. Walker resurrected over six thousand records of inhabitants of the College Memorial Park Cemetery, the second oldest African American cemetery in Houston, Texas. She lifts the skeleton of stories from not only archival records but also gravestones, news clippings, funeral programs, and oral history to bring them to the fore, fleshing them out in authentic, creative dialogue. *Distant Voices* unfolds in the tradition of African American pageants as first exemplified in the work of W. E. B. Du Bois with *Star of Ethiopia* (1913). Narration, chronological development, and museum-like montages (displays) interspersed with a blend of period music from 1840 to 1970 penetrate the airwaves from a ghost radio. Walker presents the folksy rhythms of a diverse group of African American Houstonians, from the uneducated to the college educated—slaves, ex-slaves, entrepreneurs, politicians, and preachers. The pageant structure is episodic rather than climactic, but the playwright astutely provides closure with characters reemerging at the end of the play, wrapping up their experiences with messages that lift up hope and possibility.

Walker's sweeping view takes Black Houston as a microcosm that sheds light on the macrocosm. It contributes to the understanding of the American story writ large.

Walker's historical drama *Greenwood: An American Dream Destroyed* reimagines the 1921 destruction of over thirty-five blocks of a prominent oil-rich African American community and the massacre of over three hundred citizens. From historical records, with the skillful development of fictional characters—the Boley family and friends, a representative composite of the people caught up in the tragedy—Walker brings the tragedy to light in its compelling emotional intensity.

The ambience in the brightly colored, cheerful setting of the restaurant where the major action of *Greenwood* takes place complements the talk of Solene Boley's sojourn in Paris, Black soldiers' glorious parades in Harlem after World War I, Black women involved in the women's suffrage activities, and the good food Bill is preparing for the Memorial Day festivities. Nonetheless, the happy talk in this cozy, homey, public environment is peppered with foreshadowing of trouble to come as they discuss the jealousy and greed of their White neighbors. As they gather, with little immediate concern other than where they should be placed in journalist Pritchard's photo, Walker effectively slashes the peace with the entrance of Jimmie rushing in with the shocking and terrifying news that he has been accused of attacking a White woman.

The playwright shapes a fast-moving collage of narrative images of the atrocities visited upon the Black community as the atmosphere quickly shifts to anxiety and fear. She adds technical notes for flashing lights, gunfire, and explosions to create an atmosphere of the community under a relentless siege. Horror is piled upon horror as the outsider journalist Pritchard and the Boley family and friends detail burning, bombing, theft, and murder in reactive monologues filled with fear and despair until silence reigns. Then with the epilogue, the playwright caps the shocking denouement with a gathering of the dead and survivors for a final dirge. The quality of the storytelling keeps the audience on edge until the despicable end.

Walker's *Greenwood* made history in Tulsa, opening in 2021 during the one-hundred-year anniversary of the destruction of the Black town from which the play takes its name (produced by Theatre North at the Tulsa Fine Arts Center). Now available in film, produced by Karamu House in Cleveland, Ohio, *Greenwood* is rising as one of Walker's most significant contributions to the history genre.

Reunion in Bartersville and Serving the Community

With *Reunion in Bartersville* (1983), featured at the National Black Theatre Festival in 2019, Walker not only contributes an entertaining and compelling work but also expands the African American literary canon with the murder mystery genre. In the play, the Bartersville High School class of 1933 gathers for its fiftieth reunion at the home of classmate Janie Mae Hopper. As the classmates and their spouses and friends gather and reminisce, they have a shocking and unhappy surprise addition to the party: A. J. Hamm, a former classmate and convicted murderer presumed dead. What then unfolds is a hilarious and suspense-filled investigation of the crime Hamm claims sent him unjustly to jail.

Walker's well-rounded characters are fleshed out with language, clothing, experiences, and interactions that come across as believable and natural. Diction changes from character to character based on their education (or lack thereof) and affectations. The style is heightened realism, and the audience members are made to feel as if they are listening in on the conversation as metaphorical flies on the wall.

Reunion is a tightly organized climactic plot in which each scene evokes the next in a pattern of cause-and-effect actions and reactions, with each character's story overlapping with others. It has all the popular techniques of the "Who done it?" drama—fear, menace, suspense, and surprise. Intertwined in the details of this murder mystery are thought-provoking themes regarding the face and the mask, the pull of relationships, and the need to go home.

As *Reunion* demonstrates, variety abounds in Walker's canon. Her other full-length plays include *Praise the Lord, and Raise the Roof!*, a foot-stomping gospel musical; *The Wreckin' Ball*, a story about a community and a family going through gentrification; *Brothers, Sisters, Husbands and Wives*, a provocative soap opera about a zany dysfunctional family; and *Harlem after Hours*, a swinging musical about nightlife during the Harlem Renaissance. The one-act plays include histories, fantasies, and comedies as exemplified by *Noble Lofton, Buffalo Soldier, The Red Blood of War, Adam and Eve, Revisited, Spirits, Smokes Bayou, The Boule, Jack Yates, Blacks in the Methodist Church, Hip Hoppin' the Dream, Reparations Day,* and *The History of Wheeler Baptist Church.* Performed before thousands of students over the years, Walker's youth theater includes *Freedom Train, The African Talking Drum, Where My Girls At?, Giants in the Land, Fabulous African Fables, Black Diamonds,* and *I, Barbara Jordan.*

With diverse genres, bold subject choices, meticulous research, and authentic language and characters, Celeste Bedford Walker, a sassy mama herself, has enriched American theater while preserving and ennobling in art African American history and culture.

Sassy Mamas
and Other Plays

The Wittliff Collections *present...*

A staged reading from:

CAMP LOGAN

The award-winning play about the mutiny of black soldiers in Houston, Texas — and the largest murder trial in U.S. History

Written by Celeste Bedford Walker

T.C. Hawkins, court-martialed and hanged, 1917 Texas

Interviewer
Sandra Mayo

Director
Sidney Rushing

A selection from the play will be read by Texas State students.

| Javuan Butler | Kiara Daniels | Jack Durham | Jordan Gregson | Malik James | Evan James Ledet | Michael Moody |

Camp Logan

A World War I Military Drama in Two Acts

Synopsis

On the night of August 23, 1917, after weeks of harassment from the city police and White civilians, about a hundred members of the 24th Infantry Regiment marched to the west end of Houston from their bivouac at the construction site of Camp Logan. Along the way, they fired on startled civilians who blundered into their path. When they arrived in the San Felipe district, they fought a running battle with members of the Houston police, other military units, and armed citizens.

The men of the 24th were Black; their opponents White. Before the confrontation ended, twenty persons were dead or mortally wounded in the only racially motivated riot in US history to claim more White lives than Black.

Less than four months later, thirteen soldiers of the 24th were hanged without appeal or review under sentence by the largest courts-martial ever convened in the United States. Within a year, six more soldiers were hanged on the same spot.

Celeste Bedford Walker's depiction of the incident offers us a riveting glimpse into the hearts and souls of seven soldiers—a Black sergeant, five of his infantrymen, and their White captain, who eventually betrays them. By containing the action in the barracks, Walker concentrates on the reasons behind the attitudes and acts of a loyal division of soldiers who eventually come to the conclusion that they must march against an American city. In the process, Walker creates a diverse and unforgettable cross section of characters, putting flesh and blood to a cold, infamous paragraph of American history.

August 23, 2017, marked the one hundredth anniversary of the Camp Logan incident. Performances of this timely and timeless play continue

3

to prompt discussions about the racial divide that pervades American society today.

Cast of Characters

<u>Sgt. McKinney</u> Forty years old. A spit-and-polish career soldier from Kentucky. Dedicated to the Army, almost to the point of fanaticism. Illiterate, but a natural leader, he's a strict disciplinarian, but respects his men.

<u>Gweely Brown</u> Thirty years old. A big, fun-loving fellow from Texas, he's been in the Army for twelve years. He chooses to fight the oppression of the era with laughter. However, he's fierce when finally riled.

<u>Joe Moses</u> Thirty years old. Small of stature, quick tempered, he's been in the Army ten years. If he wasn't in the Army, he'd probably be in jail. From New York, he and Gweely are best friends.

<u>Jacques "Bugaloosa" Honoré</u> Twenty-five-year-old Creole from Louisiana. He plays a musical instrument and does minstrel shows with Gweely. Haunted by memories of a lynching attempt on his life, he finds comfort in whiskey and the Virgin Mary.

<u>Robert Franciscus</u> Twenty-five-year-old "ladies' man" from Chicago. Ambitious and handsome, he's one of the few in his company with a high school education. Although more educated than many of the others, he gets along well with his fellow soldiers and officers alike.

<u>Charles Hardin</u> This nineteen-year-old has been in the Army only six months. Fiercely patriotic and highly intelligent. From Minnesota, he has been exposed to very few members of his own race.

<u>Capt. Zuelke</u> Thirty-five-year-old White officer of Company "I." Career soldier, also from Kentucky. An alcoholic. He has an ambivalent relationship with the men.

Scene

Outside the Army camp, Camp Logan, in Houston, Texas

Time

Summer morning, 1917

> *(CADENCE: "Oh here we go, oh here we go, we're at it again, we're at it again, we're moving out, we're moving in, etc.!")*

PROLOGUE

SETTING: Outside Camp Logan, Houston, Texas.

ON RISE: It's a rainy morning, around 6 a.m. In the BLACKOUT, we hear the sound of a TRAIN ENGINE coming to a halt, delivering the soldiers to the camp. Offstage we hear the Camp Logan Quartet singing an a cappella rendition of "Buffalo Soldier." CAPT. ZUELKE enters, dressed in an Army-issue rain slicker. He salutes and addresses the audience as the townspeople of Houston. As he talks, slides from the Camp Logan Exhibit may be shown.

CAPT. ZUELKE

Good evening folks, I'm Captain Harris Zuelke of the 24th Infantry, Company "I." Now that Colonel Gentry has briefed you on the battalion in general, I'm glad to get the chance to tell you something about my men in "I" Company in particular.

For the past eleven months, these boys have been stationed in the desert of Columbus, New Mexico, chasing Pancho Villa. And let me tell ya something, after being out there in that desert, we're mighty happy to be here in this good ol' Houston rain.

(Beat)

This battalion has a fine record. We've pulled duty out west in the Indian Wars, served in the Philippines, and in the Yellow Fever camps in Siboney, Cuba, and went up San Juan Hill with Teddy Roosevelt. These boys are bearcat fighters and I'm proud to serve with them! Sergeants!

(SGT. MCKINNEY marches the men onstage to CADENCE)

SGT. MCKINNEY

Tent-hut!

(Company brought to ORDER ARMS. CAPT. ZUELKE inspects the troops)

CAPT. ZUELKE

Parade!

SGT. MCKINNEY

Parade!

CAPT. ZUELKE
Rest!

SGT. MCKINNEY
Rest!
>   (*THE MEN stand at parade rest*)

CAPT. ZUELKE
I know the idea of 654 colored troops being stationed near your town has got some of you White citizens of this town worried. But let me assure you, no need for alarm with these boys. I ought to know, I've served with colored soldiers all of the fifteen years I've been in the Army, and I can truthfully say that these boys are the best of their race—they're intelligent, hardworking and as disciplined as any White soldiers I've seen.
>   (*Beat*)

Now, I understand that some of you still remember the Brownsville, Texas, incident a few years back. But that was just an isolated incident. There are some ten thousand colored soldiers in the regular Army, and for the most part they're happy, cheerful, easygoing fellows, who aren't looking to do any violence against White citizens.
>   (*Beat*)

But to help soothe some of your fears about any violence occurring here, let me give you the rules and regulations of the camp: First, only sentries on duty will carry firearms, and they won't be allowed to <u>load</u> those weapons except in case of an emergency, such as somebody trying to break into camp or somebody trying to steal supplies. And of course no White folks'll be doin' that. The soldiers are divided into four grades, and only the first three grades will be allowed to leave camp. So, set your minds at ease folks, you don't have to worry about any hotheads walking among the civilians, only soldiers with good conduct will be allowed into town. And you men of the press will get your chance at the soldiers, but first I want the citizens to observe the well-organized way these boys put up camp. They'll have the latrines dug, grass cut, tents up, in record time! Thank you for coming out, and we look forward to a pleasant stay here in Houston.
>   (*A TOWNSMAN planted in the audience jumps up, shouting hate-filled remarks*)

TOWNSMAN
Put those monkeys back on the train!

CAPT. ZUELKE
Sergeants!
> *(SGT. MCKINNEY leads THE MEN offstage)*

SGT. MCKINNEY
Tent-hut!
> *(THE MEN snap to attention, eyes straight ahead)*
> Your left, your left, your left, right, ha!

THE SOLDIERS
> *(Singing)*

Oh here we go, oh here we go, we're at it again, we're at it again, we're movin' out, we're movin' in!

SGT. MCKINNEY
Your left, your left, your left, right, left . . . etc.!

TOWNSMAN
They touch our women, it'll be a lynching!

SGT. MCKINNEY
Your left, your left, your left, right!

TOWNSMAN
Remember Brownsville!

THE SOLDIERS
Oh here we go, we're at it again . . . !

TOWNSMAN
You niggers better not come into town!

THE SOLDIERS
> *(Eyes straight ahead, singing)*

We're movin' out, we're movin' in!

END PROLOGUE

ACT I

SCENE 1

SETTING: The giant US flag on scrim provides the backdrop of the tent barracks
set of "I" Company. The living accommodations consist of a bunk bed upstage
center for SGT. MCKINNEY and FRANCISCUS. *(FRANCISCUS on lower
berth)* A wooden set of shelves, with water basins, ladle, water bucket, towels
and other prop items, is on one side of the stage. The stacked rifles are on the
opposite side. The US flag and the yellow 24th Infantry blockhouse flag are
prominently displayed. Four cots, two to the right, two to the left, with footlockers and duffel bags for GWEELY, MOSES, BUGALOOSA, and HARDIN, are
downstage. A colorful Mexican blanket is placed at the foot of MOSES' cot.
Next to BUGALOOSA's cot is a crude altar to the Virgin Mary, and his cornet.

ON RISE: A few minutes later. The lights FADE UP to the sound of a STEADY RAIN
and CLAP OF THUNDER. Hot, tired and wet, the men run in from the rain.
MOSES gets a wash basin from the shelf, and begins washing up. He's quickly
followed in by BUGALOOSA, who immediately drops to his knees before
his altar, and FRANCISCUS, who's trying to get egg stains off his shirt. As
HARDIN puts away his belongings, he's dismayed to discover that the tent is
leaking over his cot.

MOSES
(Running in)
These Southern crackers acting up already!

FRANCISCUS
(Taking off his shirt)
Damn rednecks. Look at this, eggs all over my uniform!

BUGALOOSA
Welcome to the South boys.

FRANCISCUS
I finally get a uniform with just the right fit and now—I'm sure glad
Priscilla wasn't out there to see this.

MOSES
They better be glad they didn't hit me.

BUGALOOSA
(*Getting whiskey bottle*)
They say we better not come into town tonight.

MOSES
Hell, I'm going into town!
(*GWEELY runs into the barracks, shaking out his rain slicker*)

GWEELY
Well, at least we got camp up before that downpour come.

BUGALOOSA
Yeah, I think we broke our record this time.

MOSES
Rain and nothing else going keep me in camp tonight. I can't wait to see what old Houston town's got to offer. Gweely, you sure they got plenty colored girls here?

GWEELY
Do a snake crawl?

MOSES
Well, how come we didn't see any out there? You and Bugaloosa swore up and down they were going to swamp us.

GWEELY
They is, they is. But ain't no colored gal gon' be out before day in the morning, in the rain.

FRANCISCUS
No decent one anyway.

BUGALOOSA
Yeah, none of 'em are that patriotic.

FRANCISCUS
Priscilla and some of her church friends were planning to meet us, but now since they sneaked us in in the dead of night—

MOSES
Like we're criminals!

FRANCISCUS
But that's all right. Priscilla sent me this colored newspaper, and listen to what it has to say about us.
    (Reading)
    "Although the White populace is experiencing some consternation about colored troops being stationed here in town, we at the Texas Freedman's Press hail these fine young men as a credit to our race. When the White soldiers from the 5th Infantry came to town, there was a big hoopla, and flags flew from every post. Let's give the 24th the same honor. Wake up Houston! This is 1917!"

GWEELY
That's right, Houston, this is 1917!

BUGALOOSA
Wake up!

MOSES
'Cause the "Deuce-Four" is here!

HARDIN
    (Looking up)
Do you fellows realize that it's leaking in here?
    (THEY seem to notice HARDIN for the first time)

BUGALOOSA
    (Good-naturedly)
Oh, that'll stop when the rain stops.
    (THE MEN laugh. HARDIN wipes raindrops from his face)

HARDIN
These tents need mending.

GWEELY
Where you say you from, boy?

HARDIN
Minnesota.

GWEELY
Min-ni-sota? Hear that place so cold, it freeze the balls off a brass monkey.

HARDIN
Well, yes sir, it does get pretty cold at home.

GWEELY
Didn't even know they had no colored in Min-ni-sota.

HARDIN
Not many like they have here in the South, sir. In my hometown there were only two colored families—the Nesbits and us Hardins.

MOSES
Still haven't figured out why they'd throw a draftee like you in with us regulars.

HARDIN
    (Peeved)
I'm not a draftee, I volunteered. I quit college to join up and I've been in the Army six whole months now and I—

BUGALOOSA
Y'all hear that? Six months he say. Well now, I suppose that make him a real soldier all right.
    (THEY laugh)

GWEELY

Tell you one thing boy, you lucky to be in the 24th, especially "I" Company. We'll learn you how to be a soldier.

FRANCISCUS

So, you quit college to join up huh?

HARDIN

Oh yes. It was quite evident to me from newspaper articles that this country was going to have to go to war, so I joined up to be ready.

FRANCISCUS

I went to college at home in Chicago for a while.

HARDIN

Then you quit to join the war effort too?

FRANCISCUS
        (Laughing)
Hell naw. I quit to join the <u>Franciscus</u> effort. When my pa got sick, I took over his job at the slaughterhouse. But I got tired of looking at those bloody sides of beef, and decided to hitch up about five years ago.

HARDIN
        (Fervently)
Yes well, my conscience dictated that I put my education on hold, because I feel that any man, colored or White, who is not willing to fight and die for this country, is not worth his weight in salt!

GWEELY
        (Rolling a cigarette)
Speak boy, speak!

HARDIN
        (Sheepishly)
Well . . . I guess I do feel rather strongly about this war, sir, but I—

MOSES
Will you stop calling him sir?

GWEELY
Shut up, Moses. Let the boy show some respect if he want to.

HARDIN
Well, I feel as William Burghardt Du Bois feels, he says that—

GWEELY
Who??

FRANCISCUS
W.E.B. Du Bois.

GWEELY
Oh yeah, I remember now, that's the feller you be telling us about, 'Cis-
cus. The one with the N-A-A (beat) A-C-P?

HARDIN
          (Passionately)
Du Bois says that this war is "an end and also a beginning." He says
"never again will the darker people of this world occupy just the place
we have before . . ."
          (MOSES crosses the tent to throw out dirty water)
    "And after we have proved ourselves worthy by fighting and dying for
this country, a grateful nation will gladly give us the recognition and
respect that the White man now enjoys!"

GWEELY
          (Impressed)
Boy, you sound like a professor.
          (A CLAP OF THUNDER as MOSES rushes back in)

MOSES
It's coming down in buckets out there.

BUGALOOSA
    (Shining his cornet)
Hope it slack up before we get out tonight.

MOSES
I don't care if it's raining horseshit, I'm going into town tonight.

GWEELY
Me too, if I got to paddle a canoe.

MOSES
Anyway, this rain looks good, after being stuck out there in the desert, chasing Pancho Villa's ass.

HARDIN
You chased Pancho Villa?

MOSES
Yeah, me and Gweely were in Pershing's special guard for a time.

GWEELY
But I'm the one almost caught him. I come that close . . .
    (Snaps fingers)
  That close to catching ol' Pancho single-handed . . .

BUGALOOSA
You believe that lie, you believe anything.

GWEELY
Hell, I did, you don't know.
    (Arm around HARDIN)
  It was evening, boy, along about dusk dark, and I was out patrolling for Mexican federales . . .

ALL/GWEELY
. . . all by myself!
    (THEY laugh, as GWEELY waves them off)

FRANCISCUS
Gweely wasn't the only one out there that evening.

MOSES
Yeah, we had ol' Pancho dead in our sights—
(Holding up his rifle)

GWEELY
(Lovingly caressing his rifle)
With these pretty new Springfield rifles. Ain't she a beaut? Thirty-ought caliber, battle sights, ladder sights up to a thousand yards . . . (Plants a big kiss on his rifle)
Sweet Jesus, what a weapon!

FRANCISCUS
Yeah well, I'm glad to be shed of Columbus, New Mexico.

GWEELY
Place wasn't so bad—them senoritas was nice.

FRANCISCUS
Yeah, but eleven months of nothing but rock and sagebrush was starting to get to me. I'd forgot what a tree looked like.

BUGALOOSA
Damn a tree, I forgot what a colored gal looked like.

MOSES
Me too. I got so sick of looking at Mexican faces and hearing talk I didn't half understand. Tonight I'm going get my hands on a colored girl, the Blackest one I can find!

BUGALOOSA
That Selena sure was crazy about you, though. She couldn't say nothing in English but "I love Joe Moses too much, I love Joe Moses too much."

MOSES
I taught her how to say that.

GWEELY

Use to wear me out with that shit. Hell, I met her first, don't know what she seen on you—you ugly and you sure don't part with no pesos.

MOSES

(Smugly)

I'll have to tell you my secret one day, Gweely.

FRANCISCUS

(Shining his boots)

Ol' Selena's probably hooked up with some other soldier by now.

MOSES

Say Franciscus, you still writing that cross-eyed pen pal of yours?

FRANCISCUS

(Good-naturedly)

Yeah, and she's not cross-eyed either.

MOSES

(Winking at GWEELY)

You hope. You ain't never seen her.

FRANCISCUS

Going to see her tonight.

MOSES

Me, I couldn't write a woman all this time without knowing what she look like.

GWEELY

Me neither. But Moses, we got to remember, Franciscus ain't interested in what a gal look like—all he interested in is how much book learning she got.

BUGALOOSA

And how much money her folks got.

FRANCISCUS

Aw, you two just jealous because those pen pals you had in 'Frisco turned out so bad.

BUGALOOSA

Didn't they though?

MOSES/GWEELY
(*Waving them off*)
Aw man, forget that, don't nobody want to hear about that, etc.

FRANCISCUS

Hardin wants to hear it, don't you Hardin?

HARDIN

Yes, yes I would like to hear about their exploits.

BUGALOOSA

Y'all hear that—ex-ploits?

FRANCISCUS

Well Hardin, my boy, they finally met these two sisters they'd been writing to in San Francisco. Twins they were . . .

BUGALOOSA

O-ra and Do-ra.
(*MOSES and GWEELY groan in remembrance*)

FRANCISCUS

Well, Ora turned out to be cross-eyed—

BUGALOOSA

And Dora was big as a bale of cotton!
(*Laughing, BUGALOOSA spreads his arms and lumbers across the tent*)

GWEELY

Well, I just might put all these women down over here, and marry up with one of them French senoritas.

MOSES

Let you tell it, you always going "marry up" with somebody.

FRANCISCUS

Yeah, remember he said the same thing in the Philippines.

GWEELY

But I ain't shucking and jiving this time though. Bugaloosa even much been learning me some of that French lingo.
    (Takes a deep breath)
    Pol-ly Vouse Frances? Comin' Alice too?

BUGALOOSA

Man, they not going to understand a word you say. Permittez-moi de presenter. J'ai m'pelle Jacques Honoré. Comment-allez vous?

GWEELY

Oo-wee, listen how that trip off his tongue! Be glad when I learn how to whisper it like that in them French senoritas' ears.

BUGALOOSA
    (Disgustedly)
Mademoiselles, man, mademoiselles. How many times I got to tell you, you call French women mademoiselles?

GWEELY

Yeah, well, me and you got to get together on that stuff. Yep, after the war I just might settle down overseas. They say a colored man get treated with respect overseas.

HARDIN

We're going to be treated with respect right here in America after the war.

MOSES

Yeah, things better be different when we get back.

BUGALOOSA

If we get back.

FRANCISCUS
If we don't get back, then our little children'll get the respect.

GWEELY
Yeah, that's right.

FRANCISCUS
Black Jack Pershing here we come! Finally going to see some action!
Tent-hut!
> (*THE MEN snap to attention as SGT. MCKINNEY strides in. He's holding a burlap sack and a tin cup. He puts these items on the shelf*)

SGT. MCKINNEY
As you were. All right, all right, listen up!
> (*All THE MEN, except HARDIN, resume what they're doing. HARDIN continues to stand at ramrod attention*)

OK. We in a Southern town now. And a colored soldier can run into a lot of trouble in a Southern town if he ain't careful. Houston ain't like some of the other places we been stationed in, where they lets colored come and go like they please. It ain't like that here.

They got a lot of rules for colored here. Got signs all over the place, telling colored where to eat, where to sleep, where to get on the trolley, where to get off the trolley, where to sit.
> (*Pause*)

OK. Some of these rules might be a bit irksome to some of you, but I expect y'all to go along 'em, because they the law here. You men from the South understand all this, but some of you boys from up North might have some problems with it, but I don't aim to have no problems.
> (*He stops in front of MOSES*)

So, anybody got any questions, best speak 'em now.

MOSES
Now, I just want to make sure I understand. If I catch a trolley car and all the seats in the colored section are all filled up, but it's plenty empty ones in the White section, you saying I still have to stand up?

SGT. MCKINNEY
That's what I'm saying.

MOSES
Don't make no sense.

SGT. MCKINNEY
Ain't got to make no sense, they the rules. You just follow 'em. It don't need to be a whole lot of trafficking back and forth on them trolley cars no how. Walk—you need the exercise.

MOSES
I hear a colored man can't hardly walk the streets because of the White police.

SGT. MCKINNEY
You soldiers ain't got to worry about the city police.
        (Amid murmurs of approval)
    You answer to you own MPs like you always do. And while we here, we gonna put on some extra MPs. Franciscus! You one of them.

FRANCISCUS
Yes sir.

SGT. MCKINNEY
And you can start your duty by taking this here sack—
        (Throws it to FRANCISCUS)
    . . . and going around collecting all that whiskey y'all snuck in from New Mexico.

THE MEN
        (Trying to sound innocent)
Whiskey? What whiskey? We ain't got no whiskey, etc.

SGT. MCKINNEY
In the sack.

BUGALOOSA
        (Pained)
Lord have mercy, Sarge.

(FRANCISCUS goes around to MOSES and GWEELY with the sack. They grudgingly give up a bottle each. HARDIN, of course, has nothing. Throughout the collection, SGT. MCKINNEY holds forth on the evils of liquor)

SGT. MCKINNEY

I can't understand what make a colored man drank liquor. Let the White man drank hisself to hell. He get drunk, go out, do something foolish, no harm done. But don't you fools know a colored man can't afford to get all liquored up! Next morning he find hisself swinging from a tree.
(At this point, FRANCISCUS is at BUGALOOSA's cot. BUGALOOSA is pulling out bottle after bottle after bottle from his footlocker. SGT. MCKINNEY is unaware of what's going on at BUGALOOSA's cot)
I ain't gonna abide no drinking in this company—either in barracks or in public. We gonna leave a real good impression on these White folks. Ain't gonna be no congregating on the street corners, no cussing or spitting in public, and no <u>drunkenness</u> in "I" Company.
(Suddenly aware of the constant "clink" of bottles coming from BUGALOOSA's direction, he whirls around to see BUGALOOSA sadly putting a final bottle in the sack)

HARDIN

Yes sir!

SGT. MCKINNEY

Sit down, Hardin.
(HARDIN sits. FRANCISCUS exits with the sack)
Now to cut down on a lot of going back and forward into town, the White folks done give up some of their own buildings right close to camp and turned it into a dance hall for y'all soldiers. Somewhere over on Washington Street, they say.

GWEELY

(Doing a little jig)
Hoo-ray! Just point me in the direction, Sarge, 'cause I got my dancing shoes ready.

SGT. MCKINNEY

Just hold your horses, Brown. Before y'all go out and blow your pay on some gal, I want your money for your liberty bonds.

(He gets the tin cup from the shelf, while THE MEN go in their pockets)
And dig deep. Them bums in "M" Company beat us out last time.
(SGT. MCKINNEY goes around with the cup, stopping at GWEELY first)
I'm taking up money for them folks in East St. Louis too.

GWEELY
I sure aims to give to that. I hear some of them folks ain't got the money
to bury they dead.

SGT. MCKINNEY
That's what some of this here money's for.

GWEELY
What they do to them White National Guards?

SGT. MCKINNEY
Nothing.

BUGALOOSA
Got clean away with murder.

SGT. MCKINNEY
(Sharply)
You watch your choice of words, Honoré. You talking about men in
uniform.

BUGALOOSA
I know, Sarge, but those colored folks wasn't nothing but civilians, didn't
have nothing to fight with but rocks and sticks.

HARDIN
Sergeant McKinney? What do you think started that riot, sir?

SGT. MCKINNEY
Ain't got no time to waste speculating. I wasn't there, don't know the
straight of it.
(SGT. MCKINNEY rattles his cup before BUGALOOSA)

(BUGALOOSA *drops in two coins*)
(*Disgustedly*)
Is that all you giving Honoré?

BUGALOOSA
(*Shrugging*)
That's all I got—deaux sous.

SGT. MCKINNEY
Two pennies?

BUGALOOSA
That's all I got, Sarge. I just bought a new cornet, don'tcha know, and I'm a little short.

SGT. MCKINNEY
You <u>always</u> a little short.
(*To HARDIN*)
Boy!

HARDIN
Yes sir!

SGT. MCKINNEY
Can you count money?

HARDIN
Yes sir, I can count!

SGT. MCKINNEY
(*Giving him the cup*)
Count this.
(*Back to the men*)
One more thing. The colored folk in town is got it planned to treat y'all like you some kind of heroes or something—got all kind of festivities planned for ya. But don't none of y'all get the big head about this. And Colonel Gentry figured it would be good for morale to throw the

camp open, and let y'all have visitors from thirteen hundred hours to right before curfew . . .

(He holds up a restraining hand at the men's approval)

As long as you men not on duty and done finished all assignments.

(Pause)

Now, they say some Italian woman, name-a . . . uh . . . Miss Step-nu-chi or something—she live cross the way and she say you soldiers is welcome to use her telephone . . .

THE MEN
(Excitedly)
Telephone?! We can use a telephone, etc.!

SGT. MCKINNEY
But I don't want none of y'all trooping in and out of that White woman's house, I don't care what they say.

(Pause)

Now, y'all all know how Colonel Gentry always want to be the one give out the good news, and leave it to us noncoms to give out the bad. So, when he call assembly at eighteen hundred hours this evening, y'all act like you ain't heard none of this.

GWEELY
Sarge? Them visitors? That mean women too, don't it?

SGT. MCKINNEY
(Dryly)
Yeah Brown, that mean women.

SGT. MCKINNEY
(At GWEELY's big grin)
But let me tell you something, Gweely Brown: I got my first time to catch a female in these barracks and ain't gonna be no more women visitors for "I" Company period. Understand?

GWEELY
Oh yeah, sure, I understand that.

SGT. MCKINNEY
You done counting that money, boy?

HARDIN
Yes sir! Five dollars and thirty . . .
> (*Looks pointedly at BUGALOOSA*)

<u>two</u> cents, Sergeant McKinney, sir.

SGT. MCKINNEY
Humph. Curfew same as usual. And any soldier out pass that time got me to deal with.
> (*SGT. MCKINNEY strides out of the tent*)

GWEELY
> (*Imitating SGT. MCKINNEY*)

And any soldier out past that time, got me to deal with—

SGT. MCKINNEY
> (*Reenters*)

And remember this here . . .
> (*GWEELY jumps to attention as THE MEN cut short their laughter*)

SGT. MCKINNEY
You soldiers of the United States Army, and if some of these White folks don't respect your color, they bound to respect that uniform. So, compote yourselves at all times so's you don't bring no dishonor on that uniform.

THE MEN
> (*Solemnly*)

Yes sir.

SGT. MCKINNEY
OK, that's it.
> (*SGT. MCKINNEY exits. GWEELY makes a point to be sure that SGT. MCKINNEY is gone before speaking this time*)

GWEELY

Yeah, and I bet he'll be standing guard too, making sure every man is in at curfew.

BUGALOOSA

Much as I plan to do, curfew needs to be at sunrise.

GWEELY

Wish he was like some of the other noncoms around here. The boys in "M" Company have to cover for Murphy all the time.

BUGALOOSA

Yeah, he be going AWOL, carousing and drinking with the best of us.
(*BUGALOOSA takes another whiskey bottle from his footlocker*)

MOSES

McKinney ought to get a woman. I don't think I ever saw him with a woman before.

GWEELY

Last woman he was with was in 1907.

MOSES
(*Laughing*)
Man, how you know that?

GWEELY

I was with him. Tried to fix him up with this little gal, but he runned her off, same way he run all his women off—treating 'em like boots—
(*Demonstrates on BUGALOOSA*)
  Straighten up that spine! Throw back them shoulders, pull in that gut!
(*They laugh*)
  I ain't lying, he run 'em all off like that, so I quit trying to fix him up y'know, and then after he made sergeant, we just kind of went our different ways.
(*GWEELY starts looking for FRANCISCUS's hair pomade and mirror, finds it, takes it back to his cot*)

HARDIN

You've been in the Army as long as Sergeant McKinney?

GWEELY

Damn near. Been in longer than any of these fellers.

HARDIN

You could be a sergeant, maybe even an officer.

GWEELY
        (Flattered)
Oh, they done come to me about it, but I don't want to be in charge of
nobody but me.
        (FRANCISCUS reenters, puts the empty sack back on the shelf)

BUGALOOSA

You didn't get rid of all of it, did you?

FRANCISCUS
        (Breezily)
Those were my orders.
        (Beat)
    And guess who came out to help me get rid of the contraband?

BUGALOOSA
        (Disgusted)
Captain Zuelke.

FRANCISCUS

Down his gullet.
        (Looking through his belongings, puzzled)

BUGALOOSA
        (Heatedly)
That drunk bum!
        (MOSES laughs)
    Hey man, that not funny, no! That was some good liquor all gone to
waste, yeah. Bonjé senye!

GWEELY

That's all right, Boog, don't cry over spilt whiskey, plenty more where that come from.

FRANCISCUS

(*Absently, as he searches*)

I guess Zuelke figured we owe him . . . he's the one who told Colonel Gentry it would be good for morale to open up the camp. But Gentry'll come in here and take all the credit.

GWEELY

McKinney beat him to it this time.

MOSES

Yeah, now we'll have to hear that same shit all over again.

(*BUGALOOSA starts to play on his cornet the song "Over There." ALL join in as they put finishing touches on their uniform*)

GWEELY

(*Concluding the song*)

Hey! Way I figure it, we'll go by this dance hall on Washington Street first, see what the house got there, then . . .

(*At this point, FRANCISCUS spies his pomade, starts over to GWEELY's cot*)

. . . then we'll mosey on into town, check out the juke joints there.

MOSES

All right by me.

FRANCISCUS

(*Snatching pomade*)

You're welcome!

GWEELY

Oh yeah—thanks. Gotta buy me some of that stuff one day.

FRANCISCUS

You been saying that ever since I met you.

GWEELY
(Looking in the mirror)
Look-a-there, make my hair look kind of wavy, don't it?
(FRANCISCUS takes the mirror)
You gonna paint the town with us, Franciscus?

FRANCISCUS
Not tonight. Tonight I'm going to meet Miss Pris-cil-la.

GWEELY
Well, have fun with your preacher gal, but preacher gal ain't exactly what I'm looking for tonight.

BUGALOOSA
Me neither.

FRANCISCUS
She may be a preacher's daughter, but her letters sound mighty lively.

GWEELY
What about you, boy? Wanna come with us?
(HARDIN's been lounging on his cot, reading pamphlets. He eagerly sits up)

HARDIN
Well, what do you fellows have planned to do?

GWEELY
Find some poontang and get drunk.

HARDIN
Oh—well—I was just planning to go sightseeing.
(THE MEN try to keep a straight face. HARDIN runs over to them with a pamphlet)
I have this little pamphlet here on Houston, and they have these two skyscrapers I'd really like to see—the Carter Building, which is sixteen stories high, and the Rice Hotel, with twenty-two stories.

GWEELY

Colored allowed in them?

HARDIN

Well—uh—I don't know, I was just planning to stand outside and look
up at them.
> (*THE MEN burst out laughing*)

MOSES

Boy really know how to have a good time, don't he?

GWEELY

Come on boy, we gon' break you in tonight. You can see a tall building
any time, but bet you ain't never had no poontang.

HARDIN
> (*Afraid to ask*)

Uh . . . exactly what is that?
> (*Roar of laughter from THE MEN*)

GWEELY
> (*Slapping him on back*)

Naw, you ain't never had none. Come on, boy, you going with us tonight.

HARDIN

OK, if you fellows really want me.
> (*HARDIN heads for his cot, BUGALOOSA sidles up to him*)

BUGALOOSA

You got any money?

HARDIN
> (*Reaching into his pocket*)

Well yes, as a matter of fact, my mother just sent me—

GWEELY

Don't worry Bugaloosa, me and Moses got plenty money, we take care
of you.

MOSES

Hey nigger, don't be loaning out my money. He ain't got no money, let
him stay in camp.

(The call for ASSEMBLY SOUNDS)

FRANCISCUS

(Snapping to attention)

As-sem-bly! Look smart, men, look smart!

*(THE MEN snap to attention. By this time they are sleek and sharp in their
uniforms, except HARDIN. BUGALOOSA starts playing "Over There," and THE
MEN join in)*

THE MEN

(Singing)

*Over there, over there, tell the men to beware over there, 'cause the yanks are coming, the yanks
are coming and we won't stop marching 'til it's over, over there . . . Over there, over there etc.!*

*(They dance a little jig on out the tent. HARDIN scurries after them, tucking in his
shirttail)*

<u>FADE OUT</u>

<u>END ACT I, SCENE 1</u>

ACT I

SCENE 2

<u>ON RISE:</u> Two days later. The Barracks of "I" Company. MOSES is sitting on his cot, holding a crudely painted sign. GWEELY is sitting on his cot, twirling a colorful parasol. He has a loopy grin on his face. FRANCISCUS flips through a magazine; BUGALOOSA is losing a hand of solitaire to himself.

MOSES
(Reading the sign)
<u>"No Negroes, No Mexicans, No Dogs Allowed."</u> I don't believe this!
(Turns the sign around)
We don't take no shit like this up North!

GWEELY
(Twirling the parasol)
That's the way it is in the South.

MOSES
(Pacing)
And these White conductors act like they're giving a colored man a free ride. Hell, we pay our fare, we ought to be able to sit anywhere we want to!

GWEELY
Aw, you make too big a deal out of it. Don't matter where I sit, strap me on top, long's I'm riding.

MOSES
Comparing us to dogs! How the colored here take this?

BUGALOOSA
Way of life here. They used to it.

FRANCISCUS

Bound to respect the uniform, huh?

(*Closes the magazine*)

These Whites here don't act like they're bound to respect anything that belongs to the colored man.

BUGALOOSA

A bunch of them tried to run me off the sidewalk last night. They better be glad I didn't have my sidearm.

(*MOSES takes another sign from under his cot*)

MOSES

And look at this one here, fellers. Got it off the trolley car . . .

(*Reads*)

"No Colored Seated beyond This Point"

FRANCISCUS

(*Coming after MOSES*)

No wonder we have so many complaints about missing signs!

MOSES

(*Dodging FRANCISCUS*)

Gonna keep these as souvenirs.

(*Puts them in his footlocker*)

When I show them to my buddies in New York, they ain't going to believe this shit.

(*Beat*)

I kept inching up and inching up behind that conductor until I was breathing down his White neck.

FRANCISCUS

All right, Moses, these White folks here take those trolley cars real serious. You going to find yourself in stockade, or worse, in the city jail. And if I catch you confiscating any more of those signs, Moses, I'm going to have to report you.

MOSES
(Drops to his knees)
Oh please, Mr. Corporal Franciscus, Mister MP, sir! Can I just keep those signs sir! I want to show them to my son when he grows up, so he'll know how it was for us, Mr. Corporal Franciscus MP, sir?

FRANCISCUS
Get away from me. You're not going to make me feel bad about doing my job. If I don't do my job, I get in trouble with the Sarge and Zuelke.

MOSES
You always worried about getting in trouble.

GWEELY
(Blowing smoke)
Ain't he though? Don't you know we don't get in trouble in the 24th? We kicks trouble's behind.

MOSES
(Lying on his cot)
Yeah, we lead a charmed life, don't you know? They loved us in Manila, they loved us in San Fran.

GWEELY
In Manila they give the Deuce-Four the keys to the city. Told us we was welcome back any time. And the same thing gon' happen here, Franciscus. We gonna win these White folks over too. All we got to do is—grin.

BUGALOOSA
(Not looking up from his cards)
And don't look at the White women.

MOSES
Damn these crackers. They don't have to like me. The colored here sure treating us right.

GWEELY
Ain't they though?

(*Twirling the parasol*)
I got to return this here parasol to a pretty little gal I met yesterday.

BUGALOOSA
Man, I'm still full from that picnic yesterday. I never seen that much food in my life.

FRANCISCUS
Me either. Tubs full of rice and potato salad . . .

BUGALOOSA
All different kind of cakes and cookies. And creole food almost as good as Grand-mère used to cook.

MOSES
It seemed like all the colored in the world was there . . .
(*Overlapping*)

FRANCISCUS
Young folks, old folks—

GWEELY
Women.

BUGALOOSA
Preachers, teachers—

GWEELY
Women.

MOSES
Army of Black faces, spread all over the grounds—

GWEELY
Women.
(*Smacks a kiss to the air*)
I could of just hugged and kissed 'em all—

FRANCISCUS
Church choirs singing—

BUGALOOSA
Preachers preaching—

GWEELY
In their pretty little parasols and dresses . . .

MOSES
They were following after us, trying to touch us, just like we was Jesus or somebody.

GWEELY
Just like being in a candy store . . .

BUGALOOSA
Little boys running up to us, wanting to shake our hands—

FRANCISCUS
Old men calling us soldiers of freedom.

MOSES
I believe they would've done anything we told them to do that day. I believe they would have followed us right straight into hell.

FRANCISCUS
Yeah . . . it was something all right . . . I'll never forget that day . . .

ALL
Yeah . . .
    (Beat)

FRANCISCUS
Hey, so . . . what you fellows think of Priscilla?
    (They make a "so-so" gesture with their hands and a sound that says they're unimpressed)

ALL
Eh . . .

GWEELY
I guess she ain't bad for a preacher daughter. But what was all that crazy talk she was talking and all them papers she was passing around?

FRANCISCUS
(*Proudly*)
Priscilla's what you call a suffragette.

THE MEN
A what?

FRANCISCUS
A suffragette. She thinks White women ought to have the right to vote.

MOSES
What she care about White women getting the vote, when a colored man can't even vote.

FRANCISCUS
Well, she's in this group that figures if White women get the vote, maybe then it'll come on down to the rest of us.

MOSES
How's a bunch of colored gals going to get us the vote? When we men win this fight overseas, that's when we going to get the vote.

FRANCISCUS
Hey fellows, let me tell you what you have to see: You have to see her father's house. It's a palace, I tell ya, a real live palace!
(*He eagerly waits for them to ask for further details, they don't*)

BUGALOOSA
(*Finally looking up from his solitaire*)
So, what it look like, Franciscus?

FRANCISCUS
It's got <u>electric</u> lights.

THE MEN
(Impressed, despite themselves)
Electric . . . ?

FRANCISCUS
And <u>inside</u> bathrooms—

THE MEN
Inside bathrooms . . . naw, for real, etc.?

FRANCISCUS
Two of them! Five bedrooms, a library—everything!

GWEELY
(Rolling a cigarette)
He must really be passing around the collecting plate.

FRANCISCUS
He pastors a mighty big church all right, mighty big. Priscilla says all of the best colored families attend there.

GWEELY
Boy you shitting in high cotton now.

FRANCISCUS
I told her father the Camp Logan quartet would sing at his church next Sunday.

GWEELY
Next Sunday? Man, by next Sunday I plans to be waking up beside the most prettiest gal in the world. Mavis. Works at the dance hall. Beautiful. Ain't she Moses?

MOSES
(*Shrugging*)
She all right.

GWEELY
Pretty woman like that can have all my money.

MOSES
She did.

GWEELY
(*Ignoring MOSES*)
She tall, Franciscus, big-hipped, like I like 'em, y'know, and she got this smooth brown skin, and kind of slanted-like eyes, and—oh Lawd—I gits weak about the knees just thinking about her.

MOSES
(*Beat*)
They say she belongs to the meanest White police in town—name of O'Reilly. They say he just came off suspension for killing two colored civilians.

GWEELY
(*Unperturbed*)
She ain't mentioned no O'Reilly to me.

FRANCISCUS
O'Reilly? Yeah, he's with the Mounted Police. We met him last night when the city police briefed us. Tall, red-haired peckerwood, mean as a hornet. They say he rides a big black horse called Nigger. Say he'll go upside a colored man's head as soon as look at him.

GWEELY
(*Unperturbed*)
I'm going 'round to her house tonight.

BUGALOOSA
Bet not let that cracker catch you.

GWEELY
(Breezily)
He don't bother me, I won't bother him.

MOSES
Man, she ain't worth it.

GWEELY
(Sharply)
How you know what she worth? You just jealous 'cause Selena showed up and plucked that sweet blackberry out your hand.

MOSES
Selena don't stop me from nothing!

GWEELY
(Laughing)
Tell her that, not me.

MOSES
(Frustrated)
She don't understand no English, dammit!

FRANCISCUS
I still can't believe she followed you here.

MOSES
Well, she did. I don't know how she did, but that crazy Mexican did.

GWEELY
He'd met this pretty little colored gal too, Franciscus. And she was buying him beer by the barrel—matter fact, the whole house was buying us soldiers beer—

BUGALOOSA
Didn't have to spend a nickel. I won ten dollars off those civilians too—

MOSES
I came that close—
> (Snaps fingers)
—that close to taking that little colored gal in the back room—
> (MOSES is unaware that GWEELY is sneaking up behind him. GWEELY slips
> MOSES' Mexican blanket off MOSES' cot and wraps it around his shoulders)
—when out of the blue—man I thought I was hearing things—

GWEELY
> (A coquettish Spanish voice)
Joe! Joe Moses? Joe Moses?
> (Minces around the tent, batting his eyes)
I just love Joe Moses too much, I just love Joe Moses too much!
> (MOSES holds his head in anguish as THE MEN roll on their cots with laughter)
You could of bought Joe Moses with a penny.
> (He throws the blanket over MOSES' head)

BUGALOOSA
> (Winking at FRANCISCUS)
Hey Mose! Guess who got that little colored gal of yours?

MOSES
Who!

GWEELY
> (Gleefully)
Hardin.

MOSES
Hardin?!

GWEELY
Well, he coulda had her, but he didn't know what to do with her.

BUGALOOSA
She started batting her eyes at him, but he just sit there—

GWEELY
Looking like a scared little rabbit, ready to bolt.

SGT. MCKINNEY *(Offstage)*
Mo-ses!

MOSES
(Under breath)
Damn.
(FRANCISCUS exits as SGT. MCKINNEY enters and crosses to MOSES' cot)

SGT. MCKINNEY
Moses! Heard you threatened to turn over the Franklin Street trolley
last night.

MOSES
(At attention)
Turn over a trolley?

SGT. MCKINNEY
You heard me, you heard me. I'm sure you wasn't the onliest one in on it . . .
(Looks around at the others)
   . . . but the conductor remembers hearing your name loud and clear.

MOSES
(Trying to bluff)
A trolley car? I don't know nothing about turning over no trolley car. I
just know it was the last trolley running back to camp before curfew, and
a lot of us kind of pile on—

SGT. MCKINNEY
—and spilt over into the White section of the car.

MOSES
(Decides to come clean)
Look Sarge, it wasn't but a few White men sitting in the White section of
the bus that time of night, and I figured—

SGT. MCKINNEY
Oh, you figured—?

MOSES
Yeah. It didn't make sense for half of us to have to get off the bus, and be late for curfew, when we were already on a trolley car full of empty seats.

SGT. MCKINNEY
Look, I told you not to try to make no sense outta these rules. I told you, you just follow 'em, and that's all you do. You understand that?

MOSES
(Long sullen stare)
Yeah . . . I understand.

SGT. MCKINNEY
(In MOSES' face)
Don't you be bucking me, boy! I'll bust you down to the lowest tin can of a buck private, I'll have you on dirty detail 'til the day you die!
(Reluctantly, MOSES averts his gaze. SGT. MCKINNEY walks toward other MEN)
Ain't had no dis'plinary problems in this company, and I ain't gon' have none now, even if I have to keep half of ya locked up in stockade. Wonder how y'all expect to hold up under fire in France, if you lose your head with a conductor on a trolley car. We soldiers, dammit! Our fight ain't here in this muddy bayou town with these civilians, it's overseas with them godless Huns!
(Beat. Walking toward MOSES)
Maybe I had you pegged wrong, Moses. Maybe I had all y'all pegged wrong, maybe I needs to weed through this company, and find out who ready to fight with the White boys in France and who ain't.

MOSES
You know I'm ready for France and anything else they throw at us, but if you'd heard the way that conductor <u>talked</u> to us—

SGT. MCKINNEY
Oh? So you didn't like the way he <u>talked</u> to you, that it?

(Circling MOSES)

Well, how you likes to be talked to Moses . . . huh . . . ?

(Mocking, feminine voice)

Words got to be poured over you like blackstrap molasses, all so-o-o-ft and swe-e-e-t, like a gal?

(Beat, then lays it on thick, as others snicker)

You know Moses, they got a-plenty of them German Huns just dying to sweet-talk a colored boy like you right on over to they side. Yeah, that's how come the gov'ment scared to send colored troops overseas, you know that? They scared that when them sneaky Huns gets through telling you what a hard time you got over here, you just might turn your weapon on your own officers! That's what they scared of, Moses. And maybe they got good reason to be scared, 'cause I'm wondering what you gon' do when one of them godless Huns slides up in your face with all that sweet talk. *(In his face)* What you gon' do, Moses? *(Disgustedly)* Follow 'em like a lamb to the slaughter.

(Turns on his heels and starts for exit)

MOSES

(Calls after him)

Naw. *(Beat)* I'm gonna mow them White sons of bitches down like a boll weevil going through cotton!

(SGT. MCKINNEY calmly strides back)

SGT. MCKINNEY

Oh yeah? (Smirking) Well . . . we'll see, Moses . . . we'll see. Double guard duty for you, starting . . .

(Pulls chain watch out of his pocket)

Now!

BLACKOUT

END ACT I, SCENE 2

ACT I

SCENE 3

SETTING: The small office of CAPT. ZUELKE. The office consists of an old beat-up desk, two chairs and an American flag. The desk is cluttered with stacks of paperwork, coffee cups, old food, etc.

ON RISE: Midmorning, and already hot. CAPT. ZUELKE is seated at his desk, fanning himself as he shuffles paperwork. He's florid and sloppy from the heat and too much whiskey. SGT. MCKINNEY stands at ease before him, all spit and polish. These two, both loners, have worked together for years—unwillingly united in the command and discipline of the men.

CAPT. ZUELKE
Another note from that damn Harris County Patriotic League. Blast that group to hell! I believe they'd report their own mothers for "seditious" and "traitorous" behavior.

SGT. MCKINNEY
What they sayin' now, Capt. Zuelke?

CAPT. ZUELKE
That the soldiers in this company are consorting with Mexican spies.

SGT. MCKINNEY
(Snorts)
Mexican spies?

CAPT. ZUELKE
I know, a bunch of hogwash, but we can't just ignore these folks, we have to give 'em some kind of report.

SGT. MCKINNEY
Well, we was in Mexico so long, a lotta the soldiers picked up that Mexican lingo. Reckon maybe that's what they talking about.

CAPT. ZUELKE

Maybe—but spy around into it. You never know what these boys might let themselves get talked into.

MCKINNEY

Yessuh.

CAPT. ZUELKE

Now, this trouble between the White construction workers and the soldiers is going from bad to worse. Construction workers say they're going to walk if the attitude of some of these soldiers don't change. You know the ones I'm talking about in "I" Company.

SGT. MCKINNEY

Well suh, from what I can see, it's them construction workers that's causing all the trouble—

CAPT. ZUELKE

Wait a minute, McKinney. We got to try to be fair about this.

SGT. MCKINNEY

Well suh, I figure I'm being fair. I'm in camp all the time and I see—

CAPT. ZUELKE

Wait a minute, McKinney. You trying to say I'm not in camp long enough to know what's going on with my men?

SGT. MCKINNEY

Naw suh, I ain't saying that. I know <u>you</u> in camp all the time, sir, but well—Colonel Gentry and some of the other officers—

CAPT. ZUELKE
          (Reprimandingly)
—are away from camp a lot, yes. But an officer's got more to do than just run camp, McKinney. He's got to keep up good relations with the folks of a town, and sometimes, yes, that might mean going to dinner or playing a game of billiards.
          (Taking a sip of coffee)

All in the line of duty.

SGT. MCKINNEY
Yessuh.

CAPT. ZUELKE
Now. The White construction workers and businessmen say that some of your boys take every chance they get to act insolent to them.

SGT. MCKINNEY
Insolent?

CAPT. ZUELKE
Yeah, insolent, you know—hos-tile. They say the soldiers keep on insisting on being called colored.

SGT. MCKINNEY
Instead of nigger.
 (*A BEAT as CAPT. ZUELKE tries to assess if SGT. MCKINNEY is being insolent or not*)

CAPT. ZUELKE
I know the men are not used to being called names. But they've got to try to understand that these folks don't mean no harm, that's just what they're used to calling their colored here.

SGT. MCKINNEY
I don't reckon the soldiers mean no harm, neither, Cap'n, they just trying to let them workers know they don't cotton to being called nigger.

CAPT. ZUELKE
 (*Beat*)
Of course they don't. But I understand that it's the tone of voice the men use with the White workers that's upsetting them.

SGT. MCKINNEY
 (*Dryly*)
Well, I'll speak to the men about the <u>tone</u> of their voices.

(Catching the sarcasm this time, CAPT. ZUELKE gives him a hard look, forcing SGT. MCKINNEY to add)

SGT. MCKINNEY
Suh.

CAPT. ZUELKE
(Jumps up from his desk)
And <u>your</u> tone is pretty damn close to insubordination, boy!
(A beat, then, good-naturedly)
   Aw hell McKinney, we're both from Kentucky. You know how it is in the South. Little things—tone of voice, expression on your face—can set off a riot. And we don't want another East St. Louis on our hands, do we?

SGT. MCKINNEY
Naw suh, we don't.

CAPT. ZUELKE
Well, the soldiers are going to have to get off their high horses in this town. They're going to have to realize that they're colored first in this town, and soldiers second.
(Sits, resumes shuffling papers)
   Now, Colonel Gentry says that the White citizens have even been complaining that since the soldiers came to town, the colored civilians have started acting funny toward the White folks.

SGT. MCKINNEY
"Funny"?

CAPT. ZUELKE
Yeah—funny. Disrespectful. Like they think the soldiers are going back up anything they do. Why, Colonel Gentry even says that a socialite friend of his complained that her servants have been acting mighty sassy since the soldiers arrived.

SGT. MCKINNEY
(Holding back a smile)

Well sir, what you expect me to do about that? I ain't got no control over nobody's sassy maid.

(CAPT. ZUELKE is up from his desk like a shot, in SGT. MCKINNEY's face)

CAPT. ZUELKE

I expect <u>you</u> as the so-called leader of that outfit over there to be aware of such things!

SGT. MCKINNEY

Yes suh!

CAPT. ZUELKE

And if any of the boys in this company are encouraging misbehavior among the colored civilians, I expect <u>you</u> to put an end to it, that's what I expect <u>you</u> to do! Is that clear!

SGT. MCKINNEY

Yes suh!

CAPT. ZUELKE

(Fussing with things on his desk)

Thought being in town with so many of their own kind would be good for morale, but looks like all this hero worship's just giving them the swelled head.

SGT. MCKINNEY

Most of 'em adjusting just fine, Cap'n. It's just a few of 'em acting up, and I'll straighten them out.

CAPT. ZUELKE

See that you do. Or else I've got a good mind to suspend this company's privileges.

(Shuffling papers)

And another thing—why in the Sam Hill are so many of our boys being thrown in the city jail? Where the hell are the MPs?

SGT. MCKINNEY
   (Plaintively)
They right out there, Cap'n, trying to do their job, but the civil police
won't let 'em. If a soldier get into trouble on the street, civil police haul
him off to jail, and if the MP complain about it, they throw him in jail
right along with the wrongdoer.

CAPT. ZUELKE
   (Hoping to give the impression he has influence with the colonel)
Well, Colonel Gentry is having dinner with Chief Brock tonight.
I'll have him bring the matter up.

SGT. MCKINNEY
Oh? You mean they invited you? To supper?

CAPT. ZUELKE
   (Testily)
I'm sure I _will_ be invited, McKinney.

SGT. MCKINNEY
   (Beat)
Well, if you _do_ get to go, Cap'n, can you tell them the MPs need to be
able to carry they sidearms, like they always do?

CAPT. ZUELKE
Out of the question, and you know it. Colonel Gentry assured the townspeople that the soldiers wouldn't be allowed to walk the streets with weapons.

SGT. MCKINNEY
But this the military police. How can they keep the peace when they ain't
got nothing to keep the peace with?

CAPT. ZUELKE
   (Dismissively)
Those are the colonel's orders, nothing I can do about it.
   (Big sigh)
   And about these dadburn water barrels. The workers say they've caught
the soldiers drinking out of the barrel clearly marked "White."

SGT. MCKINNEY
(Carefully)
That's 'cause for "some reason" the colored barrels keep running dry.

CAPT. ZUELKE
(Just as carefully)
You think the construction workers are emptying water out of the colored barrel?

SGT. MCKINNEY
It's crossed my mind.

CAPT. ZUELKE
Still—the soldiers have to follow the regulations. So tell 'em to leave that White water barrel alone.

SGT. MCKINNEY
(Holding in rising anger)
And what the men gon' do for water?

CAPT. ZUELKE
I'll tell the foreman to keep a better eye on his workers—

SGT. MCKINNEY
Been told that before, didn't do no good.

CAPT. ZUELKE
I guarantee you that there will be water in the soldier's barrel, if I have to stand out there with my rifle and guard it myself.

SGT. MCKINNEY
Thank you, suh.

CAPT. ZUELKE
Now, let's see here . . . one of the townspeople has made a complaint against Moses and—

SGT. MCKINNEY

I know about that, Cap'n, and to my way of thinking, Moses was in the right this time, he was—

CAPT. ZUELKE

This is not a matter of right or wrong, it's simply a matter of keeping things running smoothly.

SGT. MCKINNEY

But all Moses done was ask to see the civilian's pass, it's the sentry's duty to ask to see the pass each and every time for security—

CAPT. ZUELKE

Don't you quote the regulations to me, dammit! I know the regulations, I'm the officer in this outfit!
    (As though explaining to an idiot)
   But the White men coming in and out of here on business ain't used to having to identify themselves to a colored man. A lot of them are city officials, get it, friends of Colonel Gentry's, and they've complained about the procedure. So, from now on, White visitors don't have to show their passes to the colored soldiers, only to the White gatekeeper. After all he's the one who's actually supposed to check the passes anyway, the soldiers are just there to guard the construction.

SGT. MCKINNEY
    (Pushing it)
All right, I'll tell 'em, but the men already feel like they can't half do their job, they already feel like—

CAPT. ZUELKE
    (Slams fist on desk)
Dammit McKinney! Don't you make no federal case out of this! I always thought that you ruled those boys with an iron hand, but all I hear out of you lately is . . .
    (Whining voice)
   —the men don't like this, the men don't like that. You got to stop mollycoddling them! They're soldiers, dammit, and they have got to bear up under pressure just like any White soldier.

(Takes a few steps toward SGT. MCKINNEY)

You know the government is scared to send colored troops overseas, and you know why. Well, now is a chance to test that, to see what a colored boy is really made out of. But if they can't take a little hassling from the local yokels, how in the Sam Hill do they expect to perform on a real battlefield?

SGT. MCKINNEY

(Quietly)

I understand all that, sir. I just thought you'd like to hear the soldier's side of it, so's you would have all the facts.

CAPT. ZUELKE

(Shaking papers in SGT. MCKINNEY's face)

I have all the facts! I have more doggone facts than I know what to do with! But the fact of the matter is, the battle is not here in this muddy bayou town, it's over there in France! Against those godless Huns!

(CAPT. ZUELKE takes a few deep breaths, wiping his hand across his lips. He needs a drink badly. He takes a liquor flask out of the drawer, pours himself a large drink, takes a deep swallow)

(Cordially)

Sit down, McKinney, sit down.

(SGT. MCKINNEY sighs, reluctantly lowers himself to the edge of his chair)

(Expansively)

Relax yourself. That's what's wrong with you, you don't know how to relax.

(Extending the flask)

Have one?

SGT. MCKINNEY

(Self-righteously)

Naw suh, you know I don't drank.

CAPT. ZUELKE

(A beat, as he decides to respond good-naturedly)

Bad habit, not drinking. Granddaddy always said never trust a colored fellow who won't take a nip of Kentucky bourbon every now and again.

>   *(Confidentially)*
>
> But I can trust you, can't I, McKinney?

SGT. MCKINNEY

Yessir. I just don't like the taste of the stuff, is all.

CAPT. ZUELKE

You don't drink it for taste, dummy.

SGT. MCKINNEY
>   *(Standing)*
>
> Well sir, if that's it, I'll just—

CAPT. ZUELKE

This here's about the only little pleasure I get out of life, McKinney, just a quiet little drink every now and again.

>   *(Trapped, SGT. MCKINNEY sits back down. He pulls out his pocket watch and sneaks glances throughout CAPT. ZUELKE's whining)*

I don't rate getting invited to their little dinner parties and such, like the other shiny new officers in this outfit. But I'm the one they call on when they need their little amusements from you boys. Tell Gweely, I want him to get up that minstrel show for the Chamber of Commerce next week.

SGT. MCKINNEY
>   *(Rising)*
>
> Yessuh, I'll get right on it—

CAPT. ZUELKE

Naw . . . *(SGT. MCKINNEY sits back down)* I'm not like the other officers in this outfit . . . especially those high and mighty lieutenants from West Point. *(Bitterly)*

Damn apple polishers, flitting around the brass like fireflies.

>   *(CAPT. ZUELKE takes a deep drink, lost in bitter thoughts. SGT. MCKINNEY slowly rises)*

SGT. MCKINNEY

Well suh . . .

CAPT. ZUELKE

Naw. (*SGT. MCKINNEY sits back down*) I ain't ever going get no higher than I am right now. I never went to West Point. I clawed my way up through the noncom ranks, like you, McKinney. But those West Point looies in this outfit got their bright young futures ahead of them. And this here battalion, with you colored boys is just practice until they get a commission over White troops.

> (*FRANCISCUS enters and tries to get SGT. MCKINNEY's attention without attracting CAPT. ZUELKE's. SGT. MCKINNEY is divided between trying to figure out what FRANCISCUS wants and giving the appearance of listening to his superior*)

SGT. MCKINNEY

> (*Distractedly*)

Well—uh—who knows, Cap'n, you might get a White commission one day—

CAPT. ZUELKE

I don't want it! They couldn't hand it to me on a silver platter! I don't want no White troops, I like things just the way they are, me and the colored boys.

> (*Raises his glass in a toast*)

That's why "I" Company's got to bear up, so I can show 'em!

SGT. MCKINNEY

Uh—don't worry, Cap'n, uh—we ain't gonna let you down.

CAPT. ZUELKE

> (*Warmly*)

I know you're not McKinney, y'all some good boys. (*Takes a drink*)

But the first one of ya turn tail and run, I'll have lined up and shot.

> (*Suddenly spotting FRANCISCUS*)

What the hell you want, Franciscus?

FRANCISCUS

> (*Steps forward, snapping to attention*)

Uh—sir! Uh—yes sir, we-uh—

CAPT. ZUELKE
Speak up, boy, speak up!

FRANCISCUS
Well—uh—we need to see the Sarge outside right away—

CAPT. ZUELKE
What the hell for?

FRANCISCUS
Well—uh—

CAPT. ZUELKE
Speak up, speak up!

SGT. MCKINNEY
        (Standing)
Trouble?

FRANCISCUS
One of the White laborers turned over the colored water barrels—again.
And now one of the soldiers is threatening to run him through with his
bayonet.

CAPT. ZUELKE
Who the hell is it—Moses?

FRANCISCUS
No sir, Gweely.

ZUELKE/MCKINNEY
Gweely?
        (SGT. MCKINNEY starts for the exit, CAPT. ZUELKE pushes past him)

CAPT. ZUELKE
I'll handle this.

(As a MINSTREL TUNE starts to play, they exit, with CAPT. ZUELKE leading and FRANCISCUS and SGT. MCKINNEY following, whispering and gesticulating together)

<u>FADE OUT</u>

<u>END ACT I, SCENE 3</u>

ACT I

~~~~~

SCENE 4

SETTING: The barracks of "I" Company.

ON RISE: It's evening, about a week later. In the BLACKOUT, as the MINSTREL
TUNE plays, we hear the SOUND OF COINS being dropped into a tin cup.
The LIGHTS SLOWLY FADE UP on GWEELY and BUGALOOSA sitting
on their cots. They have just returned from performing a minstrel show and
are still in BLACKFACE. GWEELY was released from stockade to do the show
only hours earlier. Under his comical face, he's stiff with anger. BUGALOOSA
is gleefully counting the change he made for doing the show. HARDIN lies on
his cot, reading his Bible.

BUGALOOSA
(Dropping the coins)
Man, I'm sure glad Zuelke sprung you out of stockade in time to do the
show.
(GWEELY is holding a mirror, looking at his blackfaced image)

GWEELY
(Sullenly)
Yeah.

BUGALOOSA
I was broke as a skunk and, man, them White folks paid off. Stay you butt
out of lockup, so we can make some more money.

GWEELY
(Rigid with anger)
I don't know what come over me. I know I don't let these Southern crack-
ers get next to me, but all of a sudden I seen blood in my eyes.
(Pause, as he relives the moment)
Good thing Sarge come out there when he did, else I would have
been in a heap a trouble. And the bad thing about it was, I thought he
was a pretty good ol' White boy, y'know. We'd been passing the time,

playing cards, shooting craps, he was even talking about us maybe doing the show at his lodge. Then later on, I heard him and this other worker laughing and joking, saying "It cost twenty-five dollars to kill a buzzard in Texas and five dollars to kill a nigger." I didn't say nothing. Then after that, I seen him and this other cracker empty the water out of the colored barrel, I turnt my head, let it go. Then this poor hot colored worker come to get him a dip of water, barrel was dry. I still ain't said nothing. But then this cracker spits in the barrel and tells the colored feller, drink that, nigger. Well—when I come to myself, I was in stockade.

HARDIN
And now O'Reilly's riding around camp on that big black horse of his, looking for you.

GWEELY
Well, let him find me.

BUGALOOSA
(Getting angry)
Gimme something to take this mess off my face.

GWEELY
Here.
(GWEELY throws him a jar of cleansing cream)

HARDIN
Why do you have to wear that stuff?

GWEELY
(Sarcasm)
Got to put your blackface on.

HARDIN
You already have a Black face.

GWEELY
White folk just don't like a colored man to entertain 'em in his own face. They just don't get no kick out of it.

BUGALOOSA

That's how come I hate to do these minstrel shows—you got to look like a clown.

It's not like that in New Orleans. Wish I was in New Orleans right now . . . if I was I'd be in the section called Back o' Town, catching a set at Ponce's or maybe sitting in with the boys at Matranga's. My brother wrote me they got a boy play at Matranga's now—Dipper Armstrong—they say he got fire in his horn. Say he may even take the crown away from Joe Oliver. But I don't believe that. Oliver is the king.

HARDIN

The king? The king of what?

BUGALOOSA

(Impatiently)

You know, the blues, the Dixieland, the king.

HARDIN

Can he play as good as you?

BUGALOOSA

(Flattered)

Well—yeah. Hell, I'm good, true enough, but Oliver, well, he got the chops, yeah. He's the king. Yeah . . . in New Orleans the White folks would pack in to hear us, and all we had to do was play the music, didn't have to put nothing on our faces.

(Continues taking off the makeup)

GWEELY

Well, in New Orleans you was playing real music. But here all they want us to do is clown around . . . and grin . . .

(He jumps to his feet, shaking off depression)

Yep, minstrel show ain't nothing but clowning around.

(Grinning, he hops up on HARDIN's footlocker)

Fox had his eye on this here turkey atop a tree. The fox called up to the turkey. Hey Brer Turkey, is you heard about the new law?

(BUGALOOSA jumps up on his locker, flapping his arms and gobbling)

BUGALOOSA
Gobble, gobble, gobble . . .

GWEELY
The new law say foxes can't eat no more turkeys, and hounds can't chase no more foxes. So, come on down from that tree, Brer Turkey, and let's jest talk about it for a while.

BUGALOOSA
Gobble, gobble, gobble . . .

GWEELY
Brer Turkey say, nothing doing, Brer Fox, I'm staying right up here in this tree, where I is, we can talk about it right where we is. All of a sudden Brer Fox heard some hounds coming over the hill . . .
    (BUGALOOSA starts barking)
    Well, I guess I'll be running along, said Brer Fox. Brer Turkey said, I thought you said the new law say hounds can't chase you foxes no more? And Brer Fox hollered back over his shoulder, that's right, that's what the law say, but them hounds'll run right over that law!
    (HARDIN falls on his cot laughing)

GWEELY
Then we give 'em a little "Ballin' the Jack."
    (Sings "Ballin' the Jack" as he dances)
    Come on, boy, get up from there, and ball that jack! Come on, boy, ball that jack!

HARDIN
I can't dance—

GWEELY
    (Pulling him up)
Yeah you can, come on boy . . .
    (HARDIN stiffly tries to imitate GWEELY's movement)

GWEELY
That's right, that's right, move boy, I knew you had it in you, etc.!

(HARDIN gets into the spirit of the thing)

HARDIN
(Singing, as he concludes)
"And that's what I call ballin' the jack!"
(Enter MOSES and FRANCISCUS)

MOSES
That's the last time, the last time! I ain't standing for this no more!

FRANCISCUS
Calm down, Moses, calm down—

MOSES
Don't tell me to calm down! I'm sick of this shit! I'm a soldier of the United States Army, and, dammit, I aim to be treated like one.

GWEELY
What happened?

FRANCISCUS
White civilian flashed a blank piece of paper at him, and walked right on in camp.

GWEELY
(Shrugs)
They done flashed all kind of fake stuff at me, one time or another—baseball passes, tickets, blank piece of paper—

MOSES
Then he stood there grinning at me, like I was some kind of dummy or something!

FRANCISCUS
Zuelke says we're not supposed to worry about checking their ID anymore, so I just ignore them—

MOSES

I ain't ignoring nothing no more! The next one pull a trick like that on me is getting a bullet!

BUGALOOSA

Fool around and get yourself court-martialed.

FRANCISCUS

Look who's talking. You tried to make a White National Guardsman salute you last night.

BUGALOOSA
        (Jumps up)
Tried! Hell, I made him salute!
        (Salutes)
    Next thing I knew I was hauled off to the city jail. Soldier ain't supposed to go to the city jail, the MPs supposed to handle us.

FRANCISCUS

Yeah well, I <u>was</u> "handling" it, but you kept running off at the mouth, so I <u>let</u> them take you down.

MOSES
        (Pacing)
Then they bring us back to camp in those damn paddy wagons. The MPs supposed to be bring us back!
        (Disgustedly)
    But the MPs ain't worth their weight in cat shit in this town.

GWEELY

Hey, be quiet Moses—

FRANCISCUS

Let him talk! Let the nigger talk. That's all he's good for anyway is running off at the mouth!

MOSES
> *(Charging)*

I'll show you what I'm good for!

FRANCISCUS

Come on then, come on—!
> *(GWEELY and BUGALOOSA struggle to keep the two men apart. FRANCISCUS breaks away, paces)*

FRANCISCUS
> *(Pacing)*

Look, we do the best we can out there with no weapons and no respect! Damned if we do, damned if we don't!
> *(Pause. ALL of the men look at each other, then down at the floor)*

I can't even pack a weapon to handle military business, but Zuelke and McKinney just got through bawling me out because I didn't stop some colored civilian from jumping a White man! And I'm supposed to do that with my bare hands! Then I got to come back to barracks and hear you niggers run off at the mouth! Damned if I do, damned if I don't!
> *(FRANCISCUS looks around for something to kick, slams his foot into BUGALOOSA's locker. Bugaloosa hurries to it, praying that none of his whiskey bottles are broken)*

MOSES
> *(Grudging apology)*

Yeah . . . yeah, I know . . . it's just this town, man . . . it's just this hot, Southern town . . .
> *(Accusingly)*

Gweely, I thought you said this town was OK.

GWEELY
> *(Rolling a cigarette)*

It is OK. Plenty of colored here.

MOSES

Yeah, but they all act like slaves.
> *(Beat)*

I saw this old colored man downtown today. He was standing in the middle of the street, with tears running down his face, getting cussed out by some young White gal. She was talking to him like he had a tail, because he'd dropped some packages he was carrying for her.

GWEELY
Well Mavis say since we hit town, the colored done started speaking up some for themselves.

MOSES
They need to do something.

GWEELY
Well, I hope I ain't here next weekend. Put in for a three-day pass to my home. Hey Mose, why don't you grab Selena, since she <u>still</u> in town, and come go with me and Mavis?

MOSES
Naw. I got my fill of Texas.

GWEELY
I ain't gon' be up there long, just want to see my baby sister, and walk around the old homestead. Ain't nobody living up to the old place no more. Used to be eight of us children—two boys and six girls, but they done all died off with that TB . . . before Mama died, she give me this here watch, said it would bring me good luck.

FRANCISCUS
This place is worse than Stamps, Arkansas. I used to visit my grandparents there every summer, and I thought that place was bad. A colored man couldn't walk the road there. He see a White man coming, he'd have to step in the ditch. But Houston—it's worse.

BUGALOOSA
Bogalusa, Louisiana, man. You don't never want to go there. They lynch a colored man as soon as look at him.
        (Rubs the ugly scar on his neck)
    I guess I'll die with this scar.

(HARDIN crosses over to BUGALOOSA)

HARDIN
    (Fascinated)
How did you get that?

BUGALOOSA
Lynching.

HARDIN
Oh my God. But—but you're still alive.

BUGALOOSA
Something distracted 'em and Grand-mère and my brother come and cut me down, revived me.

HARDIN
    (Accusingly)
Why did they lynch you? What did you do?

BUGALOOSA
    (Sarcastically)
What else . . . raped a White woman of course.

HARDIN
    (Repulsed)
You did that?

BUGALOOSA
Fook, that's what they <u>said</u> I did.
    (Beat)
    I used to play at this café, White feller owned it. And he had this little yellow-haired gal, who loved the way I made—music.
    (Plays a riff on his cornet)
    Well, the owner and her brothers got it into their heads it was something going on between us, and got up a lynch mob.

GWEELY

Why sure boy, don't you know? Us colored men just can't keep our hands off them "pretty" White women. They all just so "pretty," don'tcha know? Why, it just ain't no such thing as a ugly White woman, naw suh, you just can't find one.

(Beat)

One thing I hope I live to see, is a pretty monkey and a ugly White woman.

(THEY laugh)

BUGALOOSA

(Rubbing the scar)

Sometimes . . . I can still feel that rope around my neck . . .

(Speaks in Creole, as he loses control)

Prends cette corde autour de mon cou . . . prends cette corde autour de mon cou, etc.

GWEELY

(Hand on his shoulder)

Come on, soldier, get a grip, that's all behind you now . . .

BUGALOOSA

(Trying to laugh it off)

Yeah, yeah . . . they thought I was dead. To this day they think I'm in my grave, but the blessed Virgin Mary was with me . . .

(Kisses the cross)

Grand-mère hid me out until I got better, then I snuck outta town.

FRANCISCUS

Consider yourself one lucky soldier.

BUGALOOSA

Yeah, I used to be an altar boy, so the Blessed Mother Mary protected me. After that I hitched up in the Army. I figured it would be better for a colored man in here than out there, but now I don't know . . . everywhere I go . . . after this war . . . I just want to get out and put me a band together . . . have some peace . . .

MOSES
    (*Rolling a cigarette*)
Well, none of these peckerwoods gonna run me off, I don't let no peckerwood push me around, I don't care who he is, I get 'em all straight.
Remember that time I had to set that little White corporal straight about
those cakes, Gweely?

GWEELY
Yeah, that was in 'Frisco, after the quake.

MOSES
Me and Gweely was helping out in the White mess, so this little corporal
came up to me and told me that the mess sergeant wanted me to cut up
two big cakes and put 'em out, so I said OK, and I cut 'em up and put
'em out. Well, those greedy White boys went at 'em like hotcakes. So when
this little corporal comes back later to get him a piece, cake is all gone.
So he comes up to me and he says:
    (*MOSES imitates a Southern drawl when speaking as the corporal*)
    Didn't I tell you Sergeant Driscoll said for you to cut up those cakes
and put them out? I said, yeah I already did that. He said you sure? I
said, yeah, I'm sure. Then he looked around and asked me again. You
sure you put those cakes out? I said yeah, I did.
    Then I could see he was getting ready to ask me that same question
all over again, so I said, Look! Don't ask me that no more! I already told
you I put those cakes out. What the hell you think, I ate 'em both up?!

GWEELY
    (*Laughing*)
That boy turned beet red.

MOSES
He said I was insubordinate to him. I said he was insubordinate to me, I
was a corporal just like he was—at the time. I said I may be colored, but
I'm a man just like you. He looked at me, shook his head and walked
off. After that, whenever he'd see me, he'd point and tell whoever he was
with, see that nigger there—he's crazy. But that's all right though, he didn't
never ask me the same question twice no more.
    (*THE MEN laugh, regaining their confidence*)

THE MEN
That's all right, Mose, tell it, you sure told him, etc.

GWEELY
Yeah, we laughed about that for time to come.

HARDIN
(Smugly, after the laughter subsides)
Well, so far, I'm not having any trouble with anybody. I just follow the rules. I think we have to prove to them that we're <u>intelligent</u> enough to follow the rules.

FRANCISCUS
And everything will be just fine and dandy huh?

HARDIN
Well—yes. I mean, I think if we just stop concentrating on the bad things and look for what's workable between the races, things will go smoother.

MOSES
For who?

HARDIN
Why for all concerned.

BUGALOOSA
Y'all hear that? This here boy ain't run up against the wall yet.

GWEELY
He live long enough, he will.

HARDIN
What wall?

BUGALOOSA
Y'all hear that?
(Mimics)
"What wall?"

(In HARDIN's chest, forcing him to back up with each sentence)

The white wall, boy. Ain't you ever seen it? It stretches all across this country. Colored man can't get over it, can't get around it, can't get under it. All he can do is butt his head up against it, 'til he bust his brains out.

GWEELY

(Shining his boots)

See—you been up there in Minnisota with all that white snow and all them White folks and they treated you good, 'cause it was just a few of ya—

MOSES

Like a little pet.

GWEELY

So you think everything's just hunky-dory. But that ain't the natural way of White toward colored. Every colored man come to learn that when he run slam up against that wall.

FRANCISCUS

He don't understand what you talking about.

HARDIN

(Peeved)

I understand what you're saying. You're talking about the wall of prejudice and ignorance that <u>some</u> White people put up toward the colored race. But not all White people are like that. I know, because I know some good White people, who are just as human as we are.

MOSES

Don't fool yourself boy. Every White man you meet, aim to keep his foot on your neck.

HARDIN

(Exasperated)

If you fellows don't have any hope for our country's future, what are you doing in the Army?

FRANCISCUS

Hey boy, we're not talking about hope, and we're not talking about the future. We're talking about how things are right here and now. You need to face <u>that</u> before you can do anything about the future.

GWEELY

Yeah, get your head out of that snow.

HARDIN

So, what you're all saying is that the only way for the colored man to progress, is to hate the White man?

MOSES

We're saying you better believe they hate you.

HARDIN

    (Stubbornly)

Not all of them.

MOSES

The ones who don't hate you, don't count.

HARDIN

I think you have it backward.

    (Fed up, FRANCISCUS strides over to HARDIN)

FRANCISCUS

Look boy, don't be arguing with us! You supposed to be so smart, why don't you learn when to shut up!

HARDIN

Why don't you make me shut up!

    (FRANCISCUS starts toward HARDIN. BUGALOOSA and MOSES intervene. GWEELY grabs HARDIN. FRANCISCUS fakes returning peacefully to his cot, then manages to tap HARDIN upside the head, and returns to his cot. HARDIN comes after him)

HARDIN
>*(Struggling, but not too hard)*
Let me go, let me at him, etc.!

GWEELY
Come on boy, come on now, etc.
>*(Getting pencil and paper)*
Now listen—calm down now boy, calm down. Listen, I been trying to call my woman all day, but she ain't been in . . .

MOSES
>*(Under breath)*
Probably with that red O'Reilly.

GWEELY
>*(Sharply)*
What's that?

MOSES
Nothing.

GWEELY
>*(A beat. Then back to HARDIN)*
I go on duty in a few minutes, and when I leave I want you to go around to Miss Stephanucci's and try to get a hold of Mavis again.
>*(GWEELY turns HARDIN around so that he can use HARDIN's back as a desk to write down MAVIS's phone number)*
This is Mavis telephone number. I want you to call her and tell her don't she go nowhere tonight, 'cause I'm coming around there after I get off duty.
>*(Puts paper in HARDIN's hand)*
Got that?

HARDIN
I got it.
>*(HARDIN exits, giving FRANCISCUS a wide berth)*

BUGALOOSA
Hey, want me to go around to the house and tell her something?

GWEELY

I don't want you to do nothing, but keep your French eyeballs off my woman.

BUGALOOSA
    (*Innocently*)
Aw man, you can trust me, yeah.
    (*GWEELY gathers his things, preparing to go on duty*)

GWEELY

I don't trust you no further than I can run my hand up a wet paper bag. I know about you Louisiana men, you be done put some kind of hex on her.

BUGALOOSA

Not me. I ain't going to mess with that woman, no. I ain't crazy like you, no, I ain't going to have that White police after me.

FRANCISCUS

They say he already killed one colored man over that woman.

GWEELY

That peckerwood don't scare me none. Anyway, she gon' cut him loose just as soon as she pick the right time to break the news.

MOSES
    (*Winking at the others*)
Oh, I see, he ain't got the "news" yet. No wonder he's always dropping in the dance hall, hugging and squeezing on "your" woman.

GWEELY

That's all going to come to a halt right soon.

MOSES

Man, you ought to leave that woman alone. They say she's been hooked up with that White boy for six years and not about to give him up for no colored man.

GWEELY
     (Unperturbed)
That was in the past, before she met up with Gweely Brown. And we done talked about why she took up with that White boy in the first place. It wasn't for love or nothing like that, naw it was just so's she'd have some help feeding her children.

BUGALOOSA
Yeah well, that youngest one of hers got red hair.

MOSES
Man, you better be careful. That kind of gal will get your neck stretched.

GWEELY
     (Getting angry)
It's my neck.

MOSES
All right, all right.

BUGALOOSA
But seriously, Gweely, he just saying you need to watch your back, that's all.

GWEELY
     (Pointedly)
I'm always watching my back. 'Specially when I gets all this "brotherly" concern.
     I told y'all I ain't worried about no O'Reilly. He ain't no more man than me.
     (Hoisting rifle)
'Cause this here rifle makes me just as much man as he is.
     (GWEELY snatches up his rain poncho, exits in a huff. LIGHTS FADE OUT on a stanza from "Buffalo Soldier": "When will they call you a man?")

INTERMISSION

ACT II

SCENE 1

<u>ON RISE:</u> In the BLACKOUT we hear the mournful sound of TAPS. The LIGHTS
SLOWLY FADE UP on "I" Barracks.

Offstage or behind SCRIM we see BUGALOOSA playing TAPS. SGT. MCKINNEY
is shaving with a knife, peering into a broken mirror by lantern light. As the last
notes of TAPS fade, a HOOT OWL calls out in the night.

HARDIN enters, with rifle, from guard duty. Suddenly, SGT. MCKINNEY lets out a
blood-curdling scream.

SGT. MCKINNEY
(*Frantically wiping at his face*)
Aw-w-w! Aw-w-w!

HARDIN
(*Running to SGT. MCKINNEY*)
Sergeant McKinney, what is it! What's the matter?

SGT. MCKINNEY
Blood! Blood! All over my face, blood!

HARDIN
Blood??

SGT. MCKINNEY
All over my face, all over my face—!

HARDIN
But—but there's no blood on your face, sir, no blood at all. (*Holding up
mirror*)
Look.

SGT. MCKINNEY
> (*Peering into the mirror*)

But . . . but . . . I . . . was trimmin' my moustache in the glass here . . . when . . . when all of a sudden-like my face . . . I seen blood streamin' down my face . . . like rain . . . blood . . .
> (*SGT. MCKINNEY wipes at his face with a towel, then looks hard into the mirror*)

HARDIN

I-I don't see any, any blood, sir. You must have fallen asleep. You had a nightmare.

SGT. MCKINNEY

Naw, I was awake, wide awake . . . I . . .
> (*Pauses, collecting himself*)

. . . maybe . . . maybe you right . . . maybe I just . . . fell off . . .

HARDIN

Yes, that's what happened. We've all been having bad dreams lately. Bugaloosa woke up screaming the other night.

SGT. MCKINNEY

Yeah . . . maybe . . . I remember when my pap died. Before I even so much as heard a word that he'd went down in El Caney, I seen his face in this here looking glass.
> (*Pause*)

I was trimming my moustache then too, when Pap's face kind of just appeared-like, then it just kind of faded away. Right after that, we got word, he'd went down in battle.
> (*He takes a small photograph from his pocket*)

This here's a picture of him.

HARDIN
> (*Respectfully*)

He looks like a real tough soldier, sir.

SGT. MCKINNEY
> (*Proudly*)

He was. A real Army man, Pap. He were born a slave, though. But he runned off from his Marster when he was fifteen, and joined up with the Union troops. Reckon that's why soldiering's so strong in my blood. I was born to the Army. Even my mammy, she was a soldier.
>   (*Chuckles at HARDIN's look*)

HARDIN
Really?

SGT. MCKINNEY
Well—she was a cook for the Union troops.

HARDIN
Is that right?

SGT. MCKINNEY
Oh yeah. They both used to tell me stories 'bout the battles during the Civil War.
>   (*SGT. MCKINNEY takes the US flag from the stand*)

They said them slave soldiers fought right alongside the Union troops, fighting for they own freedom, and they held Ol' Glory high! Held Ol' Glory <u>high</u>!
>   (*Waving the flag above his head*)

They never let her touch the ground, never let her touch the ground!
>   (*Fiercely*)

And we ain't gon' let her touch the ground neither, Hardin! We gonna show 'em! This town ain't gonna make us forget our duty!

HARDIN
Yes sir! Sergeant McKinney? How long have you been in the Army?

SGT. MCKINNEY
Twenty-two years.

HARDIN
That's a long time. I bet you've seen a lot?

SGT. MCKINNEY

Seen all is to be seen. You young fellers always griping about how hard you got it. But colored soldier done come a long way. When I was training in Newport News, Virginny, we slept out in the open, rain or shine, wasn't supplied with no eating utensils and such, had to eat with our hands, and we had to work, sick or well. Remember back in '98, a bunch of us from the 24th volunteered to care of the White soldiers in the Yellow Fever camps in Siboney, Cuba. We was forty days and forty nights nursing them dying White boys. They said us colored boys had some kind of im-im-munity to the fever.

(Pause)

But a lot of us died helping out.

(Beat)

Almost died myself. Yep. I done seen all it is to be seen.

HARDIN

Do you really think the colored troops will see any action?

SGT. MCKINNEY

We better. I ain't been a soldier all these years for a war to come and I don't fight in it.

HARDIN

But *Crisis Magazine* says that they're not going to send regulars overseas, because they might come back with fancy notions of equality. Du Bois says they're just planning to send the draftees overseas, because they'll be easier to handle and—

SGT. MCKINNEY

(Disdainfully)

Aw, that Du Bois feller don't know nothing about the military. He just sit and spin them tall tales to sell that magazine of his, and you fool enough to buy 'em. Us regulars _is_ going to France and we gon' fight for their freedom and ours too. Just like President Wilson say, we gon' spread democracy all over this world, even to the South. That's what's gon' happen because colored ain't gon' stand for nothing else to happen. Our chance done come!

HARDIN
(Eagerly) Yes, that's the same thing Du Bois is saying! He's saying there's
a colored renaissance all across the land, there's a change coming for
colored people. And after the war we're going to come back home heroes.
The sky is going to be the limit for the colored man!
(GWEELY and MOSES rush in, out of breath. They spot SGT. MCKINNEY and
stop in their tracks)

MOSES
Wait a minute, now Sarge—

GWEELY
Yeah, you got to let us explain—

MOSES
Got to let us tell you—

GWEELY
—what happened—

SGT. MCKINNEY
Y'all thirty-five minutes pass curfew, that's what happened—

GWEELY
Yeah, but it wasn't our fault, see, we had to walk all the way from town
and—

MOSES
That conductor, you know the one I had the run-in with—?

GWEELY
Zipped right past us—!

MOSES
With plenty of empty seats on the trolley—

SGT. MCKINNEY
Hardin?

HARDIN
Yes sir?

SGT. MCKINNEY
Get my book there. Mark down Gweely Brown and Joe Moses out pass
curfew.

HARDIN
        (As he gets the book)
But that conductor is always passing up soldiers, Sergeant, especially at
curfew.

GWEELY/MOSES
Tell him boy, uh-huh, that's right, tell him.

SGT. MCKINNEY
Hell, you can't get a ride back to camp, don't go into town. You two was
late last night. I let it pass. Give y'all a inch, you take a mile. Mark 'em
down, Hardin. KP duty all next week.
        (SGT. MCKINNEY goes back to his bunk. HARDIN writes in the book)

GWEELY
        (Pacing)
This here ain't right . . . it just ain't right . . . !

MOSES
That conductor need him some chastising. And I'm just the one to do
it. Next time I see him . . .
        (Pounding his fist into his palm)
    I'm going to beat him 'til his heart get <u>right</u>!

<u>BLACKOUT</u>

<u>END ACT II, SCENE 1</u>

ACT II

SCENE 2

<u>SETTING:</u> CAPT. ZUELKE's office.

<u>ON RISE:</u> Midmorning. One week later. SGT. MCKINNEY sits in a chair, hat on his
knees, pleading with CAPT. ZUELKE. A stone-faced CAPT. ZUELKE sits at
his cluttered desk, rolling a cigarette.

SGT. MCKINNEY

It's this here town, Cap'n. It's got the men acting like this. You know
Franciscus ain't never been in no kind of trouble before.

CAPT. ZUELKE

And that Hardin boy too. They're corrupting him already—taken to the
city jail for gambling. I bet that drunk Honoré was behind that.

SGT. MCKINNEY

Well Cap'n, I don't think—

CAPT. ZUELKE

No excuses. These men are soldiers, Franciscus, an MP at that. He ought
to be able to take a little pressure.

SGT. MCKINNEY

That's just it. These men been soldiers too long to take this mistreating
without a fight.

CAPT. ZUELKE

Sounds like you can't handle your men no more, McKinney.

SGT. MCKINNEY

I can handle the men, suh, but I can't handle this town and them
police, I can't—

CAPT. ZUELKE

If the men would try to follow the rules of this city with a little better spirit, I'm sure the town would meet 'em halfway.

(Looking through papers)

So, Colonel Gentry's give out some more rules to try and keep some order in this place.

SGT. MCKINNEY

And that's another thing, Cap'n. Look like all these here rules just make things worser. Like sending the men back to camp in them paddy wagons after they spends a night in jail—it's bad for mo-rale. The men feel like they criminals—

CAPT. ZUELKE

Swinging on a civil police officer _is_ a criminal act. Franciscus brought it on himself.

SGT. MCKINNEY

Yessuh, but it make the men feel like the Army's siding with the civil police.

CAPT. ZUELKE

Well, you know that's not the truth.

SGT. MCKINNEY

Yessuh, I know that, but the men, they—

CAPT. ZUELKE

(Exasperated)

So what the hell you want me to do, McKinney?

SGT. MCKINNEY

(Desperate to get his point across he stands, leans)

Well, Cap'n Zuelke, I been hearing "talk" among the men, y'know grousing and grumbling . . .

(Desperate whisper)

I know 'em, I know what they can take, and I know what they can't take, and I don't think they can take much more of this without—I don't think the men ought to be let go into town no more, naw suh, and I don't think the colored civilians ought to visit camp no more. 'Cause see, they got a hand in all of this too, y'know, they eggs the soldiers on, makes 'em do stuff they wouldn't ordinary do.

CAPT. ZUELKE

I don't hear none of the other noncoms whining about closing up camp.

SGT. MCKINNEY

Well . . . that's just how I feel about it, Cap'n, that's all.
    (Sits back down)

CAPT. ZUELKE
    (Scratching his head)
Hell man, I'm the one who suggested the colonel throw open the camp. I'm supposed to be the "expert" on you colored boys and now you want me to go tell him I made a mistake, that we officers can't handle the soldiers?

SGT. MCKINNEY

It ain't you officers suh, it's the men.
    (CAPT. ZUELKE listens with pursed lips and steepled fingers)
    The men can't handle theyselves out there. All this—this—freedom done gone to their heads.

CAPT. ZUELKE
    (Thoughtfully)
Hum . . . I don't know . . . maybe you're right . . .
    (Making a little joke)
Give a nigger an inch, he'll take a mile.

SGT. MCKINNEY

Yessuh. You sure know how they is.
    (Beat)
    And now this here thing with Franciscus is got 'em all riled up. They figure the police ought to be done released Franciscus by now. They figure maybe something done happened to him, they figure maybe—

CAPT. ZUELKE
  (*Absently searching desk*)
Franciscus is all right, nothing's happened to him.

SGT. MCKINNEY
Yessuh.

CAPT. ZUELKE
I want you to go in there and let the men know that.

SGT. MCKINNEY
Yessuh.

CAPT. ZUELKE
He'll be released when they get through processing him.

SGT. MCKINNEY
Yessuh.

CAPT. ZUELKE
Ah, here it is. This is the weekend pass Gweely wanted.
  (*He snatches it back*)
   Ordinary I'd give it to him, just like that. But I got a good mind to
deny it this time.

SGT. MCKINNEY
How come?

CAPT. ZUELKE
Don't like his attitude lately. Ain't you noticed? He used to be a pretty
fair soldier. Now he's getting as bad as that dadblasted Moses.
  (*Pockets the pass*)
   I want you to talk to him.

SGT. MCKINNEY
Yessuh.

CAPT. ZUELKE

And uh—I'll think on going to the colonel with what you said. Maybe it wouldn't hurt to close up camp for the remainder of the time.

SGT. MCKINNEY

I hopes you get on it real quick, Cap'n, 'cause I don't want these men to do something crazy and miss out on France where the real fight is. 'Cause they good men, they don't want no trouble over here, they want to fight them heathens overseas, they want to—

CAPT. ZUELKE

So do we all, McKinney, so do we all.
> (*Conversation at an end, he stands up, stretching*)
> (*Beat. Carefully, watching for SGT. MCKINNEY's reaction*)
But guarding this campsite is every bit as important as being on the front lines in France. Or guarding the borders, stateside. Everybody won't be going to France, y'know.

SGT. MCKINNEY

> (*Unworried*)
I reckon they won't. But I know we going, a good seasoned outfit like us, been waiting for this all our lives, I know we going.
> (*Gets no response*)
Ain't we, Cap'n?

CAPT. ZUELKE

> (*Walking away from SGT. MCKINNEY's gaze*)
Border duty's just as important.

SGT. MCKINNEY

But we going to France, ain't we Cap'n Zuelke?

CAPT. ZUELKE

We'll go wherever the Army sees fit to send us.

SGT. MCKINNEY

But the 24th? We going to France? Ain't we, Cap'n?

CAPT. ZUELKE
> *(Without anger)*

Dammit McKinney, I got work to do, you do too, so let's—oh yeah, that Hardin boy, I got transfer papers here for him.

SGT. MCKINNEY
> *(Slowly rising from his chair)*

You telling me we ain't going to France.
> *(CAPT. ZUELKE takes his time putting out cigarette)*

CAPT. ZUELKE
> *(Sighs regretfully)*

None of the four colored regiments are going, McKinney. You're all staying stateside.

SGT. MCKINNEY

Stateside? How come?

CAPT. ZUELKE

A soldier don't ask why, soldier just do his duty.

SGT. MCKINNEY

So Hardin was right. He said wasn't nobody going but colored draftees, it ain't right, he said the Army—

CAPT. ZUELKE

You tell Hardin to keep his big mouth shut! He going to question the brass? They know what they're doing. Why, you boys are the cream of the crop of your race. They want to keep you out of harm's way.
> *(SGT. MCKINNEY stands like a stone statute)*
> *(Trying to win him over)*

Why, I hear they even got a colored officers training school some- where in Iowa—can you believe that—that's where these papers here are sending Hardin—and they're going to start pulling colored noncoms from the four regiments. Why, some of you noncoms'll get promoted to officers *(chuckling)* can you believe that? I know you can't read or write, but depending on what I say about you, you just might qualify—

SGT. MCKINNEY
 (*Sullenly*)
The war ain't in Iowa.

CAPT. ZUELKE
 (*Getting angry*)
You arguing with your orders?

SGT. MCKINNEY
I ain't arguing with my orders. I just don't know how the men will take
it, I just—

CAPT. ZUELKE
 (*In SGT. MCKINNEY's face*)
You don't tell the men a thing, not a damn thing, until I give you official
orders, is that understood!

SGT. MCKINNEY
Yessuh.

CAPT. ZUELKE
Had no business telling you myself. Don't know why I did, but well—I
figure you kind of deserve to know, what with all the years you put in . . .
I just figured you ought to know.

SGT. MCKINNEY
Thank ya.

CAPT. ZUELKE
Aw hell, McKinney, I don't know why. It ain't no figuring the brass, you
know that. I thought you boys were going, I really did . . .
 (*Takes a folder from his drawer*)
But the War Department sent around this report on how the colored
regiments are to be dealt with.
 (*He flips through it*)

SGT. MCKINNEY
What that report say?

CAPT. ZUELKE
Well, it all boils down to—the 24th ain't going.
  (*Puts the report back*)

SGT. MCKINNEY
Cap'n? Ain't it something you can do about this?
  (*CAPT. ZUELKE lights up another cigarette, shaking his head no*)
  I mean, these is good, seasoned men to go to waste—

CAPT. ZUELKE
  (*Shrugging*)
I know it. Ain't a dadburn thing I can do about it. I'd rather be in the trenches with you boys. I know ya, know what you made out of, but these here White troops they're giving me—

SGT. MCKINNEY
White troops? You mean <u>you</u> going? You mean <u>you</u> got a command over <u>White</u> troops!

CAPT. ZUELKE
  (*Chuckling, fit to bust*)
Damndest thing, ain't it? I finally got me a White command, McKinney.

SGT. MCKINNEY
  (*Devastated*)
But what about us?

CAPT. ZUELKE
I begged for you boys, you know I did.

SGT. MCKINNEY
Cap'n can't you go in there and talk to the colonel, again?

CAPT. ZUELKE
Nothing the colonel can do about this, these orders came straight from the top—

SGT. MCKINNEY

Tell him you got to fight with "I" Comp'ny, sir, tell him we trained and ready, tell him we got a right to fight, tell him we earned the right to fight—!

CAPT. ZUELKE

(In SGT. MCKINNEY's face)

You breathe a word of this to the colonel and I will break you down to the lowest tin can of a buck private, I will have you cleaning latrines until the day you die! You understand that!

SGT. MCKINNEY

(Snaps to attention)

I understand it.

CAPT. ZUELKE

(Beat) What you boys so all fired up to fight for, I don't know.

SGT. MCKINNEY

(Eyes straight ahead)

We just wants a chance to die for this country, like any other soldier.

CAPT. ZUELKE

Nobody wants to die.

SGT. MCKINNEY

Naw suh, nobody want to die. We just want to show the world we willing to do our part.

CAPT. ZUELKE

Well, you'll be doing your part—stateside. Now let's get out of here, I've got a meeting to go to. (Beat) McKinney?

SGT. MCKINNEY

Yessuh?

CAPT. ZUELKE

Take a nip of this.

(Sets bottle on desk)

It'll keep you from being so pent-up. Why, after a couple of minutes with that bottle, you'll see things in a whole new light. Put the bottle back when you finish.

(CAPT. ZUELKE exits, shoulders thrown back, whistling a happy tune. SGT. MCKINNEY puts the bottle back, untouched. He takes out the report, puts it in his jacket pocket and exits)

<u>LIGHTS FADE</u>

<u>END ACT II, SCENE 2</u>

ACT II

~~~~~~~~

SCENE 3

SETTING: "I" Company Barracks.

ON RISE: Later that same day. THE MEN angrily pace the barracks. ALL are present, except FRANCISCUS. ALL are holding rifles, except HARDIN, who's
holding his head in his hands. SGT. MCKINNEY is perched up on his bunk,
surveying the chaos.

MOSES
We got to do something—!

GWEELY
We ain't gon' sit still for this—!

BUGALOOSA
Them rednecks tasted colored blood, nothing can stop 'em now—!

MOSES
They call us nigger when we walk down the street—

GWEELY
They throw us in jail at the drop of a hat—

MOSES
And now they've killed Franciscus! We got to <u>do</u> something!

SGT. MCKINNEY
        (Jumps up from his bunk)
All right, all right, keep your heads, calm down—!

BUGALOOSA
But they killed Franciscus—!

ALL

We ain't gon' stand for this, we got to do something, we gotta clean up this town, etc.!

SGT. MCKINNEY

Calm down, I say! And put them rifles down!

GWEELY

We gotta get out there and show 'em, we can't stay cooped up in here like cowards—!

MOSES

I'm ready to march down to that police station, and kill us some White police!

SGT. MCKINNEY

Ain't nobody marching nowhere. Nobody leaving this camp tonight, unlessen I give the order. Now, the brass gon' handle this. If the police at fault, they'll be punished.

BUGALOOSA

Sarge, you know Slim the shoe shine boy? He says he was in Captain Zuelke's office, shining his boots, and he heard Zuelke talking on the telephone to the police chief about a White mob coming this way.

ALL

Yeah! What about that, a mob, etc.!

SGT. MCKINNEY

Shut up, all of ya! Squawking like a bunch of scared hens! That ain't nothing but talk, ain't nobody crazy enough to march on a armed camp!

HARDIN

(Speaking for the first time)
Oh God!
(Hands over his face)
I can't get the sight of Franciscus out of my mind! His head and face was covered with blood, just covered with it . . . !

SGT. MCKINNEY
   (*Harshly*)
If you had minded your own business, none of this would of happened!

HARDIN
   (*Almost crying*)
I know, I'm sorry, but I just couldn't stand by and watch that police officer beat up that colored woman.

SGT. MCKINNEY
She was a prostitute!

GWEELY
No she wasn't! But it doesn't matter what she was, she was colored and they had no business putting their hands on her!

BUGALOOSA
All it was, Sarge, was a little crap game, yeah. Then out the blue O'Reilly and his partner show up on their horses, aiming six-shooters at us. The civilians I was playing with scattered—one went under this woman's house and I—well—I took off running back to camp. Hardin, he just stood there looking like a dummy, so they grabbed him—

HARDIN
   (*Rapid-fire delivery. Fighting to keep the tears and emotion out of his voice*)
I was going to go peacefully with them, Sgt. McKinney sir, but then O'Reilly started to hit this colored lady, Mrs. Travers, because she couldn't tell them where the other fellow had gone, and when I tried to help her, they started to hit me. At about this time Franciscus came along and inquired as to what was going on, and O'Reilly said: You want some of this too . . .
   (*Shudders at the word*)
   . . . nigger!
And he pulled his weapon and started firing at Franciscus. Well, Franciscus had to take off running down the street for his life . . . then O'Reilly and Daniels got on their horses and chased him down the street. I saw Franciscus in jail . . . after they'd beaten him and . . . and . . .

GWEELY

If Franciscus had been armed, none of this never would of happened! These yeller crackers too scared to fight a colored man on equal terms!

SGT. MCKINNEY

A good man, kilt over a prostitute!

HARDIN

Sgt. McKinney, Mrs. Travers was not a prostitute. She was a decent, hardworking colored woman, but they treated her like a dog. She was in her home, ironing, but they dragged her out, barefooted, and in her underclothes, and took her to jail. And when she asked if she could take her baby with her, they threw the baby on the grass.

MOSES

We're sick and tired of this shit! Seeing our people done any kind of way in this town!

SGT. MCKINNEY

Civilians ain't none of our concern.

HARDIN

How can you say that? We're getting ready to put our lives on the line for the civilians of this country, colored and White and I think—

SGT. MCKINNEY

Don't be giving me no speeches boy.

GWEELY

Hell, the war ain't over there, the war is over here! But we ain't gon' let 'em git away with killing Franciscus, we ain't gon' let 'em get away with that!

SGT. MCKINNEY

Hardin, you sure Franciscus was . . . ?

HARDIN

He was dead. I saw him. He wasn't moving, he wasn't breathing . . . he was just lying there. They beat him to death.

(*Finally gives way to sobs*)

SGT. MCKINNEY

(*Grabbing HARDIN's shoulder*)

Don't do that. Damn!

BUGALOOSA

(*Nervously trying to roll a cigarette*)

I just wish we was transferred out of here, that's all, just transferred out of here . . .

SGT. MCKINNEY

No need a-wishing and a-hoping. We gonna be right here 'til we get orders to pull out.

(*Pause*)

Nothing we can do about Franciscus now. He's a soldier gone down.

(*Silence*)

SGT. MCKINNEY

Hardin? You can read fancy writing, can't ya?

HARDIN

Yes sir, I can read.

SGT. MCKINNEY

(*Pulls report from pocket*)

Read this.

GWEELY

What's that Sarge?

SGT. MCKINNEY

Something I got off Zuelke's desk.

HARDIN
  (Reading)
"The Disposal of the Colored Drafted Men." Disposal?

SGT. MCKINNEY
Read it.

HARDIN
  (Reading)
At the present contemplated rate of calling the draft, we can count on approximately Two Hundred Seventy Thousand colored men being drafted. It is the policy to select colored men of the best physical stamina, highest education and mental development for combatant troops, and there is every reason to believe that these specially selected men, the cream of the colored draft, will be fully equal to the requirements and make first-class combatant troops.
  (Murmurs of approval from THE MEN)
But—the mass of colored drafted men, the illiterate day laborer class has not the mental stamina or moral sturdiness to put him in the line against opposing German troops . . . therefore it is recommended that these poorer-class, backwoods Negros be organized into labor battalions. In this way, instead of laying around camp all day, they'll be kept out of trouble by doing useful work, plus the medical department can be working on them in the meanwhile, curing them of venereal diseases and putting them in shape. However—

SGT. MCKINNEY
That's enough.

GWEELY
Catching VD and doing day labor?

BUGALOOSA
Is that all they figure we good for?

MOSES
  (Holding up his rifle)
I'll show 'em what I'm good for.

HARDIN
This report seems to be specifying newly inducted draftees.

SGT. MCKINNEY
That's how they feel about all of us.

BUGALOOSA
Yeah, they don't think we colored soldiers worth nothing.

MOSES
But we'll show 'em in France.

GWEELY
I'd like to get the peckerwood who wrote that in my line of fire, over in France.

SGT. MCKINNEY
Well, you won't.

BUGALOOSA
No, you won't catch the brass in the trenches with the real men.

GWEELY
Naw, they'll be laid up with some German gal, while us poor "backwoods VD niggers" is taking a snoutful of mustard gas.

MOSES
Hey Hardin, what's that report say about us regulars?

SGT. MCKINNEY
I can tell you that. We ain't going to France.

THE MEN
        (Puzzled)
What . . . ? Not going to France . . . ? What you mean not going?

SGT. MCKINNEY
Find it, Hardin, in that report.

HARDIN
    (Flipping through the report)
. . . it says here that . . . while the ten thousand regulars in the four colored regiments are the cream of the crop, well trained, and proven in service, it is in the interest of the United States' stability and security to keep these men stateside.
    (The stunned MEN are mute with betrayal)
    (Reading)
  . . . it is believed that the tractability of the colored draftee, under the leadership of White officers will be more suitable for the role the colored soldier will play in this war.

SGT. MCKINNEY
Won't be no fight overseas for us.

MOSES
Not going to France . . . ?

BUGALOOSA
Why? What we do? Is it 'cause of the trouble here?

SGT. MCKINNEY
Naw, they wrote that out way before we even come here. It's just like Hardin said, they ain't sending nobody over but draftees. Hardin here, he might be going.

HARDIN
But I don't understand. Why aren't they sending you, you're the real soldiers, you're the regulars?

MOSES
    (Bitterly)
They don't want us to prove ourselves. They're scared we'll go over there and come back heroes.

SGT. MCKINNEY
And they always want to be the heroes, and us to be the cowards.

HARDIN

But that's not right. You're not cowards.

SGT. MCKINNEY

Naw it ain't right, but that's the way it is. They always want to put the sorriest coloreds out front.

GWEELY

We the ones trained to fight, we the ones done give our blood and sweat for this outfit, and you telling me they gonna send a bunch of backwoods draftees in our place?

BUGALOOSA

Maybe that drunk Zuelke don't know what he talking about.

SGT. MCKINNEY

He know what he talking about, you just heard the reading.

BUGALOOSA

Well, let them keep their precious war, they all White anyway, let 'em kill each other.

SGT. MCKINNEY

Naw, they never meant for the colored soldier to fight in this here war. They don't want no colored fighting men, all they want is colored cleanup men—mend the roads, dig the graves, unload the supplies, cook the mess—Tent-hut!
    (ALL the men snap to attention as CAPT. ZUELKE enters with a short riding crop under his arm. He paces the ranks in disapproving silence)

CAPT. ZUELKE

I'm disappointed in this company. Real disappointed. I want you to know that. I went to bat for you boys with the colonel. I want you to know that. I told him he'd be doing the whole camp a real favor if he let you mingle freely with your own kind. I want you to know that. But it looks like the coloreds in this town is a real bad influence on you. So, since you boys can't seem to handle yourselves in town, from now on, for the duration of our stay, you will be confined to camp. You will have no more passes into town whatsoever. You will have no visitors allowed in camp, what-soever. Is that understood?

GWEELY
What about my pass home suh?

CAPT. ZUELKE
(*Struts over to GWEELY, gets in his face*)
De-nied.

SGT. MCKINNEY
What about Franciscus?

CAPT. ZUELKE
(*Whirls around to SGT. MCKINNEY*)
What about Franciscus?

SGT. MCKINNEY
Hardin here says he seen the police beat him to death down the jailhouse.

CAPT. ZUELKE
(*Struts over to HARDIN*)
So, you're the one spreading them damn rumors?

HARDIN
Well sir I—

CAPT. ZUELKE
(*Slams him on the arm with the riding crop*)
I didn't tell you to speak boy!
(*He circles HARDIN*)
You saw Franciscus get roughed up a little bit, you overreacted. It's been a lot of that in this outfit lately, overreacting, and I've had just about enough of it. I haven't heard no report of no soldier being dead in this company. And believe me, I'd be the one to know about it and not Hardin here. I'm sure Franciscus will be back in camp in a short while, and I don't want to hear no more of them damn rumors. Is that understood!

THE MEN
Yes sir!

CAPT. ZUELKE
(Curtly to SGT. MCKINNEY)
Step outside, I want to speak to you a minute.

SGT. MCKINNEY
(To THE MEN as he exits)
As you were.
(CAPT. ZUELKE and SGT. MCKINNEY step downstage, out of THE MEN's hearing. THE LIGHTS DIM on THE MEN in barracks as they huddle, grumbling. SPOTLIGHT on CAPT. ZUELKE and SGT. MCKINNEY, side by side, at parade rest, eyes straight ahead, speaking in rapid-fire fashion)

CAPT. ZUELKE
Colonel wants all the rifles and ammo taken up tonight, and locked in the equipment tent.

SGT. MCKINNEY
Take up the rifles? But why?

CAPT. ZUELKE
(Testily)
Just as a precaution. And don't mention this to the men until we get ready to take 'em up at roll call.

SGT. MCKINNEY
Expecting trouble out the men tonight, Cap'n?

CAPT. ZUELKE
(Testy)
This ain't no disciplinary action against the men.
(Proudly)
But some of us officers will be away from camp tonight at a symphony.
We just want to make sure every weapon is accounted for, that's all.
(Beat)

There's talk of a group of Whites coming this way tonight, and we're going take up the weapons, so we don't come back to camp, and find all hell broke loose.

SGT. MCKINNEY
But I ain't understanding. If we take up the weapons, what the men supposed to do if a mob <u>do</u> come?

CAPT. ZUELKE
Who said anything about a mob? I'm talking about maybe a few young boys sowing their wild oats.

SGT. MCKINNEY
What if they come "sowing their wild oats" with weapons and my men ain't got nothing?

CAPT. ZUELKE
    (Catching the sarcasm)
Look McKinney, we're just trying to nip this shit in the bud. We officers'll have our weapons, we'll keep the peace.

SGT. MCKINNEY
    (Under his breath)
Y'all won't be in camp . . . be out on the town . . .

CAPT. ZUELKE
How's that?

SGT. MCKINNEY
I say yessuh, I'll see the weapons git took up.

CAPT. ZUELKE
No. We officers have to see to that personal. I'll be back at oh six hundred hours for roll call and I want every weapon accounted for, and every man in camp and answering for himself. And I'm not just talking a voice check either. I got to see the whites of their eyes.

SGT. MCKINNEY
Yessuh.
> (*CAPT. ZUELKE salutes, turns and exits. SGT. MCKINNEY follows suit. As the LIGHTS GO UP on THE MEN in the barracks, they erupt into loud talk*)

MOSES
You believe that lie about Franciscus?

GWEELY
Hell naw, that damn O'Reilly killed him.

BUGALOOSA
Yeah, Zuelke's just trying to throw us off. If Franciscus is all right, why ain't he back in barracks?

MOSES
Because he's dead, that's why!

HARDIN
Maybe—maybe I was wrong. I mean, I don't think Captain Zuelke would lie, do you?
> (*THEY groan at his naïveté*)

ALL
Man . . . !

HARDIN
> (*Hopefully*)

But—but maybe, somehow, Franciscus is alive, maybe—

GWEELY
> (*In HARDIN's face*)

You know what you seen, don'tcha boy?

HARDIN
Well . . . I thought . . .

GWEELY
You thought! Don't you know what you seen!

HARDIN
Well, I-I-I . . .

GWEELY
Don't you know what you seen!

HARDIN
Yes . . . yes! I saw Franciscus—dead!

MOSES
    (Grabbing his rifle)
That's enough for me.

GWEELY
    (Holding up rifle)
Me too.

MOSES
Franciscus is dead and this town's gonna pay!

BUGALOOSA
I knew this place wasn't going to be no good, ain't no place in the South no good. I just wish we was out of here, that's all, just out of here—!

MOSES
Well, I'm ready for a fight! They're not going to let us go overseas, right? Well OK then, we might as well have our own war right here.

GWEELY
I'm spoiling to chastise me a White boy anyway. And the first one I'm looking for is that damn O'Reilly.

BUGALOOSA
Yeah Gweely, after what he did to you—made you get up from the table with your own woman.

GWEELY

If I of had me a pistol on me I'da kilt that peckerwood right dead on the
spot.

HARDIN

(*Obvious disappointment*)

Yeah Gweely, why <u>did</u> you get up from the table like that? I mean, Gweely,
why didn't you just stand up to him and—?

(*Hurt by HARDIN's lack of understanding, GWEELY covers it with anger*)

GWEELY

(*Grabs him by the collar*)

Boy, I ain't had nothing on me but a pocketknife. He had a six-shooter
on his hip—what was I supposed to do . . . ?

(*For a beat, HARDIN and GWEELY stare at each other, reliving the incident in
their minds. GWEELY turns away*)

. . . get my head blowed off over some nappy-headed gal!

(*Walking over to MOSES*)

You was right about Mavis, man. Did you see how she just laughed
and grinned all up in that peckerwood's face? Just like I didn't even
much exist . . .

MOSES

What else you expect the woman to do, Gweely? He could've went upside
her head with that six-shooter.

GWEELY

Yeah . . . maybe . . . but still, I don't know about that gal no more . . .

HARDIN

Franciscus!

(*FRANCISCUS enters the barracks, very badly beaten, his pride as deeply
wounded as his body. He's in a silent rage as THE MEN eagerly gather around him,
overlapping in their comments*)

HARDIN

Franciscus!

(*THE MEN put a stool under FRANCISCUS*)

BUGALOOSA

Man, are we glad to see you! This here boy had us thinking you was dead—

HARDIN

Well, he looked dead—!

GWEELY

For a second there I thought I was seeing a ghost—!

MOSES

For once it's good to see your ugly face—!

GWEELY

You all right, soldier?

FRANCISCUS

(*Clenched teeth*)

I don't want to talk about it! I'm through talking!

GWEELY

O'Reilly—he was in on it, wasn't he?

FRANCISCUS

The ring leader.

GWEELY

Don't worry, he gon' get his.

MOSES

Yeah, and that conductor too.

SGT. MCKINNEY

Tent-hut!

(*SGT. MCKINNEY enters with CAPT. ZUELKE. THE MEN jump to attention, helping FRANCISCUS up*)

CAPT. ZUELKE

Well. I see you have Franciscus back with you?

SGT. MCKINNEY

(*Surprised and glad to see FRANCISCUS*)

Yessir, yessuh, and mighty glad to have him back.

CAPT. ZUELKE

Yeah well, that'll teach you to monitor your mouth, Hardin.

HARDIN

Yes sir.

CAPT. ZUELKE

(*Very put-upon*)

And now, as if I don't have enough to deal with, the city police have sent a detective to camp. It seems one of you soldiers swiped a shoe shine kit from some store and we've got to search all the barracks.

MOSES

A shoe shine kit—!

SGT. MCKINNEY

Shut up. Don't worry, Cap'n, if it's in here, of which I don't believe it is, I'll find it.

(*To THE MEN*)

All right, turn your stuff out.

CAPT. ZUELKE

(*Looking at his watch*)

And make it snappy.

(*Grumbling under their breath, THE MEN throw open their footlockers, shake out their duffel bags, etc. SGT. MCKINNEY goes down the line, with CAPT. ZUELKE behind him. SGT. MCKINNEY stops in front of GWEELY and looks at a beat-up shoe shine kit*)

GWEELY

You know I been had that kit ever since I been in the Army.

SGT. MCKINNEY
        (Putting it back)
Yeah, I know.

CAPT. ZUELKE
Here, let me see that.

SGT. MCKINNEY
Oh, he been had this old raggedy thing.
        (CAPT. ZUELKE knows it's not the kit but wants to assert his authority)

CAPT. ZUELKE
I <u>said</u> let me look at it.
        (SGT. MCKINNEY lets it drop into CAPT. ZUELKE's hand)
    No, this can't be it, McKinney. I told you the one we're looking for
is spank brand new.

SGT. MCKINNEY
Probably find it in "M" Comp'ny. You know how them boys is.

CAPT. ZUELKE
        (Chuckling)
Yeah, they'll steal the wet out of water, and the stink out of shit . . . hey,
what's this?
        (At BUGALOOSA's cot, holding up a new kit)

BUGALOOSA
Sir, I didn't steal nothing, no. It's spank brand new, yeah, but I paid for
that kit, I bought it at a store in town, I'll take you to the store.

MOSES
I was with him when he bought that kit.

BUGALOOSA
Tell him, Moses, I ain't stole nothing.

CAPT. ZUELKE

Maybe, maybe not. But I got to collect all new shoe shine kits and you got to come with me.

> *(Starts to lead BUGALOOSA away)*

BUGALOOSA

But—but I ain't done nothing.

SGT. MCKINNEY

What they gonna do to him, Cap'n?

CAPT. ZUELKE

If he didn't steal it, nothing. All the men with new kits have to be taken down to city jail where the store owner can look them over. If he's innocent, he'll be let go.

MOSES

You'll be back in a minute, Boog.

BUGALOOSA

> *(Hopeless)*

Yeah.

CAPT. ZUELKE

> *(To BUGALOOSA)*

Wait here a minute.

> *(He walks over to GWEELY)*

Damn good minstrel show you gave the other day Gweely. I want you to do it for the men in camp tonight.

GWEELY

I can't do the show without Bugaloosa, sir. Me and him does the show together.

CAPT. ZUELKE

Well—get Moses.

GWEELY
Suh, Moses can't dance nor sing.

CAPT. ZUELKE
    (Looking at MOSES)
Sure he can.
    (To GWEELY)
    Do the show.

GWEELY
Yessuh.

CAPT. ZUELKE
    (Aside to SGT. MCKINNEY)
Figure the show is a good way to keep them occupied tonight, you know
what I mean? See it gets organized.

SGT. MCKINNEY
I'll get right on it.

CAPT. ZUELKE
Come on, Bugaloosa.
    (CAPT. ZUELKE and BUGALOOSA exit)

SGT. MCKINNEY
    (To THE MEN)
I'll be right back. Brown, get that show together.
    (He exits)

MOSES
    (Slams lid on his footlocker)
A shoe shine kit! A damn shoe shine kit!

GWEELY
A minstrel show!

MOSES
Can you believe that!

GWEELY
It be a minstrel show tonight, Zuelke'll be the one to do it.

HARDIN
I've never stolen anything in my life! And if I ever would, it sure wouldn't be a damn shoe shine kit!
(*Slams the lid of his footlocker*)

GWEELY
Tell it boy.

HARDIN
And Moses, you told him you were with Bugaloosa when he bought that kit, and he still took him down.

MOSES
Hell, I don't know where Bugaloosa got that kit from, and I don't care. But it still don't give them no right to come in here on us like we're a bunch of criminals.

FRANCISCUS
This place just gets worse and worse. The jail and the infirmary were full of coloreds who'd been beat half to death by the police.

HARDIN
I know, I saw them.

FRANCISCUS
I heard O'Reilly and the Mounted Police making plans to come out here and put us "uppity niggers" in our place.

GWEELY
We heard the talk.

FRANCISCUS
(*Stands up, sights his rifle into the audience*)
Well, let 'em come.

MOSES
    (Sights his rifle into audience)
Yeah, we'll be ready for 'em.

GWEELY/MOSES
    (Sight rifles into audience)
Let 'em come.

FADE OUT

END ACT II, SCENE 3

ACT II

SCENE 4

<u>ON RISE:</u> Company "I" Barracks. A few hours later. We hear the distant sound of
  THUNDER and a light DRIZZLE. MOSES is skulking in an area outside the
  barracks; GWEELY paces with his rifle; FRANCISCUS tends his wounds;
  BUGALOOSA is on his knees at his altar. MOSES takes a final look around,
  then ducks into the barracks with an ammunition box.

MOSES

Hey fellows, I got some more ammo.
> *(THE MEN crowd around as MOSES puts the box on the floor and opens it.*
> *SGT. MCKINNEY quietly enters at one of the tent entrances and watches the men,*
> *who are unaware of him)*

MOSES

I figure we can make a couple more trips to the supply tent before eight
o'clock tonight.
> *(Hiding ammo)*

  We got to be able to get enough of the men to stand with us, though.
That's the thing, some of these yellow cowards. If just one or two of us
go out after that mob, we going to get our butts court-martialed. But if
we all go out, they can't court-martial us all.
> *(MOSES is on his knees passing out the ammo to THE MEN who stash it in their*
> *duffel bags, gun belts, etc.)*

GWEELY

Stop worrying, I talked to the boys in "M" and "J," they with us.

MOSES

I ain't worried, I been court-martialed before, did three months hard
labor.

FRANCISCUS

If they heard the talk I heard down at the jailhouse, they'd all be with us.

MOSES
Yeah, but some of these uncle toms . . .

FRANCISCUS
In the jitney on the way back to camp, the looie they sent to pick me up tried to get me to come back here and smooth things over. Told me to keep you fellows "calm."

GWEELY
    (Small laugh)
What'd you tell him?

FRANCISCUS
I told him—OK. Give me some more of that ammo.

SGT. MCKINNEY
That all you men gonna do . . . ?
    (The surprised MEN jump to attention)

SGT. MCKINNEY
. . . sit around and grumble? I say, that all y'all gonna do—talk? Huh?

MOSES
    (Unsure)
Well Sarge, what you want us to do?

BUGALOOSA
We can't just wait here like sitting ducks.

GWEELY
Yeah, we figure if trouble coming, we got to meet it head-on.

SGT. MCKINNEY
Head-on huh? With your bare hands?

GWEELY
    (Holding up his rifle)
Bare hands?

SGT. MCKINNEY
          (*Calmly*)
They planning to take up the rifles at roll call.

THE MEN
          (*Outraged*)
What—? Take up the rifles? Take up the rifles? They can't do that!

SGT. MCKINNEY
Gentry's orders.

BUGALOOSA
What they trying to do, get us killed?

SGT. MCKINNEY
Say he don't want no trouble in camp tonight.

BUGALOOSA
Trouble? This town is causing all the trouble.

FRANCISCUS
But the Army don't care about us, so long's no White folks get hurt.

MOSES
So what we supposed to be—target practice?

SGT. MCKINNEY
We ain't gonna be target practice for nobody.

FRANCISCUS
So, what do we do when they come for the rifles?

SGT. MCKINNEY
          (*Sizing up the men*)
Soldier don't give up his rifle.

GWEELY
So, what you saying, Sarge?

MOSES
Sound like you saying we go down first! Well, I'm for that!

SGT. MCKINNEY
Oh you is, is you? You got a lot of mouth Moses. All of y'all got a lot of mouth this evening. But what I heard y'all planning to do, take more than mouth. It take guts! It take being ready to put everything on the line, 'cause if you buck this town, ain't no turning back.
　　(He looks them in the eyes one by one)

MOSES
I don't want to turn back.

FRANCISCUS
All I know is, no White man's putting his hands on me again, that's all I know.

GWEELY
I'm ready to put my rifle where my mouth is.

BUGALOOSA
We don't want no trouble, Sarge, but don't look like we got no choice—we can't sit here, waiting for that mob to take us. We ain't got no choice!

SGT. MCKINNEY
Damn right, we ain't got no choice. This here town done took everything we come in here with—our respect, our chance for glory in France, and now the Army want us to give up our weapons so's they can come in here and slaughter us. Well, if this be the only battle they let us fight, it ain't gon' be no slaughter!

MOSES
Damn sure ain't! The hell with France!

GWEELY
We ain't giving up our rifles!

FRANCISCUS
We'll go down first!

BUGALOOSA
And die like fighting men!

GWEELY
Let's get to work right here, clean up this goddam town!

SGT. MCKINNEY
Awright! Y'all sound like the regulars you was trained to be, and I stand with ya! Your bootlicking superiors done deserted you, they ain't gonna protect you. But y'all my men and I'll go down with you. I'ma round up the rest of the company, weed out the cowards from the men . . . and all who ain't with us, is against us. Understand?

THE MEN
    (Gripping their rifles)
We understand.
    (HARDIN runs in, out of breath, with a shirt full of loose ammunition)

HARDIN
Hey fellows, I got some more ammunition. Sorry it took so long but I—
    (Spots SGT. MCKINNEY)
  Oh! Sarge!
    (He jumps to attention, dropping the ammunition to the floor)

SGT. MCKINNEY
At ease boy. And pick up that ammo.
    (HARDIN scrambles to pick it up, looking to GWEELY for an explanation)
  I stood out there about half a hour, watching you get up the nerve to go in the supply tent.

HARDIN
    (Gulps)
You did?

SGT. MCKINNEY
It was clear as water what you was up to.

HARDIN
It was?

SGT. MCKINNEY
A looie was coming your way, I had to head him off with some cocka-mamie story.

HARDIN
You did?

GWEELY
Relax, Sarge is with us.

HARDIN
He is?

SGT. MCKINNEY
Stash that ammo, boy. Zuelke'll be in here in a minute. And when he come in, everybody just go along with whatsoever I do.

MOSES
What about when he ask for the weapons?

SGT. MCKINNEY
I said just go along with whatsoever I do.
        (THE MEN nod, satisfied, and continue hiding ammo in different items of equipment)
    And whiles you stashing that ammo, save a bullet for yourself.
        (THE MEN stop, understanding what's really being said)

HARDIN
        (Puzzled)
Sir?

SGT. MCKINNEY

This ain't no chillun's game we playing tonight, boy. We could swing for what we about to do tonight. Only, a soldier don't die by the rope, criminals die by the rope. A soldier go down in battle. That's why I say, save a bullet for yourself.

> (*SGT. MCKINNEY holds up a bullet, then puts it in his shirt pocket. THE MEN do the same*)

You understand boy?

HARDIN

> (*Solemnly*)

I understand, sir.

SGT. MCKINNEY

You ready?

HARDIN

Count me in.

SGT. MCKINNEY

Tent-hut!

> (*Enter CAPT. ZUELKE, holding a lantern, and wearing a sidearm for the first time*)

CAPT. ZUELKE

All right, McKinney, fall the men in for roll call!

SGT. MCKINNEY

Y'all heard your Cap'n, fall in!

CAPT. ZUELKE

> (*Handing the lantern to SGT. MCKINNEY*)

Hold this up to each man's face, as you call his name.

> (*Holding up the lantern, SGT. MCKINNEY goes down the row*)

SGT. MCKINNEY

Brown!

GWEELY
Here!

SGT. MCKINNEY
Hardin!

HARDIN
Here!

SGT. MCKINNEY
Honoré!

BUGALOOSA
Here!

SGT. MCKINNEY
Franciscus!

FRANCISCUS
Here!

SGT. MCKINNEY
Moses!

MOSES
Here!

CAPT. ZUELKE
    (With his back to SGT. MCKINNEY)
All right, McKinney, you can take up the rifles now.
    (Pause, as he waits for SGT. MCKINNEY to give the order)
  I <u>said</u> you can—
    (CAPT. ZUELKE hears the sound of a RIFLE COCKING. He whirls around to find
    himself looking down the barrel of SGT. MCKINNEY's weapon. The OTHER MEN
    train their rifles on him too. Except HARDIN, who watches open mouthed)

CAPT. ZUELKE
What . . . ? What the hell . . . !

SGT. MCKINNEY
We ain't giving up our rifles.

CAPT. ZUELKE
What is this?
        (Takes a step)

SGT. MCKINNEY
Take another step and I'll bore you. Gweely, get his weapon.

CAPT. ZUELKE
        (Upraised hands)
What is this? What's behind this?

SGT. MCKINNEY
We ain't gonna let this town lynch us, that's what's behind it.

CAPT. ZUELKE
        (Angrily)
I told you we would handle that.

MOSES
Yeah, we just bet you would—

CAPT. ZUELKE
Shut up Moses!

MOSES
You shut up!

CAPT. ZUELKE
McKinney—stop, think. You're putting your head in a noose. You're going to throw twenty-two good years down the drain, and for what?

SGT. MCKINNEY
I done already throwed twenty-two "good" years down the drain, working and sweating for this outfit. And now the Army tell me, me and my men ain't good enough to fight with the White boys in France.

CAPT. ZUELKE
So that's what's behind this insurrection?

SGT. MCKINNEY
They taking our chance at glory in France, but we gonna get that glory anyway.

CAPT. ZUELKE
Glory? Hell, you're crazy!

GWEELY
        (Poking CAPT. ZUELKE with his rifle)
You keep talking, we'll show you who crazy.

CAPT. ZUELKE
I can't believe this shit.

MOSES
Keep talking, you gonna believe a bullet in your gut.

CAPT. ZUELKE
Look, you boys have been—
        (THE MEN raise their rifles)
    I mean, you men have been under a lot of pressure lately, I know that, and if you just put those weapons down, I'd be willing to forget this whole thing.

SGT. MCKINNEY
Now you talking crazy.

CAPT. ZUELKE
        (Putting in his bluff)
Listen to me and listen good, all of you! If you don't put those rifles down, every last damn one of you is going to be court-martialed, and hanged!

BUGALOOSA
Ain't nobody gonna put a rope around my neck no more.
        (Starts speaking in Creole)

CAPT. ZUELKE

Franciscus? I can't believe you're going along with this, you, an MP—

FRANCISCUS

That don't mean nothing in this town.

CAPT. ZUELKE

Franciscus! These men are disobeying an officer, I command you to arrest them!

FRANCISCUS

I take my orders from Sgt. McKinney.

SGT. MCKINNEY

That's right. These men is mine. Franciscus, check outside.

FRANCISCUS

Yes sir.
        (FRANCISCUS limps out)

CAPT. ZUELKE

Franciscus! Come back here! Arrest these men, I'll see it goes easy on you!

SGT. MCKINNEY

You wasting your breath—boy.

CAPT. ZUELKE

McKinney, we been through a lot together. As one career man to another—

SGT. MCKINNEY

One man to another? You ain't never seen me as no man. You done showed me that in all kind of ways. All these years us colored soldiers done took seconds in everything—food, uniforms, 'quipment, whiles you White boys got the best. But we took it, 'cause we always figured the day was coming when we'd get our chance to prove ourselves to the world. Not to you, the world!
        (Raises his rifle)
    Well, that day done come. We marching outta here tonight, and we gon' meet that mob head-on!

THE MEN
Yeah!

MOSES
Finally gonna see some action! And the first one I want to run into is that White conductor!

CAPT. ZUELKE
McKinney, you go marching these men out of here, looking to harm White civilians—

SGT. MCKINNEY
We ain't looking to harm no White civilians, we after them civil police who ain't give us nothing but trouble since we come here.

CAPT. ZUELKE
You'll be finished in the Army.

SGT. MCKINNEY
I'm already finished in this White man's Army. Fed up! We all is. We gonna march through this town and teach colored how to stand up!
        (FRANCISCUS reenters)

GWEELY
Yeah, let's head for that police station and wipe out all them no-good police!

BUGALOOSA
And let all the colored prisoners go free!

MOSES
I'm ready to go to town and get to work!

CAPT. ZUELKE
You'll never make it.

SGT. MCKINNEY
We'll make it.

CAPT. ZUELKE
    (Pleading)
What about me? What about my career? You go marching these men out
of here, what do you think the brass'll do to me?
    (SGT. MCKINNEY circles CAPT. ZUELKE, looking him up and down in disgust)

SGT. MCKINNEY
    (Spitting out the words)
Brass shoulda got rid of you long time ago. The other officers laugh at
you behind your back. You drunk eighteen hours out the day, you sloppy
and undisciplined—a disgrace to that uniform. And yet the Army see fit
to send the likes of you to France.
    (He dismisses CAPT. ZUELKE with a wave of his hands, turns away)

CAPT. ZUELKE
    (Sarcasm)
So, this is how you "prove" yourselves huh? You wouldn't catch White
troops doing this. But then, I always knew you niggers wouldn't make
the grade—!
    (THE MEN are incensed)

GWEELY
Let me put a bullet in him and shut his goddam talk!

CAPT. ZUELKE
McKinney—!

BUGALOOSA
Kill the son of a bitch!

CAPT. ZUELKE
McKinney—!

FRANCISCUS
Don't listen to him Sarge, put a bullet in him!

MOSES
Yeah, let's mow this motherfucker down!

CAPT. ZUELKE

McKinney listen . . . I saved your life in the Philippines . . .

SGT. MCKINNEY

(*Beat*) Tie him up.

    (*Suddenly, CAPT. ZUELKE makes a dive for his gun*)

GWEELY

He's going for his gun, he's going for his gun—!

    (*SGT. MCKINNEY pulls out his knife, heads him off. The two men wrestle over the knife as THE MEN watch. Finally, SGT. MCKINNEY stabs CAPT. ZUELKE*)

BUGALOOSA

Sweet mother of Jesus . . .

    (*Breathing hard, SGT. MCKINNEY takes a handkerchief from his pocket and wipes the bloody knife. HARDIN is transfixed*)

    (*Overlapping*)

GWEELY

He brung it on hisself, Sarge, he brung it on hisself—

MOSES

Yeah, it wasn't your fault, he was going for his gun—

FRANCISCUS

He was going to turn us all in—!

BUGALOOSA

    (*Going around in circles*)

Holy mother of God, Holy mother of God, Holy mother of God . . .

GWEELY

Come on, we got to get out of here fast!

SGT. MCKINNEY

Wait! Get a grip, don't lose your heads.

HARDIN

Sergeant . . . maybe—maybe you should just throw yourself on the mercy of Colonel Gentry, explain to him—

SGT. MCKINNEY

Mercy? Boy, I done kilt a officer—ain't no mercy, no mercy on this earth.
    (Pause)
    And that goes for all of us—you too boy—we all in this together. Stand by your race.

HARDIN

Yes sir, yes sir.

SGT. MCKINNEY

All right. Get plenty of ammo. Make sure your canteens full. From now on we gonna be on the move, so I'll say it now. You a good bunch of men, real soldiers, regulars, and I'm proud to serve with you.
    (SGT. MCKINNEY and THE MEN salute each other)
    Moses you take the point.

MOSES

Sir!
    (Gathering his equipment)

SGT. MCKINNEY

Gweely, you bring up the rear.

GWEELY

Suh!

SGT. MCKINNEY

And remember, any yeller coward who ain't with us is against us.
    (The sound of GUNFIRE)

BUGALOOSA

Sarge! Sarge! They're out there!

SGT. MCKINNEY

Get your guns! Shoot out the streetlights as we go. And remember—we mean business, save a bullet for yourself. Right face! Forward march!

(As THE MEN file out, GWEELY stops HARDIN. They are the only two left in barracks, except for CAPT. ZUELKE's still body lying in the middle of the floor)

GWEELY

Where you going, boy!

HARDIN

With the rest of you—!

GWEELY

Naw, naw, you ain't! You going to France—!

HARDIN

(Desperately trying to push past)

No, I'm going with the company—!

GWEELY

Naw! It ain't too late for you—

(Takes HARDIN's rifle away from him)

You run away from here boy!

HARDIN

(Still struggling)

No! Let me go—!

GWEELY

Run! Run like the devil hisself is after you! Run to some—some White person's house, yeah, go to Miss Stephanucci's, ask her to hide you out—

HARDIN

But Gweely I don't want to hide out, I—

GWEELY

Shut up!

(The GUNFIRE escalates)

GWEELY

You got to do what I say!

    (Pleading)

We at the end of the line, but you—you got to go on and fight for the 24th in France. You gotta show the world.

    (He takes off his watch)

Here, take this. And remember me in France. Gone! Run, Hardin! Run!

    (GUNFIRE)

    (HARDIN runs a few steps, stops, turns. He and GWEELY exchange quick salutes, then take off running in opposite directions. The LIGHTS DIM to a bloody red glow. SOUNDS of FIGHTING, GUNSHOTS, SHOUTS, HORSES NEIGHING, ETC.)

<u>FADE OUT</u>

<u>END ACT II, SCENE 4</u>

EPILOGUE

SETTING: An auditorium.

ON RISE: Two years later, 1919. HARDIN, in an officer's uniform, with lieutenant
insignia, stands behind a lectern, addressing the audience. His hat and notes
are on the lectern. The barracks behind HARDIN are in DIMMED LIGHT or
behind CLOSED CURTAIN.

HARDIN

Good evening, folks, I'm Second Lieutenant Charles W. Hardin of the
373rd Infantry Regiment, 92nd Division. I'd like to thank you for inviting
me to speak to you this evening about the incident in Houston, Texas,
back in 1917, and of my war experiences in France.

In this tumultuous "red" summer of 1919, colored civilians are riot-
ing out of frustration all across this nation. Many of us colored soldiers
have returned home from the war to be spat upon, ridiculed and even
lynched. But schools and organizations like yours have chosen to honor
those of us in uniform, by having us speak of our experiences in the war. I
think it is good that we have these meetings, for it is the only way our race
can gather a fair accounting of the colored soldier's role in the military.

After the incident in Houston, Texas, I was transferred to one of the
few colored regiments that actually got a chance to fight overseas. A group
of mostly Southern draftees, we weren't expected to amount to much,
but we "showed 'em, we got our chance at glory! We went through the
enemy like boweevil going through cotton!" The French Army awarded
our entire unit the Croix de Guerre with palm for bravery.

(Briskly reading from notes)

In reference to the so-called Houston riots in 1917: On the night of
August 23, some members of the 24th Infantry mutinied, and marched
into the city to take revenge on the civil police for various and repeated
indignities perpetrated upon individual soldiers of the regiment. When
that confrontation was over, some twenty Whites lay dead or seriously
wounded, including five police officers. The same night of the mutiny,
Sergeant McKinney stood beside a Southern Pacific railroad track and
executed himself with a gunshot wound to the head—with the bullet
he'd "saved" for himself. Captain Zuelke, the officer of "I" Company,

wounded during the uprising, later committed suicide, also with a gun-shot wound to the head.

In a sensational trial, held in Fort Sam Houston, San Antonio, which lasted one month, sixty-three defendants were tried. None of the accused testified, all pleaded not guilty. When the trial was over, forty-one men were sentenced to hard labor for life, four to shorter prison sentences, five were acquitted and thirteen were sentenced to be hanged by the neck until dead.

Four of those sentenced to be hanged were good friends of mine—Corporal Robert Franciscus; Private First Class Gweely Brown; Private First Class Joseph Moses; and Private First Class Jacques Hon-oré. Some hail these men as heroes; others say that they have irreparably damaged the colored soldier's reputation in the military. But whatever is said of these men, they met their deaths like soldiers. They had requested a military execution by firing squad, but they were hanged like criminals.

Strangely enough, we have an eyewitness account of the hanging in the words of a Northern White soldier, an Illinois Guardsman of the all-White 19th Infantry, Company "C." They were assigned to guard the prisoners during the trial and execution, and during that time these White soldiers of Company "C" became close to the doomed men. In a letter home to his mother, the Illinois Guardsman writes:

(Matter of fact to keep emotion at bay)

"Early on the next morning, Mother, the day of the execution, my post was at the front of the guardhouse. What a cheerless, miserable morning it was! Five o'clock and pitch dark—no trace of moon or a single star anywhere. The air was damp and cold, and a bleak wind blowing made it feel colder than zero. In the darkness, I could hear the jingle of the chains . . .

(We hear the JINGLE OF CHAINS)

"The men were coming to be placed in the trucks that would take them for their last ride . . . to the hanging site . . .

(In EERIE, INDISTINCT LIGHT, we see GWEELY, MOSES, BUGALOOSA and FRANCISCUS shuffle onstage in chains. Each stands ramrod straight at his cot)

"What a horrible ride it was! The road was full of bumps and hollows. Before our gloomy procession reached its destination, the doomed men took off their watches and rings, and gave them to us White soldiers as keepsakes. Gweely Brown made a speech to us.

(Voice coming out of the gloom)

'You soldiers in Company "C" didn't treat us like criminals, but you treated us like brothers. And if my thanks is worth anything to you men, I want to give it to ya. If any of you fellers ever git to France . . . I want you to go through the enemy like boweevil goin' through cotton!'"

(SGT. MCKINNEY appears onstage)

HARDIN

(Still reading)

"As the ropes were fastened about the men's necks, Gweely Brown suddenly broke into a hymn . . ."

GWEELY

(Singing)

Coming home, coming home, never more to roam, etc.

HARDIN

"And the others joined him . . ."

THE MEN

(Harmonizing)

Coming home, coming home, never more to roam. Open wide the arms of love. Lord, I'm coming home, etc.

HARDIN

"When they'd finished, and after a prayer, a major spoke to the doomed men: 'Just as soon as I give the command, "At-ten-tion!," I want you men to stand up! Tent-hut!'"

(THE MEN snap to attention)

THE MEN

(Wearing a proud smile)

Goodbye Company "C"!

(SGT. MCKINNEY raises his handgun and fires at his head, simultaneously with the sound of THE TRAPDOOR. Each SOLDIER simulates hanging by letting his head roll to his shoulder as though snapped—or as director stages it)

HARDIN

    (Crisply)

After the war, I returned to the States and resumed my education. For I strongly believe that the only way for me, as a colored man, to deal with the wall of prejudice that surrounds this country, is to take advantage of any opportunity that allows me to open a door that was once closed to my race. And I still remain confident that if the colored man continues to chip away at that wall whenever, wherever and in whatever form he can, one day that wall must crumble to the ground. For if France can honor the colored soldier, can America, the greatest country on earth, do less?

    (HARDIN steps to the side of the lectern and puts on his hat. We observe for the first time that he has lost an arm)

And now to the men of the 24th, and for all the soldiers of every race, who have given their blood, sweat and tears for this country—I, Second Lieutenant Charles W. Hardin, salute you!

    (HARDIN salutes the audience, turns sharply and marches up through the barracks, and on into the future. OPENING CADENCE begins)

VOICES OF THE MEN *(Offstage)*

Oh here we go, oh here we go, we're at it again, we're at it again, we're moving out, we're moving out, we're moving in, we're moving in! Your left, your left, your left, right, left! Your left, your left, your left, right!

    (At this point, AN ANNOUNCEMENT is made: Out of respect for the tragedy that happened at Camp Logan, there will not be a curtain, but the men will meet the audience in the lobby. THE MEN, still in uniform, form a reception line in the lobby to greet the audience)

THE END

Sassy Mamas

Synopsis

Sassy Mamas is a sassy romantic comedy about three women of substance and of a certain age who flip the script on gender stereotypes and become involved with younger men.

Cast of Characters

<u>Wilhemina Calloway Sorenson</u> Fifty-three. National security advisor to the president. Uptight, never been married. She meets a young man who becomes her first real love. Athletic physique. Conservative dresser, but a shoe freak. Wears distinctive eyeglasses and clothing of different nations when she wants to go incognito.

<u>Jo Billie Massey</u> Sixty. Hospital administrator, outspoken widow on the prowl for a young man. Looking for "thug love." Robust figure.

<u>Mary Wooten</u> Fifty-seven. Married for thirty years to a US ambassador, suddenly divorced, good Catholic girl. Still slim and petite, former beauty queen, can be a little judgmental.

<u>Wes Washington</u> Early thirties. Handsome young man, with character, a former football player turned sports journalist. Hopelessly in love with Wilhemina.

<u>LaDonte</u> Thirty. Jo Billie's love interest.

<u>Colby</u> Twenties. A gardener from a small town whose friendship with Mary develops into more.

Scene

Exclusive Washington, DC, high-rise apartments

Time

April–August, around 2013–14

PROLOGUE

<u>ON RISE:</u> Three sexy, sophisticated, well-dressed OLDER WOMEN dance onstage
to original song, "Sassy Mamas."

JO BILLIE
(Onstage, addressing audience)
There is nothing lovelier than the flowering blossom of a <u>young</u> woman.

MARY
The shiny skin . . .

WILHEMINA
The shiny hair . . .

MARY
The bright eyes,

WILHEMINA
Their taut young bodies,

JO BILLIE
Nothing lovelier . . .

MARY
Flat hard bellies . . .
(Overlap dialogue)

WILHEMINA
Twenty years younger . . .

JO BILLIE
Nothing lovelier . . .

MARY
Firm derriere . . .

WILHEMINA
Their taut young bodies,

JO BILLIE
Nothing lovelier . . .

MARY
Supple breasts . . .

WILHEMINA
Twenty years younger . . .

JO BILLIE
Nothing lovelier . . .

WILHEMINA
. . . Just taut, taut, taut <u>young</u> bodies . . .

JO BILLIE, WILHEMINA, MARY
Nothing can compare . . . !!

JO BILLIE
BUT,

(MUSIC revs up. JO BILLIE talking into cell phone recorder)

We mature women are giving these young sisters a run for their money these days. We're fabulous at forty, fantastic at fifty, sexy at sixty, sensuous at seventy, elegant at eighty, and naughty at ninety. We're younger in heart, body, mind and soul than many men our age. So why should we limit ourselves? Men have been expanding their options for generations. Why should they have all the fun? Why don't we mature women expand our opportunities and think about a young man. A much younger man. Full stop. Period.

(MARY and WILHEMINA go to their respective apartment spaces, WILHEMINA holding up dresses, MARY watering garden)

I am a widow, the general administrator at one of the largest hospitals in the District of Columbia, and I need to let my hair down, have some fun in my life again. So, I'm changing the tone and rules of the game. It's like this. If my new man were on a ship, I'd be his captain. If he were in the Army, I'd be his general and if he were a defendant, I'd be his judge, jury and sex-a-cutioner. So, I'm searching for some eye candy today—chocolate, caramel, vanilla . . . it's all good!

MARY

(In her garden)

A young man? What would a young man want with me? I'm fifty-seven. I couldn't even keep the old one that I had. The ambassador's wife—chairing committees, throwing dinner parties, eating weird exotic foods that made me sick, dragging our two daughters from country to country and taking care of his ailing mother. All the while trying to hold onto Jesus, trying to be the good catholic girl I was raised to be. I ought to write a book. But, all of that is behind me now—we returned to the States, the mother-in-law is dead, the children are grown, but not gone . . . my husband, Jerome, is retired and just when I thought we were both trying to work on our relationship, he kicks me to the curb for a younger woman! If I could catch a new man I would, but all this talk about catching a boy toy . . . is ridiculous! I can't even catch a cold. Which reminds me I need to get my flu shot.

WILHEMINA

(Down center stage)

I won't tell you exactly how old I am. Any woman who will tell her age will tell anything and my political position requires that I keep government secrets. I know how close the world is to sudden destruction and as of late, that has made me aware of what I've missed out on life. Oh, I have been wined and dined by the great and powerful men of this world . . . I have sat with kings, been photographed with plenty of handsome men . . . but, I have never been married. I have always been single minded.

You know, I find that older men sometimes seem threatened by us. While younger men are often attracted to powerful older women. It's flattering and, in the past, I have never really taken it seriously. How-some-eever, I have a new young escort who's kind of piqued my interest. My friend Jo Billie says I should just . . .

JO BILLIE

Live . . . !

WILHEMINA
My friend Mary says . . .

MARY
Love . . .

WILHEMINA
And, I'm supposed to follow that up with SHINE! But, I'm not sure what that looks like for me right now. So, I'm just going to exercise discipline and end this silly infatuation of my mind.

END PROLOGUE

ACT I

SCENE 1

<u>SETTING:</u> Upscale apts. / Watergate-esque. Each woman has a space on the stage, representing her apartment at this expensive, posh building. Some of the elite of Washington live in these apartments. A few basic pieces, such as a chaise lounge, small table, chest, for JO BILLIE; African art and garden for MARY; for WILHEMINA, who has the largest space, a small desk, sofa, chair, exercise bike (which can be brought on later), mirror, bookcase/bar.

<u>ON RISE:</u> MARY and WILHEMINA are in WILHEMINA's apt. WILHEMINA is holding up a dress for MARY's opinion. By the scene's end, WILHEMINA has on a lovely gown that shows her toned figure. Throughout play she sports eye-catching shoes and purses.

WILHEMINA
(Holding up gown)
Well . . . ?!

MARY
No . . .
(MARY holds up another gown for WILHEMINA's approval)

WILHEMINA
No.
(JO BILLIE enters, dressed in killer suit, carrying briefcase, head down, texting on phone. WILHEMINA holds up a dress)

WILHEMINA
Jo Billie . . . ?

JO BILLIE
No!

MARY
Wil, why don't you wear that new dress?

JO BILLIE
Yeah . . .

WILHEMINA
What new dress?
(*MARY, at desk, writing in her daily planner*)

MARY
The one you got from that young new designer.

JO BILLIE
Yeah. Wear that one.
(*WILHEMINA crosses into her bedroom to change her clothes, taking the gowns with her. JO BILLIE takes her phone out of briefcase/purse*)

JO BILLIE
(*To MARY*)
Mary, I finally got one of those young kids at the hospital to teach me how to use the voice memo on my phone . . . for my book . . . technology . . .
(*Speaking into the voice recorder on her smartphone*)
"The young men were quick to read through the feigned indifference of her glance, comma, that lingered a fraction too long over their broad shoulders comma, flat abs comma and rippling muscles . . . Full stop. Period."

MARY
How long have you been working on that novel, Jo Billie?

JO BILLIE
Ever since I realized I didn't want to go on another date with a man my age.
(*Speaking into recorder*)
"She first started looking for him as she traveled the streets, just looking. Pumping gas or running into the store, she'd try sneaking little peeks at their hard, young, muscled bodies, just tuning in to that Mandingo heat . . ."

MARY
Sounds like pure erotica.

JO BILLIE
It is. Erotica is big these days, Mary.

MARY
I don't know why you don't write about the hospital? I'm sure you have tons of interesting stories there.

JO BILLIE
Too many. I tried to write a book about the hospital at first, but hot, steamy sex kept coming out, so I'm just going to go with it.

MARY
Cameron must be turning over in his grave.

JO BILLIE
Honey, Cameron would say go for it, God rest his soul. He was always my biggest cheerleader, I miss him so much. *(Thoughtfully)* But that's what happens to good men—they work hard all their lives, then they get sick and die. Seeing him go like that . . . *(shaking head)* no, I don't ever want to go through that again. When I get a new man, I don't want an <u>old</u> new man, I want a <u>young</u> new man! *(Fanning)*
    (WILHEMINA enters, fanning)

JO BILLIE
I know what you mean, Wil.

WILHEMINA
I'm fanning because of this menopause, Jo Billie.

MARY
Girl, what are you doing about that?

WILHEMINA
Nothing, I'm hoping it'll just go away . . .

MARY
Wilhemina, it's not just going to go way. I have some herbs from Africa that are helping me get through. I'll bring you some.

WILHEMINA
OK. Oh, I'd better hurry.
(*Goes back into bedroom*)

MARY
(*Calling as WILHEMINA goes toward bedroom*)
Wilhemina, I'm chairman of the International Humanitarian Award
Dinner Committee.

WILHEMINA
(*From bedroom*)
No!
(*WILHEMINA and JO BILLIE laugh*)

MARY
We need a keynote speaker.
(*WILHEMINA is back and forth, calling from room, appearing in doorway, in
various stages of dress, etc.*)

WILHEMINA
My schedule won't allow.

MARY
I'm looking at your schedule. You <u>will</u> be in the country on that date.
Anyway, I've already told them you could attend, everybody's excited
about it.

WILHEMINA
Well gee, thanks for letting me know, Mary.

MARY
You need this, girl. This will give you a chance to show you're really a
dove—

JO BILLIE
Instead of a hawk in sheep's clothing—

WILHEMINA
 (Back in living room)
Of course I'm not a hawk. I'm just strong on national security. I have to
be. I agree with Roosevelt. America should walk softly, and carry a big
stick. *(Back into bedroom)*

JO BILLIE
 (Raising hand)
I vote for the big stick.

MARY
Well, leave your big stick at home. Our theme is "Promoting Peace and
Prosperity in the World."

WILHEMINA
Perfect. I always welcome the opportunity to speak on peace.

JO BILLIE
 (Getting contract out of briefcase)
OK, Wil, you're a lawyer, when you get a chance I want you to look over
the contract I've drawn up for the young man.

MARY
 (Grabs it)
What is that?

JO BILLIE
The contract for my indecent proposal.

MARY
You're actually writing up a contract?

JO BILLIE
You better believe it. Nowadays you have to have a contract for every-
thing you do.
 (Shows MARY the contract)

MARY

The older you get the crazier you get. You really have lost your mind.

JO BILLIE

Oh no, honey, I've found my mind. Rich old men buy sex all the time. Why can't I? At this age, I just want what I want, I don't care how I get it. Yes ma'am, I'm going to have the lucky young man sign right here on the dotted line.

WILHEMINA

(Entering living room, in gown, no shoes, goes to bookshelf/bar)

Jo Billie, I don't know what happened to you after Cameron died, you used to be such an intelligent woman, but seems like the older you get . . .

JO BILLIE

Honey, it's simple, when I was younger I tried to please everybody else, now that I'm older I just please myself.

WILHEMINA

But what could you possibly have in common with a young man? What would you two talk about?

JO BILLIE

Absolutely nothing.

(THEY ALL laugh)

WILHEMINA

You make it all sound so tawdry.

MARY

Doesn't she?

WILHEMINA

You're stereotyping the relationship between a younger man and an older woman as being totally sexual. Older women pair with younger men all the time—for love, companionship, and yes, physical intimacy, but—(Takes seat on sofa)

JO BILLIE
Just say sex, Wilhemina.

WILHEMINA
I'd like to know what's wrong with all the men I've introduced you to?

JO BILLIE
        (Up, walking)
Well, OK, let me count the ways. So far you've sent me on a blind date
with a half blind man, on another one with a guy with a wooden leg,
one with a fellow who farted all during dinner, and the pièce de résistance,
a guy who made obnoxious comments about every sweet young thing that
walked through the restaurant door. And those were the good ones.

WILHEMINA
Oh come now—

JO BILLIE
No, no, let's just face it, older men have not treated me well. They've
been cranky, rude, died on me, and cheap. They don't want me, and I
don't want them.

WILHEMINA
But all the men I've introduced you to have been of the highest
quality—statesmen, lobbyists—

JO BILLIE
        (At bar)
I don't need a high-quality man, I just need a hunk.

WILHEMINA
You're being very superficial.

JO BILLIE
That's easy for you to say, you always have some handsome distinguished
gentleman on your arm. But most men our age just don't keep themselves
up. Now, if I could find an older gentleman, who looks like some of the
ones you get, I'd take him.

WILHEMINA
They're only colleagues, Jo Billie, with—

JO BILLIE / MARY
—high security clearance.

JO BILLIE
Whatever, they look good. And now you've got this handsome young jock turned reporter coming for you tonight.

MARY
Again. What's that, his third or fourth rotation?

JO BILLIE
And what's he play, football?

WILHEMINA
Not anymore. He was a star player until he had a catastrophic injury that ended his career a few years ago. Now he's in journalism.

JO BILLIE
Oh, another dumb jock in broadcasting. But, as good as he looks, who cares?

WILHEMINA
He's quite articulate and intelligent, Jo Billie. I understand he has degrees in journalism and law. I've caught a couple of his reports, and I find his presentation to be very nuanced and professional. I'm impressed.

JO BILLIE
I bet you are. And what's his name again, your young man?

WILHEMINA
Wes. And stop calling him my young man. (*Emphatically*) He is a friend of Coach Berry, you know, one of my usual escorts, who's recovering from an illness. As a favor to Coach this young man, Wes, has volunteered to act as my escort until he gets back. I've explained it all to you. (*Going into bedroom*)

JO BILLIE
Oh, so carefully.

MARY
(Crosses from desk to chair)
I've seen the boy on TV a few times. He started out as a sports photojournalist, then he and that other reporter, Barbara Ali, did such a great job
reporting together on Hurricane Sandy, and Typhoon Haiyan, that the
station sends them out to cover all kinds of disasters now. I think there's
something going on between them, you can tell from the body language.

WILHEMINA
(From bedroom)
Oh really?

MARY
I could be wrong.

JO BILLIE
Whatever, he sure looks good in a suit.

WILHEMINA
(Entering living room, has put on shoes)
Oh, stop it, Jo Billie. Mary, can you help me with this? *(Holding necklace)*
He's been bugging me to do an interview.

MARY
(Clasping a necklace)
I don't see how an interview with him could benefit you particularly,
he's not in politics.

WILHEMINA
He said he would come at it from a different angle, my love of sports,
how I used to play tennis, you know, humanize me.

JO BILLIE
He just wants to get in your pants.

MARY

Right. You tell that young man to email his request to Media Outreach and get in line just like the other reporters. This necklace is to die for.

WILHEMINA

Isn't it? It's a gift from one of my ambassadors. *(Beat)* So Mary, it's really over between you and Jerome?

MARY

Kaput. Fini. Over and out. I received the final papers today. Who would have thought it would end this way?

JO BILLIE

Life is tricky. You never know where this journey will lead.

MARY

Thirty years down the drain. Cheers. *(Holds up wineglass as she goes to chair)*

WILHEMINA

Not totally, you have two lovely daughters.

MARY

Who blame me for the divorce.

JO BILLIE / WILHEMINA

What?

MARY

They do.

WILHEMINA

How can they blame you? Jerome left you for a girl young enough to be one of their sisters.

MARY

They say it's all my fault. They say I spent too much money. *(At their looks)* Maybe I did, but I had to do something to fill the hole in my life . . . so . . .

I bought things. I guess after being assigned to poor countries all those years, I went a little crazy when I got back here to the States and discovered the Home Shopping Network. *(Testily, at their looks, gets up)* Well, you'd think a man would buy his wife a few clothes without getting a divorce.

WILHEMINA
Ha!

JO BILLIE
A few clothes?

MARY
OK, maybe the whole house had become one big closet . . . and . . . I guess when the garage started to fill up, and he couldn't find a place to park his beloved Jaguar . . . I guess that was the final straw—

JO BILLIE
Ya think? And you don't even wear the clothes, you just buy them. You're turning into a clothes hoarder.

MARY
    (Big sigh, back at desk)
I'm so lonely. The girls are right. I should have tried harder.

JO BILLIE
Awww . . . *(To WILHEMINA, who is sipping her drink, lost in her own thoughts)* Wil, a little help here.

WILHEMINA
    (Rushing over)
Oh! Don't berate yourself, you did your best. At this stage in life, we all have some regrets. Look at me.

MARY
Look at you? You're national security advisor to the president.

WILHEMINA

But I have no family. I've given my life to this country, and I don't regret it but, I have no children, no husband to grow old with.

MARY

Well, hell, neither do I . . . thirty years down the drain. *(Pouring a drink)* Cheers.

WILHEMINA

You can't drown your loneliness in wine, Mary—

JO BILLIE

That's right—

WILHEMINA

You need to do something to get Jerome out of your system. You need to get a life.

JO BILLIE

Yes.

MARY

(Going to sofa)

I have a life. I'm helping you with your social calendar, until you can find another assistant, I'm helping take care of my grandkids, I raise millions with my charity work, I tend my plants . . . Oh, which reminds me, I have a meeting with that gardener—

WILHEMINA

What about that old classmate of yours who keeps calling—what's his name—?

WILHEMINA / JO BILLIE

Bill?

MARY

(Disinterested)

Bill Bryant—

JO BILLIE
Yes. At least go out to dinner with him or something.

MARY
He wants more than dinner. He wants me to go to this out of town conference with him next weekend.

WILHEMINA / JO BILLIE
Go, for goodness' sakes, go.

MARY
    (Sniffling)
Maybe I should have tried harder . . .
    (Doorman buzzer)

DOORMAN
A Mr. Wesley Van Washington is here to see you.

WILHEMINA
Send him up please, thank you.

MARY
(Starts to cry) It's been a year since he filed for divorce . . . I thought I was
all cried out by now, but these tears just keep coming . . .

JO BILLIE / WILHEMINA
    (Giving her tissue)
Aw Mary—

WILHEMINA
    (Patting her)
You poor thing. That's all right, Mary, We're here for you, get it all out
of your system—*(MARY boo-hoos loudly. The doorbell rings)* That's him! *(Excitedly
modeling)* How do I look, how do I look?

JO BILLIE
Hot.

WILHEMINA
(*Fanning*) Oh no, am I perspiring?

JO BILLIE
As in sexy, Wilhemina.

WILHEMINA
Really?

JO BILLIE
Get the door.
    (*Calmly, WILHEMINA opens the door. A HANDSOME YOUNG MAN stands
    there, dressed in tux, with flowers*)

WES
Hello again.

WILHEMINA
Hello Wes. You remember my friends, Jo Billie Massey, and Mary Wooten
who live right down the hall?

WES
Oh yes, a pleasure to see you ladies again.

MARY
Nice to see you too.

JO BILLIE
The pleasure's all mine.

WILHEMINA
Well, we'd better get going.

MARY
Remember you have an early morning on the hillll—
    (*Dashes out, crying*)

JO BILLIE

And don't do you two anything I wouldn't do.

(*Exits*)

(*WES puts wrap around WILHEMINA's shoulders, his hands lingering a brief moment, then they exit*)

<u>FADE OUT</u>

<u>END ACT I, SCENE 1</u>

ACT I

SCENE 2

<u>ON RISE:</u> One week later, the weekend. JO BILLIE's apartment. From offstage JO
   BILLIE calls out to MARY as MARY enters her remodeled sex(y) room.

JO BILLIE *(Offstage)*
Go on in, Mary. Tell me what you think of my remodeled room.

MARY
   (Entering)
Oh! It's so . . . so . . . wild . . .

JO BILLIE
   *(Enters with shopping bag. Removes picture of CAMERON from small table, takes
   sex toys out of bag as they talk)*

JO BILLIE
I know! Just getting ready for the young man, girl.

MARY
Oh . . .

JO BILLIE
So how was your weekend, Mary?

MARY
It was very relaxing. I actually enjoyed it. We stayed at the Ritz Hotel,
with a breathtaking view of the beach.

JO BILLIE
Good. So, what did he look like, Bill, after all these years?

MARY
Well, he'd put on weight, but he wasn't fat. He seemed shorter, I remembered him taller—

JO BILLIE
They never look like you remember. That's why I swore off class reunions, they mess with your fantasies.

MARY
He was gray as a possum—

JO BILLIE
Oh Lord—

MARY
He didn't look bad, he just didn't look like himself, but then neither do I. *(Beat)* He had arthritis in his left knee—

JO BILLIE
Oh Lord—

MARY
Yeah, well I have arthritis in my right knee. He was smelling a little like liniment—

JO BILLIE
 (Laughing)
Oh no! Romeo came to the rendezvous with his unrequited love smelling like Bengay?

MARY
They gave us the handicap room because he was limping rather badly.

JO BILLIE
Lord, that's so funny. They just looked at you two and knew you needed a handicap room.

MARY

It was <u>him</u>, not me.

JO BILLIE

OK. Then what did you two swingers do?

MARY

Well, we unpacked.

JO BILLIE

That's exciting.

MARY

He's very neat, he put all of his stuff out on the dresser—his liniment, his pillbox, his denture cup—

JO BILLIE

His denture cup! Oh, no he didn't!

MARY

Well—yes, he did. He has most of his teeth, he only had a very small partial, and he wanted to keep it fresh—

JO BILLIE

I'm too through. He got that comfortable with you?

MARY

Well, we go back a long way. Then he laid out his little blue pills on the dresser.

JO BILLIE

Girl, no. The brother came there on a cane, smelling like Bengay, with a pocketful of Viagra?

MARY

Yes.

JO BILLIE
I can't take this!

MARY
He's recovering from prostate cancer surgery, and his doctor gave him
a prescription for 120 pills and—

JO BILLIE
A hundred and twen—and he plans on trying them all out on you, huh?

MARY
Apparently.

JO BILLIE
I am <u>too</u> through. (*Beat*) Well—did they work?

MARY
(*Sings*) Vi-va Vi-a-gra!

JO BILLIE
Details . . . details. I want some details . . .

MARY
He bought me some really nice gifts too. And he wants us to meet again
next month.

JO BILLIE
I'll just bet he does. I am too through. (*Beat*) Are you going to meet him?

MARY
(*Big sigh*) I don't know. He was very romantic, and quite a lover. But the
connection just wasn't there, you know what I mean? But he's done quite
well. I'd be sitting pretty—if we got married . . .

JO BILLIE
Married? Who's talking marriage?

MARY
He is.

JO BILLIE
Already? Listen Mary—

MARY
I don't like being alone, Jo Billie. I'm afraid of being alone. You know
that. I'm afraid I'm going to wake up one night and find a predator
standing at the foot of my bed.

JO BILLIE
And lover boy is going to take him on with his cane?
    (MARY finally bursts out laughing)
    Seriously Mary, you are freshly divorced, Mary, give yourself some
time alone, have some fun. Believe me, you do not want to nursemaid a
man with prostate cancer . . . not unless you really love him.

MARY
Look, I know how hard it must have been for you watching Cameron
deteriorate from that stroke, but Bill <u>had</u> prostate cancer, he's cured
now.

JO BILLIE
(Beat) OK. (Looking at watch) Oh! I'm not going to be able to make the
baby shower.

MARY
Why?

JO BILLIE
    (Mischievously)
I think I finally found him.

MARY
Who?

JO BILLIE
    (*Excitedly*)
The guy I'm going to make the indecent proposal too! He'll be here soon.

MARY
And you're giving me advice.

JO BILLIE
Found the dear boy right under my nose.

MARY
Oh?

JO BILLIE
I was on my rounds, when suddenly I turned down the hall headed for the lab and there he was. Mandingo. Slinging a mop. And then I saw him later waiting at the bus stop and—

MARY
Well, I'd love to hear more, but I have to meet the gardener. I don't want to be late, the girls are already upset with me for being out of pocket all weekend. You be careful.

JO BILLIE
    (*Waving bye*)
Don't worry about me, see you later. (*Speaking into recorder*) "Standing at the bus stop, he boldly returned her look, checking out her ride, her jewelry, her clothes with eyes that said, 'Bring it on Mama.' And so the games began . . ." Full stop.
    (*LIGHTS DIM. MARY exits. JO BILLIE takes her place on the chaise lounge*)

<u>END ACT I, SCENE 2</u>

ACT I

SCENE 3

<u>ON RISE:</u> Same time. LIGHTS UP on WILHEMINA's apartment. She's exercising on a pedal bike, while WES interviews her, taking notes. JAZZ plays softly in the background. WES's equipment, camera, bag, motorcycle helmet, is on floor.

WES

He just got in a lucky hit, that's all. You know how they like to do the quarterbacks.

WILHEMINA

I know. That must have been terrifying for you.

WES

Yeah, it was kind of scary . . . lying there on my back, looking up at the sky, total silence. I tried to get up, but I couldn't move. I prayed.

WILHEMINA

Thank God the paralysis was temporary.

WES

Yeah, it was a miracle, but the doc said I couldn't risk playing football anymore. That was hard.

WILHEMINA

But you've made a name for yourself in journalism. My, you've accomplished a great deal for one your age—scholar, a star football player, journalist, yes for your age—

WES

I got injured when I was twenty-eight, I've been in journalism for five years, I'm thirty-three years old. I know you've been trying to ask me that since we met.

WILHEMINA
I most certainly have not. I was just—thirty-three, is that all?

WES
Is that a problem?

WILHEMINA
What?

WES
My age?

WILHEMINA
What kind of problem could it possibly be to me?

WES
That's what I'm talking about. Because age is just a number, right?

WILHEMINA
Right, but I don't know how we got on this subject, it's not related to anything, is it?

WES
Is it?

WILHEMINA
No it's not. Shall we get on with the interview?
    (Resumes pedaling bike)

WES
    (Taking out pad and pencil)
I want to thank you for giving me this shot, it'll look good on my résumé. So, what made you decide to give tennis up professionally? You were good, you were a top seed—

WILHEMINA
That's it, I was good. I wasn't great. But with politics, it's a lot like tennis in its approach, you know, the back-and-forth, the serve, return.

WES

Tennis is too fast for me. Golf's my game these days. Maybe you'll take me to the tennis court one day, give me some tips.

WILHEMINA

OK, you know the ground rules?

WES

Well, I know that in tennis scoring love equals—

WILHEMINA

Zero. I'm talking about the rules for this interview we're doing.

WES

Oh right. On the record, I can quote you directly; background, I can't quote you directly off the record, nothing may be used in the story; the information is strictly for the reporter's education only.

WILHEMINA

That's right.

WES

OK, the people already know the highlights of your meteoric career more or less—university president, ambassador to France, national security advisor, you speak what four, five languages . . .

WILHEMINA

Six.

WES

Seven.

WILHEMINA

No, I only speak six.

WES

But I speak seven. A Rhodes Scholar, Yale.

WILHEMINA
Harvard . . .

WES
My condolences. So, let's start off with the question all America really wants to know: Who's your significant other?

WILHEMINA
I thought we were going to talk sports.

WES
It's taken me several weeks to get this interview with you, just need to get a little background first.

WILHEMINA
I don't have a significant other. My life is just too hectic.

WES
I know what you mean. I haven't been able to find anyone willing to fit into mine either.

WILHEMINA
Oh come now, don't try to make me believe you have trouble getting a girl.

WES
I can get 'em, but I can't keep 'em, because of this job.

WILHEMINA
I'm sure the right one will come along.

WES
I sure hope so. (*Beat*) I like that tune, so mellow and romantic, "Bridget." Freddie Hubbard wrote it for the woman he loved . . .

WILHEMINA
You're familiar with Freddie Hubbard?

WES
I'm something of a jazz aficionado.

WILHEMINA
Oh really?

WES
You think I should love rap? *(At her laugh)* I do. I also love opera, funk, rock . . . a little country, and soulllllllllll! *(said à la Soul Train)*
(Grabs her to dance to song)
(Referring to music)
This cat, Freddie Hubbard, was brilliant. He wrote his first hit tune when he was . . .

WILHEMINA/WES
Nineteen.

WILHEMINA
Yeah, look at you.
Youth has its advantages.
(He dips her. They have a moment and he lets her go)

(WES looks at photos displayed)

WILHEMINA
That's my mother. That's Mom and Dad Sorenson. They adopted me, as you know, when my mother died. They're originally from Sweden, but they've built an empire in Texas. Dad was the one who introduced me to sports. In Texas, they're fanatical about their sports.

WES
Yeah, I know. That's where I took my hit.

WILHEMINA
I know. *(Suddenly, wiping tears)*

WES

(*Softly*)

What's the matter?

WILHEMINA

I'm fine. I'm sorry. Just looking at the picture there of my mother, I don't know what got into me. I haven't done that in years . . .

WES

You don't have to apologize.

WILHEMINA

I've just been thinking about her a lot lately. She was my true inspiration. One of the things she taught me even as a young girl was that I should constantly seek to expand my options . . . she was quite a character . . . I lost my mother when I was eleven. (*Sigh*) I just wished she'd lived to see some of my accomplishments . . .

WES

I think she sees you.

WILHEMINA

You do?

WES

Yeah. (*Thoughtfully*) I think mothers see all of our accomplishments from on high and applaud us. At least that's what I tell myself.

WILHEMINA

That's a good way of looking at it. (*Beat*) Well. I'm going to get something cold to drink. Would you like something too?

WES

Sure. I'll have what you're having. (*Calls to her in kitchen*) Let me get a little more background. So, what's your favorite food? (*Writing in notebook*)

WILHEMINA
Oh my . . . well I love French cuisine and soul food, but originally, I'm from Philly. So, you know my favorite is a—

WILHEMINA/WES
Philly cheesesteak.

WILHEMINA
Oh yes! Sometimes I get such a craving, I want to take off to one of my favorite little cafés and get a real one . . . you know? Others try to duplicate it but—

WES
I know. I'm from Baltimore, and when I get a craving for blue crab I have to go home. You should let me take you to Philly sometime and pick up that cheesesteak . . .

WILHEMINA
(Laughs dismissively. Gives him his drink)
Secret Service would have a fit.

WES
Oh, I'm a quarterback . . . I know how to dodge Secret Service. *(Takes drink)* Thank you.
(He takes a sip, almost spits it out)
That's water!

WILHEMINA
(Laughing)
Yes, H2O, that's what I'm drinking. I drink eight glasses a day.

WES
I thought you meant a real drink.

WILHEMINA
I drink very little. I have to stay in shape.

WES
You're in great shape.

WILHEMINA
For a woman my age?

WES
Period.
  (WILHEMINA's PHONE SOUNDS or VIBRATES. She reads message)

WES
Problem?

WILHEMINA
Yes. We have to cut this short. I have to get ready to go.

WES
To the White House?
  (She doesn't answer)

WES
Something breaking?
  (WILHEMINA doesn't answer him, leads him to the door)

WES
Wait, when—when will I see you again?

WILHEMINA
Listen Wes I—I think you've gotten all you need—I don't think there's any reason for us to continue—

WES
Wilhemina, please. I've got to see you again.

WILHEMINA
Wes I—*(Quick decision)* OK, I'll call you when I get back.
  (WES exits. WILHEMINA leans against door, fanning)

Ooooo . . . this damn menopause.
   (Dashes to offstage bedroom)

<u>BLACKOUT</u>

<u>END ACT I, SCENE 3</u>

ACT I

SCENE 4

<u>ON RISE:</u> Same time. LIGHTS UP on JO BILLIE stretched out on chaise lounge in
loungewear, reading from her contract. LADONTE is bouncing around taking
in the surroundings.

LADONTE *(Offstage)*
Man! You ballin'! On the twenty-third floor, lookin' out on the, the
Potomac . . . this crib is laid! Feel like I'm on that show, y'know, uh—*Cribs
of the Rich and Famous*, yeah. Hey I'm not on TV am I?

JO BILLIE
No, you're not. First off, young brother, you don't have to make conversation with me. Matter of fact, I'd prefer that you not speak unless
spoken to.

LADONTE
What?

JO BILLIE
Be quiet and listen up. I've invited you here to offer you a contract—

LADONTE
Hold up, hold up, wait a minute.

JO BILLIE
No, baby I'm driving this train . . .

LADONTE
Well, go on then. I'm listening.

JO BILLIE
I've created a document for your services, and depending on services
rendered I am prepared to offer you—

LADONTE

Services rendered? *(Pause)* May I—uh—conversate?

JO BILLIE

Hm-hm.

LADONTE

Now I know you not just talking about mopping the floor, so I think I got an idea what you talking about but, I got to be sure I get this straight, since you got a contract and all y'know. So, exactly what kind of services rendered you talking about?

JO BILLIE

Services of a sexual nature.

LADONTE

Ah, that's what I thought, but whew! Man, I ain't never had nobody just come right out and say it like that, you know?

JO BILLIE

Well—LaDonte—is it?

LADONTE

Yeah. But my friends call me Tay-Tay.

JO BILLIE

LaDonte, I'm a businesswoman as you know, and I like to be upfront and specific about everything I do.

LADONTE

Yeah, but, how come you pick me? I mean I could be anybody coming up in here—

JO BILLIE

Oh baby, I had you checked out. Trust. *(As he takes selfies on phone)* You're clever, but not too intelligent, in financial need, but not dangerous, street smart, but not criminal.

Let's just say I'm looking for something special and I think you have most of the qualifications I'm looking for—

LADONTE
Like what?

JO BILLIE
You're very fine . . .

LADONTE
Hey, thanks, you're not bad looking either, y'know, for a y'know . . . *(At her look)* You think I'm a thug, don'tcha, you looking for that thug love, ain'tcha?

JO BILLIE
Well, I'll say this: I think you'll scrub up nicely, you'll look good in the clothes I'll purchase for you, but there are still some things I have to check out, of a personal nature, you understand?

LADONTE
Yea. You want to check out the goods. No problem. But let me ask you this here—let's just say I go for this, not saying that I will, but if I did go for it, what's in it for me? In dollars and cents.
  (JO BILLIE shows him the dollar amount on the contract)

LADONTE
I'd be making bank!!!

JO BILLIE
Yes. All of the funds and resources you will receive from me will be considerable. It's all spelled out there in the contract. You may spend it as you please, it'll be your money, what you do with it is of no concern to me. But, I would suggest you save it, so that when our little arrangement is over, you'll have a nice nest egg.

LADONTE
When it's over, huh? So, how long is this supposed to be for?

JO BILLIE

I don't know how long it's going to last, we'll see how things go, I'm just going to go with it.

LADONTE

(Mulling it over)

Well, where would I live then, what you gonna do, put me up in my own condo, like this?

JO BILLIE

Not hardly. You'd live right here with me, sweet thang. I want you near me, so that at night I can just reach over and squeeze you.

LADONTE

(Sudden thought, looks around)

Wait a minute—is LaKeisha behind this?

JO BILLIE

(Looking at notes)

You mean one LaKeisha Foster?

LADONTE

Yea. I knew it, I knew—

JO BILLIE

No, no LaDonte. I found out about LaKeisha when I was vetting you.

LADONTE

So you know uh—she my baby mama then, but it ain't nothing between us.

JO BILLIE

You're not engaged to be married?

LADONTE

Well it was on and off . . . mostly off—

JO BILLIE

For the past two years, now.

LADONTE
Yeah, but it's off now, we went our separate ways.

JO BILLIE
I hope for your sake you're telling the truth, because I'm not interested in breaking up a family. I'll ask you no questions, so you tell me no lies.

LADONTE
We're not together. I ain't lying. I had to let her go, that girl is too crazy for me. I see you did your research though, so you know I got plans for my life, it ain't like I don't have nothing going for me, I got a job—

JO BILLIE
Slinging a mop.

LADONTE
Well, yeah, but at least I ain't selling dope, I'm getting ready to go to school for my respiratory license and everything . . .

JO BILLIE
And, you need money . . .

LADONTE
. . . So, I'm not just some dumb janitor—

JO BILLIE
I like dumbness in a man. I hope you don't disappoint.

LADONTE
Huh? So let me get this straight—all I got to do is move in with you, quit my job, sex you up, and I'll make all that money?

JO BILLIE
Look, I have things to do, do you want the job or not LaDonte?

LADONTE
Well—hell yeah, sassy mama!

JO BILLIE
Don't call me mama.

LADONTE
OK—Ma—Jo Billie, cool, cool. *(Pulls out cell phone)* Wait 'til I tell my homies about this!

JO BILLIE
Your "homies" are off-limits to this place. And your baby mama too. It's spelled out quite clearly here, on page five, paragraph two.

LADONTE
OK, OK, OK! Dang.

JO BILLIE
Now, I have only one cardinal rule, dear boy.

LADONTE
I knew it was a catch. What?

JO BILLIE
Well two.

LADONTE
Man—

JO BILLIE
	(Holding up fingers)
Number one. Do not bore me.

LADONTE
OK, but—

JO BILLIE
Two. When I say zip it, you shut up . . . And, when I say unzip it—well, I don't think that needs any explanation.

LADONTE
O-K, but if I can't even talk, I mean right there it's—

JO BILLIE
Zip it.

LADONTE
     (Under breath)
—going to be boring as hell—

JO BILLIE
Zip it. We'll find a way. Any questions? (As he hesitates) You may speak.

LADONTE
     (A little hesitant)
   Uh—yeah. Where do I sign?
     (She gives him the agreement)

JO BILLIE
And you can get started on your duties right now.

LADONTE
Right now?

JO BILLIE
Right now.

LADONTE
     (Taking off his shirt)
OK.

JO BILLIE
No, no, no, baby. Keep your clothes on sweetness. First, a cup of tea, please.

LADONTE
Tea?

JO BILLIE
Yes.

LADONTE
Oh, OK. How you like your tea?

JO BILLIE
Two lumps of sugar.

LADONTE
Two lumps of sugar . . .

JO BILLIE
Stirred . . .

LADONTE
Stirred . . .

JO BILLIE
(She grabs his index finger) with this finger right here.
> *(He stirs tea, and she puts finger in her mouth)*
> *(LIGHTS OUT, as MUSIC blares)*

<u>END ACT I, SCENE 4</u>

ACT I

SCENE 5

ON RISE: A few days later. MARY's apartment. A GARDEN AREA, maybe the PATIO or WINDOWBOX. MARY is tending her flowers as she talks to the gardener, COLBY. They move flowers around in the tight confines trying to avoid touching each other, and realize they are talking about more than the garden.

MARY

My Garden of Eden project . . . Since my husband was an ambassador, for many years, to many African countries . . . I just fell in love with the continent. And, I want to re-create the floral delights of an African garden. I miss the flowers and plants of Africa. This is a cutting from the Hottentot sugarbush.

(COLBY brings plant over to her)

And this is the Japanese lantern, one of my favorites. You find it in Kenya, Mozambique and Tanzania. It's from the hibiscus family you know, you make various drinks with it. I love hibiscus tea. Look how beautiful . . . delicate pinkish-red petals, and like many of the hibiscus species the staminal column is long and sticks out.

COLBY

Yes ma'am.

MARY

And of course we must have the aloe plant, succulent stem. It is native to KwaZulu-Natal in South Africa.

COLBY

This is a beautiful plant. It's got a lot of names, the miracle plant, medicine plant . . .

MARY/COLBY

. . . the burn plant. Yeah, yeah . . .

COLBY

There's a clear gel inside the leaves that when you break it open it's used for healing, soothing and . . .

MARY/COLBY

. . . and rejuvenating.

COLBY

It's real easy to grow too.

MARY

Where should we put this? Perhaps we'd put it here.
          (*She puts plant down, bending over. COLBY fights not to ogle her*)

COLBY

I wrote another poem.

MARY

Oh, you did? Well, lovely. Regale me.

COLBY

Say what?

MARY

Read it . . . just read it . . .

COLBY
          (*Maybe a song or poem*)

Where's the love in the city?
I don't see no love or compassion.
In the city, I can see sickness in the faces of the elders,
so I make planters for them to put in their windows
and on their porches with healing herbs in them.
I can see pain in the eyes of little children, too
But love and compassion release the hormones.
Like the love between a child and a mother
Love and compassion release the healing hormones . . .

Like the love between a man and a woman
The love stirs up healing hormones in one another.

MARY

I lived in Africa for years. It's awesomely beautiful but it has a lot of poverty and pain.

I never realized how much I loved it until I left. It's God's sanctuary for animals.

COLBY

That's right up my alley. I love animals. I'm a country boy. I love the land, and guns, and flowers but l can't talk about these kind of things to girls my age, they just don't get me. But I can talk to you, Miss Mary . . . Wooten.

MARY

(Giggle) My ex-husband and I have seen herds of elephant, gazelles, zebra. Heard lions roaring in the distance. We've seen the orange sun setting on the Serengeti plains. You'd think that after viewing all of that beauty together it would have brought us closer.

COLBY

Yeah.

MARY

But it didn't. He used his ambassadorship to impress other women.

COLBY

I think my girl found herself another man. She said I wasn't spending enough time with her, so she called off the wedding. But I was working two jobs, six days a week, saving to buy her a house and to pay off the wedding.

MARY

Aww, I'm sorry. Colby . . . Let me feel your guns.

COLBY

Beg pardon?

MARY

Your muscles. *(He flexes his muscles, she kneads them)* Ooooh . . . I think you would like Africa.

COLBY

It sounds so pretty.

MARY

(Excitedly)

There's this place in Zambia, Colby, called the Victoria Falls. Can you believe I started to bungee jump off of it once, but I didn't?

COLBY

Sound like that would of been fun. How come you didn't jump?

MARY

It was foolish. My ex-husband stopped me, he was right. I was too old to do something like that. It was too dangerous, I could have broken my bones, and I already have a little arthritis.

COLBY

I got something for that. *(At her look)* Oh no, I don't meant that, I mean I got some ointment—

MARY

Thank you, but I don't want to smell like ointment around you, Colby.

COLBY

Oh, this is something that I made up, it smells real good. I'll bring you some next time and rub you down—uh—I didn't mean it like that, I meant—

MARY

Oh . . . ummmm.

COLBY

Naw, naw, not that, I mean—ummm—

MARY
I love the rosebush you bought me—

COLBY
Yeah, I know how to make 'em grow real big, the roses, I mean, in the garden I mean—!

MARY/COLBY
Um—ah—um . . .

COLBY
Well, guess I better get back to the chrysanthemums . . .

MARY
Perhaps you could put the Hottentot . . .

COLBY
sugarbush . . .

MARY
Yes . . . That's what it's called. (*MARY's words trail off. Their eyes meet*)

<u>FADE OUT</u>

<u>END ACT I, SCENE 5</u>

ACT I

SCENE 6

ON RISE: A few weeks later. Early morning. WILHEMINA's apt. In silence, WILHE-
MINA brings in teapot, pours a cup for JO BILLIE as JO BILLIE enters. WIL-
HEMINA looks through newspaper. JO BILLIE sips tea, stretching sensuously
with a satisfied smile on her face.

JO BILLIE

Let's get some music on in here.
(JO BILLIE crosses to remote for music. Turns on. Low volume. Jazz comes on)
I don't want to hear that. *(Goes through a few choices)* I don't want to hear
that either. *(Country music)* Nooo. *(She then lands on "Super Freak" by Rick James or
another appropriate song)* Yes!
*(The volume is low. JO BILLIE lets it play at a low volume and then it feels good to
her and she turns it up SLOWLY and starts to dance. Enter MARY, with planner)*

MARY

G'morning . . . sorry I'm late.

WILHEMINA

G'morning . . .
*(JO BILLIE and WILHEMINA start singing to song. JO BILLIE dances over to
WILHEMINA. MARY crosses into offstage room to get something, but does not
engage in the antics)*

JO BILLIE

Oh, come on, Wilhemina. You know you want to . . . Rick James!
. . . *(Dancing)* "Ow! Come on!"
*(WILHEMINA gives in a little. And, then . . . a little more . . . gets funky with it.
MARY reenters, dancing and singing)*

MARY

(Singing)
"It's super freaky, owww!"

(LADIES get into a little singing group routine, until MARY makes a wrong step on her arthritic knee and brings it to an end. MARY turns off music)

MARY

All right ladies, ladies, we have work to do.
(WILHEMINA's PHONE RINGS. It is the PRESIDENT'S RING. It has a different tone from the other ring)

MARY

Oh! That's the president's ring, Wilhemina! *(Hands WILHEMINA her phone)*

WILHEMINA

Good morning Mr. President! *(Steps aside for brief conversation)*

JO BILLIE

You are really working it. Good assistant, Miss Mary.

MARY

It's been a month. I'm on it now.

MARY

(To WILHEMINA, who's off the phone)
You have interviews with all of the major TV stations today. And we have to find time to work on your speech for the Kennedy Center Honors Dinner.
(WILHEMINA is getting a text message)
Wilhemina?

WILHEMINA

I'm getting a text, from Wes . . . He says he's going out of town on an investigative assignment. He'll be gone for a week.

MARY

Thank God.

WILHEMINA

But he needs to see me before he leaves—

JO BILLIE
Ooooo . . .

MARY
(At desk)
You know, he's a mighty cool customer to make a move on the national security advisor to the president of these United States, and you don't want to jeopardize your career, carrying on with a reporter—

WILHEMINA
Calm down Mary. I'm not "carrying" on with him, and he didn't make a "move" on me. We're both two very busy people, who find that we have some things in common and I just—just—enjoy chatting with him, just like I do with my other male friends.

MARY
But he's got your hormones going. Believe me, your body is raging over that boy.

JO BILLIE
I have one word for you Wilhemina.

WILHEMINA
What?

JO BILLIE
Condoms. You don't know what else these young boys are packing nowadays, besides those baby makers.

WILHEMINA
(Dismissively)
We don't have that kind of relationship!

MARY / JO BILLIE
Yet.

WILHEMINA
And even if we did I'm past—babies.

JO BILLIE
Not really. You still have that last little vestige of youth left. Enough to
get you knocked up. I see women your age in the hospital all the time
from complications of pregnancy. Don't get caught with your pants
down, girl.

WILHEMINA
Jo Billie, please.

MARY
Wil, you have your pick of distinguished older gentlemen . . . your age.

WILHEMINA
I think that Wes is very mature for his age.

JO BILLIE
Huh-huh . . .

MARY
Oh is he? Well, was he mature when he talked you into ditching security,
and running around the city alone with him for hours. On a motorcycle.
Security was hysterical. They're dying to get their hands on that boy—

WILHEMINA
If they touch a hair on his head, I will skin them alive. It was a good test
for them. And it was my idea. Keep them on their toes. Suppose they lost
the president like that? They'd better get their stuff together. Besides, I
was incognito, nobody knew it was me. Jo Billie come 'ere.
      (Sipping tea, JO BILLIE sits next to WILHEMINA)

WILHEMINA
We ended up at his apartment—
      (Deep intake of breath from MARY)

WILHEMINA
—and when we got there, he had a surprise for me—
      (Another deep intake of breath)

JO BILLIE
I bet he did.

WILHEMINA
—a genuine Philly cheesesteak.
        (*MARY exhales*)

JO BILLIE
I am too through . . . He must really care for you. He braved that city for cheesesteak? But then he's from Baltimore you say, so I guess it didn't faze him.

MARY
Listen Wilhemina, seriously, you have got to end this thing with this boy before it gets started.

WILHEMINA
Stop calling him a boy, he is a grown man—

MARY
Oh—that reminds me I've got to call the gardener.

WILHEMINA
Speaking of boys.

JO BILLIE
        (*Cat sound*)

MARY
What, what?

WILHEMINA
You've been spending a lot of time with the "gardener" lately.

MARY
        (*Dismissively*)
Don't be absurd, he's the gardener. He's helping me transform my balcony into paradise.

(WILHEMINA and JO BILLIE look at each other)

JO BILLIE
He's weeding her garden.

WILHEMINA
(Looking at phone)
Oh, it's him again—

MARY
Goodness—

WILHEMINA
Yeah, it is a little annoying, but I don't know, it's kind of cute too. He's practicing his Swedish on me, so he's texting me in Swedish. When I was in bilateral with the minister of Japan yesterday, I kept losing the thread of conversation because he kept sending me messages with little hearts.

JO BILLIE
Well, look, I have to go. I have a staff meeting to get to. They want me to figure out a way to cut the budget by twenty million *(groans from the girls)* without cutting services.
   (Another groan)
   Plus, somebody's been complaining to State about the way I'm running the hospital. I think some of my own staff is helping them, the traitors. Now, the State Hospital Commission is sending out a special inspection team.

MARY
Oh no, after all you've done for that place? You went in there and turned things around—

JO BILLIE
Tell me about it.

WILHEMINA
Do they know about LaDonte?

JO BILLIE
I have sense enough not to let a little lust interfere with my livelihood—

WILHEMINA
OK, OK, for goodness' sakes, I wasn't implying that you—

JO BILLIE
I know, I know. *(Sitting back beside her)* But speaking of which, that La-don-tay! *(Grinning)* Tay-Tay . . . Oooh, Lawdy chile, be careful what you pray for, you just might get it.

WILHEMINA
Wore you out huh?

JO BILLIE
To the bone. *(As WILHEMINA laughs)* So, I say go for it with your football player girl—
  (Enacts throwing football)

WILHEMINA
Touch down!

MARY
Would you listen to you two—successful, sophisticated woman at the top of your game—

WILHEMINA
  (Laughing)
What's happening to us?

JO BILLIE
The secret lives of menopausal broads, that's what. But I guess it could be worse. We could be sitting in a hospital with some old dude watching him go through an MRI scan.

MARY
Uh—actually . . . Bill wants me to go with him for his MRI scan.

JO BILLIE

Oh no, Mary, I told you not to let that man entrap you in his illness.

MARY

It's just a checkup, he's doing fine. This will be a part of our lives, if I decide to marry him.

WILHEMINA / JO BILLIE (*Overlapping*)

You're going to marry Bill—?

JO BILLIE

You're still thinking about marrying Bill?

MARY

I'm thinking about it.

JO BILLIE

So, you're going to stick with the old guys, huh?

MARY

If that's the way you want to put it.

JO BILLIE

Well, I have to go.

MARY/WILHEMINA

Bye, Jo Billie.

JO BILLIE

See you, ladies.
     (*JO BILLIE exits*)

MARY

We do too. Come on, Wilhemina.
     (*Reading off her schedule*)
  You have a press briefing today at twelve thirty.

WILHEMINA

Twelve thirty? Darn. Wes and I were going to have a luncheon interview in the café.

MARY

How long do you think people are going to fall for that interview business? It's been four weeks now.

WILHEMINA

All right, all right, I'll cancel it.

MARY

(Horrified)

The press conference?

WILHEMINA

Of course not, the luncheon with Wes.

MARY

Thank God.

WILHEMINA

I don't have anything serious planned for tonight, do I?

MARY

Oh Wilhemina—

WILHEMINA

No, Mary, you're right . . .

(While WILHEMINA speaks, MARY is back and forth to other offstage room, gathering things)

WILHEMINA

I'm going to meet with Wes tonight and I'm going to be very clear with him that these interviews are over. Don't worry. I have defensive measures in place. I can handle myself. I've shut down flirtatious dictators, amorous ambassadors and every manner of touchy-feely politician there is. I can certainly handle one Wesley Van Washington. (Exits to bedroom)

(Back in living room, MARY gives one final look around, gathers papers, exits unknown to WILHEMINA)

WILHEMINA
(Reenters with purse)
Yes, Mr. President, of course Mr. President, I'm on my way. OK, I'm ready Mary, let's go. Mary . . . ? *(Looking around for MARY)* Mary! I can't believe she left without me.
(Exits)

<u>BLACKOUT</u>

<u>END ACT I, SCENE 6</u>

ACT I

SCENE 7

ON RISE: Later that night. MUSIC: Mood-setting music of love and seduction as LIGHTS shift to MARY and COLBY. Colby uncaps oil, starts to rub MARY's shoulders, arms. Seductively, she takes his hands and shows him how to massage her as he speaks.

COLBY
I . . . uh, Miss Mary . . .

MARY
Mary.

COLBY
Mary. I feel like I'm kind of behind with the girls, y'know.

MARY
Well, you know these young girls nowadays, sometimes they just don't appreciate gentleness.

COLBY
The last girl I was with since I been here, well, I was taking my time, y'know, leading up to things, the way they say they want you to do—taking her out to supper, trying to have conversation, but I couldn't think of nothing to say. Well, come to find out she just wanted to hop into bed, but I didn't know that, so she got tired of waiting and went and told all her friends that I didn't know what to do, and now whenever they see me, they laugh. What I'm supposed to do, act like gangsta?

MARY
Don't compromise yourself Colby. Be yourself. Don't be so apologetic. You give a woman a normal amount of respect the way a man should, then let her earn the rest, don't put her on a pedestal.

COLBY

I guess I just don't have no game.

MARY

Well, one can always be taught, Colby. Can't one?

COLBY

(*Giggling*) You <u>talk</u> like a teacher.

MARY

(*Archly*) Well. I've always wanted to teach.

COLBY

I wish somebody would teach me what these girls want so maybe I can get my girlfriend back.

MARY

If you want to get your girlfriend back, Colby, you have to put your arms around her—like this.
　　　(*Wraps his arms around her*)

COLBY
　　　(*Hugging her*)
Like this?

MARY

Yes, yes. Then, whisper sweet messages to her.

COLBY

I'm listening.

MARY

You whisper to her—
　　　(*She whispers in his ear*)
　　　(*He's heated by her whispers*)
　　Use the words from your poem, Colby . . .
　　Love and compassion releases the healing hormones . . .
　　Oh, your arms are so healing . . .

COLBY
The love between a man . . .

MARY
. . . and a woman.

COLBY/MARY
. . . stirs up the healing hormones . . .
(*LIGHTS shift to WILHEMINA and WES in WILHEMINA's apartment. WES sipping drink as Wilhemina talks*)

WILHEMINA
Wes, this is getting out of hand, clearly it will not work, even you must see that. (*He gives her a drink, she downs it, he hands another drink, she downs it*) I'm afraid that rumors will start flying, I have a position to uphold, I have to be circumspect, I—
(*WES leans over and stops her with a kiss. Her glasses steam up*)

(*LIGHT on JO BILLIE and LADONTE*)

(*LADONTE starts to perform a striptease for her, as JO BILLIE smiles, and directs him from the chaise lounge*)

JO BILLIE
That's it, Sweetness! Turn this way, baby, now turn that way baby. Ooow let the games begin!

LADONTE
I'm gonna take it off, I'm gonna take it all off—!
(*Overlapping*)

JO BILLIE
Zip it! Now unzip it . . . and come to mama . . .

WES
(*To WILHEMINA*)
Come to papa . . .

(Insistent buzz of PRESIDENT'S RING that WILHEMINA ignores, throwing off her eyeglasses)

MARY/COLBY

Release the healing hormones in one another . . .

(LIGHTS slowly go down on ALL THREE COUPLES. In a free-for-all, in their separate areas, hot and heavy. And all the while the PRESIDENT'S RING is buzzing)

INTERMISSION

ACT II

SCENE 1

ON RISE: Two months later. WILHEMINA's apartment. THE THREE WOMEN are getting ready to go to a church event. GOSPEL MUSIC PLAYING. They are dressed in Sunday attire, hats, gloves, pearls. WILHEMINA is going over a speech. Her cell phone keeps RINGING, distracting her.

WILHEMINA
   (Speaking)
And as we stand here today—(Phone rings) . . . as we stand here today on the shoulders of our female ancestors—(Phone rings) And as we stand here today, their grace and beauty surround us. Again (Phone rings) thank you for inviting me to this momentous occasion. (Phone rings)

MARY
The National Baptists Women's Conference is going to love your speech.
   (PHONE RINGING)

JO BILLIE
   (To WILHEMINA)
Are you going to answer that?

WILHEMINA
No.

MARY
You might as well talk to him Wilhemina, and get it over with. He's not going to stop calling.

WILHEMINA
Eventually he will.

MARY
You owe him an explanation. You've been seeing him for . . .

JO BILLIE
Two months . . .

MARY
And now you're running from him. He thinks you two have a tennis date.
You're going to have to confront him, Wil. For the past week you've been
making dates with him—

JO BILLIE
—breaking dates—

MARY
I can't believe you. Every week you keep saying you're going to break it
off with him. But, instead—

JO BILLIE
You just keep giving it up! Hey, I ain't mad at you, girl.

WILHEMINA
        (Overlap)
What can I say? I'm just going to cut him off cold turkey. Just like I did
with cigarettes.

MARY
He's not a pack of camels, Wilhemina.

WILHEMINA
No, but he's temptation, and I just have to put forth effort to resist him.
        (Fanning)
   Oh, but last night I woke up in a cold sweat.

MARY
Night sweats?

JO BILLIE / WILHEMINA
No!

WILHEMINA

A cold sweat—at the thought of what I'd done. I've made a terrible, terrible mistake. I've allowed myself to be seduced by a young man I hardly know.

JO BILLIE

Well, it happens to the best of us, Wilhemina.

WILHEMINA

But, then again, I feel like I know him. Oh, how could I be so undisciplined? Even now I can't stop thinking about him and his—smile. Being with him was like nothing I'd ever experienced before. I felt the depths of my being yielding, utterly, like fountains of water. I was being emptied, and I was being filled. I couldn't stop crying, and I couldn't stop laughing. It was almost spiritual.

JO BILLIE

It was an orgasm, Wilhemina.
    (THE PHONE RINGS. WILHEMINA is torn)

    (DOOR BUZZER rings insistently)

WILHEMINA

(Goes to buzzer) Yes?

DOOR KEEPER

Wesley Van Washington here to see you.

WILHEMINA

(Frightened) It's him. How do I look, how do I look!

JO BILLIE

Hot.

WILHEMINA

As in sexy?

JO BILLIE

No, as in hot and sweaty.

WILHEMINA
Oh God—(*Fanning*)

JO BILLIE / MARY
Well, send him up, let him come up, deal with it, girl, we have your back, etc.

WILHEMINA
    (*Deep breath*)
You're right, I can't allow this crisis to escalate. I must isolate and let die.

JO BILLIE
All this military talk. Just get the door.

WILHEMINA
Send him up, please.

JO BILLIE
We'll wait for you in the lobby.

WILHEMINA
No! No. Please don't leave me here alone with him. I can't trust myself just yet—stay with me.

BOTH
Well, OK.
    (*JO BILLIE and MARY sit back down, looking forward to the show*)

    (*WILHEMINA paces, biting her fingernails. DOORBELL RINGS. WILHEMINA freezes*)

MARY
Answer the door Wilhemina.

WILHEMINA
Of course.
    (*Opens door*)

(Enter WES, dressed in tennis outfit, with racket)

WES

    (Amicably)

Hi! You don't look like you're dressed for a tennis date . . . ?

WILHEMINA

I forgot I'd promised Mary that I'd go to an event with her.

WES

We need to talk.

    (JO BILLIE'S RAP SONG RINGTONE goes off)

JO BILLIE

Oh, that's Tay-Tay. Got to go, got to go. *(To WILHEMINA)* We'll meet you down in the lobby.

MARY

No—

JO BILLIE

Yes. *(To WILHEMINA)* You got this.

    (MARY and JO BILLIE go past WES. JO BILLIE smiling broadly, MARY looking concerned as they exit)

MARY

Hurry, Wilhemina.

JO BILLIE

Take all the time you need.

WES

    (After they exit)

Wilhemina, what's going on? You break our dates, you don't return my calls. I don't understand, why are you avoiding me? Did I upset you? Did I do something wrong?

WILHEMINA

Wes, rumors are starting to circulate.

WES

Well, talk to me then, you can't just dismiss me like this.

WILHEMINA

Wes, I've been down to Texas on the ranch. The family read me the riot act and they were right. I realize what a fool I've been, exposing myself to a possible—possible—

WES
        (Perplexed)
Possible what—? To what? To a relationship? To—?

WILHEMINA

Let's face it, a reporter is always looking for a story, it's just the nature of the beast—

WES

So, you think I'm looking for a story? I thought you knew me better than that. You think that's what this is all about? A story?

WILHEMINA
        (Pulling away)
Oh Wes, can't you see this—this just can't go on.

WES

Why not, baby? You're single, I'm single . . .

WILHEMINA

Will you stop staying that! Discipline and control . . . are the guiding lights of my life . . . and you've got to help me put them back into play. You've got to help me, I'm not myself, I'm menopausal, I'm crazy, I'm out of control—!
        (WILHEMINA throws hat up in air, runs out of the room)

WES

(To nobody)

What in the hell just happened?

(WILHEMINA walks back in the room, calmly pulling on gloves as though nothing has happened)

Wilhemina, how can I help you when I can't help myself? I want the world to know—!

WILHEMINA

No! No, the timing is so inconvenient. Maybe, when I'm out of the public eye, maybe when I'm a private person again, maybe then we can "come out," so to speak . . . but by then you'll probably be with a woman your own age.

WES

Why do you keep saying that?

WILHEMINA

Don't you like young women?

WES

Sure I do. But it's not about your age, it's about you. It's about us. Young women have their advantages, they have their disadvantages too.

WILHEMINA

Disadvantages? Like what?

WES

Oh, I don't know . . . well . . . sometimes they're still discovering who they are, y'know, and sometimes they aren't as interesting . . . I like interesting women. You know who you are, so you have nothing to prove to me, no axe to grind, you can just be yourself, and let me be myself.

WILHEMINA

And that turns you on?

WES
Yes. It's very appealing to me.
> *(Beat)*

I can't believe that <u>you</u> want <u>me</u>. Let's keep it real. You have the strength of diplomacy and the might of the military behind you. You don't know how scared I was to make that first move, do you? *(They laugh)* Never thought I'd be holding one of the most powerful women in the world in my arms.

WILHEMINA
And that turns you on?

WES
Oh yes.

WILHEMINA
So, I'm a trophy. *(Gets up)*

WES
. . . that, I can't show off.

WILHEMINA
Are you turned on by me or by my position?
> *(PHONE BUZZES. She picks it up, scrolls as WES begins talking)*

WES
All of what you are . . . makes you who you are . . . including your age and position.
> *(Takes phone from her)*

Wilhemina, listen. You're having doubts with this whole age thing, so I'll be honest with you. I never thought I'd fall for a woman years older than I, but I really don't have a problem with it. What it boils down to is I'm a man, and you've got everything I'm looking for in a woman. I want you. And I always go after what I want.

WILHEMINA
That's what turns me on about you, you go after what you want. But you're young and virile, and you want me now, but tomorrow you might want—

WES

    (Gathering her hands, kissing them)

Wilhemina, let's just live in the moment, sweetheart. Tomorrow anything could happen, but today we have each other . . . let's not throw that away. I've traveled the world over to find what we have. Let's just enjoy this moment.

    (They embrace)

<u>FADE OUT</u>

<u>END ACT II, SCENE 1</u>

ACT II

SCENE 2

<u>ON RISE:</u>   A few days later. JO BILLIE's apartment. JO BILLIE, in sheer robe over sexy
outfit, LADONTE in exotic costume, both engaged in some kind of freaky sex
game. JO BILLIE in control, holding a whip, other sex toys on display. FRANTIC
KNOCKING AT DOOR.

JO BILLIE
Yes?!

MARY *(Offstage)*
It's me, Mary.

JO BILLIE
Damn. Just a minute.
> *(Offstage MARY continues pounding on door while JO BILLIE and LADONTE
> scramble to gather sex toys and put them in offstage bedroom. ENTER MARY,
> obviously upset, wrapped in a sheet, carrying a large half-empty bottle of
> wine)*

MARY
Where are you? Where are you? JoJo, JoJo, Jo Billie?

JO BILLIE
> *(Reentering)*
Mary . . . ?

MARY
I used my key and came on in . . .

JO BILLIE
What is it Mary? *(Pulling robe around her)*

MARY
  (Slurred)
Oh, JoJo, JoJo, Jo Billie—I-I know it's in the middle of the night, I hope I'm not 'sturbing you—Have you seen Colby?

JO BILLIE
Have I seen Colby—? Why would I see Colby—?

MARY
It's the girls! They've gone off the deep end! The deep end! They called me everything but a child of God! Their mother! *(Flops on couch)*

JO BILLIE
Mary, why are you in my house, wrapped in a bedsheet?

MARY
The girls! They walked in on me and Colby!

JO BILLIE
Oh no.

MARY
Yes, yes! I was so embarrassed I wish the bed had just swallowed me up. They say if I ever see him again, they will totally disown me, and tell mother! What am I going to do? I don't want to lose my little girls' respect, they're all I have.

JO BILLIE
I told you not to give them the keys to your apartment—
  (During dialogue, chugs wine from bottle)

MARY
I gave it to them in case they ever had to come inside and find me dead or something. But they still should have knocked! I'm not dead yet. They should have considered that I just might have company over. I may be a grandma, but I'm still a sexual being. I'll bet they wouldn't go barging into their dad's house all hours of the night—

JO BILLIE
Uh—would you like a glass for that—?

MARY
Oh it was devastating, devastating! We didn't hear anything because the
air conditioner was on, and you know how it is—plus I can't hear well
out of my right ear, and I just didn't expect anybody to come over that
time of the night. Well, when the girls heard the screams coming from
my bedroom they—

JO BILLIE
Screams?

MARY
    (Dismissively)
You know how it is . . . *(Scream)*
    (At scream, LADONTE runs in, in only a towel. JO BILLIE waves him away.
    MARY doesn't see this, continues talking. Behind MARY's back, LADONTE comes
    to bedroom door from time to time, teasing JO BILLIE, and she shoos him back)

MARY
—well, they just knew I was being attacked, so they rushed in, they had
the grandbabies with them, and started to pound poor Colby, oh it was
just awful—poor Colby didn't know what to do, whether to run or hide
under the sheets. Then when I tried to explain to them that I-I-I wasn't
being attacked, and please don't call the cops, I thought I would just die
at the look of disgust on their faces.
    (Finally LADONTE comes out in some kind of costume that makes JO BILLIE laugh
    to herself. MARY turns to face her just as she's laughing)

MARY
It's not funny.

JO BILLIE
I know, I'm sorry—
    (Can't stop laughing, then stretches, feigning a yawn)
I really do feel badly for you, but I really have to get back to bed—

MARY

And that's not the killer.

JO BILLIE

What could be worse than catching you in the act?

MARY

Jerome.

JO BILLIE

He caught you too?

MARY

No. But the girls called him, hysterical, and he called and told me that he knew this was all about him, that I was with a young man just to get back at him for him for having a young woman, and that I should start going back to Mass, and be careful about the company I keep because he didn't want a pervert around his daughters and grandchildren, meaning me, I'm the pervert!

JO BILLIE

What? Where's Colby, now?

MARY

I don't know. (*Waving*) Gone! In the wind, poor thing, he ran away, naked!
    (*Big sigh*)
    Thanks for letting me vent. I guess I'll—just go back home. I would go to Wil's but she has so much on her plate these days—bringing democracy to the Muslim world, and that boy and all—we've got to do something about her—

JO BILLIE
    (*Walking MARY to door*)
Come on Mary, we'll talk later, OK?
    (*As MARY sniffles and nods, COLBY suddenly appears again*)

MARY

    (Suddenly takes in the scene)

Ohhh . . . LaDonte . . . ! I love his costume.

    (To JO BILLIE, taking in her outfit for the first time)

    Pretty . . . I'm sorry—here I just barged right in on you, without even—oh God, I'm worse than the girls, I feel so foolish—

JO BILLIE

No big deal. We'll just take up where we left off.

MARY

Well, I'm going to look for Colby. He's probably in the gardener's shed.

JO BILLIE

Sure you're going to be all right?

MARY

    (Nodding)

Yes I'm just down the hall. Thanks, Jo Billie. You, nymph, you. Bye Tay-Tay.

    (MARY exits. JO BILLIE and LADONTE resume their activities, going into offstage bedroom)

LIGHTS FADE

END ACT II, SCENE 2

ACT II

~~~~~~~~

SCENE 3

<u>ON RISE:</u> Two weeks later, evening. LIGHTS UP. WILHEMINA's apt. WES, shirtless, in socks, has photos spread out on a table, going through them. At some point he fixes a drink, looks at his phone.

WES
(Calling to WILHEMINA offstage)
Wish I were taking you to the party tonight. I hate to see you with anybody else.

WILHEMINA
(Enters in lovely gown)
I know, me too. But we promised each other not to become possessive. I think it wise that I should continue to see my usual escorts. It's just Coach, our mutual friend.

WES
I saw our "mutual friend" at the gym the other day, and he's not speaking to me anymore.

WILHEMINA
Men.
(Looking at the photos)
These pictures are quite good, Wes.

WES
You think so?

WILHEMINA
Yes. You were a terrific photojournalist.

WES
Still am. I just got bumped up to on-air. But . . . I still love capturing
the moment.

WILHEMINA
Remarkable. Utterly transporting.

WES
(Looking at her) Yeah . . .

WILHEMINA
Zip me. How do I look?

WES
Delicious . . . Can I have a little snack now?
    (Share wicked laughter, as WES gets a text)

WILHEMINA
You naughty boy. No. I've prepared a little repast for us, but you can't
eat until I get back. I've arranged to leave early, then you and I will have
our *own privalt litten fest.* (Swedish for "private little party")

WES
    (Thinking)
Private little party . . . ?

WILHEMINA
    (As she exits to bedroom)
Ahhh . . . ahhh . . . You will be here when I get back tonight?
    (WES's PHONE RINGS)
    (From bedroom, when she gets no answer)
  Wes?

WES
Well—uh—actually, wait a minute, I'm getting a message that I have to
leave town, tonight.

WILHEMINA
But you said you were going to be free tonight.

WES
Well, I thought I was but I just received this text from the station—you know how it is, sorry.

WILHEMINA
Oh? Breaking news?

WES
Kind of.

WILHEMINA
Well what is it?
    (WES doesn't answer)

WILHEMINA
If it's private and you can't discuss it with me all you have to do is say so.

WES
    (Gathering his things)
I'm up for an award. The Dart Journalism Award, for balanced and thoughtful reporting on survivors of traumatic events: From Katrina to the Philippines.

WILHEMINA
    (Running back out)
Oh! Babe, congratulations, I'm so proud of you!

WES
Thank you.

WILHEMINA
Oh! We'll really have to celebrate tonight. Surely you don't <u>have</u> to leave tonight. *(Exits back into bedroom)*

WES

Yeah baby, I do, you see, the station was already planning to do a retro-
spective on Katrina and now, they want to push up the filming timeline
to correspond with the award. So, they've asked . . . Barb and me to leave
for New Orleans tonight to get started.

WILHEMINA

    (Reentering holding shoes that she puts on at some point in scene)
Barb? Barb?

WES

    (Gathering up pictures)
Barbara, yes. That's why I didn't want to mention it, you always seem to
bristle whenever I mention her name—

WILHEMINA

Oh, come on!

WES

See.

WILHEMINA

Oh, come on! I certainly don't want to give the impression that I have
a lock on you.

WES

Wait now, I didn't mean it like that—

WILHEMINA

Wes. Forgive me for wanting to think that I'm the only woman in your
life, just because you're the only man in mine— *(In mirror)*

WES

You are the only woman in my life. This girl is a fellow reporter, a
colleague.
    This is my career. *(Pause)* Look, don't go to the party. I still have a little
time, stay here with me.

WILHEMINA
    (Pulling away)
That's not an option, it's a state dinner.

WES
OK, I understand. I'll be back in a few days and we'll—

WILHEMINA
I'll be in the Middle East.

WES
For how long?

WILHEMINA
You know I can't tell you that.
    (Beat)
  Do you have to go? Tell them you have to interview me, tell them to send someone else.

WES
It's an assignment, Wil, it's my job, I have to go. I <u>want</u> to go.

WILHEMINA
Oh, I'm sure you want to go. Well, I'm asking you not to go.

WES
I . . . I don't like the way you're asking. I'm not one of your underlings.

WILHEMINA
Of course not, but Wes, there is one thing you have to know about me.

WES
And what is that?

WILHEMINA
I give, but I don't share.

WES
I don't know what you're talking about. This is my career. You've got to trust me, just like I trust you.

WILHEMINA
I'm certainly not going to sit here arguing with you about another woman—

WES
We're not arguing, we're just talking—

WILHEMINA
It sounds like an argument to me.
    (Getting her wrap)

WES
Look—I'm not LaDonte.

WILHEMINA
What! And what is that supposed to mean?

WES
It means I'm here because I love you.
    I was going to wait for a better time to do this but . . . *(Gets on one knee)* Wilhemina, will you marry me? I always said when I found the right woman I'd make a full commitment. We've been seeing each other for months now. When we're apart we miss each other, when we're together we can't get enough of each other. We say we're in love. Then we need to be together, we need to take care of our business, take care of each other, like an old married couple.

WILHEMINA
My . . . Wes . . . you have it all figured out, don't you?

WES
Yeah, I do. *(Beat)* So . . . will you marry me?
    (BUZZER)

WILHEMINA

I . . . I . . .

WES

Wilhemina Callaway Sorenson, will you marry me?
>   (*No answer from WILHEMINA. INSISTENT BUZZER*)

WES

>   (*Gets up, after he gets no answer*)

Well . . . I guess that's my answer. There's your date. (*As they walk to the door, she holds out her wrap for him to put around her shoulders. His hands full with his equipment, he declines*) After you.

<u>BLACKOUT</u>

<u>END ACT II, SCENE 3</u>

ACT II

~~~~~~~

SCENE 4

<u>ON RISE:</u> Two days later. JO BILLIE's apartment. Toys are strewn around. JO BILLIE
is listening to a message on her phone as she waves MARY in. MARY enters,
loaded down with shopping bags.

JO BILLIE
Girl, listen to this message I got from that little . . . just . . . listen.

LAKEISHA *(Voice from JO BILLIE's voice mail)*
I KNOW YOU DON'T WANT TO STEP TO ME! TAY-TAY IS MY MAN
AND MY BABY DADDY! YOU DON'T LOVE HIM. I DO! YOU JUST
WANT TO USE HIM, WITH YOUR OLD ASS. YOU DON'T WANT
NOTHIN' WITH HIM BUT SEX, OUGHT TO BE SHAME OF YO'
OLD SELF! BUT YOU DONE MESSED WITH THE WRONG ONE
NOW! YOU GONNA LEARN NOT TO MESS WITH KEE-KEE. YOU
BETTER WATCH YO' BACK 'CAUSE ME AND MY GIRLS GONNA
MESS YOU UP! BITCH!

MARY
      (Stunned)
Oh my. That sounds like a threat. I thought you said that LaDonte and
whatever her name is, didn't have a relationship?

JO BILLIE
They don't. But you know how these young girls are nowadays, always
trying to cause trouble.
      (MARY accidentally steps on squeaking toy, jumps, screams)

MARY
My goodness, Jo Billie, what are you running here, a day care?
      (Steps on another toy)
   Toys all over the place—

JO BILLIE
For LaDonte's little boy when he comes to visit. Which is all the time now. What have I gotten myself into? That heifer keeps bringing that baby over here for us to keep while she goes off to God knows where—to get her weave tightened I guess—

MARY
Well I have to dash, just wanted to drop off these bags—

JO BILLIE
(Frustrated) Mary, when are you going to stop stashing all of your stuff at my place?

MARY
This is the last batch, I promise. My wedding trousseau. I can't let Colby see my wedding . . . "stuff."

JO BILLIE
He doesn't know you're getting married next week?

MARY
No, I'm trying to hold on to my good thang as long as I can.

JO BILLIE
You're getting greedy in your old age.

MARY
I know, but I've been hungry so long. I just can't bear to let him go.
        (Enter WILHEMINA, in scarf, dark glasses, with a valise)

WILHEMINA
Ladies! I need your help!

JO BILLIE
Enough . . . Y'all need to give me back my keys.

MARY
Oh Lord I don't have time for this—I'll miss my afternoon delight—

(Notices what WILHEMINA is wearing)
Where in the world are you going in that disguise?

WILHEMINA
To New Orleans. I need your help.

MARY
To New Orleans? For what?

WILHEMINA
On official business.

MARY
Wilhemina, Wes is there isn't he? Filming that Katrina special, isn't he?

WILHEMINA
Supposedly. But my sources have not been able to locate him anywhere. Or that Barbara Ali person. I called his room but he wasn't there and called Ms. Ali's room and she wasn't there either. He called me briefly from a bar in the French Quarter but we were cut off and I could swear I heard a woman giggling in the background—and I haven't heard anything from him since. They're out there, somewhere, together, I know it.

JO BILLIE
Well, when you're in New Orleans laissez les bon temps rouler. *(Lazay-Lay-Bon-Tom Roulay)*

WILHEMINA
I am not trying to hear that. Mary, I need you to charter me a flight to the French Quarter—

MARY
The French—Wilhemina? Are you out of your mind?

WILHEMINA
Probably. But . . . I guess this is what happens when you wait to be my age . . . to fall in love . . .

MARY

Awww, you poor dear . . .

JO BILLIE

Yeah . . . Wil, your soul mate comes along maybe once in a life time, and he might not be in the package you're expecting but I say if you find him don't let go, no matter what age he is.

MARY

What are you talking about? She can't go lurking around New Orleans searching for that boy.

WILHEMINA

Are you coming with me or not?

MARY

Not. I have a funeral to pre— *(quickly)* I mean a wedding to prepare for.

WILHEMINA

I'm sorry I won't be able to attend the wedding, but I'll pick you up something in the region.

Jo Billie—?

JO BILLIE

Don't look at me. I'm trying to cover my own backside. I've invited that traitorous lab director to lunch. I think she's the one making these false reports to State.

MARY

This is crazy, Wil. Now you're going to have to snap out of this fever that you're in and get a grip.

(*MARY signals for JO BILLIE to hide WILHEMINA's valise*)

WILHEMINA

Fine. I'll go alone.

(*Starts to exit, looking for valise*)

(*JO BILLIE and MARY go through a* Three Stooges—*like routine with WILHEMINA, passing the valise from one to the other, trying to elude WILHEMINA during the following dialogue*)

JO BILLIE
So what are you going to do? Go down to the French Quarter and kick butt. (*Throws case*) Catch Mary.

WILHEMINA
Give me my valise—!

MARY
Honey, you don't want to tangle with one of those young girls down in New Orleans. You may be ready to take on Kim Yong Un or ISIS, but one of those young girls will kick your butt—

WILHEMINA
Give me my valise!!!
        (*The LADIES tumble on the chaise lounge, laughing, out of breath*)

WILHEMINA
This is ridiculous! We're too old for this!

MARY / JO BILLIE
We know—!
        (*PHONE BUZZES. They fumble around, looking for WILHEMINA's purse. JO BILLIE finds it, takes out the phone, gives it to WILHEMINA. WILHEMINA looks at the caller ID*)

WILHEMINA
        (*She whispers to MARY and JO BILLIE*)
It's Wes!

MARY / JO BILLIE
Put him on speaker, put him on speaker.

WES
Wil . . . ? Wilhemina?

WILHEMINA
(*Catching deep breath*)
Yes?

WES
Wil! Listen. Sorry, we got disconnected on that last call, but listen, I'll
be in Paris next week. Can we meet at that soul food café we talked about
for a cup of coffee?

WILHEMINA
Congratulations on your award . . .
(*JO BILLIE looks at her with a "What are you doing/saying?" look*)

WES
Thank you. Wil . . . ?
(*No answer*)

(*WILHEMINA shoos the LADIES out to talk to WES privately. But they listen from
inside the hallway, poking their heads through the doorframe*)

WES
Are you there?

WILHEMINA
Wes? Did you mean it . . . when you . . . asked . . . me . . . you know . . .
that . . . thing . . . ?

WES
(*Teasing her*)
When I asked you what . . . ?

WILHEMINA
Wes . . .

WES
Oh, you mean when I asked you to marry me? Of course I meant it.

WILHEMINA
(Shyly)
I've been asked a lot of things . . . but actually I've never been asked that before.

WES
And I caught you off guard, sorry, I'll try not to do that again . . .

WILHEMINA
What, catch me off guard or ask me to marry you?

WES
Well . . . I've got my pride, but girl, I love you, I love you more than blue crab.

WILHEMINA
(Laughs)
You do? And I—I miss you . . .

WES
More than a Philly cheesesteak?

WILHEMINA
You're pushing it . . .
        (WES laughs)

WES
Meet me in Paris, Wil. We'll tour the city, no strings attached. Wilhemi—?
        (PHONE suddenly cuts off. WILHEMINA hangs up)

MARY
What happened?

WILHEMINA
It cut off again.

JO BILLIE
Well? Are you going to meet him in Paris?

WILHEMINA
(Gathering her things)
Thanks ladies.

JO BILLIE
Are you going to meet him—?

MARY
You can't go to Paris, you're leaving for the Middle East—
(WILHEMINA blows them a kiss, exits)
Too-da-loo.

MARY
(To WILHEMINA)
I'll call you in the morning. Bright and early.

JO BILLIE
(A sly smile/laugh at the possibilities)
She's really in love.

MARY
Yep. (Beat) He must have tapped that good.

(JO BILLIE can't believe what she heard. MARY runs down hall to her apartment)

<u>END ACT II, SCENE 4</u>

ACT II

SCENE 5

<u>ON RISE:</u> Minutes later. MARY'S garden. COLBY in garden with massage oils.

MARY (*Offstage*)
Colby!

COLBY
Mary!!!

MARY
Oh baby, you know I don't want to miss my afternoon delight!

COLBY
Want me to start where we left off?
> (*MARY rushes in, smiles and nods, while sitting down on outside stool or chair.*
> *COLBY massages her shoulders*)

MARY
Colby, can we talk?

COLBY
Yeah.

MARY
I've decided to marry Bill.

COLBY
Huh? Marry Bill? How can you do that? Me and you going together.

MARY
Colby, we have a very sweet relationship, but Bill and I move in the same circles, we have many of the same things in common—

COLBY

But me and you are at the same stage in our lives, remember you said? We both want to go to Africa together, and bungee jump off the Zambezi River, like you said. Right?

MARY

Right, but you don't understand—

COLBY

Naw I don't understand.

MARY

Try to understand, sweetheart. *(Massages his shoulders)* I now realize that I may never have gotten divorced in the first place if I'd had sense enough to take a lover.

(Looking into his bewildered eyes)

A lover would have made the marriage bearable. But no, there I was suffering in silence, being the good little Catholic wife. I've decided I can't make that same mistake again.

COLBY

So you not going to marry Bill?

MARY

Oh, I'm going to marry Bill.

COLBY

So . . . you asking me to be your dude on the side?

MARY

There won't be any problems, I promise you.

COLBY

(Seems to think it over)

But I got a problem with it. I don't want to be your man on the side. I been done wrong, I don't want to do another dude like that. I know how that feels.

MARY

But we won't be hurting anybody.

COLBY

(Interrupting. As much to himself as to her)
We'll be hurting him. I don't know what you want.

MARY

I'm years older than you, Colby . . .

COLBY

So? What do you want? I don't know what you want. Do you even know what you want?

MARY

(Struggling)
What do I want? I want . . . I want people to not be mad at me when I do things I want to do. Because people stay mad at you sooo long, Colby, my mother, Jerome, the girls. I can't bear it. Things are running smoothly now that I'm going to marry Bill, everybody's happy, nobody's mad, and I don't want to rock the boat. Just work with me.

COLBY

But, it won't work.

MARY

(Getting angry)
How can you say that to me? After all we've been to each other. You could at least try to understand what I'm going through.

COLBY

I understand you, but you don't understand me. You taught me a lot of things, like how to have confidence in myself as a man, how a woman should treat me as a man and stuff. Now you're upset because I learned the things you taught me. Mary, all I'm saying is if you get married on me, I can't be in the picture. You got to choose him or me.

MARY

Oh my God. I've created a monster.

COLBY

I'm no monster Mary. I care for you. You mean a whole lot to me. But you the one who told me don't compromise myself with a woman. And, you're trying to get me to go along with something I can't do. If you're gonna talk the talk, you gotta walk the walk.

(At MARY's angry look)

And now you mad at me. Well . . . I guess I better be going. Everything's looking pretty good in the garden. It's gonna be hard for me to find a woman to come up to you, Mary. Don't forget to prune the rosebush.

(COLBY walks away, MARY arranges flowers)

<u>END ACT II, SCENE 5</u>

ACT II

~~~~~~

SCENE 6

<u>ON RISE:</u> JO BILLIE's apartment. LADONTE ending a phone conversation. JO
  BILLIE enters.

LADONTE
Yeah man, she's at lunch with her now. I know I should have told Jo Billie
about that lab director . . .
  (DOOR SLAM. JO BILLIE enters the apartment)

LADONTE
. . . but—

JO BILLIE
  (Screaming / calling out)
LADONTE . . .
  (JO BILLIE moves to another part of the house)

LADONTE
. . . gotta go.
  *(LADONTE quickly hangs up the phone and starts picking up and putting away the
  baby toys)*

JO BILLIE
  (Screaming / calling out)
LADONTE . . .
  (JO BILLIE enters the room)
  I just left having lunch with—!

LADONTE
Oh yeah, I know about that, I can tell you all about that . . .

JO BILLIE
I'm listening.

(He begins slowly, expecting to be stopped, then picks up steam)

LADONTE

Look, I know I should of told you about the lab director, but see, I worked with this lab broad at another hospital before me and you hooked up. And the chick was going through brothas over there like baby wipes, man. At first I thought she was just messing around with me, but come to find out she was banging everybody, excuse my French. So, they fired her. But then the chick got hired at your hospital and, y'know, she saw me and we hooked back up. But I didn't even know you then. So, when you offered me your deal, I cut the chick loose, so she was trying to get back at me by taking you down.

JO BILLIE

Yeah, I found that out too. Why didn't you tell me about it?

LADONTE

Well, every time I try to talk to you, you tell me to zip it, or unzip it. But you don't think I had nothing to do with her trying to take you down, do you?

JO BILLIE

No, I don't. That would be stupid of you. And even you're not that stupid.

LADONTE

(Big sigh of relief)
Whew! Man, that's a load off my mind. Whew!

JO BILLIE

But, the lab director didn't show up for lunch.

LADONTE

But I thought you just said she—

JO BILLIE

I ended up having lunch with LaKeisha . . .

LADONTE
        (Overlap)
Ah, hell naw!

JO BILLIE
        (Overlap)
A.k.a. Kee-Kee.

LADONTE
Aw man . . . What you do that for?

JO BILLIE
Well, I had no choice.

LADONTE
I told you there was nothing between me and her. I told you I would
handle her!

JO BILLIE
I sat at the table, waiting for the lab director, who never showed
up . . .

LADONTE
        (Overlap)
Oh man . . .

JO BILLIE
. . . and Kee-Kee slid into the seat.

LADONTE
Oh man—

JO BILLIE
You broke the contract. You've been bringing that girl in my home,
while I'm at work.

    I want you out of here, today!

LADONTE
(*Offstage to get his suitcase*)
Aw you too cold. You got to let me explain. What I'm gonna do, where I'm gonna go, I mean, I live here with you.

JO BILLIE
(*Back in with suitcase*) Not anymore. (*Putting baby toys, sex toys in suitcase*)

LADONTE
You can't just throw me out like this, you got to give a young brother another chance.
    Come on now.

JO BILLIE
(*Picks up her cell phone*) Am I going to have to call security?

LADONTE
(*He backs off*)
So it's like that. You know what? I got a case against you, I could take you to court, we had a deal, and you letting LaKeisha mess it up. You mad at her and you taking it out on me. True enough she did drop in a couple of times, but nothing happened, we was just kicking it, whatever she said, it's not true. (*Beat*) What did she say—?

JO BILLIE
She said she can't compete with me. She said she loved you, but I just want you for sex. Oh, and then she said she's pregnant again, but you don't have to worry about it because she and Little LaDonte can make it without you. You lied about your relationship!

LADONTE
(*Gathering baby toys off floor*)
I didn't lie! Things with me and LaKeisha was off and on, and at the time me and you, I mean you and I, met up it was off. What the hell, you said you didn't care what I did anyway so long as I took care of my responsibilities with you. I saw an opportunity for the come up and I took it. You just got caught up in your own game.
    (*JO BILLIE is stone still, furious*)

JO BILLIE
I want you out of here, now!

LADONTE
(*Big sigh as JO BILLIE takes out CAMERON's picture*) Look, I know I'm not all that, but I'm doing the best I can, I didn't have a daddy to teach me, I'm learning on the fly. I'm not a big deal like that Cameron dude you were married to—

JO BILLIE
You do not put his name in your mouth! Cameron was my god! He was my hero! He was my rock! He was a genius. He engineered parts for guided missiles! But then, you wouldn't understand that.

LADONTE
Well, dawg man, I had a job too, but you made me quit it and now you firing me from this one—

JO BILLIE
You could never be the man he was.

LADONTE
I ain't trying to do no dead dude. I'm trying to do me!

JO BILLIE
Well, do you, LaDonte, do you. Give me my keys and get out!

LADONTE
But—wait, we got to talk about this. (*She holds out her hand. He drops keys in hand*) Well can I at least get my job back?

JO BILLIE
No. (*JO BILLIE continues throwing his items into suitcase*) It was fun while it lasted, LaDonte, but it's over. I would never come between a man and his family. You lied. So go home to them. (*Angrily slides his suitcase to door*) They need you, such as you are. But I don't need—

LADONTE

Zip it! I'll get out. I can't win in this situation no way. You holding all the cards, so, this ain't working for me either. I'm out of here. I'm gonna do like LaKeisha say, yeah, I'm gonna get my own, get my respiratory license, take care of my family, and save lives.

    (JO BILLIE throws wad of money at him)

I don't need that. I took your advice, I saved the money I earned. *(At JO BILLIE's look)* Don't hate the playa, hate the game.

    (He squares his shoulders, exits. After he leaves, JO BILLIE breaks down crying, talking to CAMERON's picture)

JO BILLIE

I'm sorry, I'm sorry . . . I don't know what happened to me. How did I get involved with a boy like that, so different from you? But you left me baby . . . you left me! *(Grabs recorder)* "His widow is facing her own reality now . . . and not trying to bury her grief in fantasies any more . . . she's forced to come to terms with her beloved husband's death. I'm lost without you Cameron . . . full stop."

<u>END ACT II, SCENE 6</u>

ACT II

―――――

SCENE 7

<u>ON RISE:</u> WILHEMINA's apt. WILHEMINA and MARY are chatting about what has transpired in the past few weeks. MARY is helping WILHEMINA put finishing touches on elaborate African garb and headdress. WILHEMINA is already in her basic outfit, but the outfit involves some item of clothing and/or accessory that requires further work onstage, like head wrap, shawl, draping, etc. MARY looks fabulous.

WILHEMINA
I was in a meeting with the vice president, discussing the ever-present threat of nuclear destruction hanging over our heads, when I suddenly had an epiphany.

MARY
Hold still.

WILHEMINA
A hundred years from now, we'll all be dead, no matter what age we are. So what was I waiting for? I knew I'd never love another man the way I love Wesley Van Washington, no matter what age he is.

MARY
Uh-huh.

WILHEMINA
The press will have a field day. You really think this disguise is going to get me pass them Mary?

MARY
It'll work. They'll think you're a beautiful African queen. The press will never know it's you. The key word is incognito. But it's not fair that you feel you have to hide. You have a right to happiness too.

WILHEMINA

Of course I do, but breaking it to some of the higher-ups was rather difficult. You could see they were having a hard time holding in the smirks, but the president loved it.

MARY

If you were a man with a bride twenty years your junior, they would be giving you high fives.

WILHEMINA

Don't you know it? When is your flight?

MARY

Don't worry about me, I'm leaving tomorrow. I just want you out of here on time to catch your flight. (*Accusingly*) Since you didn't tell me you were leaving until the last minute—

WILHEMINA

Well Mary I—

MARY

I know, I know, you thought I'd try to talk you out of it, and maybe I would have—

WILHEMINA

That's the reason why I didn't tell you or Jo Billie. Although she seems to have disappeared for a few weeks and I can't find her anyway. It's not like her to not let us know what's going on.

MARY

I think she's finally mourning Cameron. She's back in town. She called last night and I've filled her in. She'll be here before you leave. She says she has a surprise for us.

WILHEMINA

Oh no. And you're really going back to Africa?

MARY
Oh yes.

WILHEMINA
Good for you.

MARY
The girls are having a hard time with it though. One of them is begging
me to take her with me.

WILHEMINA
Oh Mary.

MARY
And the other wants me to delay my trip until the newborn, is
older—

WILHEMINA
Mary.

MARY
And of course mother is displeased.

WILHEMINA
Mary . . .

MARY
But every time I think about trying to stay and help, it just feels like such
a chore. I don't want to stay here and change baby diapers, dammit!
    (Accidentally sticks, or pulls something too tight)
    Oops, sorry. I changed diapers when I was older, but I'm younger
now. (Beat) So I told them that I love them all dearly, but it's time for
me to shine like platinum! I'm going to Africa and bungee jump off
Victoria Falls—
    (Enter COLBY, looking like a male model in new clothes)
    —with Colby! Hi honey.

COLBY
Hello, sunflower.

MARY
You can take this luggage right here, please. Thank you baby.
(COLBY picks up luggage, it's heavy as lead)

COLBY
Ooo, what's in here?

WILHEMINA
Thank you for helping Colby.

COLBY
(Exiting)
My pleasure, Wil.

WILHEMINA
Wow, Colby has certainly come a long way, hasn't he?

MARY
Scrumptious isn't he? But not only does he look good; he is good for
me. Strange as it seems I think he's helping me grow up.

WILHEMINA
Really?

MARY
I know you might find this hard to believe Wilhemina, but sometimes I
think I might be a little immature.

WILHEMINA
Really?

MARY
I was really upset with him at first for refusing to go along with my plan,
but I was really proud of him for not compromising himself. I learned

something from him. It's just like Colby said, we may be from different generations but right now we're at the same place in life. I'm so excited!

WILHEMINA
I know, it's the same with me and Wesley. I can't wait to get back to him.

MARY
In Sweden?

WILHEMINA
Yes. We got married in Paris, but of course, I had to run back here on business, so we're going to start our honeymoon in Sweden. I don't know how the press got wind of our marriage so soon, but I just can't deal with their questions right now. When I get back with my "young husband" that will be soon enough to face the fire.
    (*Ushered in by MARY, enter WES disguised as Secret Service, in suit, dark glasses, followed by COLBY*)

WES
With me by your side!

WILHEMINA
Wesley! Darling! (*Looking from WES to a grinning MARY*) What—? Mary—? What are you doing here?

WES
Special Agent Van Washington at your service ma'am.

WILHEMINA
But I thought you were in Sweden—?

MARY
You're not the only one with surprises, Wil.

WES
Do you think I'd let my beautiful bride fly alone? And I have special clearance now, so Mary arranged this with the agents. The car is coming

around, my dear. There's a gaggle of reporters outside but I know how to dodge them.

WILHEMINA
Oh, I love you. I love you . . . did I tell you I love you . . . !

COLBY
Come on, man. *(Gathering bags)*

MARY
Yes, Wes, you better hurry. *(Giving him WILHEMINA's valise)*

WILHEMINA
You guys . . .
    (Laughter)

WES
Thanks, Mary. *(To WILHEMINA)* Hurry baby.
    (At door COLBY and WES pose à la Secret Service men, both in dark glasses. They exit and encounter JO BILLIE, who swings into the still open door, and exchange greetings. JO BILLIE has new hairstyle, new fashion style)

MARY/WILHEMINA
Jo Billie!

JO BILLIE
I was hoping I'd catch you before you left.

WILHEMINA/MARY
Look at you!

JO BILLIE
    (As they take it in)
New day. New me. New look. What do you think?

MARY
> (*Circle her*)

Love!

JO BILLIE

And look at you two! Mary, sexy baby, oooo . . . and Wilhemina! That's a different look for you.

MARY

You and that book of yours were our inspiration.

WILHEMINA

Well, like you always say Jo Billie, life is tricky. You never know where this journey will lead.

MARY

Too bad it didn't work out for you.

JO BILLIE

Oh, I'm doing all right. I fired that lab director, decided to give LaDonte a recommendation to another hospital, found a way to cut the budget, and the CEO gave me a raise. What the devil meant for evil God turned to good.

MARY

Even got a little religion along the way.

JO BILLIE

I just wanted to show you guys how to keep your options open. Sometimes the option is to be alone at a particular time in your life. I realize that grief is the price of love. I've made peace with that. Full stop. Period.
> (*RING. Text for MARY*)

MARY

That's Colby. The car is waiting.

WILHEMINA

Oh! How do I look? How do I look!

MARY

Like a beautiful butterfly. Now, flutter, flutter . . .
(WILHEMINA takes last look in mirror. MARY gives JO BILLIE a business card)
Here's Bill's phone number. I hate to see a good man go to waste. So check on him sometime, will you?

JO BILLIE

Oh, Mary . . .

MARY

Just as a friend. He could use a friend . . .

WILHEMINA

. . . and you could too, JB.

MARY

JoJo . . . ?

JO BILLIE

(Looking at card)
Hum . . . anything is possible. No, everything is possible.

WILHEMINA

Well, are we ready?

ALL

Yes!

WILHEMINA

Let's go!

JO BILLIE

But first . . . let's claim it girls . . .
(Each toast glass of champagne)

ALL

Let's Live! Let's Love! Let's Shine!

MARY

And remember, incognito.

> *(They put on sunglasses, exit laughing or dancing to "Sassy Mamas," then take bows)*

THE END

Reunion in Bartersville

A Comedy/Mystery in Two Acts

Synopsis

The 1933 class of Bartersville High is having its fiftieth reunion at Janie Mae Hopper's house. All of the guests have arrived, ready for an evening of gaiety. But . . . they're in for a heart-stopping surprise when an unexpected guest arrives and turns their party into an evening of hilarious suspense.

Cast of Characters

Janie Mae Hopper A sixty-eight-year-old spinster and retired school teacher. Obsessed with keeping up appearances, her politeness and soft-spokenness hide the fact that she's a little mad, as in crazy. She has a hidden envy of her friend Pollina.

Cous Pickett Janie's sixty-eight-year-old cousin, a less educated, "poor" relation. A gossip and a tease, he's under Janie's thumb. He's a janitor at the Texas Wax Museum.

Pollina Davis Brassy, well-to-do owner of a string of nightclubs. Married five times, her current husband is forty years her junior.

Perry Roussel Also sixty-eight, he was a dancer and a ladies' man in his youth. A snappy dresser and heavy drinker, he's been in show business most of his life, and resides in Hollywood with his White wife. He speaks with an affected accent.

Ronnie Davis Pollina's fifth husband. A hunk, he used to be an exotic dancer. He may have married Pollina for her money, but she's getting her money's worth out of him.

Liz Roussel Perry's forty-five-year-old wife of twenty years, from a wealthy family. Dedicated to Perry, she's concerned about his health and frustrated with his drinking.

A.J. Hamm Contends that he's spent most of his life wrongfully jailed. Cunning, vengeful, he comes to the reunion to discover who "framed" him.

Scene

In the home of JANIE MAE HOPPER, in Bartersville, Texas

Time

A summer day, around noon, 1983

ACT I

SCENE 1

<u>SETTING:</u> The living room of JANIE MAE HOPPER. It's an old lady's room, busy with antique pieces, old photographs, a phonograph, lace dollies, roses and potted plants from her garden. Two jars, one with gall stones, the other with kidney stones, are prominently displayed on her desk.

<u>ON RISE:</u> JANIE MAE is fussing over a buffet spread, while her cousin, COUS, stuffs hors d'oeuvres into his mouth. JANIE MAE is dressed in an expensive shirtwaist dress, with a handkerchief in her belt, support hose and sensible shoes. Her hair is blue rinsed. COUS, who has bad feet, wears shoes with slits for his aching corns. He's hard of hearing but refuses to wear a hearing aid. Dressed in black pants, a short-sleeved shirt and loud suspenders, he always keeps a toothpick in his mouth.

JANIE MAE
Oh Cousin, I'm just so excited. Our fiftieth high school class reunion!

COUS
(Through mouthful)
Yeah, that ought to be somethin' awright.

JANIE MAE
(Hitting his hand)
Stop eating up all of the food!

COUS
Well, shoots, I'm hungry, Janie Mae.

JANIE MAE
We're not going to touch a thing until everybody gets here.

COUS
Hear that? My stomach's growlin'.

JANIE MAE

I don't care. Get the dust mop and give the furniture a final going over.

COUS

(As he goes for the dust mop)

Aw Janie . . .

JANIE MAE

Now, don't complain, I've already waxed it. All you have to do is hit a lick at it.

(As COUS lightly swats at the furniture)

Oh, for goodness' sake, give me that.

COUS

Well, you said hit a lick at it.

JANIE MAE

(Dusting)

Oh, I just can't wait for everybody to show up.

(Schoolgirl shy)

Especially Per-ry.

COUS

You keep talkin' about everybody. Gal, it ain't no "everybody." You know, you almost waited too late to have this reunion, Janie. Out of a class of nine, there's only four of us left, includin' you and me.

(JANIE MAE gets an album of funeral programs from her desk)

JANIE MAE

Yes . . . they're all gone now . . . poor Donny White got killed soon after we graduated . . . see, his funeral program is all yellowed now . . .

COUS

The old folks always said Don was headed for a early grave, and they proved right . . .

(Chuckling in fond memory)

I remember that boy used to go roarin' through town in that Model T of Perry's—doing twenty-five miles a hour!

JANIE MAE

Yes, he was always in a hurry . . . hum . . . has it really been five years since Kenny Lee Mason passed? Doesn't seem that long, does it . . . ?

COUS

Now les' see, Floyd Brown got killed during the war, and A.J. Hamm put Dinah's lights out.

JANIE MAE

Oh please, Cousin, don't mention that. That was the worst thing to ever happen in this town. I still shudder to think of it.

COUS
    (With relish)
Yep, he blew ol' Dinah to kingdom come. Booom!

JANIE MAE

Must you be so crude?

COUS

Well, that's what he done.

JANIE MAE

Did, Cousin, did.

COUS

Huh!

JANIE MAE
    (Loudly)
That's what he <u>did</u>, not what he <u>done</u>.

COUS

Well, whatever, he killed her.

JANIE MAE

That he did. Although he always protested he was innocent.

COUS
That's what they all say.

JANIE MAE
True, true.

COUS
'Cause if he was so innocent, how come he ran off? They found him way in Corpus Christi.

JANIE MAE
I suppose he thought that nobody would believe him, being the type of person that he was.

COUS
Doggone right nobody believed him. He was guilty as sin. And a liar to boot. After they finally caught him, remember how he tried to throw the blame on everybody else?

JANIE MAE
That was awful.

COUS
Even said it coulda been me or Perry killed her 'cause we was both courtin' her. Hell, every boy in town was courtin' Dinah, 'cause she was always willin' to—

JANIE MAE
        (Hands over ears)
I know, I know.

COUS
Oh yeah, yeah, sorry . . .

JANIE MAE
But all of his evil lies failed to save him from justice.

COUS

Doggone right.

JANIE MAE

He was convicted and died in prison. Here's his obituary . . . only seven lines for sixty-odd years of life . . . sad. But Daddy always said that boy would come to a bad end.

    (Proudly)

    They wrote a whole page on Daddy when he passed. He was such an institution.

COUS

    (Changing subject)

Yeah yeah, now les' see . . . that's Donny, Kenny Lee, Dinah . . .

JANIE MAE

Oh, and we mustn't forget Violet Dressler, poor little thing.

    (Solemnly)

    Ran over by a Greyhound bus.

COUS

    (Picking his teeth)

Bad luck, it only comes to town once a week.

JANIE MAE

Isn't life perverse? Such a huge instrument to do away with such a tiny little creature.

COUS

Yep, she mighta been a midget, but Violet was a mighty big person in this town.

JANIE MAE

Here's her program. She had a closed casket, of course. Her funeral was almost as big as Daddy's.

    (Big sigh. Sniffles)

    I still can't believe Daddy's gone.

COUS
(Dryly)
Yeah, me neither.

JANIE MAE
I miss Daddy so. Sometimes I feel like he's still right here in the house with me. But I know he's gone on to the great beyond.

COUS
(Under breath)
Or the great below . . .

JANIE MAE
What was that Cousin?

COUS
(Piously, looking toward heaven)
Uh—I said, oh yes, we all miss him so.
(Back down to earth)
  Now come on, Janie Mae, we supposed to be gettin' in a party mood around here, not sittin' up here talkin' about dead folks.

JANIE MAE
You're right. We're still going to have fun, even if there are only Perry and Pollina left to attend. Besides, they were always the life of the party anyway. Well, everything is in readiness, and the canapés do look appetizing, if I say so myself.

COUS
(At the liquor cabinet)
Well, liquor-wise, we all set up for Perry. I remember that boy used to throw back a bottle of whiskey and never come up for air. 'Course now, he might be like all those folks out there in California—on dope.

JANIE MAE
Oh, don't say that, it's only the young people who do that.

COUS

I hear they all on drugs out there.

(*JANIE MAE is dreamily looking in a mirror as she pats her hair*)

JANIE MAE

Perry Roussel . . . I still can't believe he's actually going to be right here in my living room. Oh, I feel so honored!

COUS

It ain't nobody but Perry "Russell." Went out there, changed his name, picked up a fancy accent and a White wife, and now you carryin' on over him like he's a big star or somethin'.

JANIE MAE

Don't be perverse, he <u>is</u> a big star, and you know it.

COUS

Humph, every time I ever seen him, he was in the background, dancin' and grinnin'.

JANIE MAE

(*Musingly*)

I used to have such a crush on that boy . . . but then every girl in school had a crush on Perry, he was so good looking . . .

(*Pause*)

But . . . I was always too shy to ever let him know how I felt about him. I was never the outgoing type . . .

(*Voice hardens*)

. . . like Pollina.

COUS

(*Chuckling*)

Ol' Pollina. Wonder if she's bringin' that young hunk of hers with her?

JANIE MAE
    (Agitatedly)
Oh, I don't' know. I certainly hope not. I wanted to ask her over the telephone, but I didn't want to give the impression that I was hinting for her not to bring him, so I just didn't mention the boy at all . . .

COUS
And prayed that she wouldn't bring him.

JANIE MAE
    (Defensively)
Well, I don't think the young man would fit in, do you?

COUS
    (Mischievously)
Oh, I don't know. I kinda hope she brings the young feller with her. I'd get a kick outta seein' them two together.

JANIE MAE
Well, I don't know why, it's ridiculous. The young man is sure to get bored listening to a group of old people reminiscing about the good old days. Don't you agree with me?

COUS
Huh?

JANIE MAE
I said don't you agree?

COUS
Well, I don't know . . .

JANIE MAE
Oh don't be perverse. I swear! That Pollina can put one in the most embarrassing situations! It's bad enough having to keep track of the names of all those different husbands she's had over the years, and now, she's gone and married a boy forty years her junior!

COUS

(*Laughing and slapping his thigh*)

Hot dog, ol' Pollina just won't quit, will she! On her fifth husband, and this one only twenty-eight years old. The old gal just won't quit.

JANIE MAE

Well, she ought to quit. She's almost seventy years old.

COUS

I reckon she figure if a old man can marry him a young gal, why, she can marry herself a young buck!

JANIE MAE

But that's different. A man isn't expected to have good sense, but a woman ought to know better.

COUS

Oh well, you know Pollina. She was always one to do whatever she surmised to.

(*JANIE MAE goes to the desk drawer for her medicine, holding her heart*)

JANIE MAE

I'd better take one of my nitroglycerin tablets.

COUS

That always strikes me so funny. Sound like you gettin' ready to blow yourself to kingdom come, girl.

(*Softly*)

Boom.

JANIE MAE

(*Chastening*)

Please. My heart condition is not a funny matter.

COUS

I'm sorry, Janie, I was just playin' . . .

JANIE MAE

My health is not a "playing" matter, it's very, very serious. You know that—

COUS

I know, I'm sorry, I didn't mean nothin' by it—it's just that every time I hear you say that word nitro . . .

(JANIE MAE's hard look cuts him off. COUS goes to the window)

COUS

Yeah well . . . wonder if ol' Perry's bringin' that White wife of his with him?

(Peering out of window)

JANIE MAE

(Still peeved)

I have no idea. He didn't say in the telegram. But from what I understand, his wife is from a very wealthy family, involved with several charities and committees, so she might not have the time to attend Perry's reunion.

COUS

I hope she don't come, me. 'Cause then I'll have to watch how I talk, and I get enough of that from you.

JANIE MAE

There's nothing wrong with speaking correct English.

COUS

Ol' Perry and his rich White wife . . . I can see why he married her, but what she marry him for?

JANIE MAE

Has it ever occurred to you that they may love each other? After all, they've been married twenty years now.

(Pointing her finger at him)

And, Cousin, listen to me—if he does bring his White—I mean his wife with him, I want you on your very best behavior, you hear?

COUS

Oh sure, sure Janie, you know me.

JANIE MAE

(Giving him a knowing look)

Humph. I don't know Cousin . . . maybe . . . maybe . . . I should have the affair in the den . . . ? I feel so naughty having a party right here in the living room. Daddy would have a fit.

COUS

Janie? Uncle Jack is dead and buried. This whole house is yours now, so do whatever you want to do in it.

JANIE MAE

It's just that Daddy has some very old pieces in this room, very valuable you know?

COUS

Don't I know it. Every time I'd walk through here, the old man would give me "The Speech."

JANIE MAE

It's just that he was very proud and possessive of anything that belonged to him.

COUS

Includin' you.

JANIE MAE

Well, I was the only child, the apple of his eye, and after Mother passed, I was all he had left.

(The TELEPHONE RINGS)

(Going to the phone)

It might be one of them.

COUS

What's that?

JANIE MAE
>(Louder)

It might be one of our guests. Hello, Hopper's residence . . . hello, hello . . . ?
>(Puzzled, she hangs up)

Hum . . . that's strange . . .

COUS
What say?

JANIE MAE
>(Loudly)

I say that's strange!

COUS
What?

JANIE MAE
Somebody calls, asks is this Janie Mae Hopper, and when I answer yes, they just hang up.

COUS
Probably some kook who heard about the party.

JANIE MAE
I don't know . . . there was something familiar about the voice but . . .

COUS
Hey Janie, Pollina's here! And wouldn't you know it—she's got that young buck of hers with her!

JANIE MAE
>(As she crosses to the door)

Oh my heavens! That woman's got her nerve, bringing that boy here to our reunion! I swear, sometimes she just makes me so mad I could—
>(Flings open the door)

Pol-li-na! Honey! Come on in, just come right on in!

(Enter a heavily made up, loudly dressed POLLINA, husband, RONNIE, in tow. RONNIE is wearing flashy attire that shows off his physique. He's carrying two small suitcases)

POLLINA
Well hello, everybody, hello! Phew! It's hot as hell out there!

JANIE MAE
Isn't it though? Just come on in, cool off.

COUS
OK, awright, yeah y'all just come right on in . . .

POLLINA
This is my honey, Ronnie. Ronnie, Janie Mae Hopper and Cous Pickett.

RONNIE
What's happening?

JANIE MAE
    (Taken aback)
Why, uh—we're just fine, thank you, and uh—we're so pleased that you could attend . . .

COUS
Yeah, we sho' is. Why, Janie Mae was just tellin' me, "Cous, I sure hope Pollina brings that handsome young hunk—I mean, that handsome young man of hers with her," yes sir, she was just—

JANIE MAE
    (Sharply)
Put up their luggage, Cousin. Have a seat, make yourselves comfortable, while I get you some punch and sandwiches.

POLLINA
We the first things here?

JANIE MAE
Yes, but Perry should be along shortly.

POLLINA
You know . . . as we were going down Main Street . . . I could have sworn
I saw . . . but no . . .

JANIE MAE
Who Pollina?

POLLINA
(Shrugging)
Oh, just someone who looked a little like A.J.

COUS
What she say?

POLLINA
Aw hell Cous, don't start that deaf mess with me.

JANIE MAE
(Loudly)
She said she thought she saw someone who looked like A.J.
(Serving the guests)

COUS
Musta seen his ghost, 'cause you know A.J. is good and dead.

POLLINA
I know.
(Takes a sip)
Umm . . . that hit the spot.
(Tastes hors d'oeuvres)
And these hors d'oeuvres are delicious, aren't they Ron Hon?

RONNIE
Yeah baby. Hey, Miss Hopper, why don't you give us your recipe, so we
can try 'em out in our clubs at happy hour?

JANIE MAE
I'd be delighted. I'm so glad you're enjoying them. I can't eat them because of the salt content—my high blood pressure, you know?

POLLINA
And these cookies . . .

JANIE MAE
Now the cookies I can eat—

COUS
But I can't. All that sugar. I suffers with diabetes y'know . . . ?

POLLINA
You two kill me.
    (To RONNIE)
    She can eat no salt, he can eat no sugar, and between the two of them, I bet they lick the platter clean.
    (She and RONNIE laugh)
    But really Janie, everything is delicious. Ronnie, stop me. You know I'm supposed to be watching my weight.

RONNIE
You been a good girl a whole week now.
    (Giving her a kiss)
    You deserve a treat.

POLLINA
I do, don't I? Think I'll have another cookie. Here baby, you have one too.
    (Feeding him)

COUS
    (Winking at JANIE MAE)
Whatcha watchin' your weight for, Pollina? You look mighty fine to me.

POLLINA
Why thank you, Cous.

JANIE MAE
Doesn't she look well?

COUS
Yeah, and she still got those pretty legs.

RONNIE
Prettiest legs in Texas I always say.

POLLINA
(*Pinching RONNIE's face*)
You're so sweet.
(*Turning to JANIE MAE*)
And you're looking pretty good yourself, Janie old girl.

JANIE MAE
Well, considering that I've had open heart surgery, I'd say I'm holding up pretty well, thank God. You see, they had to take a vein out of this leg here, then they had to open up my chest wall and put the vein here in my chest, then they had to take another vein from this leg and . . .

POLLINA
Oh spare me the gory details honey. I'm proud to say my heart's pumping just as good as it was the day I was born.

JANIE MAE
(*Offended*)
You're fortunate to have such good health.

POLLINA
Fortune doesn't have a thing to do with it. It's just a matter of making up your mind what you will and will not put up with. And I will not put up with being sick.
(*To RONNIE*)
Get me another sandwich, honey.

RONNIE
Sure baby.

JANIE MAE
    (Umbrage)
I certainly hope that you're not implying that I chose ill health. I don't
enjoy being unwell you know.

POLLINA
I'm sure you don't, Janie. I'm just talking in general. You know how it is
when folks get a little age on 'em? They figure there's nothing left to do,
but get sick with something, lay down and die. Well, I plan to live to be
106 years old. Don't I sweetie pie?

RONNIE
You better.
    (Squeezing her)
    You know I can't live without my girl.

JANIE MAE
Well! I certainly hope I didn't give the impression that I was getting ready
to lay down and die!

POLLINA
Calm down, girl.
    (Winking at COUS)
    You'll be here when we're all dead and buried, bad heart and all.
    (COUS grins, nodding in vigorous agreement)

RONNIE
I used to be an orderly in a hospital once, worked in the heart unit.

JANIE MAE
    (Excitedly)
Oh did you, Ronnie? Wonderful, then you understand! I was so ill,
Ronnie—Cousin'll tell you—they thought they were going to lose me there
for a while, didn't they, Cousin—?

COUS
Well they—

JANIE MAE

Two weeks I hovered between life and death, tell them Cousin—

COUS

Well, yeah, see she—

JANIE MAE

I thought I'd never leave that hospital alive, isn't that right Cousin, tell them—

COUS

Well, what the doctors said was—

JANIE MAE
    (*Joyfully*)
But here I am.

POLLINA

I hear surgeons do so much unnecessary surgery these days—especially on you older folks.

JANIE MAE

Well, I can assure you that I would never have had something as major as open heart surgery, if it hadn't been absolutely necessary.
    (*RONNIE has been wandering about the room in obvious boredom. Now he examines the jars of stones*)

RONNIE

Hey, what's these?
    (*Glad that he asked, JANIE MAE rushes over*)

JANIE MAE
    (*Proudly*)
These, Ronnie, are my stones. Those are my gall stones, and those are my kidney stones. I had them taken out about fifteen years ago, and Daddy had the undertaker preserve them in formaldehyde for me.

RONNIE
  (*Disinterestedly*)
Oh yeah?

JANIE MAE
Oh yes! I'm sure a man of your medical background must find them quite fascinating!

RONNIE
Uh—yeah, Miss Hopper, I guess they're something all right.

COUS
  (*Calling over to them*)
Well, you know I had surgery a while back on my hemorrhoids? Maybe I shoulda had them preserved, and next week I gotta go in and get these bunions took off an—

POLLINA
Now wait a minute, I'm trying to eat here! I didn't come here to listen to a bunch of old folks sitting around talking about their hemorrhoids and bunions. The only surgery I've had is plastic, and I don't mind telling it.

JANIE MAE
  (*Peering into POLLINA's face*)
Really Pollina? You know, I thought your face looked smoother.

POLLINA
My face? Honey, I haven't touched my face. I had a fanny tuck.

JANIE MAE
A what . . . ?

COUS
What she say?

POLLINA
A fanny—

JANIE MAE
    (Hands over ears)
I heard you, I heard you.

COUS
Well, I didn't. What she say?

POLLINA
    (Modeling)
You are now looking at the proud possessor of a twenty-five-year-old . . .
    (Slaps one buttock)
  . . . gluttemous . . .
    (Slaps the other buttock)
  . . . maximus.
    (JANIE MAE is mortified)

COUS
What she say? I'm lookin' at what?

RONNIE
She had her tail lifted, man.
    (JANIE MAE chokes on a sip of punch. COUS adjusts his glasses, trying to check out POLLINA's backside. POLLINA goes on, oblivious of JANIE MAE's mortification)

POLLINA
It was a simple process really, Janie Mae.
    (Putting her behind in JANIE MAE's face)
  They went in through here, see, and came out through here, and—

RONNIE
Honey, I think you're embarrassing Miss Hopper.

POLLINA
    (Hooting with laughter)
Child, I've been "embarrassing" Miss Hopper since grade school.

JANIE MAE
  (*Clearing her throat*)
Uh—you know Pollina, you haven't been to Bartersville for quite some time now, has she Cousin?

COUS
Huh? Huh?

JANIE MAE
Forget it.

POLLINA
Oh, it hasn't been that long.
  (*JANIE MAE gets her album of funeral programs*)

JANIE MAE
October of '77. You were here for Kenny Lee's funeral. That's the last time you were here.
  (*Closes album*)

POLLINA
OK, OK, I take your word for it, you don't have to drag out that old morbid album of yours.

JANIE MAE
It's not morbid. It's just my way of remembering all of our dearly departed classmates.
  (*Hugging the album*)

POLLINA
Well, when I go, don't put me in that thing. I don't even want a funeral. I told Ronnie that if I go before he does, to cremate me, scatter my ashes to the four winds.
  (*Scattering imaginary ashes*)
  And remember me alive! Remember me alive!
  (*Kicking up her leg, she falls into RONNIE's lap*)

JANIE MAE
Oh dear.

RONNIE
There's no other way I could ever remember you, baby.

COUS
Hot dog!
(*Suddenly, JANIE MAE jumps up and starts to recite*)

JANIE MAE
"Do not go gently into that good night / Old age should burn and rage at close of light."
(*Getting carried away*)
"Rage! Rage! Against the dying of the light."
(*Catches herself, then sheepishly*)
Dylan Thomas.

POLLINA
You giving me the creeps. Enough of this kind of talk.
(*Holding out her glass*)
Pour me some more champagne, Ron Hon.

RONNIE
Sure baby.

COUS
(*Holding out his glass*)
Me too, will you sonny boy?
(*A BEAT, as RONNIE looks at him, then takes his glass*)

POLLINA
Well Janie, how's retirement treating ya? You miss the classroom I bet?

JANIE MAE
Oh, indeed I do. A young girl has my literature class now. I try to keep myself busy though. I work Daddy's garden for him, although I don't have

the green thumb he had. His ivy—you know the one he'd been growing for fifteen years?

POLLINA
Uh-huh.

JANIE MAE
Well, it passed soon after Daddy died, even though I did everything I could to save it. And, of course, I have Emerson, Emily and Thoreau to keep me company.

POLLINA
Who?

JANIE MAE
My American poets, dear.

POLLINA
Oh yeah, those guys.

COUS
Well Pollina, how's the nightclub business?
        (RONNIE gives COUS his drink)

POLLINA
Smooth as silk, since I've got my Ronnie to help me now.
        (Standing behind POLLINA who is sitting on the sofa, RONNIE hands her drink to her)

RONNIE
        (Massaging POLLINA's shoulders)
But you don't let me have enough responsibility. I want to take the whole load off of your shoulders.

POLLINA
All in due time sweetikins, all in due time. If I let you spend all of your time learning the business, you wouldn't have enough time for me, now would you?
        (Pinching his cheek)

COUS
    (*Teasingly*)
Now, les' see, what's that Pollina, your fourth? Nightclub, that is?

POLLINA
    (*Catching his drift*)
No, my fifth. Nightclub, that is.

COUS
    (*Grinning*)
That's good, real good.

RONNIE
We're thinking about putting up a club on Pollina's property here in Bartersville.

JANIE MAE
    (*Consternation*)
Here?

POLLINA
Why not? I think Bartersville is finally ready for a Pollina's.

JANIE MAE
Oh my God. What we really need here is a decent restaurant. Daddy and I used to have to drive all the way to Weimer for a decent restaurant.

POLLINA
Should have come to Houston. I would have taken you anywhere you wanted to go.

JANIE MAE
You know how Daddy hated going to the big city.

COUS
Les' see . . . last time I was in Houston's was in '62. Went down there with Sylvester Jones when his daughter was in that bad car wreck. That

was some busy place, Houston. Too busy for me. Traffic was something terrible.

POLLINA
Still is. If you saw Houston now, you wouldn't know it. New buildings all over the place. You bat your eyes, they've put up a new building.

COUS
Now that's what I like about Bartersville—we keeps the old. Oh, we put up some new, but we keeps the old. Now take the Texas Wax Museum—still standing, and in good shape too. 'Course now, they've added on some new exhibits, but it's still in just as good a shape as it was when I started workin' there fifty years ago . . . Lordy, it don't seem that long . . . I was just a boy of eighteen . . . yesterday . . .

JANIE MAE
The years do fly, don't they?

COUS
Don't they though?

JANIE MAE
Our youth is but a dream . . . we wake up . . . and here we are—senior citizens.

POLLINA
Oh, you're only as old as you feel. Hey Cous, you mean you're still at the wax museum? Last time I saw you, you were talking about retiring.

COUS
Yeah, I'm still there, but I don't hit a lick at a snake, though. Mostly all I do is supervise the young boys they got workin' there now. You know these young boys nowadays don't half want to work, they just lookin' for a easy way out.
  (*JANIE MAE jumps up, trying to cover COUS's mistake*)

JANIE MAE
Uh—Pollina, won't you have another cookie?

COUS

Oh! 'Cuse me, present company expected. I'm sure Ronnie is a hard-workin' young feller.

POLLINA

(Winking eye)

In every way.

RONNIE

Uh—you get much crime around here, Cous?

COUS

A good bit lately.

JANIE MAE

We're afraid to leave our doors open now. What is this world coming to? Soon there'll be no place for the gentle and the peace-loving individual. Soon we'll be driven from the face of this earth, by the mad, the degenerate, the violent.

(Shudders)

Thank God, I won't be alive to see it.

RONNIE

We had a lot of break-ins in the clubs, until I talked Pollina into putting in a new alarm system.

POLLINA

(Tightly)

It was expensive as hell too. It better pay off.

RONNIE

It will. Have I ever steered you wrong, baby?

POLLINA

No, sweetie pie. I just don't know what I'd do without my sweetie pie. He makes me soooo happy.

RONNIE
Not as happy as my sweetie-cheeks makes me.
  (THEY gaze into each other's eyes)

COUS
Well, I'm glad everybody's happy.

POLLINA
Delirious. We've been married a year and a half now and we're still just as much in love as the day we married.

RONNIE
Oh baby, I love you more than the day I married you.

POLLINA
Show 'em our wedding pictures honey.

RONNIE
  (Whipping out snapshots)
Here you go. Doesn't she make a beautiful bride?

JANIE MAE
Every time.

POLLINA
And just think I have Harvey to thank for him.

JANIE MAE
Harvey? Wasn't that your . . . ?

POLLINA
My ex, yes. See, Ronnie was a patient of Harvey's and—

RONNIE
I hurt my foot, dancing. See, I used to be an exotic dancer, y'know and I went to her old man to get my foot fixed, but that quack made it worse.

POLLINA

I met Ronnie when he sued Harvey for malpractice. We looked across that courtroom into each other's eyes, and it was love at first sight, wasn't it Ronnie?

RONNIE

Yeah. I lost the case, but I won the girl.

COUS

    (At the window)

Well, ol' Perry ought to be drivin' up soon.

POLLINA

I don't know how I'm going to react seeing that old rascal after all these years. Fifty years and he never so much as sent me a card to find out if I was dead or alive!

COUS

Guess he just lost track of time out there in California. You know they all on drugs out there—

JANIE MAE

Cousin.

POLLINA

Don't make excuses for him, Cous.

JANIE MAE

Now Pollina, we all want this to be a fun event, you know.

RONNIE

Yeah baby, if you don't think you want to see this old dude . . .

POLLINA

Don't worry about it, everything's fine. I mean, my God, I stopped being bitter about Perry a long time ago.

    (Changing subject)

Wasn't that pitiful about Violet?

JANIE MAE
Wasn't it though?
> (*Getting album*)
Here's her program right here. She had a closed casket, of course.

POLLINA
Did she? You know, she and three of her daughters were in Houston a few years ago, and they paid me a visit.

JANIE MAE
Did they?

POLLINA
Uh-huh. How many children did she have?

COUS
> (*Before JANIE MAE can answer*)
Ten. And not a one of 'em normal size. Good kids, though. I got that oldest boy of hers a job at the museum.
> (*A KNOCK at the door*)

POLLINA
Oh my God, Perry's here, Perry's here!
> (*Going toward door*)
I'll get it!

JANIE MAE
No! I'll get it. After all, it is my house.

RONNIE
> (*To Pollina*)
Yeah woman, be cool.
> (*JANIE MAE smooths her hair before throwing open the door*)

JANIE MAE
Perry! Perry Roussel!

(PERRY and LIZ sweep in, very "Hollywood-esque" in sunglasses, and laden with gifts. PERRY's dressed in a loudly colored blazer with a carnation in his lapel. LIZ has on an expensive summer outfit)

PERRY
Janie! Janie Mae Hopper!
(PERRY gives her a Hollywood kiss, smooching the air)

PERRY
I know 'tis you, though I haven't seen you since you were eighteen years old! But you're still just as lovely as you were the day I saw you last.

JANIE MAE
(Blushing)
Oh you!

COUS
Perry Russell, you rascal you!

PERRY
(Taken aback)
And who is this old man? And the name is Roussel.

COUS
It's me, Cous. Cous Pickett!

PERRY
(Teasingly)
Cous? Pickett? Is that really you?

COUS
You know it's me.

PERRY
Of course I do, you haven't changed a bit. You still have those bad feet, I see.
(PERRY approaches POLLINA, who has been demurely waiting for his attention)

PERRY

And this lovely madam . . . must be Pollina Graves?

POLLINA
  (*Quietly*)
Hello Perry. And it's Pollina Davis now.

PERRY

Hello darling! You look fantastic! You all look fantastic!

ALL

So do you, look so good, well, real well, etc.

PERRY

And this is my better half—Liz. Liz darling, these are my classmates.

LIZ

Hi, I've heard so much about you guys, I can't tell you how thrilled I am
to meet you!

JANIE MAE

We're so glad you were able to attend, Liz.

LIZ
  (*Holding on to PERRY's arm*)
Oh, I couldn't let him attend without me, I just had to be here.

COUS

Well Miss Liz, I was just tellin' my cousin Janie here—Janie Mae, I says,
I sure hope ol' Perry brings his White—
  (*JANIE MAE clears her throat*)
  I mean, his wife with him. Yes ma'am, Miss Liz, I was just sayin' that.

LIZ

What a dear. I wouldn't have missed meeting Perry's friends for the
world.

PERRY
(Peering at RONNIE)
Now, don't tell me, young man, don't tell me. Let me guess whose son you are. Ah, you have Janie Mae's eyes.

RONNIE
Uh—naw man, I'm—

PERRY
No no, don't tell me. You're too handsome to belong to Cous . . .

RONNIE
Listen, I'm here with my—

PERRY
Don't tell me, uh—let's see . . .

POLLINA
(Taking RONNIE's arm) He belongs to me, Perry. This is Ronnie . . .

PERRY
(Fearful)
Ronnie . . . ?

RONNIE
Her husband.

POLLINA
Close your mouth, Perry.

PERRY
Forgive me, I-I-I . . .

POLLINA
Don't stutter Perry, it's a common mistake.

LIZ
    (Breezily)
I know exactly what you mean, Pollina. People make mistakes about me and Perry all the time . . .

COUS
I bet they do.

LIZ
They think I'm his daughter.

COUS
His daughter? Oh yeah, yeah, that's funny, real funny!
    (They ALL laugh overly long and loud, glad to relieve the tension. PERRY speaks as the laughter subsides)

PERRY
Now sit down everybody, sit down, while I open up my bag of goodies.

JANIE MAE
    (Clapping her hands)
Oh, you brought gifts from California, I love gifts!

PERRY
Liz picked them. She's the best little gift picker on Rodeo Drive.

LIZ
I do hope you like them. Perry told me a little something about each one of you and I tried to select what I thought each of you would like, so enjoy.
    (Throws kisses)

PERRY
    (Dispensing gifts)
This is for you, Pollina, and this, for you Janie Mae . . .
    (Throwing box to COUS)
  Catch, Cous old man. And Ronnie, is it? If I'd known you were going to be here . . .

RONNIE

Don't worry about it. Meeting a real "old-time" movie star like you can be my gift.

PERRY

Why, thank you, I'm flattered.
    (Under breath)
  I think.

POLLINA
    (Holding up gift)
Oh, look at this! It's so—so colorful! I love it. What is it?

LIZ

It's a headband, hon. You tie it around your head . . .
    (Standing behind POLLINA, sitting on the sofa, LIZ reaches for the head band, and ties it around POLLINA's head)

LIZ

. . . like this.

POLLINA

Oh, I see. At first I thought it was a sash, and I was about to tell Perry that I don't have that eighteen-inch waist that I'm sure he remembers.
    (Flirtingly, she leans toward PERRY, who flirts back)

LIZ

These headbands are all the rage in LA. So when Perry told me about the beautiful head of hair you "used" to have . . .
    (Holding up sash, like it's a dirty rag)
  I said "this" is Pollina.
    (Lets the sash drop into POLLINA's lap)

JANIE MAE

And I just love my music box, Liz.

LIZ
   (*Gushingly*)
Oh, do you, Janie Mae? I agonized over it and a book of poetry. Perry
told me you collected both.

JANIE MAE
The music box is enchanting. I'll cherish it, forever.

PERRY
Do you still collect music boxes, Janie Mae?

JANIE MAE
Well, actually I . . .

POLLINA
She collects funeral programs now, Perry, and body parts.

PERRY
I beg your pardon?

POLLINA
Tell you about it later.

COUS
Well, Miss Liz, you hit the nail on the head with me.
   (*Holding up his gift*)
   A silver needle!

LIZ
That's a silver toothpick. And please, call me Liz, Mr. Pickett.

COUS
Oh—OK. And you can call me Cous, Miss—I mean Liz. Me and Janie is
the only real kin around here, but they all calls me Cous.

LIZ
OK—Cous.

COUS

A silver toothpick! How 'bout that? Look at that y'all, ain't that something, my own personal toothpick.

(Digs between his teeth)

Works real good too, I been tryin' to get that out all day.

POLLINA

(Going to liquor cabinet)

Well, that calls for more champagne.

PERRY

(Following her)

Pour me one too, Polly, I'm parched.

(RONNIE watches POLLINA and PERRY laughing together. RONNIE comes up behind POLLINA so that when she turns to bring him his drink, he's there. RONNIE, POLLINA and PERRY pass out the drinks to all while conversation goes on)

LIZ

Janie, your home is so charming. So many beautiful antiques.

JANIE MAE

(Proudly)

Thank you. The antiques were Daddy's pride and joy, along with his rose garden.

His roses, Liz, were the talk of the town. He won many, many shows with them.

He was school principal too, you know?

LIZ

Oh was he?

JANIE MAE

Oh yes, Daddy was the pillar of this community . . .

PERRY

I propose a toast to the class of '33!

ALL

(Raising their drinks)

Toast to the class of 1933!

(PERRY leads off the school song, as the others join in, off-key)

ALL

Dear Bartersville High! / You are our pride! / You are our pride and fount of treasure / By which we measure the world's sweet treasure / Dear Bartersville High! / No matter where in this life we go /We will always remember and love you so!

(ALL collapse in laughter)

PERRY

Who wrote that?

POLLINA

Janie Mae, don't you remember?

PERRY

Ah yes, our resident Shakespeare.

(Getting camera from luggage)

All right, now everybody, its photograph time. Liz, dearest, snap us, will you?

LIZ

Surely.

JANIE MAE

Oh yes, class, we must have our reunion picture.

PERRY

Come, come, let me stage everybody. Janie you sit here, and we three will stand behind you here . . .

LIZ

Everybody ready?

ALL
Ready!

LIZ
OK, say cheese.

ALL
Cheese!

JANIE MAE
(*After the picture*)
Oh, I felt just like I was back in school again. Our school days were so happy and carefree, Liz and Ronnie, even though we graduated during the Depression.

PERRY
Ah yes, and some of our less fortunate classmates, like A.J. and Dinah, wouldn't even have had caps and gowns—

JANIE MAE
If it hadn't been for my daddy and Dr. Russell—I mean, Dr. Roussel—I mean Doctor—

POLLINA
Just say Perry's daddy.

JANIE MAE
We were all very close, always having fun.

PERRY
Except for A.J.

COUS
Yeah, he was the town bully.

JANIE MAE
And Dinah, of course. She was—

POLLINA
The town—

JANIE MAE
Pollina! We mustn't speak ill of the dead.

LIZ
And who was A.J.?
    (THEY ALL look at each other)

ALL
Well . . .

JANIE MAE
He died in prison, God rest his soul. And all the souls of our dearly
departed classmates—Violet, Floyd, Don, Kenny Lee, A.J. and Dinah.
May they all rest in peace.
    (THEY observe a moment of silence)

PERRY
Well! That calls for another drink!

RONNIE
I'll get it.

PERRY
Thank you.

LIZ
    (Admonishingly)
Per-ry . . .

PERRY
It's only champagne, darling.

POLLINA
Tell me, Liz, how are your two kids doing, Desiree and Jacob?

LIZ

Oh, you're familiar with our children's names?

POLLINA

I read an article about your family once in *Showbiz Magazine*.

LIZ

Oh yes, I remember that little write-up, don't you dear?

PERRY

Ah yes, I was working on that sitcom then.

JANIE MAE
     (Gushing)
Oh, I never ever missed that show!

POLLINA

Well, I never saw it.
     (Touching RONNIE)
   But then, I don't have much time for television.

LIZ

Well, to answer your question, Pollina—our son Jacob is in publicity at Universal Studios, and Desiree graduates Beverly Hills High this year.

POLLINA

How nice.

PERRY

What about you Janie Mae, any kids?

JANIE MAE

Oh dear me, no. I've never even been married. I live alone now, since Daddy passed last year.

PERRY

Just last year? Why that would make Professor Hopper—

JANIE MAE
Ninety-five years old when he passed.

PERRY
(Boredly) Extraordinary.

LIZ
Do you live here in Bartersville, Pollina?

POLLINA
God no! This burg's too slow for me. Everybody here's a hundred or more. Cous and Janie are the youngest things in town.

LIZ
Do you have any children, Pollina?

COUS
Now, don't rush 'em Miss Liz, they're still newlyweds, y'know?
    (ALL laugh good-naturedly, including POLLINA and RONNIE)

POLLINA
    (Pointedly to PERRY)
I have only the one son I had when I got pregnant the summer of our graduation.

PERRY
    (Choking on his champagne)

    (JANIE MAE jumps up and starts circulating with the serving tray)

JANIE MAE
    (Desperately)
Cookies anyone? Punch? Sandwiches?
    (PERRY runs to replenish his drink)

LIZ
Oh really?

POLLINA

Oh Liz, you just can't imagine how a small town like this can persecute a young girl for making a mistake, especially back in those days. None of my so-called friends would be caught dead with "that Graves girl." But it made a woman out of me—

(Looking at JANIE MAE)

JANIE MAE

(Pleading)

Punch anyone?

LIZ

I believe I'll have some, thank you.

PERRY

Music! That's what this party needs! Music!

JANIE MAE

Oh yes! I have stacks and stacks of records from our graduation year!

(JANIE MAE and PERRY look through the records)

COUS

Hey there Perry, answer me something!

PERRY

(Afraid to ask)

What?

COUS

What's it take to make it in show biz?

PERRY

(Relieved)

Oh, that's easy—10 percent talent and 90 percent contacts.

COUS

Just what I figured, ain't got to have no talent. Betcha I could make it in show biz.

POLLINA

Doing what?

COUS

Hambone! Couldn't nobody beat me at hambone!
(Slaps his thighs, singing)

Hambone, Hambone, where you been? Around the world and back again. Hambone, Hambone, what'd you do? I got a chance and I fairly flew. Hambone, Hambone, where you stay? I met a pretty gal and I couldn't stay away! Hambone, Hambone, doing that crazy hambone, etc.

LIZ

(Clapping)
Oh, how charming. I've never seen anything quite like that before.

COUS

Thank you Miss Liz.

PERRY

I haven't seen that type of thing in years. It seems so rustic now.

COUS

(Offended)
Rusty! You sayin' I'm rusty?

PERRY

No Cous, I—

COUS

Well, let's see you try to do some of that fancy steppin' you used to do.

JANIE MAE

Yes Perry, dance for us!

COUS

Go on Perry, shake some tail feathers boy, show this young pup here how we used to do it.

(*JANIE MAE puts on MUSIC: "It Don't Mean a Thing, If It Ain't Got That Swing"* *by Duke Ellington*)

JANIE MAE
Come on Perry—

PERRY
No no, I don't do much dancing these days.

COUS
What's wrong? Joints done locked up on ya?

PERRY
Of course not! I soak daily in eucalyptus oil, and it keeps me just as limber as ever I was.
    (*The MUSIC starts to play "SHOTGUN" by Jr. Walker. THEY do the jerk popular at that time*)

PERRY
    (*Snapping his fingers*)
Oh man, remember that? Boy, that was hot during the thirties. We used to swing to that at Miller's Roadhouse all night long!

COUS
Yeah, you and Pollina'd be dancin' and you'd throw her clean over your head!

PERRY
    (*Singing with record*)
Do-wa-do-wa-do-wa-do-wa, etc.
    (*PERRY starts to dance*)

COUS
That's right, shake them tail feathers, boy!

PERRY
Come on Pollina!

(PERRY and POLLINA do a few swing steps, then Perry gets winded, ends up coughing. LIZ gets an inhaler from her purse)

RONNIE

(Guiding PERRY to sofa)

Hey Pops, you all right?

POLLINA

(Rushing to his side)

Perry, Perry, are you all right . . . ?

LIZ

(Pushing POLLINA aside)

He'll be fine, he just gets a little winded sometimes. Open Perry.

(She sprays his throat)

PERRY

Guess I'm just a little out of shape.

LIZ

Actually Janie, I think the trip is beginning to catch up with us. If we could just freshen up a bit, and perhaps lie down for a few minutes . . . ?

JANIE MAE

Oh, of course, forgive my rudeness. Your room is down the hall and to the right.

PERRY

Yes, a little rest will put us as right as rain. And then, we will resume our festivities with a vengeance!

(Coughing fit)

LIZ

Come dear.

PERRY

Darling will you check and make sure the car's locked?

LIZ
But—

PERRY
I'll be fine.

LIZ
OK, I'll be right back.
>   (*LIZ exits. PERRY takes whiskey flask out of his pocket, sneaks a drink as he exits to room*)

POLLINA
Come baby, let's us catch a little peep eye too.

RONNIE
You go ahead, honey, I think I'll step out and stretch my legs a little bit.

POLLINA
No, I want you with me.

RONNIE
But I'm not sleepy.

POLLINA
>   (*Winking her eye at COUS*)
I'm not either.

JANIE MAE
Yes Pollina, you know where your room is . . . down the hall and to the . . .
>   (*JANIE MAE's voice trails off as POLLINA runs giggling to room, chased by RONNIE*)

JANIE MAE
Well I never . . .

COUS
>   (*Under breath*)
Maybe you should.

JANIE MAE

What was that?

COUS

(Snickering)

Uh—I said he mighta married her for her money, but I bet she's gettin' her money's worth outta him.

(Mortified, JANIE MAE waves him off and is grateful when the TELEPHONE RINGS. PERRY reenters to refill his flask as LIZ is reentering. POLLINA reenters to get her purse, still chased by RONNIE who has shirt unbuttoned)

JANIE MAE

(On the telephone)

Hello? Hopper's residence.

(To POLLINA and RONNIE) Shhh!

(Into phone)

Pardon me . . . ? Would you speak up please, I can't hear you clearly . . . who? Who is this!

(The OTHERS turn their attention to JANIE MAE)

Yes . . . yes . . . I'm still here . . . Of—of course you may a-a-attend, if you wish . . . yes . . . yes it's still the same address . . . yes . . . we—we'll be looking forward to seeing you again . . . A.J.

(Undone, she hangs up the telephone)

(THEY stare at each other, spooked)

<u>BLACKOUT</u>

<u>END ACT I</u>

ACT II

SCENE 1

ON RISE: A short time later, in JANIE MAE's living room. JANIE MAE is reading aloud A.J. HAMM's obituary. COUS and RONNIE are at the window. PERRY is nursing a drink, while LIZ puffs on a cigarette. POLLINA absently stuffs hors d'oeuvres into her mouth.

JANIE MAE
(Reading out loud)
A.J. Hamm, a native of Bartersville, born July 12, 1915, died in the Huntsville State Prison, June 5, 1983, of natural causes. Hamm was sentenced to life in prison for the 1933 murder of another Bartersville native, Dinah Johnson. His remains will be interred in the Huntsville Prison Cemetery.

POLLINA
That's the third time you've read that thing, and it's not going to make A.J. dead if he's still alive.

JANIE MAE
But I just don't understand how a mistake like that could be made. Not that I wish the poor man dead of course . . . *(Reading again)* "A.J. Hamm, a native of—"

PERRY
Please Janie Mae . . .
(Going for refill as she continues reading under her breath)
I understand how it could happen—the *Bartersville News* is just as inaccurate as it ever was.

LIZ
What's everybody so upset about?

RONNIE
Yeah, that's what I wanna know?

COUS
(Nervously)
Upset? Ain't nobody upset!

JANIE MAE
That's right, we have nothing to feel guilty about!

COUS
Not a thing!

PERRY
I know I don't.

LIZ
Then why are you all acting so afraid?

COUS
Did she say scared? Ain't nobody scared to face A.J. I know I ain't!

POLLINA
Oh sit down, Cous. We're all afraid and you know it.
(To LIZ)
We all testified against A.J. at the trial and he's not one to forget it.

PERRY
I did not testify at the trial.

POLLINA
I know. You'd skipped town by then.

COUS
Yeah, you skipped town.

PERRY
(Peeved) I did not "skip" town. I merely left town to seek my fortune.

RONNIE

You know what? Y'all keep picturing this dude like he was fifty years ago, all right? But now, you gotta realize, he's just a gray-haired little old dude like the rest of y'all, probably on a cane or in a wheelchair. Can't do you any harm at all.

JANIE MAE

(Hopefully)

You know Ronnie's right. We must get a grip on ourselves, we must look at this thing positively. If A.J. really is alive, and I say if, what makes us think he wants to cause trouble? Probably all he wants is to see his dear old classmates. After all, he was in the class of '33 too.

COUS

Yeah, but he wasn't never nobody's friend. You remember all the trouble he used to cause at the barn dances?

JANIE MAE

But he sounded very pleasant over the telephone.

COUS

I don't care how he sounded over the telephone, that man's a murderer!

LIZ

Don't you think you're overreacting a little bit, Cous? As Ronnie said, why be afraid of a man for something he did fifty years ago?

RONNIE

Yeah, he served his time, give the old guy a break.

POLLINA

You don't know A.J.

JANIE MAE

Well I agree with the young people, we must attempt to be open-minded about this.

COUS

OK, don't say nothin' if he whips out a pistol and kills us all.

JANIE MAE

Oh God forbid. Surely he'll understand that our testifying was nothing personal. Surely he'll understand that we simply had to answer the questions the prosecutor put to us.

PERRY

I don't think A.J. will have quite that civilized a view of it.

COUS

(Greatly distressed)

Oh Janie, Janie, why did you tell him he could come?

JANIE MAE

What else could I say, Cousin? I certainly didn't want to appear ungracious.

COUS

Ungracious! Hell, I'd rather be ungracious than dead!

POLLINA

That doggone Dinah was such a flirt. Everybody wanted to kill her at one time or another. I could never understand what the boys saw in her. All she ever had going for her was her rear end.

COUS

Which was a-plenty.

POLLINA

Which was abnormal.

COUS

Wasn't nothin' abnormal about that gal. She was about the normalest gal I'd ever seen.

JANIE MAE

She was wild as a buck deer.

POLLINA
Wanted every man in town.

COUS
And damn near had 'em too.

JANIE MAE
Cousin!

LIZ
She sounds like a very unfortunate young lady to me.

JANIE MAE
She was, poor thing.

POLLINA
She was man crazy.

JANIE MAE
She did put too much stock in a man. Mother used to always tell me: Janie Mae, never put too much stock in a man, because even the best of them will let you down time and time again. *(At their stares)* That's mother talking.

PERRY
So, A.J. is going to rise up from the grave, and come in here and wreak vengeance on us all?

JANIE MAE
He didn't say that. He simply said he'd be over in an hour.

RONNIE
Just tell the dude he's not invited, and if he comes over you're gonna call the law.

JANIE MAE
Well, as you know, I checked with the city marshall about it and he said there was nothing they could do unless somebody broke the law.

PERRY

> (*Chuckling*)

Well. This is straight out of a B movie, isn't it? And all we need now is for the eerie music to start up, while the lights go dim on each of us, staring wild-eyed at one another as we await the dreaded knock of A.J. Hamm!

> (*PERRY knocks on the table. Panic, as EVERYBODY jumps and screams. COUS dives behind the sofa. PERRY laughs uncontrollably*)

LIZ

Perry! You ought to be ashamed of yourself!

> (*But she can't help laughing*)

PERRY

> (*Still laughing*)

Come on out, Cous, it was only me.

POLLINA

My God, Perry, can't you be serious, even in your old age?

> (*COUS crawls from behind the sofa, eyeglasses askew*)

COUS

You crazy! You almost give me a heart attack!

RONNIE

> (*Trying to hide a grin*)

Come on, Cous, let me help you up, man.

JANIE MAE

My! How that caused my heart to flutter. Cousin, get me my nitro.

COUS

> (*Going for the pills*)

Need some of that stuff myself . . .

PERRY

I'm sorry, but I just couldn't let the moment pass. Oh, you should have seen yourself, Cous.

> (*Starting to cough*)

LIZ
Now look what you've done to yourself.

POLLINA
Does he need water or something?

LIZ
I think he'll be all right.

PERRY
(Deep breaths)
I'm fine, fine.

LIZ
Sure?

PERRY
Yes love. Now. Where were we?

POLLINA
Sitting here waiting for A.J. to come blow our brains out.

JANIE MAE
Oh please, Pollina, don't talk like that. Now listen, everybody, we are simply not going to let the thought of A.J., dead or alive, ruin our celebration. I know! Let's have a talent show like we used to!

PERRY
A talent show . . . ? Now really Janie, I don't think . . .

POLLINA
Who feels like a talent show? And who's got any talent anyway. Except Perry, and he's out of breath . . . Not unless my Ron Hon wants to show off some of his moves. After all he's the party motivator. Come on honey, show 'em your stuff.
(After a little reluctance, RONNIE gets into it, dancing seductively)

JANIE MAE

Stop it, stop it! I think we've seen quite enough. I've got it! I'll read you some of my poetry.

COUS
    (Groaning)
Aw naw . . .

JANIE MAE
    (Excitedly)
I've got boxes and boxes of them! Be right back.

ALL
Oh Janie please, wait up, don't, etc.

JANIE MAE
    (As she exits)
Be right back.

COUS
Well, I better get a drink, if I'm gonna have to listen to that poetry of hers.

PERRY
    (Whispering to COUS)
Refresh mine too, will you?

COUS
Say what?

PERRY
    (Still whispering)
Refresh my drink.

COUS
    (Loudly)
What's that, refresh your drink?

PERRY
    (*Exasperatedly*)
Dammit man, you can't hear thunder, can you!

COUS
    (*Going toward window*)
Is it thunderin'?

PERRY
I'll get it myself!
    (*LIZ follows PERRY*)

LIZ
    (*Hissing*)
Thanks for telling me about Pollina.

PERRY
    (*Quietly*)
That's right, I did tell you about Pollina. I told you she was crazy
about me.

LIZ
But you didn't tell me "everything."

PERRY
Believe me, love, I don't think I know "everything."

LIZ
    (*Snatching drink*)
And you don't need another drink either!

PERRY
Why don't you say it a little louder, so even that doggone deaf Cous can
hear it!

LIZ

(Hissing)

I am sick and tired of watching you destroy yourself and our lives with your drinking. You've ruined your health, you can't get work in the industry anymore—

PERRY

It's not my fault—I had that role in the palm of my hand, It was a once-in-a-lifetime role, I was born to play it, then along comes Sidney and snatches it away from me!

LIZ

He didn't snatch it Perry—

PERRY

Oh yes he did. He's been dogging my steps for forty years. I have just as much talent as he does. It's not fair.

LIZ

There will be other parts, Perry—

PERRY

Not for me. I'm sixty-eight years old, Liz. It's too late for me now. I've missed my season.

LIZ

Oh, stop being so dramatic. You lost the part because you're always sabo-taging yourself with your drinking and your temper. Maybe if you hadn't gone off on the director, they wouldn't have called in Sidney.

PERRY

I couldn't help it, it's not my fault.

LIZ

Nothing is ever your fault, is it?
    (Big sigh)

Oh Perry, I can't take it anymore, really I can't. I thought after that last fiasco you would finally give up drinking. I mean, here we are practically homeless—

PERRY
Shh!

LIZ
(Whispering)
Let them hear! I don't care anymore. I am tired of pretending that our lives aren't falling apart. I thought coming on this trip and getting away from "everything" would help you put things in perspective. I really thought you were going to keep your promise and stop drinking this time. But we get here and you start drinking all over again.

PERRY
Can you blame me? There's a murdering maniac on the way!
(PERRY downs drink)

LIZ
Well, if his coming is going to affect you this way, let's just leave.

PERRY
Leave? You know, dear, that's a novel idea.
(Raising his voice)
I'm sure none of our friends would think ill of us if we left the party a little early.

POLLINA
Oh? Skipping town again so soon, Perry?

PERRY
I am not skipping town, madam.

LIZ
We just thought that perhaps under the circumstances, we should get a hotel room for tonight . . .

COUS

What's that! Leaving you say!

LIZ

We'll be back tomorrow, but if this A.J. person is really as dangerous as you all seem to believe he is, it doesn't make sense to just sit here and wait for him.

RONNIE

(Getting up)

You know sister-girl makes sense . . .

POLLINA

(Getting her purse)

Yeah, maybe Perry's got the right idea for once, no need to be sitting ducks . . .

(JANIE MAE reenters with a shoebox)

JANIE MAE

OK, here we are. I've got bunches and bunches of poems.

COUS

They duckin' out on us, Janie Mae, they leavin'.

JANIE MAE

What? Leaving?

PERRY

Terribly sorry, Janie, we'd love to hear your poems, but—

JANIE MAE

But—but you can't leave, it's our reunion.

POLLINA

Look Janie, we're just thinking maybe you need to postpone the thing for a few days—

PERRY

Yes, just until this thing with A.J. is cleared up—

JANIE MAE

What thing with A.J.? He hasn't threatened anybody.
    (Going through poems)
  Besides, we don't even know if he is alive.
    (To COUS)
  And if he does attend, Cous, I want you on your very best behavior, don't you dare mention he's been to prison.

POLLINA

Really Janie, we think we should just go—

JANIE MAE

    (Pitifully)
But you can't leave. This is our reunion. I've gone through all of this preparation, and I-I have poems to read.
    (With a big sigh, THEY ALL sit back down)

PERRY

    (Looking at his watch)
All right, Janie, but just grace us very quickly with one of your best and then we really must be . . .

JANIE MAE

    (Brightly)
Oh, all right, if you insist. Let's see . . . ah yes, here's one I wrote in May of 1932.
    (She clears her throat)

    (Suddenly, there is a loud KNOCK at the door. EVERYBODY freezes. The KNOCKING continues. Finally, JANIE MAE starts toward the door)

COUS

Don't answer that!

JANIE MAE
But Cousin, I can't just . . .

RONNIE
Hey, I'll get it . . .

COUS
Get away from that door boy!

POLLINA
Aw hell . . .
> *(She strides toward the door)*
> Who is it!

A.J. *(Offstage)*
A.J. A.J. Hamm!
> *(ALL stare at each other)*

POLLINA
Well, don't just sit there like a bunch of dummies.
> *(Retreating)*
> Somebody let A.J. in.
> *(PERRY starts for the door, chickens out, leaning against the wall)*

JANIE MAE
I'll—I'll get it . . .

POLLINA
After all it is your house . . .
> *(JANIE MAE creeps toward the door, looking back, fearfully, over her shoulder)*

JANIE MAE
> *(Throwing open the door)*
A.J.! Hello, A.J.! Won't you come in, A.J.!
> *(Wordlessly, A.J. steps in, dressed in a cheap suit, holding a bottle of cheap wine. He surveys the group)*

JANIE MAE
It's—it's a pleasure to see you again, A.J.
> (ALL huddle together, anxiously awaiting A.J.'s reaction)

A.J.
Pleasure's all mine. Why, I just couldn't wait to see all y'all smilin' faces.
> (They ALL try to smile, then erupt into profuse greetings)

> (Overlapping)

PERRY
> (Extending his hand)
A.J.! It's a delight to see you, A.J.—

COUS
It sure is, A.J. A real delight—

POLLINA
So good to see you, A.J.—

JANIE MAE
So glad you could make it—

COUS
Real glad you could make it. Why, I was just tellin' everybody, I sure wish ol' A.J. could be here, it just ain't no reunion without A.J. Yessir, I was just sayin' that, wasn't I, everybody?

ALL
> (Nodding vigorously)
He sure was, just saying that, wouldn't be a reunion without A.J., etc.
> (Overlapping)

POLLINA
And A.J. we hope that you don't have any hard feelings about us . . .

PERRY
Yes there are some misunderstandings to clear up . . .

POLLINA
About us testifying in court, A.J. . . .

JANIE MAE
It was nothing personal, I hope you know . . .

COUS
Nothin' personal at all . . .

A.J.
(Holding up a restraining hand)
Wait a minute, wait a minute, friends! I ain't no judge here. I didn't come
to sit in judgment on nobody.

ALL
(Sighs of relief)
Thank God, so glad to hear that, didn't mean any harm, etc.

A.J.
Listen, I know I made a lot of foolish threats back then, but I'm an old
man now. I'm willin' to let bygones be bygones.

COUS
(Eagerly)
Let bygones be bygones.

A.J.
All I come here for is to meet my dear old friends and remember the
good old days.

COUS
Remember the good old days.
(ALL still looking wary. LIZ steps forward, with an outstretched hand)

LIZ
Hello, Mr. Hamm. You just can't imagine how relieved we all are to hear
you saying this. I don't mind telling you that we were a little worried
about how you would react.

A.J.
Who are you? You wasn't in the class of '33.

PERRY
This is my wife, Liz.

A.J.
That right? Pleased to meet ya, ma'am.

LIZ
Pleased to meet you.

RONNIE
And I'm Ronnie Davis, Pollina's husband.

A.J.
Pollina's old man, huh? You look familiar, boy, ever done any time?

RONNIE
Well—uh—I—

JANIE MAE
      (Quickly)
A.J. we were all having the greatest fun. Won't you sit down and join us?
Have a cookie or sandwich?

A.J.
Don't mind if I do. And here, I brought a bottle of vino for everybody.
      (JANIE MAE takes the wine reluctantly)

JANIE MAE
Why, thank you, A.J. We'll—uh—just save this bottle for later . . .

A.J.
No!
      (Catches himself, tries for milder tone)
   No, let's everybody have a drink right now.

JANIE MAE
Oh—well, all right.

COUS
I'll see to it Janie.
>*(Silence, as COUS nervously opens the bottle and begins to pour, with shaking hands)*

A.J.
You mighty nervous there, Pickett boy. Relax friend. That bottle ain't poison.
>*(Relief all around)*

JANIE MAE
Of course not. Oh you're such a cutup. Isn't he a cutup?

POLLINA
>*(Dryly)*
Ain't he though?
>*(By now, A.J. has worked himself across the stage to stand in front of JANIE MAE's chair)*

JANIE MAE
Uh—A.J. you certainly are looking well, isn't he looking well?

COUS
>*(Nervously, as he and RONNIE pass out drinks)*
Don't he look well! Real well!

A.J.
Well, you know what they say. A fellow don't age much in prison. Ain't got no decisions to make, just go along with the routine. Makes for a smooth face I reckon.
>*(By now, EVERYBODY has a drink in hand)*

A.J.
Well, drink up, everybody.
>*(NOBODY moves)*

Come on, friends, drink up!
> *(Still NOBODY moves, so A.J. takes a gulp)*

POLLINA
Oh, what the heck.
> *(POLLINA downs her drink. OTHERS follow suit)*

A.J.
Hope y'all don't mind me droppin' in like this?
> *(Plops in JANIE MAE's chair)*

JANIE MAE
> *(Looking for another seat)*
Not at all, not at all . . .

A.J.
I read about the reunion in the paper, and I didn't want to miss it.

PERRY
> *(Sitting on loveseat with LIZ)*
Well, at least the paper got the reunion right. You know they ran your death in the obituary column last year?

A.J.
> *(Unperturbed)*
That right? So, y'all all thought I was dead huh?

POLLINA
Yeah.
> *(Quickly)*
But we were real sorry about it.

A.J.
I'm sure you were, God rest my soul.

JANIE MAE
You wonder how something like that could happen.

A.J.

Some prison official probably sent in the wrong name. We cons all look alike to 'em.

RONNIE

How long you been on the ground, man?

A.J.

A year.

POLLINA

Just a year? But I thought—

A.J.

Yeah, I coulda been out a long time ago. But I got another twenty for killin' a guard.
  (At gasps)
  Just jokin'.

JANIE MAE

You're such a kidder, A.J.

LIZ

Have you been living here in Bartersville, Mr. Hamm?

A.J.

Nearby.

JANIE MAE

I see.

COUS

You mean you been this close to home and we didn't even know it.

A.J.

That ain't nothin' new. You people was always the popular crowd. Never paid too much attention to what I was doin'. But I been keepin' up with all of you awright.

COUS
  (*Gulping*)
You have?

A.J.
Real close. I know you still slingin' a mop over there at the museum, Pickett.

COUS
Yeah well, I—

A.J.
And you're a big star out there in Hollywood, Russell.

PERRY
Uh—that's Roussel.

A.J.
When the last time you made a picture?

PERRY
Well actually, I've been on something of a hiatus . . .

A.J.
What's that mean—you can't get no work?

PERRY
Of course not!

LIZ
Perry's very much in demand, I'll have you know. Offers are pouring in, he received a an Emmy nomination for his last MOW—

PERRY
My agent has a project lined up for me when I return—

A.J.

OK, OK, keep your wig on. And you Pollina, I hear you're a big-time businesswoman down there in Houston?

POLLINA

That's me, honey.

A.J.

Yeah, business suits ya. You always was cheap—

RONNIE

(Jumping up)

Hey, wait a minute—

A.J.

. . . with a buck, with a buck . . .

RONNIE

Oh—well, yeah.

POLLINA

(Laughing)

That's why they elected me class treasurer.

JANIE MAE

I've just this moment realized that Pollina was a women's libber even before it became fashionable.

POLLINA

That's me, honey. I always knew I couldn't be content just to be some jerk's wife with nothing of my own. I didn't want to end up like some of my friends I see today—old and deserted for a younger woman. More commonly referred to as up the creek without a paddle.

A.J.

And you Janie. Always figured you'd end up a spinster—'cuse me, I mean a teacher, like your old man.

JANIE MAE
Oh yes, but I'm retired now. And I do so miss the company of young minds.

COUS
I couldn't be no teacher, me. Young folks nowadays so wild and crazy, I'd have to shoot me one—uh—present company expected.

PERRY
Frankly, I find young people to be quite depressingly boring.

LIZ
Perry.

PERRY
Present company "expected" to borrow Cous's phrase. No, so many of our youth today have nothing significant to say, if you know what I mean. What they say, I've already heard, where they're going, I've already been.

A.J.
You call that old age, Russell.

RONNIE
I heard that.
     (RONNIE and A.J. high-five)

POLLINA
Well, my Ron Hon doesn't have to say anything significant to me. All he has to do is just be there.

A.J.
Just be there huh? Boy, when I was your age, I was chasing the <u>young</u> skirt tails.

POLLINA
What's age got to do with it!

RONNIE
Yeah man, what you trying to say?

A.J.
(*Getting up to replenish his drink*)
Oh 'cuse me, I ain't tryin' to say nothin' about nothin'. Folks marry who they want to marry—young, old, short, tall, Black, White, live and let live I always say.

JANIE MAE
So do I! A rose by any other name is still a rose. Right?

COUS
Right!
(*Getting album*)
A.J. you remember Violet Dressler, don't you? Well, she passed . . .

PERRY
(*Defensively*)
My wife and I met, we fell in love—

LIZ
And never even bothered about each other's color!

POLLINA
Age is a state of mind—

RONNIE
Right. I mean, I have more fun with Pollina than I ever had with any of those young chicks.

A.J.
Look, I didn't come here for no debate. I came to party. Now, when I first walked up, I thought I heard a party going on.

COUS
Yeah, you did, A.J. you sho' did . . .

JANIE MAE
    (Getting her poetry)
As a matter of fact, I was just about to read some of my poetry.

A.J.
Good, why don't you go on and read that poetry, Janie Mae?

JANIE MAE
Oh well, all right, if you like . . . let me see here . . . here's one I wrote
the year of our graduation. The title is "I Will Release You."
    (Clears her throat, reads)
  "I will release you if I must / Yet I cannot deny the experience of you.
Go / But I will remember the pretty flowers you gave me tho' your roots
ran deep in someone else / So Go / But the place where you grew in my
heart will not become a barren, fruitless spot / For the brief rains of your
love have watered the dry grounds of my heart / And made it receptive
for the seed of a deeper love / Someday."
    (JANIE MAE curtseys)

    *(COUS yawns loudly, while the OTHERS politely applaud. A.J. applauds loud and
    long, smiling broadly)*

JANIE MAE
Thank you, thank you, A.J.

PERRY
    (Looking at his watch as he and LIZ rise)
Very nice, Janie—

LIZ
Very nice—

PERRY
But now I'd like to show Liz the old homestead before nightfall . . .

LIZ
Yes, darling—

JANIE
Oh, but the party has only just begun—

A.J.
I seen that poem in Dinah's notebook one day.

JANIE MAE
Pardon me?

A.J.
Yeah, that poem, that very same poem. I remember it, 'cause me and Dinah had a big fuss about it. I thought maybe Perry or Cous had wrote it to her.

PERRY
Oh no, poetry's not my forte.

COUS
I never wrote a poem in my life.

JANIE MAE
Why yes . . . I do remember now . . . yes. It was so long ago I'd forgotten. I was helping Dinah with iambic pentameter and—

OTHERS
What?

JANIE MAE
Iambic pentameter, meter in poetry, and I used that poem as an example. She seemed to like it so much, I told her she could keep it, and I wrote myself another copy.

A.J.
There it is then. See, old friends need to get together. Rehash old things. Find out what they didn't know.

JANIE MAE

That's what a reunion's all about—to have a good time and catch up on each other's lives.

(Getting album)

A.J. you remember Violet Dressler, don't you? Well, she died . . .

A.J.

Dinah used to get my goat, braggin' about that poem. Wouldn't tell me who gave it to her. Just used to say it was a secret admirer. Then she'd break up laughing.

(Beat)

Now I know why she laughed so hard. Never thought another woman could be her lover.

(Gasps)

JANIE MAE

What . . . ? What are you saying . . . ? Why . . . I have never been so humiliated in all of my life!

POLLINA

What a terrible thing to say!

A.J.

Well, it's true!

COUS

Man! That prison done made you crazy!

JANIE MAE

Just because I wrote a simple little poem, you accuse me—

A.J.

Then why'd you sign it "secret admirer"?

JANIE MAE

Why I-I-I—did I?

A.J.
You know you did.

JANIE MAE
  (*Flippantly*)
Well—what of it? I signed it on a lark. I didn't mean anything by it.

A.J.
Oh, you didn't huh?

JANIE MAE
Of course not! Certainly not what you're implying, you—you—convict, you! I only meant that I admired her spunk. I admired the way she met the male brutality with a brutality of her own.

A.J.
Bull.

JANIE MAE
A.J. I'm disappointed in you. I welcome you into my home with the warmest regards and this is how you . . .

A.J.
In school you was always so scared of boys, so maybe you turned to a gal. Dinah, yeah. Then when you found out she couldn't be true to nobody, not even a woman, you went up there and you killed her!

JANIE MAE
Oh! My heart, my heart!
  (*A.J. whips out gun*)

PERRY
Oh my! He's got a gun, he's got a gun!
  (*Pandemonium. Shouting and screaming as EVERYBODY runs for cover*)

JANIE MAE
A.J.! A.J. my God! What are you doing—!

COUS

Comin' up in here with that gun!

(Stepping toward A.J.)

Get outta here with that gun! Go on, get out—!

A.J.

Take one more step, Cous. I'll shoot ya in your foot!

(SCREAMS, SHOUTS)

A.J.

All right everybody! Siddown and shut up!

(As pandemonium continues)

I said siddown and shut up!

(After they calm down some)

Now. Ain't nobody goin' nowhere! Not until I get the answer to a question that's been on my mind for nigh on fifty years. Which one of you shot my Dinah!

(Silence. JANIE MAE fans furiously with her handkerchief. COUS pats her back. PERRY, comforted by LIZ, has a coughing fit, while POLLINA cowers in RONNIE's arms. A.J. coolly surveys it all)

A.J.

All right, I'm waitin'! Which one of you shot her!

JANIE MAE

Prison has affected your mind. Don't you remember? You killed Dinah.

A.J.

Don't try to make out like I'm crazy, woman. I didn't kill her. I say the same thing I said fifty years ago. When I got to Dinah's house, she was already dead. Whoever done it was still on the premises. I heard 'em crashin' through the underbrush, gettin' away.

POLLINA

But what makes you so sure it was one of us?

A.J.

Yeah, it coulda been anybody, man, coulda been one of those dead folks they always talkin' about.

COUS

(*Hopefully*) Yeah, it coulda been Don or Kenny Lee.

PERRY

Or—or even Violet. Dinah used to tease her unmercifully.

A.J.

Oh sure, blame it on anybody. I can just see little Violet, tryin' to fire a rifle taller than she was. Now, I know somebody in here know somethin'. And I aim to leave here satisfied about it one way or the other. Speak up and be done with it! Come on, speak up, dammit!

(*ALL cower in silence*)

Look, I didn't come here to shootcha all. But I will.

PERRY

(*Jumping up*)

Oh this is preposterous! Everybody knows you killed Dinah!

A.J.

Why? 'Cause I came from the wrong side of the tracks and you didn't!

PERRY

Oh, so that's it. You're still jealous of me.

A.J.

Siddown and shut up!

(*PERRY obediently sits*)

COUS

Why you come in here causin' all this trouble? I wish that obituary hadda been true!

A.J.

(*Chuckling*)

I bet you do. Figured that little notice would make you folks happy. That's why I put it in there, make you feel secure.

LIZ

(*Approaching him*)

Mr. Hamm, Perry and I have come all the way from the West Coast for this reunion and—

A.J.

Lady, I don't care if you come all the way from the moon. If I don't get some answers soon, everybody in here's gonna die.

COUS

I'm a peace-lovin' feller, me, I couldn't kill nobody . . .

PERRY

I don't believe this, it's straight out of a movie . . .

POLLINA

A.J.? I think you remember me well enough to know that murder is not my style.

A.J.

Oh I remember you awright, Pollina Graves. Way I remember you, it wasn't too much you wouldn't do. The same day Dinah was killed, you and her had a fight. You told her if you ever caught her kissin' Perry again, you'd kill her.

POLLINA

But I didn't mean "kill" kill. I meant I-I'd scratch her eyes out.

A.J.

That ain't what you said.

RONNIE

Hey man, you ain't gonna lay no murder rap on my old lady. Come on, Pollina, I'm not scared of this old fool. We're outta here.

A.J.

You move and you through.
> (RONNIE locks eyes with A.J. debating whether or not to challenge him)

A.J.

Don't try to bluff me, boy. Lots of young boys like you tried to buck me in prison, and they wish they hadn't.
> (RONNIE is glad when POLLINA pulls him away)

POLLINA
> (Pulling him back to seat)

No, Ronnie, Ronnie . . .
> (To A.J.)

You can't get away with this.

A.J.

How come I can't? I ain't got nothin' to lose. I already spent mosta my life locked up for somethin' I didn't do. I don't mind bein' locked up for somethin' I'm gonna enjoy doin'.

JANIE MAE

A.J. let us reason together . . .

COUS
> (Joining JANIE MAE)

Yeah, let's reason together . . .

JANIE MAE

You don't want to do this . . .

COUS

You don't want to do this . . .

JANIE MAE
Violence will settle nothing . . .

COUS
Violence will settle nothin' . . .

A.J.
It'll settle the score!

POLLINA
Listen, A.J. maybe—maybe a mistake was made, and you really were innocent. But you can't blame us for that. It was the jury who found you guilty, not us.

A.J.
But y'all helped. Gettin' up on there in the witness stand, tellin 'em how I was always gettin' into fights. Sure, I had a short fuse, but I couldn't never hurt Dinah. I loved her. But didn't nobody mention that. Didn't nobody have one good word for A.J. Hamm.
       (PERRY clears his throat, raising his hand for permission to speak, as he steps
       forward)

PERRY
Uh—A.J. I beg to differ with you on that. If I had been in town, I certainly would have put in a good word for you, but as you know, I wasn't even in town for the trial. So really, I shouldn't even be here, you should just let me go.

A.J.
You'd like that wouldn't you, "dancin' boy"? You'd like to go dancin' right on out of here, wouldn't you? Just like you done that night Dinah was killed. Why'd you get outta town so fast that night, Russell?

PERRY
Well, I-I-I—surely you don't think that I could commit murder?
       (Tries for a laugh)
    I mean, picture me, a murderer.

A.J.

I'm picturin' it. I'm picturin' that look in your eyes when Dinah told you she was just teasin' about goin' to the dance with you. She was goin' with me, like she always did. Left you standin' there, lookin' like a fool in front of all your buddies.

POLLINA

Oh, A.J. you're just plain lying now. Everybody knew that Perry was going to the graduation dance with me.

A.J.

That's what you thought. He'd made plans to go with Dinah. He was sick of you. He'd had enough of you—

LIZ

(*Jumping up*) Oh, this is all so ugly!

PERRY

I will not have my wife listen to another moment of this!

A.J.

    (*Waving gun*)

Siddown!

    (*THEY sit. A.J. paces*)

Yeah, I'll never forget the look in your eyes when you found out she was just leadin' you on. Looked like you coulda snapped her neck.

PERRY

I assure you I was well aware of the little game she was playing, and it didn't bother me in the least. I wouldn't take a girl like her to the dance anyway.

LIZ

Why don't you leave him alone? He's not well.

A.J.

He looks all right to me.

LIZ
I mean—emotionally. His nerves, y'know . . .

A.J.
What you tryin' to say, he's crazy?
　　(Snaps)
　Well, I'm crazy too!
　　(Beat, then sneers)
　Perry Russell. Rich boy in town. Pretty boy. Had all the gals runnin'
after you. But Dinah had you runnin' after her. A poor girl from the
wrong side of the tracks. That didn't sit too good with your ego, did it?

PERRY
Even if that were—were true, it would hardly warrant murder.
　　(Shaking, he jumps up)
　I must have a drink! Can I get a drink?

A.J.
Go on. You always was a lush.
　　(Following PERRY)
　Yeah, we all know about those famous temper tantrums you used to
pitch when you couldn't get your way. I don't say you planned to kill her.
It was probably a accident . . .
　　(Stalking PERRY around room with each sentence)
　You went up there before the dance . . . to try to make her change her
mind . . . she toyed with ya . . . teased ya . . . made you feel like dirt . . .
the way she could make a feller feel like dirt . . . before you knew it, you
reached for the rifle her pa kept loaded in the corner, and you shot her
dead!
　　(By now A.J. has backed PERRY into a corner)

PERRY
　　(Wiping his face with a handkerchief)
You—you paint a very good scenario, my good man. But it never happened.
　　(As THE OTHERS look at him doubtfully)
　It never happened!

COUS

Well now Perry . . . you know you did have a whale of a temper.

LIZ

I hardly think that qualifies my husband as murderer!

PERRY

Thank you Liz.

POLLINA

(Calmly)

I remember one time we all went into Mr. Puslawski's store to buy some jelly beans, and there were only a few left. Well, Perry wanted them, and Old Lady Smiley wanted them. Naturally, Mr. Puslawski sold them to her. And when the poor man offered to sell Perry the jawbreakers instead, Perry threw the candy jar at the man's head.

COUS

Doc Russell had to work overtime to get him outta that mess.

LIZ

What is this! A "let's convict Perry Roussel" campaign!

PERRY

It's all right, darling.

LIZ

No, it is not all right! What kind of friends are these!

JANIE MAE

Pollina's just being perverse. She knows Perry wouldn't hurt a fly.

A.J.

(Grinning in enjoyment)

Let her talk. She always was the most honest of the lot of ya.

LIZ

I don't think honesty has a thing to do with it. She's just jealous because Perry was going to take Dinah to the dance.

PERRY
 (Childishly)
I was not going to take Dinah to the dance!

POLLINA
 (Equally as childishly)
Well, I don't care if you were, Perry "Russell"!

PERRY
Oh, come now, Polly . . .

RONNIE

Everybody cool it! You're all supposed to be grown folks, why don't you act like it!

PERRY
Yes please!
 (Pause)
 I think we all know why I left town so hurriedly that night long ago.

A.J.
Yeah, you'd killed Dinah!

PERRY
No man!
 (Pause, as he turns toward POLLINA)
 I-I'd gotten a young girl, who adored me, in trouble, and I didn't have the courage to face the consequences . . . so I ran. I ran away from my troubles the way I always do. I ran away from LA because, in one of my drunken stupors, I burned the mansion down, and now I'm back in Bartersville because I have nowhere else to go. I'm sixty-eight years old, and I have nowhere else to go. I've burned all my bridges, no pun intended.
 (Turning to LIZ)

I have a beautiful wife, who's stood by me through thick and thin, and I wouldn't trade her for the world . . .

(*Back to POLLINA*)

But I do regret the cowardly way I acted all those years ago.

(*POLLINA bows her head in grateful acknowledgment of his apology*)

A.J.

(*Sneeringly*)

Ain't this lovely.

(*COUS walks toward A.J. with pleading hands*)

COUS

A.J. let's us talk man to man. Don't try to throw the blame on us, 'cause it ain't no man in this room can blame you for what you done. Dinah was the kind of woman who could drive a man to murder . . .

A.J.

(*Softly*)

She drive you to murder, Pickett? That what you tryin' to say, Pickett?

COUS

Naw! I-I never touched a hair on her head.

A.J.

(*Circling COUS*)

I know she could be a frustratin' gal, Pickett. Teasin' all you fellers, but never really carin' for nobody but me. 'Cause we was two of a kind, and we knew it. But you, we used to laugh about you, Pickett. The way you used to trail behind her. Limpin' on those bad dogs of yours, beggin' for a bone.

COUS

Ain't nobody had to beg her for nothin', long as you had the price!

JANIE MAE

Gentlemen, gentlemen please!

A.J.

You went up there that night and—

COUS

Yeah, yeah I went up there!

JANIE MAE

Cousin hush!

COUS

I was sick and tired of her usin' me, spendin' all my hard-earned pennies and never givin' me the time of day—!

JANIE MAE

He doesn't know what he's saying, he—

COUS

I'm a easygoin' kinda feller, y'all all know that. But a man can only take so much . . .

JANIE MAE

Hush, hush now I say . . .

COUS

I was crazy about her . . . oh boy, was I crazy about her. Seem like no matter how bad she done me, I couldn't get that gal outta my blood. But that night I went up there to have it out with her. If she didn't go to the dance with me, I was gonna take that pretty pink dress I'd bought her and rip it to shreds!

JANIE MAE

Cousin! Hush!

A.J.

But you picked up the rifle instead!
    (In COUS's face)
    It was you all the time! You snivelin' . . . !
    (COUS falls back into a chair)

COUS

What . . . ? No, no, I never touched a hair on her head! She was dead when I got there, A.J.—still warm, and the pretty pink dress was red with her blood. Oh Lordy, Lordy, if I'd got there a little bit sooner, I coulda saved her!

(Pause)

I-I heard somebody comin' and I-I ran . . .

A.J.

You heard me comin' after you killed her and you ran!

JANIE MAE

(Stepping between them)

No! A.J. how can you be sure that Cousin did it? Suppose he's telling the truth? You wouldn't want to kill the wrong man, and have that on your conscience too, now would you?

A.J.

You ain't gonna save him. He as good as said he did it.

JANIE MAE

(Soft, reasoning voice) He said he was up there, A.J. That's all he said.

COUS

That's all I said.

A.J.

That's enough.

JANIE MAE

(Arms around COUS)

But—but maybe he wasn't the only one who went up there.

A.J.

How would you know? You in on it with him?

JANIE MAE
> (Jumping away from COUS)

Of course not! I had no reason to kill Dinah, no matter what you think. But well . . . I'm not trying to cast any aspersions on anybody, but . . . well . . . Pollina? You remember you told me that you were going to go up there and have it out with Dinah about Perry?

POLLINA
Well, my good old buddy, Janie.

JANIE MAE
Oh please, don't take this personally, Pollina. I only meant—I mean, I thought . . . well . . . you did say you were going up there and well . . . when I heard the next morning that she'd been killed, well I naturally—

POLLINA
Assumed that I'd done her in?

JANIE MAE
Oh God forbid, of course not! I just thought maybe you'd seen something.

POLLINA
Sorry to disappoint you, old buddy, but I decided that Perry wasn't worth it. So, I went to see Mama Lucy that night instead, but she couldn't do anything for me. I was too far along.

JANIE MAE
> (Embarrassed)

Oh my, I certainly didn't mean to pry into your personal business . . .

POLLINA
God forbid. But tell me, Janie, why did you write that poem for Dinah?

JANIE MAE
(Hotly) I think I've answered that quite satisfactorily.

POLLINA
Oh yeah, you admired her "spunk."

JANIE MAE

And just what are you trying to imply, Pollina?

COUS

Now Janie, calm yourself down. You always lettin' Pollina upset ya.

POLLINA

Yes, let's not take this personally, Janie.

JANIE MAE

Why Pollina, you could never upset me. Any woman who would take up with a boy young enough to be her grandson is hardly fit to sling accusations at me.

POLLINA

You're just jealous.

JANIE MAE

Jealous? Of you? Why should I be jealous of you?

POLLINA

Because I have strong young arms to hold me at night.

JANIE MAE

Oh dear God, you are perverted. I assure you I would never want to feel a young man's arms around me. It's against nature.

RONNIE

Look, let's not get off the track here . . .

POLLINA

Be quiet Ronnie.
　　(*To JANIE MAE*)
　Maybe if you had a young heart beating against yours at night, you wouldn't need that nitro.

PERRY

(*Chuckling*) Ladies, ladies!

JANIE MAE
I find your lifestyle totally immature, I truly do—

POLLINA
You just wish you—

RONNIE
Pollina, will you just cool it!

POLLINA
Ronnie I said be quiet!

JANIE MAE
Hopping from man to man—

RONNIE
Stop telling me to be quiet, dammit!

POLLINA
Don't you raise your voice to me!

JANIE MAE
Obsessed with sex, sex, sex—

RONNIE
Don't raise your voice at me! Hell, I ain't your lapdog—!

JANIE MAE
I find it disgusting, I truly do—

POLLINA
Well. I didn't know you felt that way. I thought we were happy.

RONNIE
We were, we are—I just don't go for you treating me like I'm your five-year-old one minute, then broadcasting our private lives the next minute.

POLLINA

Forgive me. I didn't know you felt that way. Maybe you'd be happier back in that three-room apartment I delivered you from, with the nagging wife and the screaming babies, maybe you'd be happier there!

RONNIE

Hey, maybe I would! Yeah, maybe I would . . .
    (Backing off) Uh—Pollina—

POLLINA

Ronnie—

RONNIE/POLLINA

Baby, I don't know what got into me—

RONNIE

We just need to cool out, OK?

LIZ

Yes, we're all overwrought here.
    (Pointing at A.J.)
  He's got you tearing at each other's throats!

A.J.

    (Gleefully)
I just make 'em tell it like it is, lady. Tell it like it is.
    (In the meantime, PERRY has positioned himself behind A.J., ready to crash the jar of stones down on his head)

JANIE MAE

    (Spying PERRY with the jar)
No Perry no! Not my stones!
    (A.J. whirls around. He and PERRY scuffle with the gun high in the air. RONNIE and COUS run to help PERRY. The WOMEN scream. RONNIE accidentally steps on COUS's foot. In the confusion, A.J. manages to hold on to the gun)

A.J.

All right, back off! Back off, I say! All of you back off!

(THEY retreat as A.J. waves the gun)

A.J.

Gonna all gang up on me, huh! Well, that's it for everybody! Line up, line up!

COUS

    (Limping badly)

A.J. A.J. Whatca gon' do, A.J.?

A.J.

Say your prayers, Cous!

COUS

Oh Lordy, Lordy!

PERRY

    (As they line up)

You can't get away with this!

A.J.

Turn around! Or do you wanna see it comin'?

POLLINA

A.J. listen, I've got money, lots of money and I—!

A.J.

I don't want your money!

LIZ

Are you aware of the punishment for mass murder?

A.J.

Yeah, and I'll meet ya all in hell!

COUS

It was Uncle Jack! Uncle Jack killed her! I practically seen him with my own eyes!

JANIE MAE
Cousin what are you saying!

COUS
(*Talking rapidly*)
Now look here, Janie Mae, the past done caught up with Uncle Jack, I
ain't gonna die for somethin' he done!

JANIE MAE
You don't know what you're talking about!

COUS
A.J. the mornin' after the murder, I come over here and seen Uncle
Jack burnin' bloody clothes. He buried the ashes in the rose garden. I
seen that!

A.J.
Uh-huh.

JANIE MAE
(*Heartbroken*)
How can you say such a thing? Daddy led a blameless life, he was the
pillar of this community, he was—

COUS
Not exactly, Janie. After Aunt Sophie died, Uncle Jack loved to chase
the young skirt tails.

POLLINA
He used to proposition me all the time.

JANIE MAE
Oh my God . . .

POLLINA
Right here in this room.

RONNIE

There it is then. A dead man did her in.

PERRY

Professor Hopper is a wonderful suspect! I love it!

RONNIE

So you can put the gun up, man.

JANIE MAE

(Weeping)

That's right, desecrate the memory of my poor dead daddy. He can't be here to defend himself, so put the blame on him . . .

COUS

(Pleadingly)

Janie, ain't no sense in us getting' killed over somethin' Uncle Jack did . . .

JANIE MAE

(Fiercely)

You hush up, that's what you do, just hush up! After all my daddy did for you. You of all people should know what a decent man he was. If it hadn't been for him, you and your slatternly mother would have gone many a day without food.

COUS

(Bitterly)

I know. And the old man never let me forget it. Never!

JANIE MAE

And this is how you repay his kindness?

COUS

(Stubbornly)

Well, facts is facts.

JANIE MAE

O, sharper than a serpent's tooth . . . ! Are you so afraid of A.J. that you'd drag your uncle's good name through the mud?

COUS

Well, everybody knew he had the eye for Dinah, and he was mean enough to do murder. Plus . . . I think Dinah was blackmailin' him, A.J.

JANIE MAE

Oh, how could you!

A.J.

Blackmailin' him huh?

POLLINA

I could see that old geezer getting himself blackmailed by somebody like Dinah, I could see that happening.

PERRY

So can I. It's a beautiful plot, made for TV . . .

JANIE MAE

A.J. I appeal to your common sense. There was absolutely no reason for Daddy to be blackmailed by anybody. He was an honorable man, he—

A.J.

Shut up Janie Mae. Keep talkin' Pickett.

COUS

Well, one night me and Dinah got drunk on some of Uncle's elderberry wine, and she told me her and Uncle had been well, y'know, rollin' in the hay . . . and if he didn't give her a bunch of money, she was gonna blab it all over town. But I didn't pay her no attention, 'cause we was both drunk, but now it's all beginnin' to add up. I reckon when she tried to blackmail him, he blasted her.

A.J.

That dirty old—! Why didn't she tell me about the scam! We coulda worked it together!

LIZ

Cous, why didn't you mention this blackmailing at the trial?

COUS

Be quiet, Miss Liz, you tryin' get me killed?

LIZ

Sorry Cous.

A.J.

Yeah, if you had spoke up back then, you coulda saved my neck.

COUS

But I didn't know for sho' A.J. And well, after all, he was my kin . . .

POLLINA

Well, the important thing is, we've gotten to the bottom of it now.

A.J.

Maybe.

COUS

What you mean maybe? It was him A.J., it was him, on my mother's grave, it was Uncle Jack!

A.J.

(Sudden rage)

But I ain't got my satisfaction! Even if it was the old man, I still ain't got my satisfaction!

(Standing in front of JACK's portrait)

That old bag of bones is layin' peaceful in his grave! Got off scot-free, while I had to take the rap. It ain't fair, and I still ain't satisfied!

(Waving gun)

Somebody's got to pay!

RONNIE
    (Sympathetically)
Hey brother, I know how you feel, but sometimes that's just the way it is, nothin' you can do about it.

PERRY
The young man is right. Sometimes we have to die with the song still in us.

RONNIE
    (Holding his hand out for the gun)
Why don't you give me that gun, brother.

LIZ
Yes, Mr. Hamm, you can still go to the authorities, and tell them who the real murderer is. You can get your name cleared—

POLLINA
And get paid, sue the state.

PERRY
A fairy-tale ending.

LIZ
Sometimes we have to make lemonade out of lemons.
    (ALL agree, except JANIE MAE)

PERRY
Exactly. Look at me, A.J. I'm stuck here in Bartersville, but I'm not going to let it defeat me. I am going to make lemonade! I am going to write my memoirs! It's going to be a best seller, then Hollywood's going to come knocking and I'm going to star in a movie about my own life!

RONNIE
Just give me the gun, and we'll forget all about this—
    (Convinced, A.J. is about to put the gun into RONNIE's hand)

JANIE MAE
Wait!

(*Calmly*) I don't intend for any one of you to leave this room thinking for one moment that Daddy could have done such a terrible thing, although that she-wolf deserved it.

(*Deep breath*) I went up there that night to see Dinah.

POLLINA
Janie, wait—

COUS
Yeah Janie Mae, please, we—

A.J.
Shut up.

JANIE MAE
Cousin is right. The past has caught up with us. The truth has to be told. When I got there, Daddy was there, as I knew he would be. I knew that Dinah was—extorting money from him.

A.J.
So you went up there . . . ?

JANIE MAE
To reason with her, A.J. only to reason with her.

COUS
Janie, don't say nothin' we done already solved this thing . . .

JANIE MAE
Daddy was pleading with that she-devil to release him from her evil grip. I don't see how one so young could be so evil. I tried to reason with her, pleaded with her in the name of whatever friendship we might have had, but she laughed in my face . . .

COUS
Don't say no more, y'hear . . .

JANIE MAE

Oh, but they must be made to understand what a truly horrible creature she really was . . .

(Caught up in the past)

Yes. I remember . . . she stood there . . . laughing at us, counting Daddy's money. And then she proceeded to call him awful, ugly, names, and so just to stop that wicked laughter . . . just to stop the filth that was proceeding from her mouth . . .

(Wonderingly)

. . . I . . . fired . . . the . . . rifle . . .

A.J.

You. You killed her.

COUS

Don't put words in her mouth!

POLLINA

Oh my God, my God.

PERRY

Sweet little Janie Mae Hopper . . .

(Something has snapped in JANIE MAE, as she continues in a singsong voice)

JANIE MAE

The money was scattered all over the floor . . . Daddy and I had to get down on our hands and knees to gather it up.

(Down on her knees, gathering imaginary money)

I remember . . . some of the bills were splattered . . . with her . . . blood . . .

(Wiping at the blood)

COUS

Ain't none of it true, she's confused . . .

A.J.

(To JANIE MAE) All those years you let me suffer . . .

JANIE MAE

(*Pleadingly, as she gets up*) Oh please, don't look at me like that, A.J. I sent you candy and cigarettes, remember?

(*A.J. shakes his head in disbelief. JANIE MAE walks slowly to her desk, talking in a little girl's voice*)

JANIE MAE

I remember Daddy sat me down at this very desk, and explained how fruitless it would be for me to waste my life in prison, because I was so very sad for you, A.J. But Daddy made me see. I had so much more to offer society, whereas you, what could you offer in the balance?

(*Brightly*)

So, Daddy and I decided on a course of action, and never discussed the matter again.

(*JANIE MAE closes a book on the desk*)

A.J.

All the years of my life . . . all my life!

(*Suddenly JANIE MAE speaks in a stern teacher's voice and taps a ruler on the desk*)

JANIE MAE

Come here and sit down, A.J.

(*As though hypnotized, A.J. takes a seat at the desk, clasping his hands between his knees. JANIE MAE stands over him, and A.J. seems to shrivel under her remarks*)

JANIE MAE

You were always maladjusted, you know? Even as a child, you stole things, you disrupted the barn dances, you made bad grades. You would have come to no good end anyway. Daddy made me see that.

A.J.

So no harm done huh?

JANIE MAE

(*Hopefully*) Then you understand?

A.J.

Yeah, I understand all right.

(Slowly rising from his seat)

I understand you cheated me out of my life, because you and your pa decided I didn't matter. I understand I lived like a caged animal, while you was free to teach school, raise flowers, recite poetry, live your life!

(Slowly takes aim)

This is for all the wasted years of my life!

(He fires the gun, JANIE MAE falls. ALL are frozen in stunned silence, then erupt into confused movement, overlapping)

COUS

(Holding her)
He killed her! He killed her!

POLLINA

I can't believe this . . . I just can't believe this . . . !

LIZ

(Going around in circles)
Oh, this is terrible, terrible . . . !

PERRY

Liz, darling—

LIZ

. . . terrible . . . !

PERRY

Liz, darling, get a grip, call an ambulance.

RONNIE

(Taking charge)
All right, all right, everybody, get yourselves together! Get back, Cous, let me look at her. Pollina, get something to cover her with, before she goes into shock!

(POLLINA gets coverlet from sofa)

(A.J. sits in JANIE MAE's chair, laughing at the confusion)

A.J.

That's right, run around, run around like a bunch of chickens with your heads chopped off.

LIZ

(On the telephone)

. . . please send an ambulance to the . . . Hopper residence . . . no, no, I'm not having a heart attack . . . no I'm not Janie Mae . . . !

POLLINA

(With coverlet) Here, put this over her . . .

PERRY

(As A.J. laughs)

How can you sit there laughing at her suffering!

A.J.

Suffering? She ain't even hurt.

PERRY

Not hurt? How can you say that, man! She's mortally wounded!

LIZ

(On telephone)

. . . no, I'm Liz, Liz Roussel . . . from Hollywood! . . .

RONNIE

(Examining JANIE MAE)

I can't seem to find the wound.

POLLINA

What do you mean Ronnie?

LIZ

Will you please just send an ambulance!

RONNIE
I don't see any blood . . . her pulse is good and steady, you know what? I
don't even think . . . I don't think she's been shot at all.

PERRY
What do you mean, not shot? Of course she's been shot!

RONNIE
Hey she's not shot, man, she's not shot.

POLLINA
But we saw him . . .

RONNIE
I think she just fainted.

OTHERS
Fainted?

COUS
Oh thank you Jesus, thank you Jesus, thank you Jesus!

PERRY
Liz, Liz honey, hang up the telly, hang up the telly!

LIZ
(*Coming over*) Hold on Janie, the ambulance is on the way.

PERRY
Forget it. She's all right, she's not hurt.

LIZ
        (*To PERRY*)
Not hurt . . . but . . . ?

PERRY
She's just fainted.

LIZ
But what happened?

A.J.
I missed.

PERRY
You what?

A.J.
On purpose.

LIZ
Thank God.

PERRY
What is the meaning of this charade?

COUS
Yeah, what you mean coming in here, scaring the hell outta everybody!
  (*Advances toward A.J.*)
 Why, I got a good mind to put my foot—!

A.J.
I got bullets left, Cous.
  (*COUS stops in his tracks*)
 I won't miss this time.

JANIE MAE
  (*Regaining consciousness*)
Daddy . . . Daddy . . . ?

COUS
It's all right, Janie. You all right sugar, you ain't hurt at all.

A.J.
  (*Standing*)
Yeah, you ain't hurt at all "sugar." Get up "sugar" and join the party.

(They help JANIE MAE to the sofa)

By rights you ought to be deader than a doorknob, Janie old girl. 'Cause I came here to do murder all right. All those years in the can, I dreamed of gettin' out, gettin' you all together, and makin' you turn on one another. Then I was goin' to blast the guilty one to hell. When I read about the reunion, I knew the devil'd answered my prayers. I come here with the purpose to blow you away—until I took aim. Then, I don't know, somethin' just went outta me. I had the truth, I didn't need your blood. 'Cause you see, Janie Mae, I might be a lotta things, but I ain't a cold-blooded killer—like you.

JANIE MAE
(Clutching heart) Ohhhh.
> *(JANIE MAE collapses again)*

RONNIE
Miss Hopper! Miss Hopper!

COUS
Janie!
> *(ALL in tense silence as RONNIE checks her pulse, puts his ear to her heart, etc.)*

RONNIE
I think she's gone this time.
> *(SOUND OF AMBULANCE in distance)*
She's dead.
> *(A.J. raises his champagne glass)*

A.J.
> *(Solemnly)*
Toast to the class of '33.
> *(A.J. downs his drink, then walks toward the door. The OTHERS are frozen in a photo of shock. A.J. quietly closes the door)*

THE END

Greenwood:
An American Dream Destroyed

A Drama about the 1921 Racial Disaster in Greenwood, Oklahoma

Synopsis

Greenwood: An American Dream Destroyed examines the tragedy that took place on May 30–June 1, 1921, in the Greenwood District of Tulsa, Oklahoma. In highly segregated Tulsa, Oklahoma, an African American community known as the "Negro Wall Street" grew and thrived. The Greenwood District boasted one of the most affluent African American communities in the country. Black citizens created entrepreneurial opportunities for themselves with a vibrant business district including banks, hotels, cafés, movie theaters, modern homes, and an excellent education system. Then disaster and devastation struck.

Tulsa police arrested a young Black man on an unsubstantiated charge. An inflammatory report in the *Tulsa Tribune* the next day spurred a racial confrontation, and the Greenwood District was looted and burned for over twenty-four hours by White mobs. Thirty-five city blocks lay in charred ruins, over three hundred Black residents were killed, six hundred African American businesses burned to the ground, and thousands were left homeless.

Greenwood: An American Dream Destroyed tells this powerful story from the perspective of three generations of the Boley family, a representative composite of an African American family that may have lived during that tragic and tumultuous time.

Cast of Characters

<u>Grandmother Boley</u> Seventies. Matriarch of the Boley family, owner of Mother Boley's Eating Establishment. She cooks and cares for family and community.

<u>Frank Boley</u> Fifties. Prosperous real estate agent in Greenwood, a leader, well educated, believes education and class will save the race.

<u>Molly Boley</u> Fifties. Socialite wife of Frank, mother of daughter Solene. Obsessed with image of her family and Greenwood.

<u>Solene Boley</u> Twenty-two. Spoiled only child of Frank and Molly Boley. She's in love with the shoe shine boy but engaged to a wealthy farmer.

<u>Bill Boley</u> Thirties. A World War I veteran, a butcher in the family restaurant, he desperately tries to put the war behind him.

<u>Della</u> Thirty. Fun-loving live-in maid for rich White family, she visits Greenwood often to see her paramour Bill.

<u>Dick Rowland (Jimmie Jones)</u> Twenty-two. An enterprising shoe shine boy, in love with Solene, accused of assaulting a White girl.

<u>Peg Leg (Horace)</u> Forty. World War I veteran, Bill's friend, does odd jobs, always in uniform, always ready for a fight.

<u>Dr. A.C. Jackson</u> Fifties. Soft spoken, prominent doctor in Greenwood.

<u>Leviticus Solomon</u> Thirty. Wealthy landowner in love with and engaged to Solene.

<u>Lawrence Pritchard</u> Unspecified age. Photographer/reporter hired by Molly to record Greenwood's prosperity.

<u>Maria Bonilla</u> Twenties. Spanish-speaking Black girl from Honduras, works at the Boleys' restaurant.

PROLOGUE

〰〰〰

History, despite its wrenching pain, cannot be unlived, but if faced with courage, need not be lived again.

—Maya Angelou

<u>ON RISE:</u>   May, 1921. MOLLY BOLEY proudly saunters through Greenwood, which is represented with ARCHIVAL FOOTAGE OF PROSPEROUS GREENWOOD. She arrives at Mount Zion Baptist Church, which may be represented by a sign, chairs. THE WOMEN'S AUXILIARY may sit in chairs, fanning, singing, then listening to Molly speak.

ALL *(Mount Zion Church Choir)*
   (Singing/humming "No More Auction Block" or appropriate music)

MOLLY
   (Begins dialogue under music)
Once upon a time in America, at the turn of the twentieth century, after slavery, Negroes acquired a strip of land on the northern banks of the Arkansas River, in the Indian Nation of Oklahoma. We took an unwanted section of town filled with old warehouses near the railroad tracks, just south of Downtown Tulsa and transformed it into a thriving community, called Greenwood. I call it paradise. Some of us happened to settle on oil-rich land and became incredibly wealthy—so wealthy in fact that we soon aroused the jealousy of our White neighbors. But that is another part of our story. Another play.
   (Chuckle)
   As president of Greenwood's Women's Auxiliary, I have invited a New York photographer, a Mr. Lawrence Pritchard to . . .
   (PRITCHARD comes out of a freeze, gathering his photography equipment, which includes a heavy camera, and small boxlike Brownie instamatic that he wears around his neck)

PRITCHARD

    (PRITCHARD reading MOLLY's letter)

". . . to come to Greenwood and record our meteoric success . . . For all the world to see the enchanted place our race has created here with our drive, our industry, and our vision . . ."

    (Walking down Greenwood Avenue, impressed)

Greenwood Avenue . . . on Memorial Day. The red, white and blue is flying everywhere! Greenwood is everything I've heard it would be—all thirty-six blocks of it. Today, in 1921, it nearly rivals White Tulsa. They have created their own American Dream here I see. They have their own school system, bus line, private airplanes, theaters, hotels, grocers, doctors, with ambulance services, funeral homes, hospitals, lawyers, professionals of all kinds live here. They have built elegant homes. Frank Boley, a real estate magnate, and his socialite wife Molly have an impressive residence on North Detroit, one of the most exclusive blocks in Greenwood. Yes, Greenwood's reputation has attracted Negroes from all four corners of the United States.

MOLLY

We tried so hard to show ourselves approved. So, on that Memorial Day evening in Mother Boley's Eating Establishment, we had no way of knowing that the trouble Jimmie Jones encountered would be the beginning of the end for Greenwood . . . and in a mere twelve hours . . . our dream . . . your dream . . . the American Dream . . . would be completely destroyed. Why?

PRITCHARD

As a journalist, I am here . . . to discover and record how and why Greenwood came to that tragic moment.

    (PRITCHARD and MOLLY leave, splitting center. THE CHILDREN [children
    optional] are frozen in a crouch, then come to life, singing and playing games)

CHILDREN

Greenwood, Greenwood, Greenwood . . .
Say, have you heard the story of a little colored town?
Way down in Indian Nation? On a lovely sloping ground?
With as pretty little houses . . . As you ever chance to meet?
With not a thing but colored folks . . . A-standing in the streets?

Oh, it's a pretty town . . .

And the Negroes own it too

With not a single White person there

To tell them what to do—in Greenwood.

    (If onstage, CHILDREN hopscotching)

PRITCHARD

Hey kids, can you point me in the direction of Mother Boley's Eating Establishment?

    (Without a break in their playing, the CHILDREN point the way. The ADULTS take up the CHILDREN's rhyme as they set the stage)

ADULTS

Oh, it's a pretty town . . .

And the Negroes own it too

With not a single White person to tell them what to do . . .

    (THE CHILDREN leave the stage, and the adults now inherit the space as the play begins)

END PROLOGUE

ACT I

SCENE 1

Greenwood—the Dream

Study to show yourself approved . . .

SETTING: Mother Boley's Eating Establishment. Redbrick facade. SIGN IN WIN-
DOW: "NO SMOKING, NO DRINKING, NO CUSSING!" A chopping block
representing butcher shop, or a display case, tables and chairs comprise the
set. A piano or Victrola may or may not be in one corner. Family living quarters
may be backstage or upstairs. Frank's Real Estate offices may or may not be
seen. There is a back door to the establishment.

ON RISE: May 25–29. In the restaurant. Early morning. The restaurant hasn't opened
yet. BILL can be heard in offstage kitchen, CHOPPING meat. PEG LEG goes
back and forth with boxes. In the background of their lives, MARIA serves the
family breakfast, cleans tables, does chores, etc. SOLENE, filled with a frantic
energy, enters, singing French song, "Champs-Élysées."

SOLENE
(*Singing*)
"*Aux Champs-Élysées, at the Champs-Élysées, at the Champs-Élysées, in the sun,
under the rain, at noon, or at midnight. There is everything you want at the Champs-
Élysées . . .*"
Bonjour Grandmama! (*French pronunciation*)

MOTHER BOLEY
Good morning Solene. You did say good morning didn't you? And
what's that you singing?

SOLENE
A French song I learned in Paris. You should see Paris, Grandmother—

MOTHER BOLEY

Baby, I'm just glad to see you back home safe and sound. It was starting to look like you weren't ever coming back.

SOLENE

Grandmother, you know what I think?

MOTHER BOLEY

What you think baby?

SOLENE

I think you should bring Mother Boley's Eating Establishment into the twentieth century, yes, you should put a few small tables and chairs outside, and create a whole little French section, like in Montmartre.

MOTHER BOLEY

Like where?

SOLENE

Montmartre. It's where I stayed, the colored section of Paris. And instead of pancakes, you should serve crêpes Suzette for breakfast.

MOTHER BOLEY

Serve Suzie who, for what?

SOLENE

Oh, Grandmother, crêpes Suzette, pancakes the French style, with straw-berries and you can serve croque monsieur—

MOTHER BOLEY

What? Child what is you talking about?

SOLENE

Eggs, cheese, and ham—

MOTHER BOLEY

Ham—that reminds me—Bill!

BILL

> *(BILL enters, sharpening knives)*

Ma'am?

MOTHER BOLEY

Son, don't forget to send a plate of meats around to Old Lady Johnson, chop it up real good for her too, you know her teeth—

BILL

Already got it ready, Mama.

MOTHER BOLEY

Oh, and you better fix up a plate for the Millers too, I hear they both doing poorly—

BILL

Mama, you give away more food than we sell—

MOTHER BOLEY

Well, I'm not gonna let nobody go hungry around here.

SOLENE

And, crêpes Suzette for everybody Maria!

> *(Taking a bite of food off MOTHER BOLEY's plate)*

Merci beaucoup.

> *(Singing)*

"Everything you want at Champs-Élysées, etc."

> *(PEG LEG and BILL join in)*

PEG LEG

Hey, I remember that song!

BILL

Yeah! They sung that in Paris all the time, Solene. Soldiers had their victory march down that street, Champs-Élysées. Well, the White soldiers did.

PEG LEG

Yeah, colored soldiers lost their lives over there just like the White, but the Army wouldn't let us be a part of the victory march.

BILL

They let the African soldiers take part, though. I was done with the American Army then.

SOLENE

Uncle Bill, how could you return to the United States after Paris? If I were you I would have never come back. I would have stayed in Paris forever.

BILL

Well, I liked France, true enough, they treated us soldiers real good, but I was homesick, I wanted to come back home, see my family. Some of the soldiers stayed over there, though. I still got friends there and one of these days, I plan to visit them.

SOLENE

How do you think I'd look with my hair bobbed, Grandmother, like this. *(Puts her hair up)*

MOTHER BOLEY

I don't think your folks would like it . . .

SOLENE

    (Big sigh)

Mother and Father have to realize that I'm a grown woman now. I'm nineteen, for goodness' sakes. They can't run me all my life. They think that just because they give me all these material possessions they can tell me what to do, even who I should marry—

MOTHER BOLEY

Baby, they just want you to have everything they didn't have coming up. Just like me, I want the best things for my children, having come out of slavery myself—

SOLENE

Oh, Grandmother, why must you talk about slavery, it's been fifty years—

MOTHER BOLEY

Thank God, no auction for my boys, and I'm just saying I want the best things for them—

SOLENE

Oh, I wish I was back in Paris again. But I want more than things. I want the world! *(Whirling around)* Since I've come back from Paris, I know that I can have it too. I met Negro people from everywhere—Harlem, Africa, the Caribbean. Look at these new books I'm reading. Gertrude Stein: "Paris is not so much what Paris gives you as what it doesn't take away." That's what I loved about it. It didn't take away my womanhood just because I was a Negro girl. In the US, all you hear is White womanhood this, White womanhood that. But there, I felt MY womanhood.

MOTHER BOLEY
    (Reprimanding)
Womanhood! What kind of way is that for a girl to be talking who 'bout to be married? Come here, child, sit down. Now you just carrying on and slinging around all those big words. You know you have to slow down for Grandmother. I'm from Greenwood, Mississippi. And don't you forget where you come from either. I'm glad you went to Paris and all, but you just calm yourself down—Now sit down, and talk to Grandmother . . . now what is it? Come on, I can tell something's bothering you. Is it Jimmie Jones? *(No answer)* Your mama was hoping that trip would take your mind off of him.

SOLENE

I know.

MOTHER BOLEY

Did it? *(SOLENE shakes head no)* Child, now, you got to get over that boy, 'cause your mama is bound and determined for you to marry that potato farmer.

SOLENE

His name is Leviticus. Leviticus Solomon, Esquire, because he's an attorney also.

MOTHER BOLEY

Um-hum. Well, how did you like touring Paris with Leviticus. Solomon. Esquire's family?

SOLENE

His mother and sisters were nice, kind of boring, but I liked them.

MOTHER BOLEY

Good thing, 'cause your mama want you to marry into that family something fierce. She hasn't stopped talking about the wedding ever since you left. You still planning to marry the boy, ain't you?

SOLENE

Oh, Grandmother, I don't know, I don't know anything anymore—

MOTHER BOLEY

Well, you better try to find out, because he's on his way here now, with a trainload of potatoes.

SOLENE

(Musing)

I'm not talking about him. I'm—I'm talking about . . . while I was in Paris, without Mother breathing down my neck, I felt free for the first time in my life. Free! I'm ready to make my own decisions. The suffragist women in Washington, DC, are having a meeting and—

MOTHER BOLEY

What you talking about?

SOLENE

Women from Africa, the Caribbean, and around the world were in Paris for the International Council of Women of the Darker Races. They were talking about the work White women are doing here in America for their own self-determination.

MOTHER BOLEY

Oh Lord . . . well, if you trying to say you not going to marry Leviticus, I don't want to be nowhere around when you try to tell your mama that.

SOLENE

(Sigh)

Oh I wish I were back in Paris again . . .

(Enter MOLLY)

MOLLY

Come Solene!

SOLENE

. . . striding down the Champs-Élysées—

MOLLY

Let's check the items again to make sure everything is here—

SOLENE

—past the Arc de Triomphe . . . the Versailles, the Louvre—

MOLLY

(Looking at boxes)

. . . Coco Chanel—

SOLENE

. . . the Sorbonne, the Eiffel Tower—

MOLLY

. . . Elsa Schiaparelli. Jean Patou—the silks, the satins—

SOLENE

Oh I had a splendid time!

MOLLY/SOLENE

Splendid!

MOLLY

Solene, I'm so happy you enjoyed Paris. You see how a change of venue makes all the difference in the world. How did you enjoy traveling with the Solomon girls?

SOLENE

Well, actually I—

MOLLY

Wonderful! You must marry up. The single most important decision a woman can make in life is whom she decides to marry.

SOLENE

I know Mother but—

MOLLY

Do you agree with me Mother Boley?

MOTHER BOLEY

Well—sometimes our children can marry folks that we don't like at all at first, but after a while they can grow on us—

MOLLY

Exactly. Now, your father and I have the real estate holdings and of course, the oil money, but what if the wells run dry or the price of crude drops? Even we can't provide like Leviticus Solomon Esquire can. A woman must always think of her future. Leviticus is a country gentleman. He owns the largest potato farm west of the Mississippi and thousands of acres of rich bottom land that they rent out, so their well will never run dry. He has the wherewithal to keep you in the comforts befitting your station in life.

Now, Mr. Pritchard's visit is coming up—I'm in the middle of gathering our papers and photos for him and—

SOLENE

Who's Mr. Pritchard—?
     (MOLLY going through boxes, oohing and aahing)

MOLLY

So much work to do. I must select the gowns that I'm going to donate to the clinic auction. But then, I'll take care of all of that after the wedding. Thank God, you're here to help me now. Let's go over our checklist, so we can stay on track . . . final review of guest list, check . . . final tasting of cake, that's tomorrow . . . complete the list of the people who will give toasts, check—oh my God, look at this, this is fabulous—*(Maybe holding up outfit)*

SOLENE

Here, Mother, I bought you and Grandmother gifts.

MOLLY

Oh, how delightful! *(Tears open small box)* Ahhh! Eau de Parfum by Chanel!
    Thank you dear. I must tell you Miss Chanel maintains two things: a woman must always carry an extra pair of gloves, and she who wears no fragrance, has no future. *(Dabbing herself generously)*

SOLENE

Mother, I must talk to you about my future.

MOLLY

Yes, my future Mrs. Leviticus Solomon Esquire.

SOLENE

Mother, there is going to be a meeting about suffragist pioneers in Washington, DC, and—

MOLLY

Oh dear, are you still talking about that women's rights nonsense? Now I'm just as independent as the next woman but these White women have gone crazy and you are to have no part of it—
    (Enter JIMMIE JONES dressed spiffily, cap, knickers, highly shined shoes, bow tie. SOLENE and JIMMIE lock eyes, loopy smiles)

JIMMIE
Hi Solene!

SOLENE
Hi Jimmie.

JIMMIE
    (To ALL)
Good morning.

MOTHER BOLEY
Good morning to you Jimmie Jones.

MOLLY
We are not open yet, Mr. Jones.

JIMMIE
Yes ma'am, I know, I—uh—I'm dropping off Mr. Frank's shoes and I need
to put in an order for my Aunt Damie at the bakery.
    (JIMMIE's eyes on SOLENE as MOTHER BOLEY speaks)

MOTHER BOLEY
Well, you tell Damie, I'm making my famous Mississippi stew today too.
That ought to give Jenkins Café a run for their money. Last week they
had lines around the block for that smothered steak and gravy they serve.
(Beat) Well, let me get myself up from here, go check on my food . . .
(Calling to BILL) Bill! How we set for tonight, son?

BILL
We'll be ready for 'em, Mama. I'm cooking up a new barbecue sauce.

MOTHER BOLEY
Oh yeah, we gonna beat out them Jenkins today, for sure.
    (As exits)
    Tell Damie, I say hello, Jimmie . . . Jimmie!

JIMMIE
    (Pulling eyes away from SOLENE)
Uh—yes ma'am, yes ma'am!
    (MARIA enters)

MARIA

The baker's on the telephone about the wedding cake, Miss Molly.

MOLLY

Oh dear, I hope there's no problem. *(Pointing)* Maria, take Mr. Jones's order, so he can be on his way, please.
> *(Hurries to telephone)*

MARIA

Yes ma'am.
> *(MARIA goes over to JIMMIE with pen and pad. Under the watchful eye of Molly, JIMMIE orders, never taking his eyes off of SOLENE. His order is delivered like a seduction)*

JIMMIE

Well . . . I'd like a nice, beautiful, sweet, lovely pound cake with just a kiss *(kisses air)* of vanilla icing . . .
> *(MOTHER BOLEY clears throat as SOLENE enjoys the moment)*

MARIA

Oh? Anything else?

JIMMIE

Huh?

MARIA

Anything else?

JIMMIE

No . . . that's all I want in the whole world . . .
> *(Enter FRANK, headed for his office)*

FRANK
> *(Upset)*

Good morning, Jim, be with you in a minute, son. I'm running late. Went by the house, and those White hoodlums had thrown trash all over our lawn again.

(Beckoning for MOLLY)
Molly, bring me the shoes please—

MOLLY
I'm on the telephone Frank.
(Enter DELLA)

DELLA
(Loudly)
Hey y'all!
(MOLLY exits with FRANK. MARIA takes JIMMIE's order, then exits. BILL comes
out, holding a package of barbecue wrapped in butcher paper. Or, if set has a meat
display case: DELLA goes to display, where BILL is wrapping up an order)

BILL
Hey there Della.

DELLA
Hey Bill, is the Huntington order ready yet?

BILL
Good 'n ready. Where you headed doll face?

DELLA
Just dropped off the girls off at the beauty shop, got to run a few errands,
then go back and pick 'em up. Umm . . . this smells so good, I can't wait
to serve it. I tell you, those White girls love your barbecue.
(BILL chuckles)

BILL
Well, they really going to like this. Just cooked up a new sauce—fresh
rubbed rosemary, garlic, basil, red onion, hint of mint an' peach wine
brandy. Best on the avenue!

DELLA
Umm, umm! Oh, and listen, be careful tonight. I think some White hoodlums from Irving Heights might be planning to cause some mischief, over
here, throwing firecrackers and stuff y'know, like they do on Halloween.

BILL

I'll be on the lookout. We still on for tonight?

DELLA

You bet. Can't wait for the fireworks.

BILL

Me neither. I'm going to slay you tonight.

DELLA

You think so, huh?

BILL

Oh yeah, I been practicing up on those dance steps you taught me.

DELLA

We'll see big daddy. Well, hello there Miss Solene! Did you and your friends have a grand time in Paris, France?

SOLENE

Oh yes, we had sooo much fun—

DELLA

I bet you did.

JIMMIE

(Under breath)

No kidding.

DELLA

Bet you were in the clubs when the sun went down and stayed there until the sun came up.

SOLENE

Oh, we had a ball, listening to musicians all dressed up in tuxedos. It was all so modern, so strange, so wonderful! Paris was like—like—one long drink—

DELLA

And you got zozzled!

    (SOLENE falls out laughing)

DELLA

You didn't have such a grand time you forgot all about your potato farmer, now did you?

SOLENE

His name is Leviticus.

JIMMIE

What kind of name is that?

SOLENE

And he's not just a potato farmer, he owns the largest potato farm west of the Mississippi.

DELLA

He sounds like a real egg. But tell me, what exactly do you and a potato farmer talk about?

JIMMIE

Yeah, what?

SOLENE

Well, we talk about a lot of things, and we talk about potatoes, yes. There are a thousand and one uses for potatoes—

    (Enter MOLLY and FRANK)

MOLLY

Solene, dear, here's another telegram from Leviticus. It says he should be here soon, and he has a new horse.

JIMMIE

    (Under breath)

Ha, ha . . . a new horse . . .

SOLENE
You opened my mail?

MOLLY
Well, I'm sorry, dear, I didn't think you'd mind—

SOLENE
Well, I do mind Mother, I do!
    (SOLENE walks away, reading letter)

DELLA
    (Looking at watch)
Oh! Gotta get a wiggle on, I can't wait to see what those gals did to their heads this time.
    (As she exits)
    Since they joined that women's group they are a law unto themselves . . .

PEG LEG
I'm on my way downtown to the parade. What about you Bill?

BILL
Nope. I don't want to be down there with all those crazy, patriotic White soldiers, with guns.

PEG LEG
Well, I figure I got just as much right to be downtown as they do. I risked my life for this country, just like they did.

BILL
See you later.

MOLLY
Thank you for helping with the packages Horace.

PEG LEG
Yes ma'am. Good day.

(PEG LEG exits. FRANK takes a seat with newspaper. Puts out his foot for
JIMMIE, who gathers his equipment and starts to shine his shoes. Frank may have
extra pair of shoes for him to shine also)

FRANK

So, how's business Jim?

JIMMIE

Not bad, not bad, sir. Business doubled since I started working downtown. I'm making good money. I'm even thinking about hiring my own
shoe shine boy on the side, to help me out.

FRANK

Very enterprising.
    Now, remember what I told you about running your own business, Jim.

JIMMIE

Take lemons and make lemonade. See, I know all the angles, I got all the
answers, just ask me—

MOLLY

    (Sarcastically)
Oh, so you're going to open up a lemonade stand now, Mr. Jones?

FRANK

    (Chuckling)
Jim Crow is the lemon, sugarplum.

JIMMIE

Yes ma'am, 'cause since we can't do business with White folks in Tulsa . . .

FRANK

—we're going to keep right on creating our own Negro Wall Street lemonade right here. Our money stays right here. Circulating in our own
community for—

JIMMIE

Count 'em—

FRANK/JIMMIE
One, two, three, whole years—

FRANK
—before a single solitary dollar leaves Greenwood!

JIMMIE
Yes sir! And if I keep working hard, one of these days I'm gonna have me a house on North Detroit and Standpipe Hill just like you and Doc Jackson.

FRANK
That's how I like to hear a young man talk.
(Reading newspaper as JIMMIE shines his shoes)
Seems we're making a spectacle of ourselves over here.

MOLLY
My God, what are they saying now?

FRANK
Well, it seems that we've annoyed the White folks with all this unseemly growth we're experiencing in Greenwood. They're accusing us of being "radical" because we take care of our own. They're just bitter because we colored men are outdoing them.

These White newspapers just agitate the races. This article is just one more thing to create tension between us and White folks.

SOLENE
Well, it seems nothing has changed in Greenwood. And, Mother, the way those White girls looked at me when I got off the ship with all my packages, if looks could kill—

MOLLY
Envious. Pay them no mind dear. Oh, and be sure to keep the all the designer empty boxes handy, Maria, I want Mr. Pritchard to take pictures of them.

SOLENE
Who is Mr. Pritchard?

FRANK
(Joking with JIMMIE)
She got in yesterday and they're still unloading her purchases off the ship.

JIMMIE
No kidding?

MOLLY
Oh Frank, how you do exaggerate. She didn't buy that much actually. I'm just trying to find room to store her things here until we can get back into our home. But soon, Solene will be gone back to Paris on her honeymoon.

FRANK
And she can let her young man pay for the trip this time.
(Winks at JIMMIE)

MOLLY
He can afford it, he's extremely wealthy. Oh! And just wait until you see Mount Zion, Solene. They spent three thousand dollars on renovations, three thousand dollars. We must remember to tell Mr. Pritchard about that—

SOLENE
Who IS this Mr. Pritchard?

MOLLY
(Fretting) I just hope they're through with the renovations in time for the wedding. *(Irked, JIMMIE gets up)* Oh, didn't I tell you? His name is Lawrence Pritchard. He's a photographer from New York City. The Women's Auxiliary of Greenwood invited him here to document our progress.

SOLENE
Progress? Greenwood?

MOLLY
Yes, Greenwood, Solene. We're an up-and-coming town. Just because
I let you go to Paris without me, you mustn't think you're too good for
Greenwood.
(ALL *have heard* MOTHER BOLEY's *stories before, and start to go about their day
speaking over her.* SOLENE *makes her way out the door*)

MOTHER BOLEY
Yes Lord, we sure have come a long way. (*All groan*) But we must never
forget from whence we come. Why I remember when me and Mr. Boley
first come here . . . from Greenwood Mississippi . . . we walked all the
way here . . .
(*Overlapping*)

MOLLY
We have lots to do today Solene . . . Maria?

MARIA
Yes ma'am.

MOLLY
Can you make sure the restaurant is ready for the breakfast crowd while
I'm gone?
Solene? We'd better get an early start . . .

SOLENE
Yes Mother.

JIMMIE
(*Finishing shine*)
How's that, Mr. Frank?

FRANK

(Examining shoes)

Not bad, not bad. Shoes make the man. *(Gives money)* Keep the change.

JIMMIE

Thank you sir!

SOLENE

You could make a killing in Paris, Jimmie. *(Getting ready to go out door)*

JIMMIE

No kidding? *(Gathering equipment)* Well, I better take off.

SOLENE

(Suspiciously)

You have to work on Memorial Day?

JIMMIE

(Sarcastically)

Well, Miss Solene, some of us working men know how to seize an opportunity on a holiday.

(Winks at FRANK. FRANK winks back)

My boss man wants me to draw in some of that parade traffic downtown. I'm one of his best workers. I'm making lots of money. Everybody wants me to shine their shoes! 'Cause I know how to make the rag sing—and do my routine!

(JIMMIE goes around putting a little shine on everybody's shoes, singing and dancing. Everybody laughs, joining in, but MOLLY, who pulls her feet away when he approaches her)

(SOLENE jumps up and dances with him. As they tear up the floor, MOLLY looks on with growing alarm)

JIMMIE

I'm Diamond Dick, that's my new name.
I'm Diamond Dick, that's my game.
Changed my name from Jimmie Jones–About
my game I make no bones.

Shine your shoes, take away your blues.
Expert on leather, make 'em ready for the weather!

Bet your potato farmer can't do like that!
    (Exits)

<u>END ACT I, SCENE 1</u>

ACT I

~~~~~~~~

SCENE 2

ON RISE: Minutes later. UNDER TRESTLE or IN TRAIN YARD. TRAIN WHISTLE OVERHEARD. JIMMIE is under a trestle smoking a cigarette. Puts it out as SOLENE runs to him. JIMMIE and SOLENE, embracing each other. OTHERS can be seen in the restaurant in the background going about their tasks. SOLENE has on her gloves.

JIMMIE
Solene, Solene, I missed you so much!

SOLENE
Oh Jimmie, darling, I missed you too!
    (Embrace)

JIMMIE
You sure? Seems like you had a real good time in Paris, dancing cheek to cheek.

SOLENE
Oh Jimmie,
    (Takes off gloves, affectionately touches his face)
  Of course I missed you!
    (Slaps him)

JIMMIE
Hey, that ain't no love tap. What's that for?

SOLENE
I heard about the good time you had while I was away.

JIMMIE
What you mean? What did you hear?

SOLENE

Mother said that you were keeping company with a different girl every day of the week.

JIMMIE

None of those girls can hold a candle to you, none of 'em.

SOLENE

Oh really? I heard that you and—

JIMMIE

Solene, sweetheart, don't believe nothing those girls say. They just crowd around me because I played football, that's all. But they don't really care nothing about me, none of them, not like you do . . . You really care about me, and what I think and what I feel . . . *(Touching her hair)* I love you Solene, and I can't stand to hear you making plans to marry another man. Remember the last time we met, before you left . . . what we said to each other? That we weren't going to let anybody separate us . . .

SOLENE/JIMMIE

It was you and me against the world.

JIMMIE

Yeah. You and me. You still going to run away with me to California?

SOLENE

Sometimes I don't know Jimmie . . . Are you really ready to settle down?

JIMMIE

I'm ready, no kidding!

SOLENE

I don't know if I'm really ready to settle down with anybody. I've been reading books, lots of books, Jimmie, about women's suffrage and I think that might be the answer for the plight of the colored race. To rise up!

JIMMIE

Oh, that's White girls talk, there. I see, you been hanging around Miss Della and those White women she works for.

SOLENE

I guess you'd know how White girls talk. Is that how Sarah talks? Oh, I heard about you out there on Cherry Hill, dancing with that White girl, showing her white ankles.

JIMMIE

Come on, cut it out, stop being so jealous. You were in Paris dancing and drinking with men in tuxedos. And here I was shining shoes, that's all. Making money for me and you to go to California. And OK, maybe I danced with her a little bit, and she danced back. And OK, maybe I went to a movie with a couple of girls, just to get my mind off you, but that's all it was to it.

SOLENE

Oh Jimmie, how could you? I bet you kissed them all too. I'll bet you even kissed that—oh, you're just a smooth talker, Jimmie Jones . . . calling your-self Dick Rowland . . . or Diamond Dick . . . or whatever you call yourself, oh I don't know. My mother was right.

JIMMIE

No she's not, your mama is dead wrong about me. She's behind all of this, can't you see? She sent you away because she thought I'm not good enough for you. But one of these days I'm going to prove myself to her.

SOLENE

She just wants what's best for me. You should be able to understand that.

JIMMIE

I DO understand it. But your mama she looks down her nose at everybody—

SOLENE

Oh, that's enough! That is enough! Don't you dare talk about my mother like that! She cares about everybody—

JIMMIE

    (Mumbles)

. . . don't care nothing about me—

SOLENE

She just wants the best for everybody. And, if you're going to talk about her like that, then we can just go our separate ways once and for all!

JIMMIE

All right then go . . . go ahead on . . . I'm not kidding . . . go on, go your separate way to your potato farmer!!! Go!

    (SOLENE, in a speechless rage, storms off stage right. JIMMIE realizes what he's done, starts after her, but changes his mind)

JIMMIE

(Frustrated, lights up cigarette) I don't need you . . . I don't need nobody. *(Kicking around)* Whenever I try to I . . . but when I don't I . . . Don't know if I should just . . . I just wish I could . . . but every time I try I . . . Sometimes I feel like I just want to . . . *(Hangs head)* But I got my pride . . . I got my pride!

CHILDREN *(Offstage)*

    (Rhyme)

Roses are red, violets are blue, Jimmie Jones loves all the girls and Solene Boley too.

<u>END ACT I, SCENE 2</u>

ACT I

SCENE 3

ON RISE: Evening, May 30. Memorial Day. Sound of FIREWORKS in background. MARIA is cleaning, tables, taking orders (if there are extras). SOLENE is at table, face in hand. BILL goes back and forth from offstage kitchen. Somewhere PATRIOTIC MUSIC plays. The American flag flies. Memorial Day decorations.

DELLA
(Rushing in)
I didn't miss the picture, did I?

BILL
Naw, doll face, you on time.

DELLA
Today of all days, wouldn't you know it, Old Lady Huntington had me doing everything under the sun! Got myself all dolled up for the picture *(modeling)* how do I look?

BILL
Umm . . . well put together . . . from a muscle-and-bone standpoint that is, like a fine rump roast . . . speaking as a butcher that is.

DELLA
(Laughing)
Bill, you slay me. You hear that Solene? Your uncle just called me a roast.
(Weak smile from SOLENE)
  Well, what are we waiting on? Where's the picture man at?

BILL
They're at the Stradford, at that fundraiser for the clinic. They ought to be on soon.

PEG LEG
 (Looking at watch)
Wish they'd get here. I got to get on.

DELLA
 (Going over to SOLENE)
Solene, you still moping over that boy, ain't you? You know the best way
to get over one man *(whispers)* is to get yourself another one. *(Laughs)* Or . . .
get you a new hairdo. You'd look really keen with your hair bobbed, like
mine. Short. Like this, see. *(Pushes up SOLENE's hair)* It's all the rage.

BILL
Oh, her folks wouldn't like it.

SOLENE
 (Explodes)
I'm tired of everybody telling me what to do! I'll bob my hair if I want
to bob my hair. And I'll smoke cigarettes too!

DELLA
 (Putting music on Victrola or playing piano)
Atta girl! A girl's got to stay in step with the times, I always say. This is
a new day for women. Have some fun. Come on, stop being such a wet
blanket, come on get up, cut a rug!

DELLA
 (Singing)
 In the morning, in the evening—Ain't
 we got fun!
 Every morning, every evening—We
 sure got fun!
 The rent's unpaid, we haven't a bus—But
 smiles were made dear
 For people like us!
 In the winter, in the summer—Don't
 we have fun!
 Times are bum and getting bummer—Still
 we have fun!

DELLA

Come on Bill! This is Memorial Day, let's have some fireworks around here!

(BILL and DELLA dance up a storm. PEG LEG joins in, stomping around. They pull MARIA in, all four dancing)

BILL

Surprised you, didn't I? Told you I been practicing.

DELLA

(Singing)
There's nothing surer, the rich get richer—
And the poor get children!
So in the meantime, in between time—Ain't
we got fun!

DELLA

All right, Maria, your turn! Come on!

BILL

Yeah come on—

PEG LEG

This ain't no funeral!

DELLA

Do some of that fancy Spanish dancing!

BILL / PEG LEG

Yeah!

MARIA

(Blushing)
Oh no, no, supposed Miss Molly walked in, Della.

SOLENE

I told you, you don't have to do everything Mother tells you to do.

MARIA

That's easy for you to say, she's your mother, but I don't want her to catch to me acting without decorum. You know how important decorum is for your mother.

DELLA

Aww, I bet Miss Molly's cutting a rug right now at that fancy party. Go head on, Maria—

ALL

Dance!

(*MARIA does Spanish flamenco—esque type dance*)

(*Enter MOTHER BOLEY, dressed to nines, with her cane. Everybody freezes. MOTHER BOLEY looks at them sternly, then bursts out singing*)

MOTHER BOLEY

(*Singing*)

In the morning, in the evening—Ain't
we got fun!

(*Speaking*)

Child, go head on and do your dance, why even King David himself danced before the Lord.

(*LOUD FIREWORKS / FLASH OF LIGHT. BILL jumps*)

BILL

What was that!

(*Overlapping*)

DELLA

No, no Bill, it's all right, it's nothing, it's nothing, it's all right.

MOTHER BOLEY

Son . . . son?

PEG LEG

Boley! He's all right, he's all right. You all right, man?

BILL
I thought I heard . . . I thought I heard—

PEG LEG
Firecrackers, man, firecrackers.

DELLA
It's Memorial Day remember? *(Caresses his arm)*
    (Enter MOLLY, FRANK, PRITCHARD in evening wear. BILL goes outside)

FRANK
And as I was saying . . . they just lynched a White boy around here not too long ago.

MOTHER BOLEY
Talking about that Belton boy?

FRANK
Yes, Mama, Roy Belton.

MOTHER BOLEY
Sure did and the police didn't do nothing about it either, 'cause he was a murderer, killed a taxi cab driver and—

MOLLY
Well, the fundraiser was quite a successful affair. We introduced Mr. Pritchard to all of the leaders in town and took in thousands of dollars' worth of pledges for the clinic and the children's home.

MOTHER BOLEY
He meet Mr. Gurley?

MOLLY
Of course.

MOTHER BOLEY
> (To PRITCHARD)

O.W. Gurley is the founder of Greenwood, you know, and he runs the newspaper too, you know—and he worked under President Grover Cleveland, you know? He started Greenwood off, bought forty acres of land and sold it only to other Negros.

FRANK
And we all followed suit.

MOLLY
Yes, he met all of the important people of Greenwood, Mother Boley—Doctor Bridgewater, Willie Williams, J.B. Stradford, Attorney Franklin—

FRANK
So—back to what I was saying—if they'll lynch a White boy just like that (snaps fingers), you know what they'll do to a colored boy—

PRITCHARD
Oh yes. I've got stories from all around the country . . .

MOTHER BOLEY
So, now that you've seen the city, and met the folks, how do you find Tulsa, Mr. Pritchard?

PRITCHARD
> (Putting up camera equipment)

Tulsa's a real pleasant surprise, a bustling little town, refreshing after the tenements and crowded streets of the North, I'll tell you. But, coming in, the automobile traffic downtown was almost as bad as the traffic up north.

FRANK
Well, everybody here has a car, you know. All that oil money. Plus you arrived in the middle of the Memorial Day parade—

MOTHER BOLEY

Humph. I still call it Decoration Day—

FRANK

That's right Mama. The White folks put their parade on every year down-town, and Greenwood has its own parade and fireworks too. The reality is there are two Tulsas—White Tulsa and Black Tulsa. And Greenwood's prospering right along with the White folks. All of us in Greenwood doing business with one another. That's why W.E.B. Du Bois called Greenwood the Negro Wall Street.

PRITCHARD

I know. And I'm looking forward to learning more about Greenwood. I thank you Miss Molly for inviting me here.

MOLLY

You're quite welcome. Are you ready for the pictures yet?

PRITCHARD

No, I like to absorb the flavor and atmosphere of the environment before I begin my work.

MOLLY

A true artiste, good. Solene! We need to add something to that outfit for the picture. Just give us a moment Mr. Pritchard. Come dear. And cheer up.

PRITCHARD

Well maybe now would be a good time for me to talk to your brother Bill. The vet?

FRANK

He's around here somewhere, I'll get him. Bill? Bill—! Bill!

MOTHER BOLEY

I think he's outside with Della, taking in the flag and watching the fireworks.

PRITCHARD

That's all right, I'll go out, and talk to him, get some pictures.
(*PRITCHARD exits outside to where BILL is dealing with the flag and looking up at the fireworks*)

PRITCHARD

Good evening Bill.

BILL

Evening. Not supposed to let flag fly at dusk you know, not unless you have a special light on it.

DELLA

They really putting on a fireworks show tonight . . .

PRITCHARD

(*Looking up at sky*)
Yeah, lighting up the night sky . . .

BILL

Like a sunrise from hell . . .

PRITCHARD

Huh . . . ?

BILL

. . . a thousand white-hot bombs lit up the sky . . . French 75s roaring . . . busting my eardrums . . . A grenade explodes not ten feet away from me . . . Fifty Germans run at us, shooting. We fire back. They're on us now, and it's hand to hand, fists, knees, gun butt, bayonet. A bayonet tears into my side— (*Holding side*) I fall but keep tossing grenades. A Kraut turns to ram his bayonet into Peg Leg's chest. I swing my blade. His head . . . falls at my feet. Me and Peg fighting back-to-back now like madmen, throwing grenades, swinging knives . . . Waves of Germans just keep coming. They keep coming—dammit! Me and Peg ain't human no more. We're killing machines. Just kill or be killed . . . ! Bodies everywhere. We fought like hell. We got letters of commendation . . . for being killing machines. (*Pause*) When I made it back to the States, it was . . . different. For a long while there I couldn't bring myself to even wring a chicken's neck.

(PEG LEG, who has walked up, puts hand on BILL's shoulder)

PEG LEG
You all right Boley?

DELLA
Sure, he's all right.

BILL
Yeah, I'm fine, it's just sometimes . . . my hearing's not as good as it used to be, but I'm all right.

I'm—I'm Bill the Butcher. That's me. I love and appreciate fine meats. And my burning desire in life is to give the people the best cuts. Now Frank, my brother, he went to the university and that's a fine thing for him. But . . . I learned what I learned at the chopping block and—

DELLA
Come on Bill, let's go back inside . . . let's take this picture, and then, we can go to Dreamland and dance the night away.

(DELLA and PEG LEG exchange looks of sympathy for BILL)

BILL
Oh, OK, yeah.

(As BILL, DELLA, PEG LEG and PRITCHARD reenter the restaurant, MOLLY sweeps in followed by SOLENE, who has added an item to her outfit. MOLLY may have made a change too)

MOLLY
Well, here we are again. Twirl Solene. Or you ready for us yet?

PRITCHARD
Not quite. So, you're one of the veterans, too, Mr.—?

PEG LEG
Taylor. Horace Taylor. They call me Peg Leg now. Yep. A vet and damn proud of it, begging your pardon ladies. Did my duty as a man and went

to war, come back home thinking we was gonna get treated better, look like things got worse.

PRITCHARD
Yes, I've noticed in my travels a certain undercurrent of anger and violence directed at the colored soldier. There've been reports of soldiers being lynched and burned alive.

PEG LEG
You from where?

PRITCHARD
Harlem.

PEG LEG
Harlem! The Harlem Hell Fighters! James Reese Europe! Oooweeee! And that drum major Noble Sissle, man! When we come back from overseas, our platoon marched straight through Harlem with the Hell Fighters. A million colored folks and White folks out there waving flags and cheering us on—it was something! Yeah! Then we come home and they have a big parade for us down Greenwood Avenue. Oh, man! I could stand to have a parade every day.
    (Sadly)
But now the war is over. Well, I better be getting on. Miss Molly, I want to get started first thing in the morning but I'm going to need to buy more Sheetrock, and I need—uh—you know . . .

MOLLY
Of course Horace. Frank—?

FRANK
    (Big sigh)
I thought we agreed on a budget Molly.

MOLLY
I know, I know, we did. (To PRITCHARD) Horace here, and his sons are doing the renovations on our home, Boley Manor.

PRITCHARD
Is that right?

PEG LEG
Uh-huh. Before I went to war, pretty much all the homes you see around here I helped put 'em up.
(*FRANK gives PEG LEG bills from a wad of money*)

FRANK
I'll meet you around the house in the morning, Peg.

PEG LEG
Good deal. Good night.
(*PEG LEG exits*)

DELLA
You been to Dreamland yet, Pritchard?

MOLLY
Mr. Pritchard.

PRITCHARD
Not yet.

MOTHER BOLEY
I didn't see you in church Sunday, Della.

DELLA
Oh, no ma'am, I had to go to service with the Huntingtons. It was dull as ditch water but I like Reverend Kerr though.

PRITCHARD
You . . . don't live in Greenwood, I take it, Della?

DELLA
No, I live-in with a White family in Irving Heights. Mr. and Mrs. Huntington and their two daughters. They swimming in money. Oil. House looks like a castle. City even put their home on postcards!

MOLLY
Postcards? Humm . . . I think our home should be on postcards too . . .
Frank—?

DELLA
Yeah, I live in T-Town, Mr. Photograph Man. Tulsa. The Magic
City. The Whitest town in Oklahoma they call it. And they proud of
it. But life is real good for colored folks over here in Greenwood. And
fun! Which is why I love to come over every off day (whispers) and to
see Bill.
      (Loud laugh, then composes herself at look from MOLLY)
      Excuse me, that wasn't very ladylike. Yeah, I been working for 'em
for five years, but I hear they're training colored girls to work the elevator now. I'm thinking about learning how to do that. But then, on the
other hand, I don't know. I'd miss the high life with the Huntingtons.
They just bought another new car, and I think they're going to give their
old one to me, then I can get ditch this Tin Lizzie I'm driving.
      (Enter DR. JACKSON with doctor's bag)

DR. JACKSON
Good evening!

MOTHER BOLEY
Evening Doctor Jackson!

DR. JACKSON
Sorry I'm late.

FRANK
Here's our world renowned doctor, Dr. A.C. Jackson.

MOLLY
He's a renowned surgeon dear.

FRANK
Right.

MOLLY
Dr. Jackson this is our photographer Lawrence Pritchard.

PRITCHARD/JACKSON
(Shaking hands)
Pleased to meet you / My pleasure.

MOLLY
Mr. Pritchard, no less than the Mayo Brothers say that our good doctor here is one of the most able Negro surgeons in the United States.

DR. JACKSON
Are they bragging on Greenwood again?

FRANK
Yes we are. And on citizens like you.

DR. JACKSON
(Self-deprecating laugh)
Oh how they do carry on. I'm just a physician who does his best to heal Greenwood's sick.

MOTHER BOLEY
Don't let him fool ya! He give me something that pretty near cured my rheumatize.

DR. JACKSON
How's your daughter Maria?

MARIA
Mejorando. Better now that you give her the medicina. Gracias.

DR. JACKSON
Nada. Well, Molly, am I in time for that grand picture you've been talking about?

MOLLY
Right on time.

FRANK
Missed you at the party.

DR. PRITCHARD
I was making a delivery.

PRITCHARD
And you've met the Mayo Brothers I take it?

DR. JACKSON
Oh, yes. Quite impressed by them too.

PRITCHARD
And you're from?

DR. JACKSON
Guthrie, Tennessee. My father was a law officer, and watching him, I learned early on that I could be part of the hurt or heal, so I attended Meharry College where I trained to be a surgeon.

I came to Greenwood to help out during the Spanish flu epidemic and was so impressed I decided to stay.

Life here is busy, but I travel a lot, which is why I hope we finish the pictures soon before I have to go to a conference in Chicago.

MOTHER BOLEY
Oh, you off again, Doc?

DR. JACKSON
Yes ma'am. For the American Medical Colleges conference. I'm learning more and more about less and less. That is how you become a specialist.

FRANK
Oh! I chased down that chain of title on that property I mentioned to you. I have some papers on the building for you to look over.

DR. JACKSON

Excellent, excellent! You're working hard, Frank, I appreciate it.

PRITCHARD

(Pacing around)

All right everybody. I think I'm beginning to get a sense of the montage I want to create. If everybody would stand up . . . now just kind of press in. Everybody.

(ALL stand up, smoothing out attire, hair, etc.)

MOLLY

(Exaggerated pose)

How do you want us to pose?

SOLENE

Take off your apron, Uncle Bill.

PRITCHARD

No—I think I want you to keep that apron on until I decide. Maybe keep the cleaver too.

I don't just shoot pictures, I tell stories.

SOLENE/MOLLY

What, but—that bloody apron?!

PRITCHARD

Don't worry. In the dark room—and I will need a room with no light—I can do magic. I superimpose images and create the stories I want.

DR. JACKSON

So, I understand you're going around the country doing pieces on Black towns, Mr. Pritchard?

PRITCHARD

That's right sir.

DR. JACKSON
Admirable. What made you decide to do so?

PRITCHARD
Well, there are fifty-eight independent Black boomtowns . . .

DR. JACKSON
Really? Fifty-eight? My, my, my.

PRITCHARD
    (As he speaks, PRITCHARD shapes group into certain poses)
And . . . each with a story to tell . . . with the New Negro Movement in
Harlem, our culture is becoming the popular thing and I want to be at
the forefront of telling and photographing our stories. And sometimes I
fear I'd better be quick about it, because as I travel, I find that as soon as
a Negro community starts to thrive, White mobs riot and destroy them.
Chicago, East St. Louis, Elaine Arkansas. Oh, they claim that some
Negro man has done this or that to White womanhood, but I find that
it's always about greed and the land. By the way, Mother Boley, are you
any relation to the Boleys of Boley, Oklahoma?

MOTHER BOLEY
Well, yeah, they are cousins of Mr. Boley's.

PRITCHARD
    (Arranging them)
Now if you will just stand here . . . I must warn you, I am . . . obsessive
about my work. So you'll have to bear with me sometimes.

BILL
So, where you planning on going after you leave here?

PRITCHARD
I'm off to interview the Goins family in a little community I've heard
of down in Florida, Rosewood. OK, everyone please gather in a little
tighter, tighter . . .

PRITCHARD

Now let me see—Mr. Frank, you get here, Della, you here—

DELLA

No, I want to be next to Bill—

BILL

And I got to be next to my Della—

PRITCHARD

All right then, Bill, get in there, without the apron this time . . . (BILL
gets hat and jacket) and Doctor Jackson, you here. Solene, if you will, come
stand here—

SOLENE

Oh Mother, do I have to?

MOLLY

Now Solene.

PRITCHARD

And, let's see, Maria . . . ?
    (MARIA looks askance at MOLLY)

MOLLY

Oh, of course you may join in Maria.
    (They start jockeying for positions)

PRITCHARD

OK, everyone please gather in a little tighter, tighter. All right everyone
take a deep breath. Smile. Hold . . . one, two, thr—!
    (SOUND OF FRANTIC KNOCK FROM BACK DOOR. JIMMIE crashes into the
    room, severely distressed)

FRANK

Jim!

SOLENE
Jimmie!

JIMMIE
Solene, oh, Solene!

FRANK
Jim! What is it son?

SOLENE
What's the matter, Jimmie?

JIMMIE
I think I'm in trouble.

BILL
What kinda trouble?

JIMMIE
Big trouble . . . with the law!

MOLLY
What did you do!

JIMMIE
Nothing! I didn't do nothing, I swear I didn't do nothing!

BILL
What happened, then, man, tell us!

ALL
Yeah, tell us, what happened!

JIMMIE
They're saying that I—that I—!

FRANK
That you what?

JIMMIE
That I put my hands on a White woman!
    (EVERYONE freezes)

ACT II

SCENE 1

<u>ON RISE:</u> Seconds later.

MOTHER BOLEY
Jimmie Jones, what are you talking about?

JIMMIE
But it's not true, none of it's true, none of it . . . (*Continued silence from ALL*)
She—she didn't bring it even with the floor!

MOLLY
Bring what even with the floor? Boy, calm down, tell us what happened,
start from the beginning?

JIMMIE
(*Breathing heavily*) I was downtown at my shoe shine stand, you know, working all day, trying to get some of that Memorial Day money, you know—

MOLLY
        (*Impatiently*)
Yes, yes, get on with it—

FRANK
Let the boy tell it, let the boy tell it—

JIMMIE
I had to use the washroom, you know, so I went in the Drexel Building
to the top floor, like I always do. It's the only washroom on Main Street
that coloreds can use. We all use it. I had permission to use it—

SOLENE
Oh, Jimmie what happened!

JIMMIE
(Pleading)

Let me tell you, I'm trying to tell you, so you'll understand! See, I just stepped in the elevator to go up to the top floor like I always do. And Sarah—

SOLENE

Sarah! What did she do! That White girl is a liar, and a tramp. She's not even as old as I am and she's been divorced twice, with two kids.

JIMMIE

—she was operating it, like she always do. But I don't know what was wrong with her today.

FRANK

What do you mean?

JIMMIE

She's still in training, you know, and sometimes she don't bring the thing even with the floor—

MOLLY

Here we go again, bring WHAT thing even with the floor?

JIMMIE

The elevator, the elevator! So when I went to step on, I tripped because the floor wasn't even! I reached out, you know, to keep from falling—and I must've accidentally grabbed hold of her arm—

BILL

Oh man.

JIMMIE

I know, I know! She started screaming and screaming. She got crazy, started beating me with her purse! Then this crazy White clerk come running out of Renbergs yelling I was assaulting her.

SOLENE
Assaulting her?! Why, you would never—

JIMMIE
Never! All I could think to do was to start running. But I didn't do nothing to her. Nothing!

FRANK
We know you didn't do anything, but—what did she tell them?

JIMMIE
She tried to tell them but they wouldn't give her a chance! They just chased me out the building hollering that I was assaulting her and—I just can't win, just when I'm thinking I'm getting ahead in life—

BILL
The best thing for you to do right now is to get off the streets in case they're on the hunt for you.
        (ALL agree)

MOTHER BOLEY
Yeah, run on home, child! And we'll pray that this will all blow over—

JIMMIE
No! I'm getting out of town, I'm going to California. (Looking at SOLENE)
Solene, I just stopped by to tell you that I'm sorry about everything—

SOLENE
I'm sorry too—

JIMMIE/SOLENE
It was all my fault!

SOLENE
I'm leaving with you—

JIMMIE
Solene, are you sure?

MOLLY
What are you talking about?

SOLENE
(To JIMMIE) Yes, I'm sure. *(To MOLLY)* Mother, Jimmie and I, we're running away and getting married—

MOLLY
What! Are you out of your mind? Leviticus is on his way—Frank do something!

FRANK
Now wait a minute, wait a minute you two. Jim what's the meaning of this?

JIMMIE
Solene and me, we love each other, Mr. Frank, and we want to get married.

MOLLY
Oh, this is ridiculous—!

FRANK
Molly!

FRANK
Now, you two just calm down. Everything's probably going to be all right. Anyway, what about Leviticus? You're already engaged to Leviticus. *(Turns to JIMMIE)* You! You run on home, young man. And we'll see what happens in the morning.
    *(JIMMIE heads for the door. SOLENE quietly sees LEVITICUS. Enter
    LEVITICUS, holding flowers. He's sexy in aviator attire, dark glasses, light-weight
    leather jacket, gloves, boots)*

SOLENE
Leviticus.

ALL
LEVITICUS!
(*EVERYBODY freezes*)

END ACT II, SCENE 1

ACT II

~~~~~~

SCENE 2

<u>ON RISE:</u>   Seconds later. Night, May 30, Memorial Day.

LEVITICUS
Good evening everyone.

MOLLY
Leviticus! Thank God you're here! Maybe you can stop her.

LEVITICUS
Pardon?

MOLLY
Solene is about to run off with Mr. Jones here.

LEVITICUS
Pardon?

MOLLY
Yes, yes!

FRANK
Molly, let me handle this. Run on home, Jim. We'll talk about everything in the morning.

JIMMIE
In the morning might be too late, Mr. Frank.

FRANK
No, you're going to be all right, you run on home—

SOLENE
Jimmie, in the morning, under the trestle—

Greenwood: An American Dream Destroyed ❦ **409**

JIMMIE
(To LEVITICUS)
You better find your own girl!
(JIMMIE exits. DELLA walking past LEVITICUS)

DELLA
Flyboy!

LEVITICUS
Solene? Can we talk alone?

MOLLY
Yes, please try to talk some sense into her. I'll get Maria to bring you refreshments.
(EVERYBODY resumes their normal activities. BILL gets his hat and coat, and he and DELLA leave. PRITCHARD gathers his equipment and exits. FRANK and MOLLY exit to offstage room. MOTHER BOLEY at cash register, counting receipts. MARIA turns sign over to closed. Or CUSTOMERS come in and out and get orders as SOLENE and LEVITICUS talk at a table)

LEVITICUS
Solene? I don't understand. You're planning to elope with another man? You and I are engaged. What happened?

SOLENE
I know I should have told you about Jimmie, but, well, when I said I would marry you I was angry with him and now he's in trouble and I can't just abandon him. (Beat) And I can't marry you either.

LEVITICUS
Solene, please don't cry. I can't stand to see you cry. You know how I feel about you.

SOLENE
But I don't—

LEVITICUS

I know, I know, you think you don't love me. But love will come. I've planned a wonderful life for us. I don't want to give up on those plans. Now, this man is on the run, I don't know what he's done, I don't know what kind of future he has, yet you want to throw your life away on him? But, if this is who you think you really want, if you think he can love you more than I do, if you think he can do more for you than I can, then . . .
(He stands up)

SOLENE

(Standing up too)
Oh Leviticus, I'm sorry I've hurt you. I hate to see you leave like this—

LEVITICUS

Oh, I'm not leaving. I won't give you up that easily. I'll be in town for the next few days. But let's just do what your father said, let's see what tomorrow brings. Look, I'm flying out to look at farmland along the Cimarron in the morning and—

SOLENE
Flying?

LEVITICUS
Yeah.

SOLENE
In an aeroplane?

LEVITICUS
Yeah.

SOLENE
Mother thought you had a new horse. But you have an aeroplane?

LEVITICUS
Just bought it. One hundred and fifty horsepower.

SOLENE
I've never been up in an aeroplane before. *(Excitedly)* It must be frightening.

LEVITICUS
You haven't lived until you've been up there, soaring so free, like a bird.
Come with me tomorrow and see.

SOLENE
But I told Jimmie that I would—

LEVITICUS
Let him wait. I mean, he's not too smart is he? How did he manage to
find himself in such tight confines with a White girl?

SOLENE
It's a public elevator.

LEVITICUS
Alone. Wait, don't get mad, we all make mistakes. In the morning?

SOLENE
Well . . .

LEVITICUS
At least do that for me.

SOLENE
OK, but—

LEVITICUS
Good. I'll see you in the morning, Buttercup.
    (LOUD POUNDING ON BACK DOOR)

    (MUSIC: "In the morning' . . . in the evenin' . . . ain't we got—!")

END ACT II, SCENE 2

ACT II

~~~~~~~~

SCENE 3

<u>ON RISE:</u> May 31, Tuesday morning, 8 a.m. MOTHER BOLEY is on telephone and sipping her coffee. We can hear her conversation intermittently. BILL may be hauling in supplies, sack flour, potatoes, etc. At a table PRITCHARD is interviewing MOLLY as she goes through photo album and looks at photos PRITCHARD has taken. MARIA is setting up for the morning customers. SOUND of CHILDREN playing outside. FRANK can be seen in his office. MOLLY has on OPERATIC MUSIC, may be CARUSO's "O sole mio."

MUSIC
> *Che bella cosa na jurnata'e'sole . . .*

MOTHER BOLEY
> *(On telephone, loudly)*

Hallo! Hey there Damie! Yeah, the police come through last night pounding on the door, but we told 'em we didn't know nothing about nothing and they left! And you say they never come around to your house, huh? Well, I reckon that means everything blowed over—! Lord, I can't hardly hear myself think, I don't know why she has to play that music so loud! No, Jimmie didn't come by this morning . . .

MOLLY
> *(Holding head)*

Oh, why must Mother Boley talk so loudly on the telephone? We have a perfectly good connection. I can hardly hear Caruso.

MOTHER BOLEY

But those two detectives, you know, Carmichael, the White one, and the colored one Henry Pack, they come around asking questions about Jimmie. They was real low key about it though. So I think everything is going to be all right. You coming to Bible study tonight? OK, see you then. Bye!

PRITCHARD

Miss Molly, have you made up your mind about which pictures you want to include?

MOLLY

(Looking through photographs)

I definitely don't want that picture you took of the Jones boy. Please don't waste my film on him. Now, these we can keep, and these . . . You're doing quite a wonderful job of capturing the spirit of Greenwood, Mr. Pritchard.

PRITCHARD

Thank you.

(KNOCK on back door)

MOLLY

(Sigh) And there's that wildcatter again. We're going to end up in the poorhouse if Frank keeps giving money to that White man.

PRITCHARD

Wildcatter?

MOLLY

An oilman who drills for oil in dried-up fields, hoping to get lucky. Quiet as it's kept, Frank is his silent partner on a field. He keeps coming back for more and more money on what I personally think is a bust. But he's got Frank believing that he's going to bring in a real gusher one day. He always knocks at the back door.

PRITCHARD

(Laughing) The back door? That's a switch.

MOLLY

He wouldn't dare come through our front door. He doesn't want other Whites to know he's borrowing from a Negro man. What he doesn't know is that he's not the only White man who comes to that door. Frank loans out money to several of them, at 8 percent interest, which is more than the banks. Don't put any of that in the article, Mr. Pritchard.

PRITCHARD
No . . . I won't.

MOLLY
    (Continuing to look through album)
Ah . . . our wedding pictures . . . that's Frank's father, Mr. Boley, he died
in the flu epidemic . . . and this . . . is an early photograph of me with
my family, my mother and father, brothers, sisters . . . obviously taken
before the Indian allotment.

PRITCHARD
I'd like to get pictures of them, are they in Greenwood?

MOLLY
No, they're dead, all dead. Oh look at Solene! Just a little bundle of love.
She was always a handful though, with a mind of her own behind that
lovely countenance. Anyway—these pictures are so very precious, the only
ones I have, so you must promise to be very careful . . .

PRITCHARD
Yes, I promise.
    (FRANK enters the restaurant. PRITCHARD blends into background, taking
    candid shots. FRANK sits at table with MOLLY. MARIA brings him coffee, then
    comes back later with newspaper)

MOLLY
Well, how much did you give him this time?

FRANK
He's drilling a horizontal well in the shale just south of the city—

MOLLY
Frank we have the wedding coming up, renovations on the house, we
can't afford to throw money away on a duster—

FRANK
I have the first mortgage on his house.

MOLLY
Oh, well, in that case . . .
    (MOLLY laughs, gives him a peck)

FRANK
That doesn't mean for you to go out shopping. Where's Solene?

MOLLY
    (Happily)
She's out with Leviticus. *(No response from FRANK)* For the life of me I don't understand why you don't like Leviticus.

FRANK
I like him. I just don't see why Solene should have to marry him or anybody else if she's not ready. If she's not ready, she can stay right here with us.

MOLLY
She won't have us around to protect her forever. She's about to become a very, very wealthy young lady and the right husband will keep away the vultures, like you did for me.

FRANK
Jim's not a vulture.

MOLLY
    (Intake of breath)
Surely you don't want her to marry him?

FRANK
Of course not. But I recognize there's a little puppy love going on, and I think if you'd stop carrying on so about it, it will die out of its own accord.
    (Enter DELLA running)

DELLA
    (Out of breath)
Hey! Have y'all heard?

(Enter BILL)

MOTHER BOLEY / BILL
Heard what?

DELLA
They just arrested Jimmie Jones down Greenwood Avenue!

ALL
What! Arrested him?

MOTHER BOLEY
Oh Lord, no! They was in here early this morning and said all they wanted to do was ask him some questions.

BILL
What they arrest him for? Jimmie said the girl didn't even want to press charges.

DELLA
Well, all I know is they hauled him off in handcuffs and looked like he was on his way to the depot before they got him, he had a suitcase with him.

MOTHER BOLEY
And I just got off the phone with Damie—

FRANK
She should retain a lawyer for him as soon as she can.

BILL
Well, he shines a lot of White lawyer's shoes, she probably needs to get one of them—

MOTHER BOLEY
B.C. Franklin! That's who he needs. B.C. Franklin, the best colored lawyer in Tulsa—

FRANK
(*Opens paper, reading newspaper*)
Look at this headline in the *Tribune* . . . (*Reading*) "Nab Negro for Attacking Girl in an Elevator. A Negro delivery boy who gave his name to the police as Diamond Dick, was arrested on South Greenwood Avenue this morning by officers Carmichael and Pack—"

DELLA
They got it in the newspaper already—?
(*ALL listen in stunned and disheartened silence as FRANK continues reading*)

FRANK
"—charged with attempting to assault the seventeen-year-old White elevator girl in the Drexel Building early yesterday. Diamond Dick will be tried in municipal court on a state charge. The girl said she noticed the Negro a few minutes before the attempted assault looking up and down the hallway on the third floor of the Drexel Building as if to see if there was anyone in sight, then Diamond Dick—"

MOTHER BOLEY
Why they keep calling him that?

MOLLY
Because that's the silly name he gave himself.

FRANK
This new sheriff, McCullough, I think he's a pretty good man.
(*Reading*)
Says here, he's not going to let the same thing happen to Diamond Dick that happened to the White boy Belton. "Not on my watch," he says.

MOLLY
Well, there. The authorities have to protect us.

FRANK
Molly is probably right. Let's just go on about our day. I'll check with some of the businessmen and see what they think.
(*FRANK and MOLLY prepare to leave out*)

(DELLA and BILL stand aside)

BILL
I got something I want to ask you tonight.

DELLA
What is it?

BILL
Tonight.

DELLA
I promised your mother I'd go to Bible study with her.

BILL
That won't last long.

DELLA
See you after Bible study then.

BILL
Copacetic.
    (Quick kiss)

    *(As DELLA starts to exit, enter SOLENE, running, with a suitcase holding up
    newspaper)*

SOLENE
Mother! Father!

FRANK/MOLLY
What is it Solene!

MOLLY
    (Sees suitcase)
And where have you been, Miss Solene. I thought you were with Leviticus, and where are you going with that suitcase?

SOLENE
    (Stuttering)
I-I was supposed to meet Jimmie, but look, it's Jimmie! They have Jimmie! Here, in the newspaper!

FRANK
Yes, we know, we've already read that and we're going to help him out—

SOLENE
They're going to lynch him tonight!

MOLLY
No, no, Solene, they've only taken the boy to jail—

FRANK
Yeah, that's all—

SOLENE
No! They are going to lynch him, Father! It's right here! *(Holding up paper)* Look!

MOLLY
Oh my God, it's on the editorial page, Frank.

FRANK
I didn't see that . . .

SOLENE
    (Reading)
"To Lynch Negro Tonight."

MOTHER BOLEY
Oh!

SOLENE
(Reading) "There is likely to be a lynching in Tulsa tonight. Whites assembling to lynch the teenager tonight."

MOTHER BOLEY

(Dialing)

Oh Lord. That's what they always do, they write up the lynching the day before, so the whole town can come see, like it's sport . . .

(LIGHTS on MOTHER BOLEY in bitter memory)

MOTHER BOLEY

I remember . . . like it was yesterday . . . it was a quiet peaceful Sunday afternoon . . . the good Christian White folk was sitting round the dinner table after church. Then all of a sudden everybody was milling around out on the town square . . . buzzing with excitement. *(Enter PRITCHARD taking pictures of her)* The town photograph man showed up . . . he always took pictures of all the big events, y'know . . . so he was setting up his equipment to take pictures and make postcards out of 'em. He sold them postcards to White folks up north for a pretty penny. Automobiles . . . wagons . . . buggies, from everywhere showed up on the town square. White folk had come from fifty mile around to see this. They had done caught a young colored boy running for his life . . . trying to get out of town . . . 'cause they said . . . he'd done raped a White woman.

They caught him 'fore he could make it out . . . stripped him naked . . . tied his hands behind his back . . . tied his feet together . . . kicked and pounded him with whatever they could find, trying to get him to beg for their mercy. But he wouldn't beg. That riled 'em up even more, they was wild with hate! They throwed a rope round his neck and hoisted the poor boy up a tree. They jeered, and shouted, and cussed up at him: "Beg nigger!" He never said a word.

Now, all while the hanging was going on . . . it was a man started to build a bone-fire. He let his little boy help him . . . little boy was so proud, helping out his pa. Now, most times in a lynching, they'd let the body hang from the tree for days before cutting it down, to put fear in the colored . . . but this here mob was in such a 'cess for blood, they cut the body down right there on the spot. When it hit the ground, they set upon it like dogs with the rabies . . . they cut off his fingers . . . and toes . . . and ears . . . they unsexed him . . . they cut out his heart and his liver . . . Oh God . . . then they poured gasoline on his body and throwed it in the fire. Smoke went up to the high heavens . . . and they let out a big ol' cheer.

All day long the mob hung around . . . men, women, children . . . watching his body burn and burn . . . laughing and joking, visiting with one another . . . 'til wasn't nothing left but ashes . . . bone bits . . . and a few teeth. But them heathens even much reached into the smoldering fire to take those teeth and bones for souvenirs, and strike poses for pictures in front of the fire . . . 'til finally the sun was going down . . . they was wore out from all their violence and started to head on back home . . . to finish up Sunday dinner.

(*Dialing phone*)

Wasn't nothing left to do but to go tell the boy's poor mama what had happened to her son . . .

(*Speaking into phone*)

Hallo, Damie? It's me Ida Mae . . .

(*APPROPRIATE MUSIC*)

<u>END ACT II, SCENE 3</u>

ACT II

~~~~~~~~

SCENE 4

<u>SETTING:</u> Tuesday, May 31. "7 p.m." flashes on the screen.

<u>ON RISE:</u> FRANK is on the telephone. PEG LEG is talking to DR. JACKSON and
PRITCHARD. BILL is in butcher shop or behind counter. LEVITICUS is at a
table.

PEG LEG

Thirty of us vets drove down to the courthouse, armed! Offered Sheriff
McCullough our help. He said he didn't need it. A thousand violent
crackers milling around outside the courthouse shouting for Jimmie Jones
head and he say he don't need no help! I'm going back down there. Now!

DR. JACKSON

Peg. Frank is on the telephone with Deputy Barney Cleaver right now
and he says the sheriff said—

PEG LEG

I don't care what Sheriff McCullough say, I was out there! I saw that
White mob!

FRANK

Hey pipe down! I've got Barney Cleaver on the phone!
    (*Listening into phone*)
He says the sheriff is doing all he can to keep Jimmie safe. They have
him in jail on the top floor of the courthouse and they've shut down the
elevator so nobody can come up— (*FRANK listens. Pause*)
    Uh-uh, OK, OK . . . Uh-huh, yeah, Barney. Good, good.
    (*Hangs up, looking at watch*)
Barney says they have six deputies all around the boy.

PEG LEG

Barney's got to look out for his job, you know, being the only colored
one up there—

DR. JACKSON
How does he say the young man's doing, Frank?

PEG LEG
How the hell you think he's doing Doc, he's scared shitless—!

FRANK
Well, it seems they're doing all they can to protect him.

PEG LEG
But that might not be enough!

DR. JACKSON
Might not be. Just yesterday I read in the newspaper that six prisoners broke out of jail.

PEG LEG
Right!

DR. JACKSON
Just sawed the bars right off the doors and windows.

PEG LEG
That's what I'm saying. If they can get out, that mob can get in—

FRANK
No, no, he's got men up on the roof with shotguns and rifles.

PEG LEG
Look, I been down there! When the sheriff came outside trying to get 'em to go home, they just hooted him down!

DR. JACKSON
Well, it's sunset. Probably they'll all go home soon and have dinner.

PEG
Ha! They'll have dinner all right.

FRANK

Let's just stay calm. *(Beat)* Now, Gurley and some of the other businessmen want to have a meeting at the Tulsa Star—

PEG LEG

A meeting! All you businessmen want to do is have meetings and talk, but we soldiers know what's got to be done—
    (To BILL, who has stepped out)
    Don't we Bill?

BILL

Maybe we ought to listen to Frank.

DR. JACKSON

Yes, much of this is just innuendo and rumors floating about—

FRANK

I think we should discuss the situation at the courthouse in a unified way. So, Gurley, Stradford, Willie Williams, Smitherman, Dr. Bridgewater, what about you Dr. Jackson? *(At DR. JACKSON's nod)*
    OK, I and some of the other businessmen are going to the courthouse and we're going talk to the sheriff.

PEG LEG

    (Intense frustration)
I already told y'all, a bunch of us soldiers already went down there and they didn't want to hear no talk—

FRANK

Well, perhaps cooler heads will prevail this time. Now listen, I think what we need to do is—
    (PEG LEG waves them off. Walks over to BILL)

PEG LEG

Bill?
    (Whispers, touches armband)
    Listen, the African Blood Brotherhood . . . we got plans . . .
    (Silence from BILL)

... They already got jitneys lined up to bring in ammunition ...
(BILL says nothing, chop chop)
They stocking up right now ... behind Paradise Baptist Church ...
(BILL brings the cleaver down on the chopping block, PEG LEG jumps back. Bill laughs)

PEG LEG
Damn man.

BILL
What you jumping for Peg? You know I got good hand-to-eye coordination.

PEG LEG
(Beat)
We need you Bill.

BILL
What was he doing associating with that ofay girl for, anyway?

PEG LEG
What? Come on man! That's just White folk talk. You know that. That boy got sense enough not to take that kind of chance with his life.

BILL
I don't know how much sense he's got. I've seen him operating out there on Cherry Hill.

PEG LEG
So?

BILL
So, you still looking for a fight, Peg. I'm not. I been to war and back, the war's over for me.

PEG
Well, you do what you gotta do, but me and the other soldiers not about to let 'em lynch that boy!

BILL

Don't go off half-cocked. Just wait and see what the sheriff's going to do—

PEG LEG

The best time to do something about a lynching is before it happen not afterwards!

BILL

Well—me and Della, we got big plans for tonight—and right now, I got beef to trim.

PEG LEG

Beef to trim—I can't believe what I'm hearing. *(Sneering)* Never thought I'd say this, but you ain't scared is you, like some of them soldiers we saw during the war, shaking in their foxholes, too scared to come to the aid of their own comrades?

BILL

Get out of my face Peg Leg.

PEG LEG

(In his face with rifle)
Or what, what!

BILL

(Going around him)
I know what I'm going to do!

PEG LEG

Huh—?

BILL

I'm going outside and raise Old Glory again, shine a light on it. When they see that maybe they'll pass over the restaurant.
(The PHONE RINGS. BILL stops to answer it)

(Enter MOLLY, MOTHER BOLEY, SOLENE from rooms offstage, holding Bibles, dressed for church. PEG LEG shakes his head in disgust)

MOLLY
(Pulling on gloves)
Frank?

MOTHER BOLEY
Son?

MOLLY
We're off to choir rehearsal dear—

MOTHER BOLEY
And Bible study, son—

FRANK
Rehearsal on Memorial Day weekend? I thought you already had rehearsal
on Wednesday.

MOLLY
We did, but this Sunday we're presenting a repertoire of patriotic songs
and I think they need more practice, plus, yours truly will be singing a
solo, so please attend dear. And you Mr. Pritchard, I'd like for you to come
along with us to get pictures of Mount Zion's impressive architecture—

FRANK
Molly, Pritchard's coming with us to a very important meeting over at
the Tulsa Star—

MOLLY
Meeting at Tulsa Star?

SOLENE
Is it about Jimmie?

MOLLY
Oh Frank, please, don't have him taking pictures of some riotous
meeting—we don't want to give the world the wrong impression of Greenwood. I think Mr. Pritchard should just stick to the agenda that I've
planned for him and—

FRANK
Molly.

MOLLY
But Frank, I already—

FRANK
Honey, you'll get a chance to take your pictures, but right now we have
something very important going on.

MOLLY
Honestly, I don't see what could be more important than your daughter's
wedding, I mean really—

FRANK
Molly! We have a young man in serious trouble here, and I don't want to
hear any more about that doggone wedding!

MOLLY
Oh . . . well . . . as you wish Frank . . . Come Solene.

SOLENE
    (Stubbornly)
I just want to know if anybody's going to get Jimmie out of jail, or just
let them lynch him?

FRANK
We men are going to handle it, you just go on to church.

MOTHER BOLEY
You reckon it's all right for us to go out, huh, son? Surely we'll be safe
in church, huh?

FRANK
I think so. All of the trouble is downtown. But don't go anywhere else
though, come straight back here.
    Pritchard? Be sure to bring all of your stuff with you. I want you to
take pictures and record this meeting.

PRITCHARD

Yes sir.

> (BILL comes over)

BILL

That was Seymour. He says three White men just broke into the courthouse demanding Jimmie be turned over to them!

SOLENE

I told you!

MOTHER BOLEY

Oh Jesus.

FRANK

But I thought the deputies—?

BILL

> (Taking off apron, goes behind counter)

Yeah, the deputies are still holding on to him, but it's just a matter of time before—

FRANK

We—we have to figure out how we're going to respond to this—

DR. JACKSON

Yes, we must be organized about it. A direct confrontation could be destructive for the whole community right now—

FRANK

> (To BILL)

Where're you going?

BILL

Downtown. With the other soldiers. Like I should have gone in the first place!

PEG LEG
Now you talking soldier, let's go.

FRANK
Bill, Billy. You have to weigh the pros and cons before—

BILL
This ain't no account ledger, this is a boy's life.

FRANK
I know, I know it, but you could get yourself killed. Now, we businessmen
will go downtown again and talk to them—

BILL
    (Hoist his rifle, as FRANK tries block him)
Frank, get out my way. You can stay here and do nothing, or take up your
weapon and come with me, but don't try to stop me!

MOTHER BOLEY
Bill, son, you go down there toting that gun, they'll shoot you down.

BILL
Mama don't worry about me. I can take care of myself.

MOTHER BOLEY
But you know we—we have to get ready for breakfast in the morning . . .

BILL
Mama, I'll be back in time for breakfast, OK. Tell Della I might not see
her tonight, but I'll see her tomorrow.

MOTHER BOLEY
Son . . . !

BILL
Tomorrow.

MOTHER BOLEY
God go with you.
    (BILL exits)

FRANK
Mama, Bill will be all right. I don't think you ladies should go to church this evening, after all. I want you all to stay put right here. Leviticus?

LEVITICUS
I'm coming.

FRANK
No, I need you to stay with the ladies. Close up shop!
    (FRANK, DR. JACKSON, PRITCHARD exit. LEVITICUS thinks a moment, starts for door)

SOLENE
Leviticus, where are you going?

MOLLY
This is not your fight! I could never face your parents if anything happened to you—!

LEVITICUS
Don't worry, Mrs. Boley, I can protect myself. We had a little trouble in Arkansas.
    (Takes gun out of boot, checks it)

SOLENE
Leviticus I'm afraid.

LEVITICUS
No need to be afraid. Just do like your father said and close up, you'll be all right.

SOLENE
I mean for you. I'm afraid for you. You don't have to do this because of me.

LEVITICUS

Well . . . it's not just for you. I can't stand by and watch them lynch a Negro man. Today it's him, tomorrow it's me. Besides, would you respect me if I didn't try to help?

(No answer)

No. That's what I thought. And I wouldn't blame you.

MOTHER BOLEY

(Giving him a rifle)

You seem like a fighting man.

LEVITICUS

Yes ma'am, I've had a scuffle or two. We just had a little trouble down in Arkansas with some of the White landowners.

MOTHER BOLEY

Here, take Mr. Boley's rifle. It helped get me and him out of many a tight spot. It's locked and loaded.

LEVITICUS

Thank you, Mother Boley.

SOLENE

(As he exits)

Leviticus! Be careful.

MOLLY

(Under breath)

That Jimmie Jones is going to be the death of us all.

(LEVITICUS exits. SONG begins as scene ends)

MOTHER BOLEY / MOLLY / SOLENE / MARIA

We are soldiers in the Army, we got to fight, although we have to cry. We have to hold it up the blood-stained banner, we have to hold it up until we die . . .

END ACT II, SCENE 4

ACT II

⁓⁓⁓

SCENE 5

Greenwood: The Nightmare

<u>ON RISE:</u> Wednesday, June 1. "12 a.m." flashes on the screen.

PRITCHARD
(To himself as he looks at his work)
It almost always begins with a White woman's scream, doesn't it? They say there are good Negroes who are kind and courteous. They say they are helpful and the Southerner has affection for them. But there is a Black man who is a beast, they say. This is a physical fact, they say! They say that a Black man is a bad man. He drinks the cheapest and vilest whiskey, they say. He breaks every law! He is a dope fiend, they say! He holds life lightly, he is a bully and a brute, they say.

MOTHER BOLEY
"The Negro said I was deprived of my ears, my fingers and genital parts of my body. I pleaded pitifully for my life while . . . the mutilation was going on . . . before my body was cool, it was . . . cut to pieces, the bones crushed into small bits . . . my heart was cut into pieces, as was also my liver . . . small pieces of my bones went for twenty-five cents . . ." Oh God.
(IMAGES of 'FRISCO TRAIN TRACKS, STANDPIPE HILL. PEG LEG at train track. BILL, heavily armed, high in BELFRY CHURCH TOWER, like a sniper)

PEG LEG
(Draws line with foot)
This here right here, this the dividing Line. Right here. 'Frisco tracks. White on that side, colored on this side. That's the way it's always been. Outnumbered by Whites, ten to one but got my 30-30 rifle and repeating shotgun. I'm defending Greenwood. Midnight. We been out here on the 'Frisco tracks for hours, holding off them invaders. I figure I done took down about twelve of them by myself. They done forgot all about Jimmie Jones now.

PEG LEG / BILL
They want Greenwood!

PEG LEG
    (Loading weapon)
Darkness slowed them down some in other parts of Greenwood, but it's
been hot and heavy here along the 'Frisco railroad tracks. We not gonna
let 'em cross it no matter what. Passenger train pulled in the depot, we
kept right on firing at each under the train, raking both sides. You could
see the scared look on the passengers' faces, ducking for cover on the
floor. They thought for sure they'd pulled into a war zone. Ha, ha! Yeah,
that White mob came for dear old Greenwood but they got to go through
Peg Leg first! *(As he dashes off)* Remember Standpipe Hill!
    *(ON SCREEN FLASHES "WESTERN UNION TELEGRAM: 1:46 AM,
    JUNE 1ST 1921. TELEGRAM READS: 'GOVERNOR J.B.A. ROBERTSON,
    OKLAHOMA CITY, OKLAHOMA. RACE RIOT DEVELOPED HERE. SEVERAL
    KILLED. UNABLE TO HANDLE SITUATION. REQUEST THAT NATIONAL
    GUARD FORCES BE SENT BY SPECIAL TRAIN. SITUATION SERIOUS . . .
    STOP.'")*

<u>END ACT II, SCENE 5</u>

ACT II

〜〜〜〜

SCENE 6

<u>ON RISE:</u> Wednesday, June 1, 5:30 a.m. The restaurant. SOLENE, attired in lovely
outfit, paces, like caged lion. MOLLY going through photo albums. MOTHER
BOLEY is on telephone. THE PHONE RINGS throughout intermittently.
Occasional sounds of GUNFIRE. FRANK and LEVITICUS can be seen on roof
of building, which might be Trestle, or in an area where they are seen returning
fire. FLAG ILLUMINATED outside. FRANK and LEVITICUS outside, firing.
LIGHT on DR. JACKSON at telephone.

DR. JACKSON
(Talking on phone to MOTHER BOLEY)
Well, I'm all right, but I've been hearing gunfire all night long. Yes,
I'm with my neighbor Attorney Oliphant. Uh-huh, the White man,
we're waiting it out together. I understand that what they are doing is
they order you out of your house. And, if you don't come out—they,
well, they drive you out, then they go in and take whatever they want,
set the house on fire—

MOTHER BOLEY
(On phone, looking out window)
Umph, umph, umph . . . There goes Billy Nowata in his wagon with his
grandchildren. Uh-huh, carloads of folks leaving town. Things getting
really bad . . . I know, Sam Shepherd piled his whole family up in his sedan
and took off . . . did you hear that Williams even has his White worker,
up on top of Dreamland with a rifle. Yeah, and we heard that the KKK
had dragged Jimmie out the jail, did you hear that? Dr. Jackson . . . ?

DR. JACKSON
Wait. I see a group of—of—armed White boys out on my front lawn
right now. *(Pause)* They're calling for me to come out.
(Pause) Oliphant is standing outside talking with them, telling them
who I am, you know . . . He's holding them a good bit with his talk,
they're even smiling now. I think they're going to move on. But no, they

still want me to come out. So, I'm just going to walk out there with my hands raised . . . I think I'll be all right, Mother Boley. I don't think I'm in any danger, but if you don't hear from me again, well, you'll know what happened . . .

MOTHER BOLEY
Dr. Jackson . . . Dr. Jackson? *(To the others)* The line went dead. I think something might've happened to Doctor Jackson . . .

MOLLY
Oh no . . . I hope Maria made it home all right.
   (GUNFIRE)
   Dear Jesus! I wish Frank and Leviticus would come back inside!

SOLENE
Jimmie, poor Jimmie.

MOTHER BOLEY
Baby, stop torturing yourself. Maybe—maybe it didn't happen that way to Jimmie, maybe he got away from 'em, maybe he—

SOLENE
They stormed into the jail! How could he get away! They dragged him out! And you know what they're doing to him right now! Oh God!

MOTHER BOLEY
Lord have mercy . . . just a boy . . . his whole life ahead of him. Damie knew something bad was going to happen . . .

SOLENE
Who do they think they are! Who do they think WE are! How can they treat us like this? How could they kill poor Jimmie! Savages!

MOTHER BOLEY
It's not all of them, Solene. There are some good Christian White folks in this town, we got to remember that. Surely they won't let this unrighteousness prevail—

SOLENE
Oh Grandmother please!

MOTHER BOLEY
No, it's mostly young riffraff that started this thing and—

SOLENE
They might have started it, but the so-called "good White folks" are joining right in. I bet you it was some of Jimmie's customers, the very men
whose shoes he shined, I bet it was them who lynched him, hiding under
their white sheets. Cowards!

MOLLY
     (Looking through pictures)
Mr. Pritchard is out there taking pictures of this disaster. Horrible.
Horrible images—broken Negro bodies, blood, humiliation, no. I don't
want him to develop any more of those photos.
     These are not the images I hired him to take of Greenwood. This is not
my Greenwood . . . I hired him to take pictures of our magnificence—Dear
Mr. Pritchard . . . (Starts to write letter)

SOLENE
Mother, Greenwood is dead. Jimmie is dead. Everything is dead.

MOLLY
No! Don't you dare say that! It's unfortunate about Jimmie Jones, but
dear Greenwood is not dead. We've worked too hard . . . we've worked
too hard to show ourselves approved!
     (MOLLY suddenly breaks down crying)

     (GUNFIRE)

SOLENE
Approved to whom, mother, approved to whom?? God?

MOLLY

To God! To everyone! Everybody! Everybody! We've built our own Black paradise right here, and instead of commending us, they want to bring us low! I can't believe it's come to this.

MOTHER BOLEY

(Whispers) But we always knew this day would come. No matter what we did or didn't do.

Ever since we started building Greenwood, deep in our hearts, we KNEW this day would come. All our lives we live with fear of what they can let loose on us. We KNEW they would only let us get so far, then we'd have to pay—

SOLENE

Pay? For living well? It's not fair. If they want what we have so bad, just let them have it, it's not worth it—

MOTHER BOLEY

Oh no, we ain't giving up nothing without a fight. The men are out there fighting for Greenwood, and we women can't get fainthearted, we got to fight too. We been through too many trials and tribulations in this land to let the devil win. But faith in the Lord brought us through it all.

MOLLY

I don't know, Mother Boley . . . maybe Solene is right . . . maybe it was better when we had nothing, before they discovered all this oil. Solene, you came into this world of comfort that your father and I created for you and I thought that having money would lift us all up, but it hasn't made one bit of difference, we're not equal at all. But because of money I lost my entire family. And I would give it all, ALL back to have them alive again.

(OFFSTAGE SOUND OF EXCHANGE OF GUNFIRE. DRUNKEN OBSCENITIES BEING SHOUTED, THE THUD OF ROCKS THROWN. ENTER FRANK, with LEVITICUS following close behind. The WOMEN run up to them)

WOMEN

Frank! Leviticus! Are you all right!

FRANK

We're OK. A carload of hoodlums just went by, firing shots—

LEVITICUS

And we returned the courtesy—

FRANK

They're running a scrimmage line along Archer. Seymour gave us this ammo. Let's get this box open.

MOTHER BOLEY

(Gives him a hammer, or hatchet)

What about Bill? Any word on Bill?

FRANK

Well, I think he might be the soldier who sparked it off. White mobster come up to him, asked where you going with that gun, nigger, well Bill said I'm gonna use it if I have to.

FRANK

(Struggling to open box)

He's all right. He's up in the tower of Mount Zion.

MOTHER BOLEY

He's in Mount Zion?

FRANK

Yeah, he and some other soldiers, they're protecting the homes on North Detroit. The tower'll give him a good aerial view. He's all right.

PRITCHARD

Well, I just saw the National Guard marching in—

MOTHER BOLEY

Thank the Lord!

PRITCHARD
(Putting down camera equipment)
But I don't know whose side they're on—

FRANK
What do you mean?

MOLLY
They're supposed to be on our side.

SOLENE
They're supposed to be defending us—

PRITCHARD
Well, some of them are, but some of them out there are nothing but a bunch of deputized KKK, in World War I uniforms. So, when one walks up to you, you don't know what you're getting. I saw one of them help a colored man escape from a mob of Whites, then I saw another one shoot a boy down.
(PRITCHARD begins to type furiously on typewriter as he talks)
On the commercial end . . . like war never ended. Running gunfights. Mobsters set fires to commercial property. Fire trucks turned away. *(Stops typing)* They're actually calling Greenwood the enemy—

ALL
The enemy?

LEVITICUS
How can they call Greenwood the enemy?

SOLENE
We're American citizens! American citizens!

PRITCHARD
The rumor is out that Mount Zion is a fortress with twenty caskets full of rifles—

ALL
What—?

PRITCHARD
(*Mirthless laugh*)
Unbelievable. I know. I'm going back out there, get more pictures, get the story—

MOLLY
(*Getting albums, clutching to her chest*)
Yes! Yes! Get the story. Tell the world. Take pictures of everything they're doing to us! Write it all down—and Pritchard! Take this (*Gives him an envelope*)
(*PRITCHARD exits*)

FRANK
(*To LEVITICUS*)
OK, young man, the wildcatter will be here in a minute to drive you to the airfield. I don't know how things will go with me, so I'm putting my daughter in your hands. This my daughter, my only child. I trust you to take care of her and to deliver her safely to your mother's home. Beyond that, well, it's for you two to decide. Just know this: if any harm comes to her by your hand, I'll kill you. Godspeed.

SOLENE
Oh father.

MOTHER BOLEY
And if y'all don't get married, you return her back just like you found her.

LEVITICUS
Yes ma'am.

MOLLY
(*Giving SOLENE valise*)
This is everything you will need for the short trip. We will be along as soon as we can. We love you. And remember what I taught you.

SOLENE

(As she pulls on gloves) Yes Mother. Always put my best foot forward and carry an extra pair of gloves. *(They laugh)*

> *(KNOCK on back door. ALL freeze)*

FRANK

That's the wildcatter.

> *(As FRANK goes to door, JIMMIE falls in, with shackle on foot or handcuffs. LEVITICUS raises rifle. SOLENE stays his hand)*

SOLENE

No, it's not! It's Jimmie!

FRANK

Jim!

SOLENE

Jimmie!

MOTHER BOLEY

Well, I declare before the Lord!

JIMMIE

Solene, I had to see you one last time.

SOLENE

Jimmie, oh Jimmie!

FRANK

> *(As ALL crowd around him)*

Let's get the chains off the boy—we thought you were—how did you get away!

JIMMIE

The mob came for me, but one of the deputies, I won't say who, helped me to the second floor, then I jumped out the window, hurt my ankle a little bit, but I'm OK—they're hot on my trail, though. I got to get out of town. I just wanted to see Solene—

(JIMMIE takes SOLENE off to a corner)

SOLENE
You're here and alive!

JIMMIE
I'm running against the wind now, Solene. All the plans we made—I can't take care of myself, much less protect you.

SOLENE
Well, stay here then, hide out until everything blows over, then we'll figure out—

JIMMIE
(Grabs both her hands)
Solene, no, you got to listen to me.
  I'm Diamond Dick remember? I'll be all right. Your mother was right, I'm full of trouble. Nothing's gonna change for me. Ever since I was a boy running from Vinita Oklahoma, I been on the run. You can't come with me. What kind of man would I be to put you in that kind of danger?
  (Holding her hand)
  No, you deserve a better man than me . . . So, you go on . . .
  (Gives her hand to LEVITICUS)
  With him.

LEVITICUS
What's your plan of escape?

JIMMIE
Why should I tell you?

LEVITICUS
Well, they're not letting any trains in, but they're still letting the freight trains go out. My boxcars will be moving out at soon. *(Looks at watch)* Get on it, if you don't mind hiding among a mountain of spuds it'll take you to Kansas.
  (JIMMIE gives LEVITICUS a suspicious look)

SOLENE
It's all right, Jimmie. It's all all right.

FRANK
Come on Jim, take this.
(*Gives wad of money*)

(*All gather around JIMMIE, giving him advice, gun, food, money, fresh clothes, bandages. MOLLY can only stand and look at things unfolding*)

MOTHER BOLEY
(*Prayer, gather hands*) Lord, protect and keep us all, in Jesus' name. Amen.

ALL
Amen.
(*The TELEPHONE RINGS. MOTHER BOLEY answers it. MOLLY has a moment with JIMMIE*)

MOLLY
Thank you Jimmie for not taking her away.

JIMMIE
Goodbye Solene.

(*Exits*)

MOLLY
Take care Jimmie.

MOTHER BOLEY
It's Maria! There's fire everywhere! Greenwood is burning!
(*SOUND OF SHATTERING GLASS as ROCK IS THROWN. Chairs, tables, barricade windows/door. EVERYBODY freezes. GUNSHOT. FRANK is wounded in the shoulder*)

MOLLY
Frank!

(GUNSHOTS. SOUND OF ANGRY MOB POUNDING AT FRONT DOOR.
BURST OF LIGHT, which are torches. *LEVITICUS and MOTHER BOLEY* level
their shotguns at door and *BLAST SHOTGUNS. FLASHES OF LIGHT, SOUNDS*
OF A GUNFIGHT IN BOLEY RESTAURANT. PRITCHARD out in the streets
reporting and taking pictures)

PRITCHARD
Martial law was declared at 11:59 a.m. on June 1, 1921. Everywhere the
smell of blood . . . Whites armed to the teeth, hanging out of motorcars,
firing at will. Fires set.

   Telephone and telegraph lines cut, so they could wipe out Greenwood
without anybody knowing. They blocked all the trains going into Tulsa.
They burned everything block by block by block. All night long, shouts,
gunfire, deathly screams—and then . . . an eerie silence. A lull. It was like
Greenwood was holding its breath. In that silence, Frank Smitherman
even managed to get out the newspaper: "At 9 pm the trouble started; by
2 am the thing was done." We didn't know it was the lull before the storm.

<u>BLACKOUT</u>

<u>END ACT II, SCENE 6</u>

ACT II

~~~~~~~

SCENE 7

<u>ON RISE:</u> June 1, Wednesday. Wandering the streets with bloody feet, DELLA
speaks, LIGHTS change from BLACKOUT to SUNRISE to FULL LIGHT
OF MORNING. In the restaurant, MOLLY, FRANK, MOTHER BOLEY
in bemused silence. Somewhere BILLOWS of SMOKE. MOLLY doctors
FRANK's shoulder.

DELLA
(In a SPOTLIGHT, holding her shoes)
All night I walked on glass for Bill. All night I searched for him. It was
shattered glass everywhere. A group of hooligans spotted me, at one
point, and chased me. I ran so hard, I ran right out of out of my shoes,
and cut up my feet. All through Greenwood, I saw the mob back trucks
up to colored folks' houses . . . they took money off folks, took jewelry,
anything they thought was valuable, they took. I saw oil barons, with their
hooting hyena wives running down the street, with shopping bags, loot-
ing the homes of Black doctors and lawyers, even taking Negro women's
underwear, and the men's silk shirts—then . . . all of a sudden, it got quiet.
Everybody started to think maybe the danger was over, maybe White folks
had got it out their system. We were grateful that we'd made it through
the night . . . I never did find my Bill that night, I'll never know what he
wanted to say to me. *(Continues walking, looking for BILL)*
(A montage of images of angry White mob)

*(Enter PRITCHARD snapping pictures as rapidly as he can, frantically jotting notes,
dodging bullets)*

PRITCHARD
George Miller. White physician. Tried to help wounded colored man
bleeding on street. Dr. Miller tried to help, but crowd wouldn't let
ambulance pick him up. Impossible situation. Miller got in his car
and just drove away. People were out on the roads, some in their night

clothes, fleeing the town and some so shocked, they were moving like zombies.

(*MARIA enters, running*)

MARIA

Que Dios me quide! Ay! I wake up to the smell of smoke. Grab Angelina, my baby, an' run out of the burning house but there are fires everywhere! Greenwood is burning!

Everyone is outside. Men, women, children—in our night clothes . . . barefoot . . . running away from everything we have, dodging bullets . . . glass.

Electric wires falling down all around. They had cut them down to electrocute us. I try to run back to the Boley's. I turn the corner and run right . . . into a White mob.

DELLA

(*Holding out hand*)
Maria! Maria! Come with me Maria!

MARIA

(*Running, doesn't hear DELLA*)
They chase me down the alley in back of the Rialto Theatre. I run inside. It is so dark. Dios me ajuda! I jump on the stage . . . in front of the pictura screen. A blinking light coming from the balcony. It . . . it is blinding me! They see me and yell, "There she is! Get that nigger girl!" I see some steps where they play la musica and run down—

(*SOUND of SHOT*)

MARIA

Ay no!

(*A BURST OF LIGHT. She freezes*)
I fell into the darkness. I . . . I don't know what happen . . . to my Angelina . . . Angelina . . . to my baby . . .

(*Bemused, finds herself in Della's arms*)
Della—?

DELLA

Come on Maria!

MARIA

My baby, my baby—

DELLA

They're hiding women and children in the basement of Reverend Kerr's church, and the Holy Family Cathedral. Maybe somebody took your baby there. *(They scramble away)*
    (To audience)
There were Whites who tried to help, tried to stop it, but the bad element was just too wild for 'em. The White mob went around to White folks that they knew had live-in help and demanded that they send 'em out. When they came looking for me, the Huntington girls cussed them White boys out and slapped a couple of 'em. Like I say, them girls is the limit! But I saw a lot of mothers shot down holding their babies. Afterwards some of the Christian White ladies tried to comfort the little Black babies, but only their Black mamas could comfort them, but they were dead.

BILL

    (Heavily armed, high in BELFRY CHURCH TOWER, like a sniper)
At Second and Cincinnati. Major casualties. Can't worry about Dick Rowland now. They ain't concerned about him now. They want Greenwood! But we got a good aerial view of Standpipe Hill.
    (LIGHTS shift like fire. SOUNDS of AIRPLANES, BOMBS)
(Looking up) What's that?! *(A beat)* Bombs! They bombin' us, dammit! Droppin' bombs an' dynamite on us! American citizens! We went to war against the Krauts, took bullets, lost limbs, then come back home and they raining liquid fire down on us! From our own planes!
    (SOUND of BOMBS)

    (BILL angrily shoots up at the sky)

DELLA

(In another spot. Still searching for BILL, she doesn't see him as she calls his name)

Bill!!!

(Burst of light, EXPLOSION)

(BILL is killed. DELLA exits)

(Lights shift. Calm. Quiet . . . dawn's early light)

PRITCHARD

(Still reporting)

All night long . . . gunshots, glass breaking, screams, shouting! Then . . . silence. It was like Greenwood was holding its breath . . . *(Pause)*

(In the pause, FRANK, MOLLY, MOTHER BOLEY, battered, slowly move around the restaurant, which still stands, setting chairs upright, maybe sweeping out debris, etc.)

MOLLY

(Checking FRANK's wound)

Dawn's early light. Greenwood, oh, Greenwood. I prayed we would live to see another sunrise.

MOTHER BOLEY

Yes, we made it through the long night with the help of the Lord.

FRANK

(Reading newspaper)

Yes, Smitherman even got the newspaper out. I think the riot has finally played itself out . . .

MOLLY

Now, we'll see if we can get ahold of Doctor Jackson for you Frank.

FRANK

It's not serious I don't think. We took some losses, but I think the storm is over.

MOLLY
Thank God Solene and Leviticus were even able to get word to us that they'd made it out safely.

MOTHER BOLEY
Nobody but Jesus.

MOLLY
(At the window)
I hope that Mr. Pritchard fared well. This is what he must write in his report: Once upon a time in America, let it be known in the year 1921, there was a Negro Paradise . . .

FRANK
Molly—come away from the window, things aren't safe yet—

MOLLY
A flowering Negro community in Tulsa—Tallassi—Oklahoma called Greenwood . . . *(MOLLY sees children out window)* Oh, look there are the Kinney children, they must have gotten separated from their family. They shouldn't be out there, it's still dangerous!
(SOUND of A LONG SLOW WHISTLE)

PRITCHARD
Then at 5:30 a.m. I heard that whistle blow. It was signal, I think.

CHILD 1 *(Offstage)*
Brother, what is that whistle, and why is the sky on fire?

CHILD 2 *(Offstage)*
I don't know, but it sure don't look good, sister.

MOLLY
(Calling) Children! Get out of the street, children—!

FRANK

I'll get them. You stay put.

> (*FRANK runs out to them, MOLLY behind him*)

Molly! Go back inside!

> (*DYNAMITE STICKS drop, MOLLY screams. FRANK throws himself over her. BOTH are struck and killed*)

END ACT II, SCENE 7

EPILOGUE

ON RISE: ALL those who have died, FRANK, MOLLY, BILL, MOTHER BOLEY, DELLA, PEG LEG, reenter the stage. They wear shrouds.

PRITCHARD

Now they say there was no whistle. But I know what I heard. I'll never forget it. Suddenly there was an invasion of Whites from everywhere. Bombs from planes overhead raining down sticks of dynamite.

During the lull, the enemy had organized during the night and was ready for a full-scale invasion . . . White rage let loose! An invasion. I think that's what they'd planned all along, to invade Greenwood at daybreak.

The colored men put up a gallant fight—fought like tigers—but they were outgunned and outnumbered. They swarmed in on Greenwood to feed and destroy. Like locusts.

(Pause)

In the aftermath of the disaster, all surviving Negros were placed under arrest and ordered to march down the streets, to the convention center downtown, with hands up. Only White employers could sign them out for work, and when they went out, they were required to wear green tags to be approved. The dead were dumped unceremoniously into mass, unmarked graves, no funeral. Fortunately, I have obtained a copy of the toll of the known dead and the wounded from Red Cross Records.

(The funeral for Greenwood's dead begins. MOLLY, who has died, sings "Crucifixion" as names of the dead are read by PRITCHARD and/or scrolled on the screen)

MOLLY

They crucified my Lord . . . and he never said a mumbling word . . . pierced him in the side . . . hung his head and died.

PRITCHARD

Ed Adams, dead, thirty-two, shot through back.

J Abernathy, wounded, shot through back.

Greg Alexander, dead, thirty-five, shot through back.

Greenwood: An American Dream Destroyed § 453

Cal Amley, wounded, shot in ankle.

Dr. Jackson, he found himself at the mercy of two young White thugs drunk with power. Even though his White neighbor Oliphant pleaded for his life, they shot him three times. Oliphant took him to the White hospital in south Tulsa since they burned down the hospital in Greenwood, but they wouldn't treat him. Rejected by the White hospital, he bled to death on the floor of the convention center . . .

William "Bill" Boley, decorated soldier, shot through the heart.

Molly Lena Boley, Frank Boley, Mother Boley, death by firebomb . . .

Della Green, death by firebomb.

Peg Leg, disappeared into the annals of legend.

(As MOLLY exits, the funeral for greenwood ends)

We've had the funeral for Greenwood's dead, but the dream Molly had for the living, lives on . . . a better American Dream . . .

(Enter SOLENE with flowers)

SOLENE

(Reading conclusion of MOLLY's letter)

Once upon a time there was a place called Greenwood . . . don't let it be forgotten . . . Greenwood. Write our story, Mr. Pritchard. Report the disaster. Record the dead but show all the pretty pictures of the living in their finery, in their elegance, in their progress, strutting down their streets, laughing, loving, living in Greenwood. *(Beat)* The horrible night I saw Greenwood for the last time. Flying in the aeroplane with Leviticus, I looked down from the skies and saw Greenwood burning. The place that had nurtured me was no more. But after only a few short years, a new Greenwood emerged from the ashes. They rebuilt better than ever. Then the city of Tulsa decided to run a highway through the heart and soul of Greenwood and destroyed our progress again. I come to lay flowers on their unmarked graves.

(She turns and sees JIMMIE)

Jimmie.

(Enter JIMMIE)

JIMMIE

Somehow, I managed to escape the Klan that night, which all turned out to be customers of mine. They had on hoods, but I knew their shoes. But they didn't have time to deal with me no more, they wanted Greenwood.

I caught a train to Kansas, but I return to Greenwood to lay flowers on the graves of the people who took me in. *(Sees SOLENE)* Solene.

SOLENE
I live in Paris now and as president of the International Council of Women, I travel the world speaking of the horrors of that night, seeking racial justice and reparations for all the businesses and lives that were destroyed. *(Turns and sees LEVITICUS)* Leviticus.
    (Enter LEVITICUS)

LEVITICUS
The City of Greenwood engaged me as their attorney to litigate their case for repair. To date no reparations have been made.

ALL
But still, we rise!
    (A montage of images of the prosperous Greenwood community)

    (CHILDREN or CHILDREN'S VOICES begin, then ALL join in)

ALL/CHILDREN
    Oh, it's a pretty town . . .
    And the Negroes own it too
    With not a single White person there
    To tell them what to do—

    With not a single White person there
    To tell them what to do—
    In Greenwood, in Greenwood, in . . .

ALL
Greenwood. Forever.

THE END

Distant Voices

Synopsis

In this enchanting theatrical collage, the dead tell their intermingled stories in an unkempt cemetery, teaching us a lesson or two about how to live, cook, sing, and die well.

The author researched and resurrected some of the six thousand inhabitants of College Memorial Park, the second-oldest African American cemetery in Houston, Texas. The cemetery was in a ruinous condition; the dead protested, came out, told their intermingled stories. The play shows a broad cross section of the lives memorialized by *Distant Voices*. The production commissioned by the Ensemble Theatre used a company of fourteen to play some seventy characters by doubling, tripling, and quadrupling roles. The producer may cast the play with as many or as few performers as are deemed sufficient. The cast of the Ensemble Theatre production was African American. They played all cultures, characters, and races. They sang songs, hymns, and nursery rhymes from 1840 to 1970, the life of this place of the dead. The technique of intertwining scenes and monologues makes it possible to perform the play in its entirety or to do excerpts. *Distant Voices* was a finalist for the international Susan Smith Blackburn Prize.

Music is an integral element of *Distant Voices*. There is a blend of period music, from 1840 to 1970, that emanates from the ghost radio somewhere on the set; there is live singing, accompanied and a cappella, by the cast; and there is a score composed by Horace Alexander Young, playable by an ensemble ranging from a trio to an octet.

Cast of Characters

African Ancestor

Drucilla Johnson

Louise Lights (child)

Lucinda Barton

Rebecka Woodard

Rev. Jack Yates

John Sessums

Vietnam Veteran

Sgt. Vida Henry

Maria Bingham Sessums

Rev. Frederick Lee Lights

Henry McPhearson

Miss Lump

Churchill Fulcher

Anthony Moore

Lutisha Rivers

Arthur Goodie

Winnie Jones

Harris Robinson (child)

P.R. Johnson

Nannie Yates Countee

Homer Gregg

Dr. Cato

Dr. Cato's Wife

Sister Mattie

Ernst Lemuel (Anglo)

Abraham King

Jack Fritz

Jennie Perry

Shenette Clifton

Wilfred Price

Ophelia Lemuel

Janie Lemuel

Shep McGowen

Susan Toliver Lemuel

John Norwood (Anglo)

Frances Toliver

Richard Allen

Jennie Nathaniel

Hardin Nathaniel

Mary

Martha

Mr. Steveson

Mrs. Steveson

Eldridge Jackson

Annie Taylor

Addie Davis

Brock Family Member (child)

Mahalia Teal

Daniel Hughes

Viola P. Cole (child)

Lillie Horton

Armenda Williams

Joseph Haller

William H. Hodge

J.D. Collins

Dock Johnson

Henry Ammons

Isaac Abney Sr.

Contractor 1 (on video, Anglo)

Contractor 2 (on video, Anglo)

Children

Unknowns

There are family members, husbands, children, and many unknowns who speak only one or two lines. Producers should refer directly to the script to see the appearance of these characters.

Scene

College Park Memorial Cemetery, a destroyed and neglected graveyard on the Fourth Ward, Houston, Texas

Time

From approximately 1840 to 1970

ACT I

SCENE I

A stylized image of an abandoned, wrecked cemetery. In one corner there is a trashed sofa, missing one set of legs. In another, what could be a pulpit. In another, a ladder that leads up into darkness. A child's rusted tricycle is on its side under the ladder. In the last corner there is a set of three steps leading nowhere. Between the ladder and the steps, a wrought-iron chair, bent and rusted, faces in. There are dark green and black thirty-gallon garbage bags, some full, some half empty, scattered everywhere. Newspapers, scraps of paper, mounds of trash and garbage and artifacts from times gone by. The mounds are topped with an apparently wrecked television set and an old-fashioned radio.

It is dark. In the darkness we see what could be bodies. Wrapped like Egyptian mummies, lying sprawled, stacked together. The television flickers to life. Faces appear. The faces you will see in the play. In the darkness, a voice begins to speak in Yoruba. A pin light illuminates the face of someone high on the ladder to nowhere. This person translates line by line.

Who can tell where the journey begins?

Where we begin to live, where we begin to die?

That place lies so far away, before consciousness, after memory, and yet, so close—a handhold away, a kiss away, a trigger, a knife, a spasm away.

Our journey's stories are also being born and dying.

What we lack to let them live is someone to listen to our distant voices.

Some of us began there, where the sun is born, and ended here, halfway to where the sun sets, a half hour's walk from where you sit listening, at College Memorial Park, a forgotten place, without a number, on a street that's changed its name.

Now, we don't ask you to ponder unduly life's reasons—why we begin at all, why we rise, how we fall—we only ask you to spend an hour's worth of life with us, with yourselves, so we can find our voices in your listening, our answers in your questions.

Come share in our prayers, our curses, our brief memories of being on this brief earth.

—Director, Peter Webster

(The AFRICAN ANCESTOR gestures, and the subliminal music that has been building establishes a rhythm. The half-seen figures start to move. They begin to dance in time to the music. We hear the names of the dead in this cemetery as part of the music. The light brightens. The music changes into a more insistent rhythm, the slap–slap–slap of a jump rope. LITTLE GIRLS begin to play)

GIRL CHILD
Mary Mac, Mac, Mac

GIRL CHILD
All dressed in black, black, black

GIRL CHILD
With twenty-four buttons, buttons, buttons

GIRL CHILD
Up and down her back, back, back
>*(TWO BOYS jump into the game, the GIRLS chase them away and start a new game)*

CHILDREN
>A tisket, a tasket, a brown and yellow basket.
>I wrote a letter to my mama, and on the way I dropped it.
>I dropped it, I dropped it, I dropped my yellow basket!
>*(A WOMAN who has been sitting on the steps to nowhere speaks. She is a laundress)*

>*(She folds clothes as she speaks and engages the LITTLE GIRLS to help her)*

DRUCILLA JOHNSON
My husband and I used to sit on these steps of an evenin', watchin' the little chil'ren play. We'd sit here, swattin' mosquitoes, feel the night air on our faces, hear a train in the distance—until we got divorced. He said I was too ticky for him, I said he was too messy for me. So I moved into a boarding house in Third Ward, on McKinney. We didn't have no children. My ex-husband said I didn't need to have no children, said I'd drive 'em loco with my clean ways. But I was taught cleanliness was next to godliness.

GIRL CHILDREN
Yes, ma'am.

DRUCILLA JOHNSON
A place for everything, and everything in its place.

GIRL CHILDREN
Yes ma'am.

DRUCILLA JOHNSON
Always leave your surroundin' better than you found them, my mama always said.

GIRL CHILDREN
Yes ma'am.

DRUCILLA JOHNSON
I'd done Miss Westheimer's washin' that morning. Oh, sometimes I'd do two, three ladies in a day, I was just that much in demand! I was gonna go pick up Miss Meineke's tablecloths that evenin'. She was havin' this big party later in the week, and she wouldn't let nobody touch them lace tablecloths but me. So, I'd laid down across my bed in between jobs—it had got to the place I had to do that. Used to be I could work around the clock. I finally went to the doctor to find out why I was so tired all the time, and he used some big, long word, I don't know, but all it boiled down to was my heart wasn't working right. Anyhow, I'd laid 'cross my bed for a while—and couldn't never get up. Miss Meineke knew something musta been wrong for me not to show up, so she sent her boy 'round the house to check on me.

Sure enough there I was, layin' 'cross the bed—dead. On clean sheets of course. There was a place for everything in my room and everything in its place. That was me, Drucilla Johnson. The day was August 21—a week before my thirty-first birthday.

(She goes into a reverie. One of the LITTLE GIRLS gets up and skips along, singing)

LOUISE LIGHTS
I wrote a letter to my mama and on the way I—
(The light changes. We hear the sound of LIGHTNING)

Ma-ma!

I didn't listen!

I'd already had one ice cream cone at the ball game. It was starting to rain, and Mama'd said one was enough, but it tasted so-o-o good, I just wanted one more, just one more, so I ran down to the store before it got dark, and I was running back home before the storm broke—but lightning struck me, and I was killed, and my name was Louise Lights, and I was eight.

(She kneels in front of LUCINDA BARTON)

LUCINDA BARTON

Children! Obey your parents in the Lord!

That's the only commandment in the Bible with a promise to it—if you do that your days will be long upon this earth.

I ought to know! I was Lucinda Barton, born 1831.

I always obeyed my parents and I lived to be ninety-six years old.

REBECKA WOODARD

Well, you beat me by two years, Lucindy.

(She rises and addresses the crowd with animation)

Rebecka Woodard. Born 1817, died 1911, at the ripe old age of ninety-four.

(REBECKA WOODARD shoos LUCINDA BARTON out of the chair)

LUCINDA BARTON

Now, before I left this earth, I desired to leave behind pearls of wisdom to the young folks. I couldn't read or nor write too good, else I'da wrote me a book, so what I done was—

REBECKA WOODARD

Thanks for the seat, beauty before age y'know—

LUCINDA BARTON

(Continuing)

—well, my eyesight started to go when I got up around eighty—

REBECKA WOODARD

—eagle eyes they called me, never had to wear glasses in my life—

LUCINDA BARTON
—so what I done was I started to string these beads together to make me a little livin'—

REBECKA WOODARD
—and had all my choppers when I went on to glory. (*Clacking teeth*)

LUCINDA BARTON
—so what I done was—every time I met a young'un, I'd give 'em a word of wisdom and one of my little trinklets—I called 'em my pearls—to remember it by.

REBECKA WOODARD
Well, I taught Sunday school at church for many a year, and I used to tell the chillun: Fear of the Lawd is the beginnin' of wisdom.

CHILDREN
Yes ma'am.

REBECKA WOODARD
You don't learn that, how you gon' learn your ABCs?

REBECKA WOODARD
Before I passed on, I told the chilluns, I told 'em, "Chillun, y'all got it made today in 1911, all these modern conveniences." 'Cause I come up the rough side of the mountain!

LUCINDA BARTON
Lord, yes!

BOTH
We come up through slavery.
    (*From the ladder to nowhere we hear a VOICE*)

AFRICAN ANCESTOR
My master used to auction off cattle and slaves.
    (*SLAVES step forth*)

FRANCES TOLIVER
Frances Toliver.

AFRICAN ANCESTOR
Born!

FRANCES TOLIVER
1811.

AFRICAN ANCESTOR
Died!

FRANCES TOLIVER
1900.

FATHER MCGINNIS
Father McGinnis.

AFRICAN ANCESTOR
Born!

FATHER MCGINNIS
1846.

AFRICAN ANCESTOR
Died!

FATHER MCGINNIS
1926.

ANGELINA RICE
Angelina Rice.

AFRICAN ANCESTOR
Born!

ANGELINA RICE
1836.

AFRICAN ANCESTOR
Died!

ANGELINA RICE
1910.

NED DIXON
Ned Dixon.

AFRICAN ANCESTOR
Born!

NED DIXON
1834.

AFRICAN ANCESTOR
Died!

NED DIXON
1921.

CAESAR GAMBLE
Caesar Gamble.

AFRICAN ANCESTOR
Born!

CAESAR GAMBLE
1840.

AFRICAN ANCESTOR
Died!

CAESAR GAMBLE
1912.

REV. YATES
Father Jack Yates.

AFRICAN ANCESTOR
Born!

REV. YATES
A slave.
    I didn't know much about my father. That's the way it was in my day.
    But my mother must have descended from African royalty.
    She was courageous, hardworking, and unselfish.
    In slavery, I worked in the fields and I worked in the house.
    I made things grow. I wielded the hammer and the saw.
    Then I went to the blacksmith's barn, and learned to forge metal, to
beat and shape metal until it became what I wanted it to become.
    I learned to read and write.
    I became an expert at oystering, and fishing.
    Little did I know that one day I would be fishing for men.
    My master allowed me to catch fish on Saturdays and sell my catch
on Sundays.
    I saved money and prospered in my condition.
    I built me a little sailing craft. When that boat got too small I built a
bigger boat, and ventured farther off into the deep.
    At sea I was alone with my God. And there I learned about fish, and
the waves, and the deep, and what is deep in man. I learned about freedom. I came to Jesus.
        (Beat)
    Saturday nights, slaves were released from work.
    They were dancing and singing, drinking and gambling.
    I looked on my people. I saw them in a way I'd never seen them before.
    I saw them with the heart of God.
    And that heart was grieved.
    My people had taken on the ways of the oppressor.
    They were in danger of losing their very souls.
    That night I accepted the charge from God:
    "Lead my people in the way they should go."
    To change their ways, I had to change my ways.
    Now at slave gatherings, instead of dancing, I'd hold prayer meetings.
    I brought them the message of the Gospel.
    (Whispers) I had to be careful with the Gospel. Truth is strong. It'll
break bonds.

Now slaves were drunk—not with corn licker, but with God.

Now slaves were dancing, but they were dancing unto the Lord.

Masters trembled: the Word set captives free in the Lord.

But though the spirit may fly in freedom, still the body is chained to toil.

In 1863, my wife and children were sold off from me.

Harriet and my children, along with 150,000 other slaves, were marched from Virginia to Texas.

Being separated from my wife and children just took all the heart out of me. So I made a new heart in the forge of faith.

I used my money to buy my freedom from my master.

I went to Texas in search of my heart.

I found my little family in Texas. The war ended. Freedom came to all.

Times were hard. Work was scarce. Poverty became our new master.

Then I heard about a little town some seventy miles north and east of us, where an ex-slave might find work.

And so, we came to Houston. We stayed, put down deep roots that were nourished in freedom.

I built a home. I helped build a church. I encouraged other ex-slaves to buy land.

I say—build temples to the Lord in your souls.

I say—build houses on the land in which to live.

I say—after God, land.

Build homes!

Plant trees!

Put down roots!

Praise the Lord!

FRANCES TOLIVER

When freedom come, slaves streamed into Houston from plantations all around Texas.

It was supposed to be a good place for colored folks to live.

CAESAR GAMBLE

We crowded along the bayou. With nothing at first but our freedom.

ANGELINA RICE

The bayou would overflow its banks, flood us out, but we'd return again, overflowing with new hope.

NED DIXON

We made a little squatter's town down at the coliseum.

REV. YATES

You mean where the coliseum was going to be built.

ISAAC ABNEY SR.

Naw, you mean where the coliseum used to be!

LUCINDA BARTON

Free Man Town.

REBECKA WOODARD

You mean Freedman's Town.

ISAAC ABNEY SR.

You mean Old Freedman's Town.

ALL

Fourth Ward!

AFRICAN ANCESTOR

I was conceived in freedom and born in slavery. My mother was already pregnant with me in Africa when they captured her and brought her to a plantation in North Carolina. I was sold off from my mother when I was nine. But I never forgot all the African words and songs and dances she taught me. When I died in 1921, my children give me a African funeral.

> (AFRICAN ANCESTOR comes down the ladder. The music grows stronger. The MEN and WOMEN move in ritual steps. The WOMEN sing the wordless "Victoria Falls Lullaby." The music shifts into the spiritual song, "Hush")

ALL

"Hush, hush, someone's callin' my name . . ."

LUCINDA BARTON

They had to have somewhere to bury the Af'kins. That's what they called us then. Couldn't put 'em in the same ground with the White folks. That's the way College Park Memorial Cemetery came about. 1840.

AFRICAN ANCESTOR

The year they say I was born.

LUCINDA BARTON

That's the year they started puttin' us out here. But they didn't name it until around 1896, when they put up that Negro college across the way.

REBECKA WOODARD

College Park Memorial Cemetery. Oh! This place was something back then, not like it is now, all overrun with weeds and trash. No, it was a beautiful resting place in my day. Families would come out here of a Sunday and brang flowers. They'd have a picnic and stay out here all day long.

LUCINDA BARTON

And then once the year, we'd have a homecoming.
 A reunion between the living and the dead.
 Right here in the graveyard.
 And no matter where our childrens was, all across the country, they'd come home and eat together, then come out here and clean up the grave-yard. Oh! It was a beautiful sight to behold. They'd take some crepe paper, y'see, and wire, and make these little flowers and decorate the headstones with 'em.
 (From the audience, in the dark, an angry VOICE calls out)

UNKNOWN

I ain't got no headstone! Vandals packed it off years ago. They use 'em around here for stepping-stones when it rains. So when them graveyard researchers come around to my grave, they had to write down "Unknown." But I know who I was.
 (JOHN SESSUMS steps into the light. He stands at attention)

JOHN SESSUMS

Captain John Sessums, at your service.

Perpetual drummer of the Houston Light Guard.

Born 1850, died 1928.

Faithful unto death.

The Guard was a volunteer militia organized in 1873.

The only men who were allowed in where White men of good moral character.

And me.

I was the only colored man ever allowed in. My drumming was the main reason the Light Guard won so many prizes and medals. In Galveston in 1885, we took first prize of forty-five hundred dollars. They said it was the most perfect drill ever witnessed in the United States.

(THE DRUMMER creates automatic rifle fire. A VIETNAM VETERAN enters, crouching)

VIETNAM VETERAN

The first one I killed really got to me. We were trailing Charlie on a night patrol somewhere around Da Nang. Out the corner of my eye, I catch something running. Next thing I know it's almost up on me. I shoot.

(Automatic rifle fire)

Hell, somebody get that close, you don't wait to check no ID.

Emptied my M-16 in him.

All the 'bloods come runnin' over to me, slapping me on the back, congratulating me on the kill.

You got a kill man, you finally got a kill. Loverly, man, loverly.

Wasn't no drill either.

I thought sure Charlie would get me in the 'Nam. But I had to come all the way back home to get it. Killed on the streets of Freedman's Town at the hands of a "brotha."

(Under the ladder, a shadowy figure speaks)

SGT. HENRY

I died by my own hand. I saved a bullet for myself, because a soldier die by the bullet.

—We'd come to the end of the line.

In a little muddy bayou town called Houston, Texas.

I could hear the Mounted Police cussin', strugglin' through the underbrush after us.

It was 1917, and it was night.

The 24th Infantry Regiment, colored, was stationed at Camp Logan in Houston in the Fourth Ward.

We'd served with honor in the Philippines, the West, fighting Mescal Eros, Kiowa, Comanche, Sioux.

We had just come off a expedition in Mexico with Black Jack Pershing, chasing Pancho Villa. And now we'd run into a little trouble with the city police in this Southern bayou town.

I'd told my soldiers: "Keep yo' heads."

When they throw you off the trolley cars, "Keep yo' heads."

When you walk down the streets and they calls you a nigger, "Hold yo' peace!"

When they pistol-whip you and throw you in jail, "Don't strike back!"

Don't do nothin' to brang no dishonor on that uniform, 'cause the fight ain't over here with these local yokels.

It's with them godless heathens overseas!

But the civil police didn't care nothin' about our uniforms.

They beat one of our soldiers half to death.

That was it. I couldn't hold the mens no mo'.

"Hell, the war ain't over there, the war is over here!"

So we gathered up our Springfield rifles and we went out.

(Sound of gunfire. SGT. HENRY seems transfixed)

After we come to ourselves, some of the men wanted to go back to camp, throw theirselves on the mercy of the military.

But we done killed White.

There wasn't no mercy, no mercy on this earth.

We was gon' swang for what we'd done.

Only a soldier don't die by the rope. A soldier die by the bullet.

(He makes a slow salute that turns into the shape of a gun. The DRUMMER creates a single sharp sound. SGT. HENRY sits slowly down on the battered couch)

Always thought my remains would rest in my own hometown in Kentucky.

But I'm here in College Park. I'm in good comp'ny, though. They got colored soldiers here from every war—

(He calls out the names of some of the soldiers interred alongside him. They answer "Sir!" after their names)

Pvt. Harvey Hogans Hendrick! Born June 22, 1886, died December 4, 1904, veteran Spanish American War!

Pvt. Ed Harris! 165th Depot Brigade. Died May 4, 1929.

Pvt. Archibald Wallace! Born October 11, 1896, died August 10, 1956, 331st Service Battalion, WWI.

Pvt. Freddie M. Jones. Born December 12, 1895, died August 4, 1958, Company "D," 412th Labor Battalion, WWI.

Commodore Reed TEC5 Army Air Force WWII—

You soldiers gave your blood, sweat and tears for this country, and I'm proud I served wit' ya!

(MARIA BINGHAM SESSUMS, wife of JOHN SESSUMS, enters. Sleek and veiled, she wanders among the headstones as though window-shopping)

MARIA BINGHAM SESSUMS

They had some of the most beautiful sculpture in the country in Olivewood Cemetery—the Methodist cemetery. I'm Maria Bingham Sessums. I passed on in 1912, and I was buried in the Methodist cemetery. John's father was a great Methodist leader, he founded the Trinity Methodist Church—the silk-stocking church they called it, because all of us ladies wore real silk stockings. Of course John was supposed to be buried in the Methodist cemetery with me. But when he died, the White folks loved him so, they just took over the funeral arrangements. They planned everything. They buried my husband here in College Park—a Baptist cemetery (Shudders) . . . so I come here sometimes looking for him. John was always a little different. I suppose it was the drums.

(She exits. LUCINDA BARTON addresses the audience and then JOHN SESSUMS. He responds eagerly)

LUCINDA BARTON

I used to tell the young'uns, "Don't worry if you different from the others.

"Don't fret if you seem outta step with your friends."

Maybe you hear the beat of a different drummer.

JOHN SESSUMS

Yes. Yes! I tried to be like other men, I tried to work a regular job!

For years I worked at the First National Bank as chief porter, and they always gave me time off to travel with the Guard. Until we got a new bank president, and he wouldn't let me go.

I was at work one day, standing at the curb, watching the Guard march off to the railroad station.

I was going to be strong. I was a man with a family, I couldn't jeopardize my job for a set of drums!

But—the drums, the drums kept calling me, calling me.

(The PERCUSSIONIST begins an insinuating African polyrhythm. The DRUMMER takes the rhythm and turns it into a more military beat. A snare drum rolls across the stage to JOHN SESSUMS. He straps it on and begins to play. The percussionist, the drummer and JOHN SESSUMS all build the music to an impossible degree)

JOHN SESSUMS

Suddenly, I couldn't take it anymore. I had to go. I quit my job right there on the spot, and ran off after the Guard. From that day forward I knew what my mission in life was.

I dedicated myself to the Guard, and I organized colored in our own militias too—the Davis Rifles, Sheridan Guard, the Cocke Rifles—until the day I died in 1928.

Oh, the Light Guard gave me a great funeral. A great funeral! It was the headline in all the newspapers. The *Chronicle*—John Sessums, Light Guard Negro Drummer, to get Military Funeral!

The procession stretched all the way down West Dallas.

The light Guard paraded.

The officers and their wives rode in open cars, waving.

A great funeral.

(SOMEONE tries to gently pull him away. He resists)

(REV. FREDERICK LIGHTS steps up and begins an oration at the pulpit)

REV. FREDERICK LIGHTS

Dearly bereaved we are gathered here together—

JOHN SESSUMS

They bought me a marble monument—

REV. FREDERICK LIGHTS

—at the home going of our dearly beloved.

It is not a time of sadness, but a time of joy.

Not an end, but a beginning.

JOHN SESSUMS

But now that Sessums monument has crumbled.

TWO UNKNOWN MEN

Unknown. My grave is sunken. My marker is gone!

REV. FREDERICK LIGHTS

Gone, but not forgotten, never forgotten by God.

I was born on the Fourth of July, 1859, died September 16, 1921.

Reverend Frederick Lee Lights.

I preached the funerals of many a one buried here in this graveyard.

Including my own. Oh yes, every man preaches his own funeral—by the life he lives.

Now God always reveals to his servants what He must do.

And when I climbed into the pulpit that last day, I knew I was standing before the Antioch congregation for the last time.

I'd finished my course, I'd run my race, I'd kept the faith, and now a crown of glory was laid up for me.

And for you too, if you do the will of God.

My last words to the flock were: "Little children, wherever you go, whatever you do, do it all to the glory of God!"

(He collapses in the pulpit, and is carried off by two DEACONS. HENRY MCPHEARSON enters with two shovels slung over his shoulder)

HENRY MCPHEARSON

The Lord giveth, and McPhearson puts you away.

Blessed be the name of the Lord.

(Doffs his hat)

Henry McPhearson here. Born 1873. Gravedigger.

Actually, I was assistant gravedigger.

The number-one gravedigger, the king of the gravediggers around these parts, at that time, was John Johnson, from the Johnson Funeral Home bunch. Now he was the expert. "Graveyard John" they called him, or "Johnny Two Shovels." Folks would be sitting out on the porch, and ol' John would go by, with his two shovels—oh yeah, you had to have two shovels. You got your sharpshooter right here, to break the ground up, then you got to scoop it out with the spade.

"Somebody musta died," they'd say, "there go Johnny Two Shovels." Folks was scared of us gravediggers. No need to be scared of me, I ain't gon' do you nothin'. I was just using the gift God give me to make a livin' for my family.

(A LITTLE GIRL enters with a lunch pail)

Ask my little granddaughter here, she'll tell ya, she wasn't scared of Paw-Paw.

(The child nods no, and exits. He opens the lunch pail and starts smacking on a sandwich)

Naw, it ain't the dead you got to fear, it's the living. Now some of them can give you the shivers.

We had a caretaker out here for years, kept this graveyard looking like a showpiece. Name of Miss Westbrook.

(MISS WESTBROOK looks in and waves)

Well, she was OK. But that sister of hers, name of Lump. Miss Lump. Now she was a one for the books.

(We see MISS LUMP in the shadows. Her face is powdered white, with lipstick smeared all around her mouth. She has on a hat, veil, and long gloves. She is engaged in ritual)

(Whispers) Hoodoo. Folks was always going backwards and forwards outta her house, all times of the night. Black and White folks. I'd catch her out here in the cemetery, all times of the night, vexing the dead.

MISS LUMP

Some people are ill at ease with the living—with their constant striving to perform. The dead are not so, they're kind and hold no judgments. They smile at me as I dip my hands into the stream of their memories, and splash them over me in the moonlight.

(Catches HENRY MCPHEARSON watching her)

Leave me.

I am accepted among the dead and cannot be vexed with the living.

(HENRY MCPHEARSON retreats under the ladder to nowhere. MISS LUMP exits slowly)

HENRY MCPHEARSON

Yep—crazy as a loon.

But me, ol' McPhearson, I was just making a living. Burying folks and making up headstones. Now them headstones was a step-by-step process.

Most of the folks was poor and couldn't afford nothing fancy. So I'd put down a paper marker. And hope it wouldn't fly away before they could get a tin one made up. Then, when they got hold of a little somethin', they'd put up a wood marker, which would rot away over the years. Then finally some of 'em would save up enough for me to pour up a block of cement and chisel their loved ones' names in it:

Gone But Not Forgotten.

At Rest.

Beloved Son.

Beloved Wife.

Asleep in Jesus.

Now the so-called rich ones could afford a slab of stone. Wasn't many of them at first: the Milligan-Roland Plot, the Brock Family Plot, the Spencers.

And I'd make a little extra sometimes pouring cement steps for folks who could afford 'em. Now see them steps over yonder? Poured them up for Abe and Lucy Brown.

(HENRY MCPHEARSON exits as CHURCHELL FULCHER enters)

CHURCHELL FULCHER

A horse is a vain thing. And I guess he ought to be. He's a beautiful creature, and he sho' nuff know it. Name's Churchell Fulcher. I learned blacksmithin' around the racetracks in Richmond, Texas.

I was born 1886, died 1960. From a boy up, I always admired hosses, the way they built. You have to have the right set of muscles to be able to stand like that, and sleep on your feet?

Somethin' real manly about a horse.

My wife, Fannie, said I was strong as a horse. We were married forty years and lived at 1409 Robin Street.

My wife's grandma got feeble and had to come up from Georgia to live with us—Miss Adelaide Green.

Now she was a hoss of a different color. But we got along just fine. She said I had a mind like a hoss. I took that as a compliment.

Magnificent animal, the horse. I jest love to see 'em standin' on their feet—in good fittin' pairs of shoes.

(ANTHONY MOORE sweeps into the room in ballet slippers)

ANTHONY MOORE

Go west, young man, go west. And so I went west to Los Angeles, and I loved it. Loved it!

The mountains, the ocean—Houston's such a swamp. I wanted to be a dancer, but a Negro man couldn't pursue a dancing career in Houston, Texas, in the 1920s. So I went to Los Angeles. And I danced! And danced!

(He proceeds to do a balletic piece with vigor and strength. He falters, coughing)

But I got sick and died out there. They brought me back home and buried me in College Park. I was Anthony—call me Tony—Moore. I was a gift! Born—Christmas Eve, 1890. Died from the consumption, December 10, 1925.

(As he exits, a young woman, LUTISHA RIVERS, is down on her knees, retching)

LUTISHA RIVERS

I knew them canned vegetables tasted funny. Don't know why I messed with them, I like my vegetables to come straight out the ground. I woke up that night soaking wet with sweat. Couldn't breathe, and my heart felt like it was gonna quit on me.

I couldn't stop throwing up. It was coming outta both ends.

I hadn't never felt that bad before in my life.

Felt so bad, I wished I could just die. And I did.

May 2, 1900. Lutisha Rivers, fifty-five years old.

(She leaves, and an ebullient ARTHUR GOODIE enters, sniffing the air)

ARTHUR GOODIE

Hey, they barbecuing over there.

You know some of them barbecue pits is sittin' on top of graves?

Yeah, they rest their barbecue racks on the headstones.

Barbecuing . . .

Now I could teach 'em how to barbecue, yeah.

Had a secret recipe, yeah! I come from Louisian', so you know when he come to cookin' this here old boy know how to throw down!

Ask anybody in the Ward about Arthur Goodie, they'll tell ya.

Everywhere I'd go, they'd make me cook.

In the Army, I was sergeant over the mess hall.

I cooked in all the best restaurants in town, and whenever the kinfolk got together I had to do all the cookin': étouffée, gumbo, boudin—I'm talking about blood boudin, chère, what most folks say they won't eat—but they ate this here old boy's!

Oh yeah, chère, I could make it taste so good, it make you want to slap yo' pappy.

(The band strikes up a Zydeco tune. TWO BOYS enter, one dancing, the other playing a washboard)

And they couldn't have Zydeco without Arthur Goodie! Et toi, et toi, et toi! Laissez le bon temps rouler!

(He exits, followed by the TWO BOYS)

(A WOMAN sits on the steps. A folded American flag is placed in her lap)

WINNIE JONES

When Solomon died, I thought about going crazy, but I didn't know how.

Solomon was all I had. Our families disowned us when we converted to the Jewish religion.

At his funeral they folded up his flag—he was a WWI veteran, y'know—and laid it in my lap. That's when I first thought about going crazy: a woman all alone, sitting there, holding his flag.

And then when I was sittin' shiva, moaning and crying, I thought about Jacquelyn Kennedy.

Thought about how she carried on after her husband died, and they'd laid his flag in her lap. And I decided to go on.

Anyway, I was too old to go crazy. I knew I'd see Solomon again one day soon, so I made up my mind to live until I died.

Winnie Jones. Shalom!

(A BOY runs out)

HARRIS ROBINSON

(All in one breath)

It was 1900, when I was nine, and it was the day before the Fourth of July, 'cause on the Fourth I was going to 'Mancipation Park, and eat watermelon and red soda water, and all kinda good stuff, and play ball, but first they was gonna read the 'mancipation pocumation, but I was in Butler's Brick Yard, 'cause I was the boy-round-the-house there, and the malaria come back on me and I died *(exhales)* and so I didn't get to go to the park. Thank ya, bye!

(He runs off, runs right back on)

Oh, my name is—was Harris Robinson. Bye!

UNKNOWN

Nobody was more surprised than me when I died.

I was pouring syrup over a short stack of flapjacks that morning when something slammed into my chest, poleaxed me—first I thought it was gas—but it drove through me like a stake!

Then I knew whatever this was, I wasn't gonna survive it. Them flapjacks sure looked good too.

(He drifts off, and P.R. JOHNSON enters, singing loudly. His WIFE joins him on the broken-down couch)

P.R. JOHNSON

Hi ho, hi ho silver, hi ho, hi ho silver!
Hi ho, hi ho silver, hi ho, hi ho silver!
Hi ho, hi ho silver, hi ho, hi ho silver!
Hi ho, hi ho silver, hi ho, hi ho silver!

Big Joe Turner.

Boy that was the song in the forties.

I saw him in person once at the Eldorado Ballroom . . .

Humph, funny the things you remember when you dying—not Big Joe Turner—but I kept seeing this old crazy woman, walking down the street, singing that song with all her might—

Hi ho, hi ho silver, hi ho silver!
Hi ho, hi ho silver, hi ho silver!

Me and my wife were sitting on the porch, drinking our coffee, when she went singing by, early in the morning.

She didn't have 'em all, everybody in the neighborhood knew that.

Singing just as loud. Hair white as snow, but she wasn't old, and she wasn't dressed right—had on some kind of old robe, and house shoes.

She waved at us and kept right on going.

Hi ho, hi ho silver, hi ho silver!
Hi ho, hi ho silver, hi ho silver!

From then on, me and my wife couldn't think what the woman's real name was, 'cause after that all we called her was "Hi Ho Silver."

"Hey honey, there go Hi Ho Silver!" And we'd fall out laughing.

I couldn't stop thinking about that woman the day I died.

My wife was sitting there by my side.

I wanted to hear her laugh one more time before I died.

She reached for my hand—

"P.R.? P.R.?' You got anything you want to say to me honey?"

(Whispers)

Hi ho, hi ho silver, hi ho, hi ho silver!

(The couple laughs together one last time. A WOMAN enters, laughing)

NANNIE YATES COUNTEE

(Laughing)

Every time I think about how people jumped ship when they found out it was going to be a cemetery out here, I can't stop laughing.

Everybody was gung-ho for this land-buying project Papa had for ex-slaves to own land.

Until they told them they were going to put a graveyard out here.

Lord, what did they do that for?

Those Negroes abandoned Papa's project like rats jumping a sinking ship. Said they were scared of being "haunted."

—Now, they're all out here, haunting each other.

I was Nannie Yates Countee, one of the last ones to be buried out here. This place was still nice then, in 1969. I was born in 1882 to Jack and Harriet Yates.

I was the baby. As far back as I could remember Papa was a leader in Freedman's Town. He was the first pastor of Antioch Baptist Church, founded by men and women fresh out of slavery.

And three things he preached to our people: be on time, work hard and keep your property clean.

(Looking around)

His grave is over there, along the fence.

The one with the trash bags on top of it.

They named Jack Yates High School after him, did you know?

Oh yes! He taught all twelve of us children to believe in education. So, you can understand why I was a teacher. I wanted to prepare our young boys and girls to be a blessing to the community.

(TWO LIVE YOUTHS enter. The light changes to a shadowy blue—the light of the living in this world of the dead. When they speak we cannot hear what they say. It comes across as a dissonant, weird sound. They are here to hide stolen goods)

You know the Negro college that used to be across the street? Well, it's a juvenile probation department now. In the old days children would escape, and run through here to get away. Nowadays hey come here to hide stolen goods.

(The TWO YOUTHS stand before her. She tries to touch them—she cannot)

Oh, I just want to reach out to them, but I can't. I want to call out to them. "You're on the wrong road. Stop!" But I can't . . .

(She exits sadly. The TWO YOUTHS exit also as a GROUP OF EXCITED CHILDREN run on)

CHILDREN

Do you see him yet? Yes, I see him! Is he coming! Do you see him?

(Enter HOMER GREGG, a happy young man, singing)

HOMER GREGG

Happy days are here again,
The skies are blue and clear again,
The days are full of cheer again,
Happy days are here again!

(He engages the CHILDREN)

That's the song I was singing the day I was killed!

I was always happy!

Always had a lotta drive!

A lotta get-up-and-go, always wanted to be somebody!

If I'd lived longer, I woulda made a mark on this world.

I died when I was only thirty-one, May 24, 1928, injured on the job!

I could do all kinds of work.

I was a waiter at W.P. Price!

(At each job, the CHILDREN ooh and aah, and the DRUMMER gives a rim shot)

I was a delivery boy for Battlesteins Department Store!

I helped build the coliseum.

(DRUMMER does a roll ending in a rim shot)

And then in 1928, I got the best job of all—driving a truck!

(The CHILDREN are agog with delight)

Me and my wife moved into a house on Colorado Street.

I was set!

I was on my way!

I was going to be somebody in life—but I died—young!

   (*He gestures in a vaudeville fashion, the CHILDREN do not respond*)

Come on kids, you're killin' me here—

   (*The CHILDREN start to sing, he joins them but cannot continue, he exits in a
   dejected fashion*)

CHILDREN

Happy days are here again,

The skies are blue and clear again,

The days are full of cheer again,

Happy days are here again!

   (*DR. CATO, DR. CATO'S WIFE and SISTER MATTIE enter. The CHILDREN
   shift their focus*)

CHILDREN

Dr. Cato, Dr. Cato! Give us some jelly beans! Please! Please give us some
jelly beans!

DR. CATO

They called me Dr. Cato, but I wasn't a medical doctor though.

   I was a doctor of the gospel.

   Sanctified!

   A physician for the weary soul.

   My wife and me had worship in a little grocery store we owned.

   See those steps there? They used to lead to our little store. During
worship service, while we had our eyes closed, praying, the little children
would sneak jelly beans out of my pockets.

DR. CATO'S WIFE

Sister Mattie would be singing and writing out her grocery list.

SISTER MATTIE

(*Singing*) Bread of heav-ven, bread of hea-ven, fe-e-e-d me 'til I want no more!

   Bread—sugar—butter—flour—'taters . . .

DR. CATO'S WIFE

We could always count on Sister Mattie for a caramel cake and a covered dish. In the wintertime, we'd have a little potbelly stove, and sometimes the sparks would shoot out from it—

   (By the stove [the pulpit] SISTER MATTIE stomps on sparks as she sings)

She'd stomp on the flames and keep on singing . . .

SISTER MATTIE

Bread of hea-ven, bread of hea-ven, fe-e-e-d me 'til I want no more!

   (One of the CHILDREN sneaks up behind her and pops a paper bag)

I'm gonna kick yo'—help me, Lord! Help me!

DR. CATO'S WIFE

All of a sudden Brother Johnson would jump up and sing his running song.

DOCK JOHNSON

I've been running, runnin', runnin', running . . .

DR. CATO'S WIFE

He's all right! The children used to make fun of him, until they found out what that song meant to him.

DR. CATO

My flock was small, but they came from all over—up Brazos River way, out Louisiana, Hallettsville, North, South Carolina, East Texas—

SISTER MATTIE

Me and my sisters came from East Texas. With all that red clay and tall pine trees. Every second Sunday in August, we'd go up home for the family reunion, and when we got back, red clay dust would be all over our clothes. We used to eat that red clay too, oh yeah, on a regular basis.

   Red clay was good for ya, everybody knew that.

   I mean, we'd just get a craving for it. They say it was the iron in it. You could use it as a poultice for strains and sprains too.

   —And kerosene oil. That was good for cuts and wounds you little children get during the summer.

I don't know what was in it—the clay I mean—but me and my sisters ate it all our lives from time to time, and didn't hardly ever get sick!

(*She exits, singing*)

Feed me 'til I want no more . . . !

(*DR. CATO and DR. CATO'S WIFE exit, the CHILDREN remain, eating jelly beans. ERNST LEMUEL enters. He never stops moving across the stage, slowly but surely*)

ERNST LEMUEL

My name is Ernst Lemuel. I came to America from Prussia. I am buried in College Park too. I lived nearby—over the bayou. I found love here. In America. In Fourth Ward. In Freedman's Town.

I was White. She was colored.

(*The CHILDREN are arguing over the jelly beans*)

CHILDREN

I got the red one! I want the white one! Give me the yellow one! I got black!

(*A GIRL tells a BOY to share with ERNST LEMUEL, he grudgingly obliges. ERNST LEMUEL takes a jelly bean and pats the BOY's head*)

ERNST LEMUEL

Love has a color of its own.

(*He shambles off*)

(*The CHILDREN are transformed to the family of ABRAHAM KING, lying on the battered couch next to his wife. They mouth the words that ABRAHAM KING speaks for them. All cluster around him, hugging him*)

ABRAHAM KING

"Daddy? Daddy?"

Every time I tried to slip away, they'd call me back.

"Daddy? Daddy? Can you hear us?"

I could hear 'em but I couldn't open my eyes or talk—that tuberculosis wore me down. They all sat around my bed, around the clock, so I couldn't escape into death.

"Daddy, we love you, Daddy."

I love y'all too, but I'm crossin' over. Abraham King, 1839 'til 1900.

*(He passes, but stands up slowly, following something we cannot see. His FAMILY
is still intent on the place where his body still [seems] to be. They have not seen the
soul leave the body. Not until later in the song does his wife sense the death, and the
FAMILY collapses in grief onto the battered couch. ABRAHAM KING makes his
way to the ladder to nowhere, slowly ascends, and turning out to the audience, opens
his arms in benediction, as JACK FRITZ enters and talks over the music. He will in
turn take up the hymn, as does everyone)*

Precious Lord, take my hand,
I am weak, I am worn, I am tired . . .

JACK FRITZ
"He still got so much life left in him" they said, whiles I laid there dying.
I went down hard, 'cause I was young and I was strong. My name was
Jack, Jack Fritz. I was a laborer, I had these muscles, and I could pretty
much tackle anything came my way. But that blood poisoning thing snuck
up on me. I snagged myself on a rusty nail, the next thing I knowed my
whole body was raging with poison.
  *(He takes up the hymn. WOMEN walk in, singing, and leading CHILDREN
  who slowly move into a line of CHILDREN lying on the floor—a sampling of
  the hundreds who died young. Sounds of INFANTS and YOUNG CHILDREN
  coughing and whining)*

WOMEN
Frank Sessums, twelve years old, acute bronchitis; Alice Young, eight
months, three days, convulsions; Beatrice Maxville, one year, eighteen
days, infant cholera; Marshall Johnson, seven months, eighteen days,
infant cholera; Child Misher, one year, infant cholera . . .
  *(The MEN and WOMEN continue to sing. One voice overtakes them all, and all
  fall silent as this great gospel voice gently leads the hymn to a conclusion. A slow,
  muffled drumbeat has built in rhythm to the hymn, and it transforms into the quicker
  beat of a young heart. A YOUNG GIRL slowly separates herself from the line of
  silent CHILDREN and begins a slow revolution, almost the dance of a baby still in
  the womb as it moves in the amniotic fluid. The heartbeat stops. She speaks)*

SESSUMS INFANT
Stillborn. The Sessums infant.
  Born, though I was never alive. Can you be born, if you never lived?

Still, I was born on March 10, 1900, to Will and Emma Sessums, and I was buried in Potters field near Strangers' Rest.

(SESSUMS INFANT is now facing ABRAHAM KING on the ladder. He extends his arms to her, and she moves toward him, singing "Precious Lord." As she reaches a high note, JENNIE PERRY of the boisterous Perry family bursts in)

JENNIE PERRY
Hi!

We were the Perrys! We were a sociable lot!

There used to be a houseful of us. Now there's a plot-full of us.

(She laughs and calls out names. The CHILDREN come to life, and the COMPANY scurries in. All answer to their names and everyone calls "Lavonne" who is always late)

Jimmy! Anita! Genevieve! LaBertha! Hazel! Freemore! Selma! Eunice! and—

ALL
Lavonne!

JIMMY PERRY
We lived in a big two-story house on Robin Street—

HAZEL PERRY
And now we reside at College Park.

LABERTHA PERRY
Our house used to be the gathering place for family and friends!

FREEMORE PERRY
That large tomb out there is our home now, and nobody comes to visit.

JENNIE PERRY
Oh, but the fun we had growing up. Taking music lessons at Madam Rochon's, going to Juneteenth at Emancipation Park, and dressing up for De-ro-Loc!

ALL
What's De-ro-Loc?

JENNIE PERRY
Why you don't know what De-ro-Loc is? That's colored spelled—

ALL
Backward!
(Everyone thinks this is grand)

JENNIE PERRY
That's what we called our Fall Festival. The Whites had a carnival every year too, and it was Houston spelled backward. Not-su-oh.
(Everyone thinks this is grand. During the laughter, EVERYONE forms an outward-facing circle and poses)
Oh yes, we had a beautiful childhood!
And every year we took a family photograph by Mr. C.G. Harris.
(C.G. HARRIS enters hurriedly and prepares to photograph them)

C.G. HARRIS
Watch the birdie. Say cheese.
(There is a flash. The pose is broken. These lines are spoken by MEN, WOMEN and CHILDREN as they represent the different vocations, with one lone male voice singing out on the cabinetmaker's line)

ALL
Che-ee-ese!
We were teachers and soldiers, movers and shakers, mothers, fathers, and cabinet makers.
We were the Perrys!
(They exit swiftly, noisily. The Lavonne character stays on, transforming into an UNKNOWN character. A WOMAN is left in the chair, a MAN on the ladder to nowhere)

UNKNOWN
I used to walk through this graveyard when it was nice and green, and wonder what it would be like to be dead, lying in my nice cool grave with my hands folded.
It wasn't so much that I wanted to die, just sometimes I didn't want to be bothered.

I decided to kill myself once, when things weren't going right between me and this fellow I was seeing.

I went to this café and there he was, jitterbugging with this woman he'd met.

I didn't say anything.

I just walked straight past 'em into the kitchen.

I knew the cook who worked there kept a can of potash on a shelf over the stove.

I remember the radio was playing, as I swallowed that potash down.

The cook was quick thinking though—he took a can of bacon grease that he saved to cook with and poured it down my throat.

I throwed up all over that man's kitchen.

My throat was raw for a while afterwards, but I was all right.

I lived a long time after that incident, and I was glad I did!

(She exits quickly. We see a figure sprawled on the battered couch, eyes open, motionless. Only the lips move, and a tear from the eyes)

SHENETTE CLIFTON

Got stabbed in a beer joint on West Clay back in 194—aaah.

(She can't remember. It is hard for her to focus)

My name was Shenette Clifton, and I could always take care of myself, but I didn't know that tramp had a knife on her though.

She surprised me.

Cut me. Cut me bad.

I didn't know what to do, so I took off running out the screen door.

Seemed like if I could just make it home to Mama, I could . . . but the blood was pouring outta me.

I thought I was running, but I musta fell down, 'cause all of a sudden, I was laying flat of my back. Looking up at the stars.

I coulda just reached up and grabbed a hand full of 'em.

I remember that.

And, you know those birds that start to sing when it's still night, and you can't see no light, but you can feel the light and you can smell the light?

Well, they were singing.

Just a-singing.

And I looked around and the world was so beautiful, and the stars were so beautiful and I just—

(Her breath fails. The eyes extinguish. WILFRED PRICE speaks from the ladder to nowhere)

WILFRED PRICE

I was a hack driver, what you'd call today, a limousine driver. I had a full load, a wedding party of White folks that day. I was in a hurry to get home to my wife Melissa and my three daughters—Ethel Mae, Myrtle, and Hazel. Hazel was going to play the piano and sing for the family that evening, and I promised I'd be home early.

(HAZEL PRICE, his daughter, enters. A clumsy piano picks out the halting song she sings)

HAZEL PRICE

Listen to the mockingbird, listen to the mockingbird . . .

WILFRED PRICE

So I was in a hurry, and never saw the train coming.

Everybody in the vehicle was killed.

I would never return to my family.

But finally, one by one—Melissa, Ethel Mae, Myrtle and Hazel—they joined me.

Wilfred Price, born 1868, died 1913.

(The band produces the SOUND OF THUNDER as they exit, and OPHELIA LEMUEL sits in the chair, speaks. Two GIRLS bring in her gloves, a stylish hat and umbrella)

OPHELIA LEMUEL

They're having my funeral today, so you know it's going to rain.

Ophelia Lemuel, born May 1875.

Oh, they laid me out like a queen.

I don't go anywhere looking any kind of old way.

(She holds a pose at center. JANIE LEMUEL rises and speaks knowingly)

JANIE LEMUEL

Oh yes, we laid Ophelia out in style. I was her sister, Janie Lemuel. Ophelia was always stylish.

(She moves in a circle around OPHELIA LEMUEL)

She was the bee's knees, she was the cat's meow, she was—well, I just wished I'd looked half as good at my own funeral.

And we did it all ourselves too.

Back then, colored folks didn't too much go to undertakers.

The body stayed right at home.

The undertaker would come, put 'em on the cooling board and do the embalming. And then they'd call for the moanin' women.

(TWO WOMEN enter, moaning under their breath. They escort OPHELIA LEMUEL to the chair, seat her, and primp her)

They'd prepare the body for visitation.

They'd bathe and lotion her down, press her hair—didn't have to worry about burning her none—put on her makeup, then lay her out in the parlor so folks could stop by and pay their respects.

(One of the WOMEN places a large black satin bow on the back of the chair)

Then at church, they tied a back bow on her seat so nobody could sit in her seat for a while. So Ophelia was still the center of attention—oh yeah, she loved to be—

(She is not allowed to finish. THREE MEN enter, escort her politely but forcibly off, and sit on the three steps, heads in hands, miserable)

OPHELIA LEMUEL

But my mourners' bench was filled with my three husbands . . .

Oh, how they wept for me!

(The HUSBANDS wail)

Now my first husband was Will Jackson—

WILL JACKSON

It took a lot to rile me up, but now Ophelia, you had to walk light around her, else she'd gather up the children and go to her folks' place. Sometimes I think she'd try to get mad about any little old thing, just so she could leave the house.

'Cause Ophelia was courting on me. Oh yeah, I know she had her—paramours—when we wasn't together.

Still, we had four children: Mabel, Monroe, Homer and Susie.

I was Will Jackson, born 1870, in Waller County.

(He sits on the steps, particularly jostling one of the MEN near him)

OPHELIA LEMUEL

M'dear was right. It's always best to have your own.

—You can't live with these men. They were all so jealous, even Will, and he was a easy type man to live with.

Even he didn't understand me having friends.

Just friends.

Like my good friend, Mr. Gregg here . . . Now, he was a friend.

MR. GREGG

Indeed. We had a son named Homer, born—

(MR. GREGG and MR. JACKSON slowly rise at the same speed, saying the same thing together)

MR. GREGG / WILL JACKSON

(With dawning knowledge) In 1897, died May 24, 1928 . . .

WILL JACKSON

They said some things wouldn't be revealed until we crossed over . . . !

OPHELIA LEMUEL

—And my third husband, Richard Roberts.

RICHARD ROBERTS

We had a child together, born in 1900. Had a bad hurricane that year. Flooded out everything. Me and Ophelia got divorced in 1910 . . .

OPHELIA LEMUEL

And I moved back in with my daddy—

(She moves swiftly to an OLDER MAN behind the pulpit. RICHARD ROBERTS exits slowly)

HORACE LEMUEL

Horace Lemuel. Born 1855 in Louisiana, moved to Washington County, Texas, when I was a young man, and got married to Susan Toliver. Before we got divorced, we had nine children—Ophelia, Ann, Douglas, the twins Mary and Martha, Janie, Charlie, Willie, Luvesta, and Clara.

Even though me and their mama wasn't together and I'd taken a second wife, who up and died on me, even through all of that, I always let my children know they could come to me, no matter what.

And I believed in working hard, so I'd have a little something to give 'em.

And I believed in giving to the next fellow, lending a helpin' hand if I could.

Other words, I tried to be a Christian man.

I died in 1911, at fifty-six years of age. Thankee.

(He exits. SHEP MCGOWEN is at the steps. He speaks thickly)

SHEP MCGOWEN

My name was Shep McGowen. I was a boarder with Horace in 1900.

I was down on my luck, didn't have no place to stay, 'cause I'd got sick and lost my place.

Somebody had give me some food though, but I didn't have no place to cook it.

It was some sausage and beans and some hoghead cheese, I was dyin' for it.

I had cancer of the throat.

But I felt like if I could just get somewhere to cook it, I'd be able to eat it. Horace Lemuel let me use his kitchen.

I cooked the food, but I couldn't eat it.

He let me board with him until I died. It wasn't long.

(He exits as SUSAN TOLIVER LEMUEL enters and sits on a rung of the ladder to nowhere)

SUSAN TOLIVER LEMUEL

The *Titanic* went down in 1912, and my hair started to fall out that same year.

Nerves.

The next year I died on February 14. I was fifty-six years old.

I was Susan Toliver Lemuel, Ophelia's mother.

I was born in February too, y'know?

—Ever notice how a lotta times people die the same month they born in?

I still can't believe it—the *Titanic* went down!

It was unsinkable.

That weighed on my mind all that year.

Now I look back, I realize it was sign of what was going to happen to me.

I couldn't get it outta my mind, kept seeing it going down slow—it took a while, y'know, to sink?

Now the year before that, Horace passed.

Oh, we'd been divorced for years.

And even when we were married, we always had our separate households. M'dear believed in that. She always told us girls, "Maintain your own." So, I did that. To please M'dear. Even though I had nine children, and sometime I felt like I wanted to try and live with Horace, but I didn't want M'dear to think that I just had to have a man.

But now, here we are, me, Horace, and the children all together now. Ain't that funny?

(She laughs a strange little laugh)

Horace left a little property when he died, and I went to court to try to get it, but they said it was all tied up, 'cause Horace had been in some kind of "enterprise" with some White man named John Norwood.

That made me so nervous, my hair started coming out in clumps.

And all the while I'm thinking about those poor souls trapped under the water, hollering and screaming.

Then I said, "Well, those rich people had all that money, and they went down—I ain't gon' worry about tryin' to get Horace's little bit."

(She pauses. She laughs again)

Ran into a iceberg!

Couldn't they see that big old iceberg?

But life is like that, ain't it?

One minute you going along fine, music playing to beat the band, and then bam!

You sunk.

(She scuttles off as JOHN NORWOOD, a rustic White man, enters. He has a plug of tobacco in his jaw)

JOHN NORWOOD

This here cold weather remind me of hog-killing time.

One time a city boy asked me, "How come you have to slaughter 'em in the winter, Mr. Norwood, how come you can't kill 'em in the summertime?" I said "Boy, you can't slaughter no hog in the summer. How you gonna preserve 'im?"

(Raucous laughter that goes into a cough)

City boy.

But now me and Horace, we could talk about things like that.

We were both farmers.

He was from Louisiana, and I was from Hempstead.

Both my folks were born in Alabama, but I was a Texas boy.

Now—I never taken nothing from Horace. Matter fact, I gave to him, he was a friend of mine.

He got in a little bind from time to time, like that time Ophelia came back home, with all her children, plus he was always helping somebody out, so I loaned him some money, from time to time.

He couldn't pay me back in cash, so he put me in his will, is the reason I was trying to get it probated.

But I never could.

I'm John Norwood, and I was born in 1874. I'm buried out here in College Park, 'cause I used to live with the colored folks, right up the street there.

> *(He clumps off. As he goes, he spits tobacco juice, and the DRUMMER zings the cymbal as the juice hits it. FRANCES TOLIVER enters. A gaggle of CHILDREN follow her)*

FRANCES TOLIVER

I was always a independent woman.

I was always head of my own household.

I was Frances Toliver, and I lived in this house in 1880.

I was sixty-nine years old and still strong. My baby daughter Susan, who was twenty-three at the time was living with me, with her three babies, Ann, five, Ophelia, three, and Douglas, one.

My sixteen-year-old granddaughter Jane and her five-month-old baby girl was living here with me too.

And my servant Henry Bell. Yes, my servant. That's how I listed him on the 1880 census. He lived on the premises, and he helped me out at a little café I had up the street. So, he was my servant. He wasn't my son, and he wasn't my husband, and he certainly wasn't my paramour.

He was my servant, and I paid him. That's how you do business.

I was born in Virginia in 1811.

When freedom come I walked to Louisiana.

Never looked back, didn't miss nothing in Virginia, but the Virginia hams.

I farmed for a while in Louisiana, then ended up here in Houston, Texas, in Green Pond.

That's what they called this part of Freedman's Town back then, on account of when it rained, the water would stand for days and turn green.

(The CHILDREN scoff)

Oh, y'all didn't know that? I bet y'all thought it was called Green Pond 'cause a little green pond used to run through here?

Naw children, it used to flood so bad out here, the men and boys would catch big old crawfish. That's when it used to be a slough here, where we got that good ole red clay from.

CHILDREN
Grandma, Grandma, we hungry!

FRANCES TOLIVER
Hush now, children, listen and you might learn something. They used to have baptisms in the bayou too, y'know—

CHILDREN
We hungry, Grandma—

FRANCES TOLIVER
Hush now, I'm trying to talk to the people—the water ran clear then, and it had this silvery sand in it that made you glow.
(PEARL LIGHTS, a candidate for baptism, enters, escorted by REV. YATES. With them are four DEACONS, each with an [imagined] depth pole to probe the bottom of Buffalo Bayou)

CHILDREN
Grandma, Grandma, we want to go to church, we want to go to Dr. Cato's church, etc.

FRANCES TOLIVER
Aw hush, y'all just want some jelly beans. The deacons would go out and mark a good spot with these long poles they had. Then you'd wade in,

and the pastor would dunk you in the water and you'd come up glowing with the silver sand and the Holy Ghost!

(PEARL LIGHTS enters the space between the deacons. After REV. YATES's blessing, she falls back into the arms of the DEACONS. Cloth is passed over her, in a motion like water. She emerges, thrown up by the arms of the four DEACONS, throwing a spray of silver dust into the air)

REV. YATES

I now baptize you, Pearl S. Lights, in the name of the Father, the Son, and the Holy Ghost!

PEARL LIGHTS

Thank you, Jesus!

I went in the bayou stained with sin! I came back up whole again!

ALL

Let the light from the lighthouse sh-iiiiine on me.

Shine on me-eeee, shine on me,

Let the light from the lighthouse, sh-iiiiine on me . . . etc.

(We are suddenly in the interior of DR. CATO's little grocery store church)

DR. CATO

Won't you come, won't you come? All are welcome, saint or sinner. Won't you come into the light with the saints?

ALL

Let the light from the lighthouse shiiiine on me.

Shine on meeee, shine on me.

(The COMPANY forms into pairs to be married. The time ranges from the Jumping of the Broom ceremony to a 1970 event. Appropriate music adorns each swift vignette)

DR. CATO

Dearly beloved—

We are gathered together to witness the union of this man and this woman in holy matrimony.

Adaume and Heile, Dayton and Eliza Hunt, Gus and Ester Holt, Andy Nathaniel and Lucinda Smith, Arthur and Harriet Fulcher, Ada and Arthur Goodie, etc.

Do you promise to love one another in sickness and in health, for richer, for poorer, until death do you part . . . ?

ALL
I do, I do.
>*(Before our eyes, children are born, grow, die, adults grow older, and pass on. REV. YATES observes all, blessing them as they swiftly go through the processes of life)*

REV. YATES
Ashes to ashes, dust to dust, as we lay this beloved husband and wife, father and mother . . . brother . . . sister . . . child, to rest.
The Lord giveth and the Lord taketh away.

ALL
Blessed be the name of the Lord.
>*(REV. YATES finishes his blessing. As DR. CATO speaks, the COMPANY comes to life, in preparation for the good food that always follows life events)*

DR. CATO
Oh yes, we had a blessed time. We were always looking for occasions to come together—hayrides on Juneteenth, church picnics, Emancipation on the Fourth of July—

HARRIS ROBINSON
Yahoo! The Fourth of July!

DR. CATO
All were welcome to our church activities, no matter what their religion. They came from Bethel, the Church of the Nazarene—some of our Methodist friends would come and eat a hound's bait. Everybody was always willing to come to your wedding or your funeral, one, and bring their famous dishes—
>*(MARIA BINGHAM SESSUMS enters)*
Welcome, Miss Sessums!

MARIA BINGHAM SESSUMS
Your forgiveness in correcting you, Reverend. That's Mrs. *Bingham* Sessums—

(She sees LUCINDA BARTON and approaches her)
Oh! Miss Barton! What did you bring?
(SISTER MATTIE interrupts her)

SISTER MATTIE
Plain ol' hoecakes—what did you bring?

MARIA BINGHAM SESSUMS
I brought Southern buttermilk biscuits.

SISTER MATTIE / MARIA BINGHAM SESSUMS
What's your recipe?

SISTER MATTIE	MARIA BINGHAM SESSUMS
2 cups yellow cornmeal	4 cups all-purpose flour
1 cup all-purpose flour	2 tablespoons baking powder
2 teaspoons baking powder	1 teaspoon salt
1 teaspoon salt	1½ teaspoons sugar
1 tablespoon sugar	1⅓ stick butter, softened
¾ cup buttermilk	1¼ cups buttermilk
½ cup water	¼ cup water
½ cup bacon drippings	¼ cup butter, melted

REV. YATES
Thank you Sister Mattie, and Sister *Bingham* Sessums, for your wonderful Breads of Life. Now, what about something that would stick to a reverend's ribs?
(This is a seduction)

REBECKA WOODARD
I've got something, Reverend. Pan-fried rabbit smothered in gravy:
　1 cup all-purpose flour
　½ teaspoon salt
　2 *young* rabbits, rinsed, and cut into 8 pieces
　1½ stick butter
　1 medium onion, *diced (flirtatious smile)*
　3 cloves garlic *(winks)*, *minced*
　1 medium carrot, *diced*

1¼ quarts *brown* stock
2 ribs celery, *diced*
2 teaspoons *cider vinegar*
1 tablespoon *finely* chopped fresh thyme *(bats her eyes)*
Salt and freshly ground *black* pepper to taste—
Reverend . . .

REV. YATES
Praise be to God!
    Sister Woodard, I'm sure going to save a spot for your *wild*, young rabbits.

DR. CATO
    (Defusing the heat)
Well, Brother Goodie—I'm sure you got one of your Recipes for Life—
    (He notices REV. LIGHTS too late)
    Oh! Rev. Lights! I know you've got a recipe—
    (BOTH MEN answer)

REV. LIGHTS / ARTHUR GOODIE
    Jollof rice. Slap yo' pappy gumbo—
    (They challenge one another)
    What's your recipe?
    (Overlapping)

REV. LIGHTS	ARTHUR GOODIE
3 1-lb. broiler chickens	1 hen
½ cup vegetable oil	2 ropes smoked sausage
4 large onions, chopped	handful of dried shrimp
4 large cloves garlic, minced	2 lbs. fresh shrimp
¼ cup grated fresh ginger root	1 bunch green onions
6 cups long grain rice	1 large, white onion
1 3-oz. can tomato paste	2 or 3 bay leaves
curry powder to taste	bell pepper, good size
2 tablespoons salt	pinch of Cayenne pepper
2 lbs. carrots, peeled, diced fine	enough prepared white
1 lb. string beans, ends trimmed	flour to make a good mix
cut into 1–1½ inch pieces	chicken stock
10 cups chicken broth, or water	roux

REV. YATES
It all sounds so good . . . but we need something *sweet*.
  Sister Barton, I know *you've* got something sweet—

LUCINDA BARTON
Oh yes, Reverend I got Southern *sweet* potato pie . . .

ALL
Aaaah! Ooooooh! Ohhhh!

LUCINDA BARTON
1 stick butter
  ½ cup packed, dark (kisses back of her brown hand) brown sugar
  1 cup cooked and mashed sweet potatoes
  ½ teaspoon ground nutmeg
  3 eggs, *lightly* beaten
  ⅓ cup corn syrup
  ⅓ cup milk
  1 teaspoon salt
  1 teaspoon vanilla
  And don't forget, one unbaked Southern pie shell!
    (*ALL fall into raptures that subside, slowly. In the silence*)

DR. CATO
What about the fried chicken?

ALL
2 cups flour
  tablespoon of black pepper
  2 eggs, beaten
  ½ cup water
  a pinch of salt
  lard
  And a nice, young, fresh, plump pullet!
    (*All exit quickly, speaking as they go*)

ALL

Humm, this sho' tastes good—You make the best cakes—I love your hoecakes—Wish I had your green thumb—Thank you for helping me out—I'll save a slice for you—I'll save some for you—I'll save piece for you—there's plenty left to go around—Money's 'scase, but we seem to always make do—money's 'scase as hen's teeth, but look like we always have food—Bye!—See you soon! If the Good Lord's willin' and the creek don't rise—If the Good Lord says so—If the Good Lords says the same . . .

AFRICAN ANCESTOR

And the richest one in the village is the one who gave away the most . . .

<u>END ACT I</u>

ACT II

~~~~~~~~

SCENE I

A happy horde of people tumble onto the stage, laughing, talking, pointing—they await the entrance of RICHARD ALLEN, running for office again at this carnival event. The crowd starts to sing a campaign song, which is interrupted by the entrance of RICHARD ALLEN.

ALL

Mother, mother can I go out to swim?

> Yes my darling son, if you hang your clothes on a hickory limb.
> And vote for Richard Allen!

RICHARD ALLEN

Friends! Houstonians! Countrymen! Lend me your ears!

> I come to bury someone, not to praise them.
> The evil that men do lives after them, the good is oft interred with their bones.
> So, let it be with Caesar.
> And with myself, Richard Allen.
> Born 1826, died 1911, state legislator, representing Harris and Montgomery Counties . . .
> > *(Applause from the people)*
> It has been said by my opponents that Richard Allen was ambitious, that I used my friendship with influential Whites of my day to become a wealthy man, with a grand home and car and several downtown businesses.
> Let the record reflect that Richard Allen will not bore you with words in his own defense!
> For I come to bury Richard Allen, not to praise him.
> > *(Applause)*
> So, I will make no mention of the fact that he rose up from slavery to become one of the first of his race to help draft Texas laws, and that he introduced a bill which created the Gregory Institute to educate ex-slaves! Did this in Richard seem ambitious?
> But I will make no mention of these things.

For I come to bury Richard Allen, not praise him.

(Applause. REV. YATES enters, to acclaim from the assembled people)

Reverend Jack Yates! My friend and colleague!

We are most honored to have you in our midst!

ALL

Rev. Yates, why don't you run for office?—We're always saying you ought to run for office—You're a good man—You got streetlamps for our street—You got us Emancipation Park—You know we'd vote for you—We want a man of God, not a godless politician—

REV. YATES

No, my children! I work for the Lord.

I believe that the colored preacher should stand aloft and free from the pernicious and pecuniary entanglement of politics.

I commend my brother in Christ, Richard Allen, to you.

We have worked together on my projects for the colored community, and we will continue to help and encourage one another.

I must remain in the pulpit, and let Brother Richard have the platform.

I cast my vote for Richard Allen!

(REV. YATES moves to the top of the steps that lead nowhere)

RICHARD ALLEN

Thank you!

So I will humbly make no mention of the fact that I helped build Antioch Church, and raised money for Emancipation Park for the recreation of your souls—so vote for Richard Allen!

(The group breaks into two segments, dueling musically. One sings the campaign song, the other, "Will the Circle Be Unbroken?" The hymn wins)

ALL

Will the circle be unbroken, by and by, Lord, by and by, etc.

(As the dust clears, we have the large family of the Nathaniels in evidence. REV. YATES has been transformed into HARDIN NATHANIEL)

JENNIE NATHANIEL

I'm Jennie Nathaniel, I was always just a mother.

Me and my husband Hardin here were blessed with twelve children.

HARDIN NATHANIEL
We were both from Limestone County.

JENNIE NATHANIEL
Oh, the times we had with them children.

HARDIN NATHANIEL
We were born in 1867—
    (A CHILD drops a tambourine, loudly)
—and back in my day children were supposed to be seen, and not heard.

JENNIE NATHANIEL
People said I spoiled my children.

HARDIN NATHANIEL
You did let 'em talk too much.

JENNIE NATHANIEL
I believed in letting the children express themselves. They were so smart
and wanted to be so many things.

HARDIN NATHANIEL
Just settle on something.

JENNIE NATHANIEL
So, I told 'em, "Children, just get a good education, and you can be
whatever you want to be!"
    But me, I never wanted to be anything, but a mother.

HARDIN NATHANIEL
Lord, those children could eat!

JENNIE NATHANIEL
I'd call 'em to supper.
    (They call rapidly. The CHILDREN answer, variously and loudly)

BOTH
Annie Lee, Elonzo, Arthur, Benjamin, Lizzie Lee, McKinley, Andy, Gertrude, Alvin, Roosevelt, Esta B, and Fred!

JENNIE NATHANIEL
Come and get it!
> (ALL exit singing "Will the Circle Be Unbroken?" MARY and MARTHA stay on, doing "Sanctified Dancing." The tempo changes. The hymn becomes slower and slower. The DANCERS follow suit. The tune segues to "Mary, Don't You Weep, Martha, Don't You Moan." The music stops abruptly as they speak)

MARY
Martha, is that you?

MARTHA
Mary, is that you too.

MARY
My sister!

MARTHA
My twin!

MARY
In life we shared everything.

MARTHA
In death we do too.
> (As they move in a circle, in an admiring and loving embrace, MARY notes an absence)

MARY
Sister, my marker is missing.

MARTHA
Then I'll share mine with you.

(In a graceful arc, MARTHA moves MARY offstage, and remains on to become MATILDA. STEVESON. MR. STEVESON enters to the Strauss waltz, "Roses from the South." They dance, then speak)

MR. STEVESON
Me and Mrs. Steveson had a model life.
   When she died, I put on her tombstone, "A model wife."

MATILDA STEVESON
I tried to be. I got his tea.

MR. STEVESON
I dressed her well.

MATILDA STEVESON
As you can tell.

MR. STEVESON
She set a good table, didn't talk too much.

MATILDA STEVESON
I always responded to his touch.

MR. STEVESON
I was a member of the United Brothers of Friendship, and Mrs. Steveson had membership in the Daughters of the Mysterious Ten, the Married Ladies Art and Charity Club, and of course, she was very active in church.
   (MATILDA STEVESON pops open a fan and fans herself)
   We were in great demand in Houston's Negro society, and often attended soirees at the famous Lubin home, where we were privileged to meet Paul Robeson and the great Booker T. Washington.
   I made a good living as a railway mail clerk, and of course, Mrs. Steveson kept the house, and prepared me well-balanced meals.
   Me and Mrs. Steveson had no children, so we were free to travel as we pleased.
   Truly this woman was beyond compare. She was my friend, my wife, and my lover.

MATILDA STEVESON

Shortly after I died, Mr. Steveson married another.

I was Matilda Steveson, born 12 August 1867, closed my eyes in death 28 January 1925.

(The couple moves toward one another. They seem about to begin a new dance, but pass each other sightlessly. A MAN enters. He picks up some of the trash that litters the stage, chooses a pamphlet and begins to read. It is a funeral program, his funeral program)

ELDRIDGE JACKSON

"Eldridge Jackson, sunrise June 19, 1875, sunset June 17, 1924. A Houston business leader, survived by his second wife Blanche Bradley, and a host of friends and relatives. His body will be interred at College Park Memorial Cemetery . . ."

(Turns over the program)

Is this all there is? Humph, I made up a many of these in my day. I operated a successful undertaking business for almost twenty years. Put away many of these people buried out here. Did excellent work. I started out with one horse and a hack, expanded little by little.

I loved life! This program doesn't mention that.

Me and my young second wife used to throw parties in our quarters above the funeral business.

We entertained until the break of dawn.

They gossiped that we were making merry over the dead. But we lived up there, that was our home.

My business was the dead, but I was alive. Alive!

When my first wife died, I was still in the prime of my life, so I married my secretary. Where was the sin in that? Live, drink and be merry, for tomorrow you die! So we ignored the whispers, the wagging tongues . . . and kept our secrets . . .

(The muffled figure of A YOUNG WOMAN approaches him. He caresses her cheek and she drops her shawl around her shoulders. She seems transfixed)

—If I disclosed all of the proposals that I received from the grieving widows of their freshly dead, dearly departed . . . well, we undertakers are the soul of discretion. We understand that grief can cause one to behave in strange ways.

(He exits. The YOUNG WOMAN suddenly becomes aware of her surroundings)

ANNIE TAYLOR

We loved each other so much, my husband and me. We'd just been married a few months when I got what you called Bright's disease, which just means I couldn't pass my water. We had a little place in Sixth Ward on Center Street. My husband took care of me all the two years I was sick, until I passed away May 5, 1900.

(She starts to leave, then stops, and speaks in a kind of wonder)

I was twenty-two.

(She seems to float into darkness. ADDIE DAVIS screams. She is captured in a red light. She is experiencing delirium tremens)

ADDIE DAVIS

I was twenty-three, and I went out screaming—DTs.

Doctor told me I was gonna drink myself to death, so I tried to stop, but I had so much hard luck in my life, I couldn't take it sober. They put me on "the ward." They kept asking me all them questions, to see if I was in my right mind—

(She sits in the chair, seems strapped to it. The only light in stage is a slash of bright white light across her darting eyes. She struggles to control her wildness and the hideous DT visions)

"What's your name?" Addie Davis.

"How old are you?" Twenty-three.

"When were you born?" 1877.

"Where do you live?" 1405 St. Emanuel.

"Who's the president of the United States?" Joe Moontalvo.

Asking me all those crazy questions!

I knew who the president was, it was—uh, uh, uh—Teddy Roosevelt, wasn't it?

I wasn't crazy, I was just drunk.

(The woman who will become MAHALIA TEAL enters, places her hand on ADDIE DAVIS's forehead and soothes her. Across the stage, a YOUNG MAN steps into the light)

BROCK FAMILY MEMBER

You're not going to find my plot out here.

Fancy apartments are sitting on it.

My mother taught me one thing in life—you have to live and let live.

On the 1920 census, they listed me as a mulatto. I'd been called worse. By Black and White.

It was a new day, and my generation demanded that we be called Colored, with a capital "C."

My mother was White, my father was a colored man. You didn't see much of that in my day, but it was a fact.

My father had done well in business, better than a lot of White men. Some of my father's family members said that was the reason mother married him. But all I ever saw in my parent's home was love and respect.

We lived in the colored section of town. My mother's family disowned her. A colored person had to have a pass to go across town where my mother's parents lived.

There were ten of us children. And thank God we had each other because sometimes the colored didn't accept us, and all the time the Whites didn't accept us.

You might not like me—even though I never did anything to you—but you have to let me live, you have to let me come to the trough. Even the lions in the jungle let the other animals drink, even they know you have to live and let live.

(MAHALIA TEAL is combing out the hair of the woman who played ADDIE DAVIS—ADDIE DAVIS is now a wealthy WHITE WOMAN that MAHALIA TEAL is ministering to)

MAHALIA TEAL

My name was Mahalia Teal. I was born in Louisiana in 1888. In 1920 I was in private service at a mansion in River Oaks, in Houston, Texas. I was married to William Buck Misher at the time and had two children by him. Buck was mean, and he was in State Shaw Prison. Life was hard, taking care of the children, my ailing parents and other relatives.

I remember one day the White lady I worked for asked me how we colored women could be so strong.

(As she combs out the White woman's hair, she imitates her voice and mannerisms)

"I just don't see how you colored women do it, Mahalia—stay so strong, I mean. Why, if it was me, Mahalia, I think I'd just collapse in a heap on the floor . . ."

I looked at that woman.

But she was a kind White lady, she always asked after my family, and gave me extra to take home. I could see she didn't mean no harm.

(*MAHALIA TEAL moves out in front of the woman in the chair. Her manner is that of a thorough district attorney, impartial, relentless, yet strangely gentle—the facts do all the accusing. As each new "fact" is mentioned, a different group enters: her CHILDREN, her MOTHER and FATHER and A CHILD, a MAN and a CHILD—the people in her life. They watch, motionless and silent*)

So, I just told her: "Ma'am, is this a time for weakness, when my mama is sick and my children is still at home, and my man's in jail?"

"Is this a time for weakness when the rent's due and food got to be bought and my man just lost his job?"

"Is this a time to be weak when bills got to be paid and folks is looking to you and your man just got lynched?"

"Is this a time for weakness when the fire is low, and the house is cold?"

"I don't have no time to be weak, ma'am, 'cause weak women don't live in row houses like me, they live in mansions."

"Meaning no disrespect, ma'am, 'cause you a kind White lady."

(*She backs away, guided by two of her children. The woman remains in the chair, transfixed. MAHALIA TEAL's children transform into another GROUP OF CHILDREN*)

HELEN HILL

Yes, Jesus loves me,
Yes, Jesus loves me,
Yes, Jesus loves me,
For the Bible tells me so.

Helen Hill, two.

SARAH MOORE

Sarah Moore, born December 9, 1872, died December 18, 1881. Nine.

THOMAS CRAWFORD

Thomas Kyle Crawford, born May 17, 1909, died June 12, 1919. Ten.

ARLETTA FLETCHER

Arletta Fletcher, born January 17, 1894, died 1899. Five.

MILDRED FLETCHER
Mildred Fletcher, born September 5, 1892, died November 22, 1893.
One.

DANIEL HUGHES
I was a college man. Tuskegee.
   My parents had big plans for me, big plans.
   I was the only boy, you see. I had four older sisters, but I was the only
one to carry on the family name.
   As a boy I went to a private school. I wanted to be a reporter, to
report on my times, so in high school I got a job at the *Houston Post* as a
copy boy.
   Then later I worked at the *Texas Freedman Press*.
   I had a nose for the news, I wanted to report on my times.
   I died before America went to war, but I knew it was coming.
   'Cause I had a nose for the news.
      (*The lights change to a fractured mix of sharp light and shade. Half-seen figures
      enter. Some stand in darkness, some in shards of light. These are the "Unknown"
      who sleep in Strangers' Rest*)

UNKNOWN
Unknown.
   You just don't know nothing about me, do ya?
   I'm just a restless stranger buried in the section of the cemetery called
"Strangers' Rest." Unknown.

UNKNOWN
Maybe I was one of the colored businessmen on the first floor of the
United Brothers of Friendship Building.

UNKNOWN
All you know is that I was.

UNKNOWN
Not who I was.

UNKNOWN
Or what I was.

UNKNOWN

Get your tickets now!

Don't wait 'til Saturday and have to stand in line!

Get your tickets to *Hallelujah!* playing at the South's finest Negro Motion Picture House, 711 Prairie Avenue, the place to be on Saturday night.

Maybe I was O.P. Dewalt, the owner of the Lincoln Theatre . . .

Business had been good that night, the lines were long.

I was feeling especially good because my theater had got first showing of the *Hallelujah!* movie.

The owners of the Majestic Theatre down the street didn't like the idea of a colored establishment like mine beating them out on first showing.

They usually got first and made the colored people sit up in the balcony.

But with me getting first showing, I was cutting into their colored ticket sales.

They sent warnings that I'd better not show it, but heck, I had a business to run.

I'd locked up for the night, and was getting ready to go home.

My buddy Julius Frazier worked for me, and ran the projector.

I told him I was on my way home, and started down the stairs.

Midway down—

(*The DRUMMER strikes a single shot*)

—a bullet ripped into my spine.

I tumbled down the stairs. While I laid there dying, I spotted Julius standing at the top of the stairs with a gun.

"Et tu, Julius?"

So, maybe I was O.P. Dewalt, theater owner.

Then again, maybe I was Julius Frazier, murderer.

UNKNOWN

Unknown. Maybe I was a fat housewife.

UNKNOWN

Or maybe I was a barber who formed his own barbershop quartet . . .

(*FOUR MEN among the UNKNOWNS step in and sing "Amen" with sweet street-corner harmony. The song trails off and the MEN drift to the periphery*)

UNKNOWN

Maybe I was all these people.

UNKNOWN
Maybe I was none.

UNKNOWN
Who knows?

UNKNOWN
Nobody knows.

ALL
We're all unknown.
> (The UNKNOWNS drift away, leaving behind an excited YOUNG GIRL and a
> WOMAN still trapped in her chair)

VIOLA P. COLE
Mother was going to let me wear silk stockings, do you hear me, real silk
stockings to the dance at the Pilgrim Temple!—If I got well.
  They were real silk, you could hold them up to the light and see.
  Mother was going to let me wear them them—if I got well.
  But pneumonia set in.
  So, I asked mother if she would buy me a pretty pink casket, and lots
and lots of flowers, and invite all of my friends from the Heroines of
Jericho.
> (Curtseys)

My name was Viola P. Cole, and I died in 1921, when I was seventeen.
> (From the chair, LILLIE HORTON, a twenty-five-year-old paralytic, speaks.
> She is twisted and moves with difficulty. Her speech is torturous. She struggles to be
> understood. As she speaks, the difficulty leaves her and she addresses us clearly, as the
> intent of her words comes across. She returns to the tortured state before being freed
> by her passing)

LILLIE HORTON
Born 1887.
  Trapped!
  Couldn't hardly put one foot in front of the other.
  But I always wanted to fly.
  Earthbound.
> (She starts to come out of it)

Couldn't do much for myself, but they said I had a pretty smile.

Earthbound.

Children made fun at first but when they got older they understood how hard it is just to put one foot in front of the other—and I'm not talking about walking either.

Earthbound.

I watched all the girls my age, dancing, while I longed to fly.

(Starts to get twisted again)

Earthbound.

I died January 17, 1912.

Earthbound no more!

(From the ghost radio we hear Otis Redding's "Dock of the Bay." LILLIE HORTON exits, as though dancing. ARMENDA WILLIAMS is revealed, a child of the sixties)

ARMENDA WILLIAMS

All I wanted to do was dip my big toe in the bay—talkin' about the Monterey Bay.

I wanted to go to the Monterey Jazz Festival in California one mo' time before I went to be with the Man Upstairs, on June 6, 1972, rest in peace.

(She makes the peace sign)

Peace.

I knew I wasn't going to be able to rest in peace unless I got to go to Monterey and catch the set of a buddy of mine who played the sax.

Loved me some saxophone!

The soul brother took first solo on a medium tempo blues. I mean, my man tore into that tune, blowing chorus after chorus of fast cascading bop lines, alternating high intense shrieks with deep muscular honks . . . !

When I got home, White contractors were riding up and down the 'hood, trying to buy up land. And they bought it up too.

But the big news in my family was: the bell at Bethel had been stolen.

Naw, lemme put it this way: it had "come up missing"?

That bell musta weighed a thousand pounds and it had been at Bethel ever since anybody could remember. But it "come up missing." It was made out of pewter, and it had the whole history of the church written on it . . .

I died before they found out who took it.

I was one of the last ones buried out here . . . peace.

*(She drifts off. The music shifts to ragtime, Scott Joplin's "Maple Leaf Rag."
JOSEPH HALLER, an energetic fast-talking barber, enters and sets up his chair,
center. Enter a FATHER and SON. The SON is scared. The FATHER insistent.
JOSEPH HALLER seats the SON and soothes him as he clips efficiently)*

JOSEPH HALLER

My name was Joseph Haller, born in 1870.

My mama's name was Annie. She used to tell me stories about slavery, and how she was so glad I just missed it.

She used to always tell me to make good use of my freedom, do something with your life.

So I became a barber.

*(He has finished with the SON. The SON and the FATHER start to exit, but
JOSEPH HALLER nabs the FATHER and sits him down for a quick trim)*

I had a uncle come outta slavery, N.H. Haller, and he became a member of the Texas State Legislature.

"Do something with your life."

In this here shop, I seen 'em come and I seen 'em go.

*(He's finished with the FATHER and SON. They exit. The SON comes back on
immediately as the SHOE SHINE AND CHORE BOY. Another BOY comes in with
a broom to sweep)*

You know what they say about us barbers? All we do is philosophize. Clip a little hair, give out a little philosophy . . .

*(REV. YATES enters. The SHOE SHINE AND CHORE BOY takes his coat and
hat. REV. YATES sits in the chair. JOSEPH HALLER begins and the SHOE SHINE
AND CHORE BOY gives him a shoe shine. The BOY with the broom listens)*

JOSEPH HALLER

Now, I'm no scholar, but this one thing I know—Christopher Columbus sailed the ocean blue, and he discovered America in 1492.

And you know why? He could smell land.

Oh yes, he could. He could smell it.

Columbus kept telling 'em, "If you want to find treasure, just outfit me a boat, and let me go to where the dark people of the world are. 'Cause that's where all the treasure is."

REV. YATES

It's been less than thirty-five years since the "Dark Race" was set free.

And in those years I have thought on the treasure of the colored people. The treasure you speak of.

I don't know what Columbus was really looking for.

Gold, or bodies for bondage, or souls.

I do know we were captured.

Our bodies were conquered.

Our souls were sequestered.

I know it looks like all the advantages of conquest go to the conqueror.

But I believe that history will show that the conquered, those who suffered, and yet were able to endure, are the ones that will really come out victorious.

Did God put us in the fiery furnace of slavery to test us? I do not know.

I do know that God pulled us from the blast and bellows of our suffering.

I do know that, with faith, all dross and impurities will be burned away, and we will come forth from our sufferings as pure gold.

This is the treasure of the dark people of the world, and of all people who endure great suffering.

(The SHOE SHINE AND CHORE BOY helps him on with his jacket and hat. As he exits, HENRY AMMONS enters to get to the barber's chair, but a self-important J.D. COLLINS cuts him off and scoots into the chair first. HENRY AMMONS retreats to the stair to nowhere, where he is soothed by a shoe shine)

J.D. COLLINS

I went to the barber every Saturday morning for a haircut and a mustache trim.

I always had to be well groomed—I was the first Negro clerk to be employed at the main post office downtown. I was right out front, all eyes were on me, so I had to do my best to look my best at all times.

(JOSEPH HALLER trims his mustache. With each family member's name he clips a hair. It makes J.D. COLLINS's eyes water)

My wife Sallie, and my five children, J.D. Jr., Hortense, Sarah, Florence and Louise, were all so proud of me.

(He rises, smarting, and shakes JOSEPH HALLER's hand vigorously)

I served as a deacon in my church, so I believed that my job was a blessing from the good Lord. My name was J.D. Collins. I was born July 27, 1876, and died March 9, 1953. Thank you.

(He exits in a hurry. As HENRY AMMONS again makes his way to the chair, DOCK JOHNSON drifts in, distracted. JOSEPH HALLER indicates to HENRY AMMONS to let him be. DOCK JOHNSON sits in the barber chair)

DOCK JOHNSON

I was Dock Johnson, born in Virginia in 1840. I was always running, running. Sold from one owner after another, and I run off from 'em all! They said I was tetched in the head, 'cause even though they laid open my back with many stripes, I refused to be a slave.

(JOSEPH HALLER dusts the nape of his neck and reacts to the welts from ancient whippings. He seats DOCK JOHNSON with respect on the battered couch)

Finally, I made it to Texas, and laid low in them piney woods. I hid out in this big old hollow log. It was a snake lived there first, and he kept comin' back. I said "Snake, you got to go."

True 'nuff you was here first, but you can come and go as you please in this here country, but I'm just a colored man, and I got to have this here log . . .

(He sits in the battered couch and falls into silence. HENRY AMMONS takes his place in the chair)

HENRY AMMONS

Who moves the world? The railroad, that's who! H&TC, to be specific.

Freigh' trains.

Nothing better than the sound of freigh' trains clicking by, bringing produce, taking out steel, bringing in flour, taking out cattle.

No better thing than standing between the rails, and watching 'em go off in the distance.

I was a railroad man. Henry Ammons, born in Maryland in 1857.

I was a student of the tracks as a young boy. Hung around the tracks, walked the ties, sat at the feet of the masters of the railroad—the hobos. They'd hop the freights and complain about the railroad owners didn't know nothing about running a railroad.

I coulda run a railroad, but I was a colored man at the time. So what I could be was the shop foreman, so I kept things running smooth there.

(HENRY AMMONS exits and ISAAC ABNEY SR. enters like a little old crab, sideways, takes his place in the chair)

ISAAC ABNEY SR.

I used to live in a two story house on Hobson Street.

Hobson Street doesn't even exist anymore. They tore everything down on it to put up San Felipe Courts for the White soldiers coming home from World War II.

I could see the handwriting on the wall.

I'd look out my window and see these White contractors cruising through the neighborhood, looking . . .

I passed on in 1964. By then White folks had moved out of San Felipe Courts, changed the name to Allen Parkway Village, and let the Negroes have it—well, let the Blacks have it. *(Testily)*

That's what they started calling themselves before I died. Black.

"In my day Black was a cuss word. But they had these young Negroes on television, talking about they wanted to be called Black. And everybody was talking about something called gentrification." All that meant was they were going to fix things up, then raise the rent so high poor folks couldn't afford to live in Fourth Ward anymore.

(REBECKA WOODARD and LUCINDA BARTON enter. LUCINDA BARTON has cookies on a plate)

Saw a lot of things tore down in my lifetime. It used to be six thousand souls buried in College Park, then the contractors came through and decided to take some land and put up those fancy apartments all 'round. Some of them apartments sitting right on top of our graves! That's right!

LUCINDA BARTON

I heard the sound of bulldozers! I felt the ground shaking!

REBECKA WOODARD

Surely, they wouldn't plow up the resting ground of the dead?

DOCK JOHNSON

Couldn't rest in my hollow log, an' now they runnin' me out my grave!

(The junked-out televisions flicker on. We see a WHITE CONTRACTOR, in full color, addressing the audience and the characters onstage)

CONTRACTOR

Think high-rise. High-rise mausoleums. Picture it! They'll be just like the cemeteries in California! This is the 1970s. You Afro-Americans are becoming increasingly affluent. You've got the bucks! This is a great investment! I think you people are ready to bury your dead in style!

(*REBECKA WOODARD addresses the television images directly*)

REBECKA WOODARD
This little plot of land I'm in is land enough for me.

CONTRACTOR
Oh no! We have wonderful plans for the development of this cemetery! Wonderful plans!

(*REBECKA WOODARD addresses the television images directly*)

REBECKA WOODARD
Humph, my master had a "wonderful plan" for me too, when I was in slavery.

Had a plan to sell me and my chil'ren off to keep from going to the po' house.

(*The CONTRACTOR makes a sound of sympathy. REBECKA WOODARD flicks the television off. She engages the audience with vigor*)

So I runned off, with my two chilluns, and hid right under they noses. In the attic at Grandma Tillie's place. Grandma was a old slave who'd been set free, and mastah didn't mess with her. He let her keep my chilluns.

Space was so small, you couldn't even stand up in it.

But I hid out there seven years!

So, I been in a close place, a tight spot.

This here little plot is plenty elbow room for me.

I don't need no high-rise.

LUCINDA BARTON
Don't remove the old landmarks. That's what the Bible say—you remove the old landmarks, you confuse the chillun.

(*The TWO LIVE YOUTHS enter. The light changes abruptly to the shadow light of living people. They have come to retrieve their loot. LUCINDA BARTON exits, shaking her head*)

YOUTH 1
Where's my stuff?

YOUTH 2

It was right here, dog, I put it right here, under Johnson.

YOUTH 1

You said this place was safe, you said didn't nobody come out here, man!

YOUTH 2

They don't. But somebody musta been out here cleaning up.! Aw man, they musta threw our stash away with the trash, aw man!

YOUTH 1

I ought to kill you!

> (*The ghost radio lights up. We hear the voice of DOCK JOHNSON*)

DOCK JOHNSON (*Voice SFX over ghost radio*)

I ought to kill you.

YOUTH 1 / YOUTH 2

What's that?

> (*The televisions flicker to life. We see and hear a ghostly image of DOCK JOHNSON*)

DOCK JOHNSON

I ought to kill you. I ought to blow your head clean off!

> (*The TWO LIVE YOUTHS exit quickly. DOCK JOHNSON stands up slowly*)

"I ought to kill you. I ought to blow your head clean off."

> (*Chuckles*)

That's what I said to this big black snake that crawled up in my hollow log with me. But I let him go. I lived in that hollow log for two years and was glad to live there.

> (*The televisions flicker on. TWO WHITE CONTRACTORS, in full color, are discussing the development of the cemetery area. As the scene progresses, the entire COMPANY enters slowly, and silently watches the proceedings*)

CONTRACTOR 1

An unforeseen legal snag has developed, concerning the mausoleum. It has been discovered that the eastern portion of the property was not properly certified for burials, because it was not legally a part of the cemetery. And without that portion, the banks won't finance us—there wouldn't be sufficient parking space.

CONTRACTOR 2
No parking, no project: this is Houston after all.

CONTRACTOR 1
But don't worry about it, the mausoleum was just the first idea. We can always put up townhouses. More money in that anyway.

CONTRACTOR 2
Great idea! But what can we do with all the bodies, they're such a nuisance.

CONTRACTOR 1
Well . . . we can abate the nuisance.

CONTRACTOR 2
Huh?

CONTRACTOR 1
"The law says that any old cemetery that doesn't have perpetual care or a legal endowment fund, and is so neglected as to be offensive to the inhabitants of the section surrounding the cemetery, it may be abated, and its continuance enjoined."

CONTRACTOR 2
I love it when you talk like that. Let the dead bury the dead.

CONTRACTOR 1
Yeah, that's in the Bible somewhere—we'll use that! We'll use the "Good Book," put a spin on it, people'll believe anything, take it step-by-step, they'll forget everything!
     (The COMPANY assembled is silent. REBECKA WOODARD speaks)

REBECKA WOODARD
They do forget.

You know what they say about cemeteries: "The children pay a lot of attention, the grandchil'ren pay some attention, after that, don't nobody care."

JENNIE PERRY
Some of us cared! Some of us went as far as we could go.
　We did what we could, we laid the foundation—don't let that be forgot!
　Don't let us be forgot!

NANNIE YATES COUNTEE
We did more than lay foundations, we erected structures on those foundations, we obtained freedoms. As an educator, I was glad I lived to see the young people of my day tear down the "colored" and "White" signs, inch by inch, step by step, generation by generation, our people moved into the mainstream!

AFRICAN ANCESTOR
　(In Yoruba)
I was trapped in the arms of my time.

ANNIE TAYLOR
　(Translating)
I was trapped in the arms of my time.

REBECKA WOODARD
I was in a close place, a tight spot!

MAHALIA TEAL
And I said, "Ma'am, sometimes all we colored women have standing between us and damage to our loved ones is our bluff." My man woulda come to my rescue, but he was all bound up!

DOCK JOHNSON
In a hollow log.

UNKNOWN CHILD
A forgotten life.

UNKNOWN CHILD
A forgotten death.

RICHARD ALLEN
Who spoke for us? We had to find a voice!

NANNIE YATES COUNTEE
The man of God spoke for us. He spoke courage into our times and encircled us with words of hope.
> (*From now until the end of the play, there is music underneath, and weaving through and into the scenes. The music moves from words to humming to the melody, to words. First is "Will the Circle Be Unbroken?" Then, the gospel song, "Running, Running, Running!" which segues into "Step by Step"*)

ALL
Will the circle be unbroken, by and by, Lord, by and by, etc.

REBECKA WOODARD
That's the song the children would sing at homecoming. They'd spread out all over the grounds, hundreds of them.

LUCINDA BARTON
The women would sit at the graves, making the crepe paper flowers and exchanging recipes for food and for life!

REBECKA WOODARD
Oh, we used to have a hallelujah good time in the graveyard, when the preachers would start dueling it out in the Seven Seals!
> (*DOCK JOHNSON again makes his run around the stage. The COMPANY joins in singing*)

DOCK JOHNSON
I been running, running, running, running!

OTHERS
He's all right!

DOCK JOHNSON
Running, running, running, running!

ALL
He's all right—soldiers of the cross!

LINDA BARTON
Then the preachers would get to dueling it out with their preaching!
> (*The FOUR PREACHERS move into place and begin to orate, to top one another. The COMPANY continues to sing and hum under the entire scene until the end*)

REV. LIGHTS
I can see Sister Lucinda Barton, with her name, written down in the Lamb's Book of Life!

REV. YATES
And over there, I can see, Sister Rebecka Woodard, faithful to the end!

TENT PREACHER / AFRICAN ANCESTOR
And if I look real hard, in the spirit, I can see the little children, dancing around the heavenly throne!

DR. CATO
And over here, help me Jesus! I can see Mother and Father McGinnis. They didn't have much in life, but now I can see them walking on streets of gold!
> (*The DRUMMER turns the beat from the "Running, Running, Running!" hymn to complex African polyrhythm*)

AFRICAN ANCESTOR
I can feel the ancestor. Can you feel them? They've been with us all the time. They're bone of our bone, flesh of our flesh. Oh, we may have forgotten them in our minds and in our hearts. But the body has a memory!
> (*The DRUMMER turns the African rhythm back into the "Running, Running, Running!" hymn*)

REV. LIGHTS
I say I can hear . . .

REV. YATES
Tell me what you hear, preacher!

DR. CATO
Say I can hear Sister Hazel, with a voice like an angel, singing in the heavenly choir!

(*HAZEL sings her song to the beat of the "Running, Running, Running!" hymn*)

HAZEL
Listen to the mockingbird, listen to the mockingbird—

TENT PREACHER / AFRICAN ANCESTOR
And I can see Brother Johnson, he's not running anymore, he's not living in a log anymore. He's taken up residence in his heavenly mansion!

DOCK JOHNSON
Thanks be to God, I crawled outta that log and stood up like a man. Sometimes I had to wiggle my way out! But—

ALL
Inch by inch—

DOCK JOHNSON
Sometimes along the way I got scraped, sometimes I got stuck, but—

ALL
Step by step—

DOCK JOHNSON
Sometimes I couldn't move at all, I couldn't see it in my time, but—

ALL
Generation by generation—we kept moving.

AFRICAN ANCESTOR
I returned to African shores again as an African American.

ALL
Step by step!

REV. LIGHTS
A race of people were delivered from bondage!

ALL
Generation by generation!

REBECKA WOODARD
'Cause Jesus fixed it!

REV. YATES
But if we forget our past, we're doomed to repeat it.

NANNIE YATES COUNTEE
If you want to know your future, you must understand your past.

REBECKA WOODARD
Don't forget. Don't let us be forgot.

DANIEL HUGHES
Remember our times, so that you can build your own.

LUCINDA BARTON
Come learn of us. Tell our stories and discover who you really are.

ARTHUR GOODIE
Arthur Goodie can give you the recipe for life, yeah chère!

JOHN SESSUMS
Dedicate yourself to your mission in life!

REBECKA WOODARD
Our lives is over. Can't add to 'em, can't take nothin' away, 'cause a life is what it is.

REV. LIGHTS
But a person is all the things he—

WOMEN
Or she—!

REV. LIGHTS
Can become.

REV. YATES
I call heaven and earth to record this day for you, our descendants. We have set before you life and death, blessing and cursing: Choose life! Remember us. We are you. We had our good times and our joys.

TENT PREACHER / AFRICAN ANCESTOR
We had the sunshine and our songs.

REV. LIGHTS
We had laughter and dancing.

DR. CATO
Hope and victory.

REV. YATES
But if we had to go through the pain.

REV. LIGHTS
If we had to go through the darkness and the tears—

DR. CATO
If we had to feel the rain on our faces, feel the sadness and the pain—

TENT PREACHER / AFRICAN ANCESTOR
If we had to suffer our losses and our shame—

MEN
If we had to do it all over again?

WOMEN
If we had to do it all over again?
  (Beat)

ALL
We would do it all over—again.

WOMEN
We would choose life—

ALL
Again.

LUCINDA BARTON
You choose life!

ALL
And remember us. *(Whispers)* Remember . . . us.

LUCINDA BARTON
Y'all come back now, ya hear? And don't forget to bring the crepe paper flowers!
  (HAZEL begins to sing a cappella the gospel song "Step by Step." The CHILDREN join in. The ADULTS join in until the entire cast is singing and circling. When they reach the end of the song, the band keeps playing the melody, and the COMPANY takes a bow)

THE END

An Interview with Celeste Bedford Walker

July 31, 2021

Sandra M. Mayo

Philosophy

You are an amazingly prolific and talented playwright whose works have graced American stages from coast to coast over forty-plus years. How would you define your mission and has it evolved over the years?
I have been working for many years, and it has evolved, but what it distills down to, I think, what really drives and inspires my writing, is a passion to present the American Black in a holistic light—present this individual as a joyful, courageous, loving human being with dignity and unconquerable will to not only survive but thrive.

Formative Years

You came of age in a historically Black community in Houston during the civil rights movement. What are some of your unique or significant memories from this time?
I graduated from high school in 1965. And for me, that's when the movement really started to kick in. So I was still very young, and things were happening around me. We were seeing different events and news items on the TV about what was going on in the nation, but I wasn't necessarily participating then because I was in high school. I graduated at eighteen. But I do remember there were events being held at Texas Southern University at that time that we would hear about. Different Black Power activists would come into the city and would come to the university and speak. And I do remember seeing Stokely Carmichael. I don't know exactly when that was—if it was after I was out of high

school, if I was still in high school—but I was very young, and somewhere between eighteen, nineteen, and twenty years old, I went to hear him speak and just became so inspired and enamored with him and the movement.

What were some of your activities or memorable teachers or students at Jack Yates Senior High in Houston?
Well, it's in the historic Third Ward, the same ward that George Floyd came from. Actually, he and I were raised in the same housing projects, a generation apart. And the project is right across the street, almost, from Jack Yates. I remember going back and forth for lunch, and I remember always being late for class because I lived so close, just like right across the street, five minutes away. But I would leave out thirty seconds before start time. I remember how it was like an extension of home because it was so very close. Like I said, I'd go home for lunch. I stayed home until the very last minute. I'd run home in between classes sometimes to look at the television. I guess I shouldn't be telling those kinds of things.

Did you have all Black teachers at the school?
Yes. I do remember I had all Black teachers. I remember particularly my English teacher, Mrs. Wheaton, and then I had a Mrs. Gloria King, a Mrs. Lockhart—and Mrs. Gloria King was the one who really got me to thinking about writing. She entered me in some kind of writing contest. I can't remember what it was now, but there was a writing contest, and they chose three people from Jack Yates, and I was one of the three people. I had never even thought about myself like that. But I guess she could see when I turned in different papers that I had some kind of potential. So when she suggested me to be a part of it, it really, really was a turning point for me to see myself in a different light.

What was it like attending the historically Black Texas Southern University in Houston, where you studied English and journalism in the late 1960s? Did you have any unique experiences at Texas Southern particularly related to Black literature and culture or Black theater?
Well, I really became involved in theater later in my twenties, but I do remember going to plays, but not necessarily at the theater. I would go

to plays with friends. There was an urban theater group out of which the TV, film, and stage actor Charles Robinson came, who just recently died. I think he was on the board, and they had a theater group. I would go to their plays, but I didn't think of myself as a playwright. I was not taking theater classes. But we did take up Black literature or some of the Black literature at that time. But this was 1965, and a lot of Black Arts movement literature didn't start to kick off or be published until after 1965.

Right, I went all the way through my university bachelor's degree without having a course in Black studies.
I'm sure; I'm sure you did. I learned it from the community, not necessarily from the college.

How did your family life in the early years contribute to the creativity that led to playwriting?
Well, they were such creative people. Of course, they were not theater people. They thought theater people were crazy, but they were so theatrical. I realize now we were theater unto ourselves. I was the creative one; I was all writing, always writing poetry and essays and making them sit down and listen to it. And my mother, L. V. Bedford, was kind of like a director in the home. She directed how things would go, now that I look back and see their positions. My daddy, William Bedford, was like the executive director; he was also a singer. He had a voice just like Sam Cooke. I had a brother, Billy, who was a singer. My sister, Ree, should have been an actor. She was so dramatic. And the baby brother Harold was the audience to our shenanigans. So it was just natural. They were theatrical, but they were not part of the theater scene. They were always very, very encouraging and very proud of me, of my writing.

How did career activities, beyond playwriting, support or influence your writing?
When I started out young, of course, I was actually working on real jobs—quote, unquote, "real jobs"—in data processing. I started out like that, but then I've been blessed for several years with writing as my main thing. I have to give it to my husband: I have to give him, James Walker, his due for his support.

Creative Roots

What inspired you to begin writing plays?

Well, what actually led me to it—I was trying to write a novel, and while trying to write a novel, I discovered that I really had an affinity for dialogue. I really wanted dialogue, and I really wanted plotting for the scene, to develop a scene and put the characters in and let them talk themselves out of it. Then I thought, well, perhaps, maybe I want to write a play. But I had no idea of how that would go, so I decided to join a theatrical group in the Fifth Ward called the Black Arts Center. It was the same center that Loretta Devine came out of, but when I went to it, she had just left. I joined this group and auditioned for a play, and I got the role as an actress; it was horrible. I just wanted to see how things went. I met a group of people there at the center, a group of writers, and we decided to put together our own group called Writers Clinic Inc., founded by Alma Carriere. This group borrowed from the tenets and the themes of the Black Arts movement. We wanted to write stories about Black self-determination, and we wanted to write stories about our own culture. We were realizing that as Blacks, we had our own unique culture, separate and apart from the mainstream. We wanted our stories to talk about the beauty and the strength of Blackness. So that is how I evolved and found encouragement to consider stories that I wanted to tell important.

And the Writers Clinic helped you produce the first play?

Yes. The Writers Clinic Inc. Out of that group came my very first play, which was originally titled *Sister, Sister*, a play about polygamy, about a man who tries to have two wives at the same time, and of course, that's not going to happen. So it was a comedy. Writers, actors—mainly actors, directors, and set designers—evolved out of the group. It was a once-in-a-lifetime gathering where we were young, and with all of these people with all of these talents that we didn't even know we had, [we] came together, and each one's talent started to emerge. We all started out trying to act, except for the director, and each one's talent started emerging, and we realized, well, maybe I don't want to act, but I sure would like to work on that costume that you have on; I don't think the lights are quite right here. Why don't I try that? So each one kind of evolved into their own gift. So it was really just a once-in-a-lifetime, wonderful experience.

I'm still friends with many of them. Many of the actors have gone on to act in plays of mine.

Amazing, and it's wonderful that you were at that place and it nurtured you the way it did. And that says something about the cultural enclave in the Black community. That was the 1970s when your first play was produced with this group. Then you went on to have over thirty plays produced from coast to coast. How did you break into the theater world and achieve the admirable feat of having theaters all over the country producing your plays?
Isn't that something? I look back and I don't know myself except to say that as a young Black female writer, I had to also have a business sense about me. I had to know that if it's going to get out, I'm going to write it, I'm going to cast it, I'm going to have to push it, but I probably will also have to produce it initially. And I didn't realize what I was doing. I didn't realize I was producing per se, but I knew I had to gather actors, and thank God I knew actors. I had to gather them, and then I had to try to find some workforce to produce the play if I wanted to see it up. Things just kind of evolved; I didn't realize what I was doing.

Creative Style

How would you describe your creative process? How do you make it come into being? What inspires you, provokes you, evokes you?
Well, first, I guess, I really have a very vivid imagination. I started to realize that that was what was going on. I'm always thinking about something; I'm always looking at somebody, wondering what's really going on in their lives. I've looked at people as characters, and everybody I would meet, I would write a story about them in my head, even as I was talking with them. Sometimes I had stopped myself from that and just really dealt with reality, but imagination was a very strong thing, and different things would spark me. Sometimes it was driven by character, a certain character may come to mind, or I may see somebody who seems like they would be a key character in real life, and that would start me off. Sometimes it's a topic, a social topic or some topic of social justice, or something is in the news that comes up and it makes—it grabs my imagination and makes me wonder what really happened, and why don't I try to write what I think may have happened to offer insight into this

subject. So . . . it just comes at you. You may hear a piece of music—it just comes at you from many different ways, and you just have to kind of go with the flow.

What writers have influenced your work?

When I started out, I didn't see plays in real life so much as on television. The very first play, I must have been very, very young. I remember it was called *Come Back Little Sheba* by William Inge. I saw that, and I was struck by that, and for weeks after, my brothers and sisters and I would quote the lines from the play. And that Inge play was about a serious struggle; I do know why we could relate to it—perhaps because one of the main characters was an alcoholic, and we had a very beloved alcoholic in our community. So we could relate to that drama, and as I said, for weeks afterward, we would recite it: "Come back little Sheba, come back little Sheba." So [there's] that, and then of course, Lorraine Hansberry, and I think the very first time I saw Hansberry, it was on TV too. And that really got me because it was like, Is that my family on television? I mean, you really felt like it was you. Is somehow somebody coming into our house and capturing our lives and writing a play about us, and putting it on TV, and we didn't even know anything about it? Lorraine Hansberry. I also loved Neil Simon. I loved his comedy and his characters, then later in life, in later years, Ed Bullins, and then of course I read *Black Theater USA* edited by Ted Shine and James Hatch.

There were forty-five plays in that first collection.

It was a lot of them, I remember that, and I've read every one of them. So those were some of my influences.

You have written plays in all the major genres—comedy, tragedy, history, and other related subgenres. What influences the choice of genre?

I was mostly all over the place. I started out in comedy because I was young and everything was funny—for example, the husband, the wife, the husband tries to have two wives at the same time. So I started out with comedy, and then as things went along, I took an interest in more serious work. I started to notice different social issues and social justice or injustice issues that I wanted to try to tackle, like the Camp Logan riot. And so just whatever strikes my fancy. Some works lend themselves to musicals. I want to write about them, but I want another element in there to help carry the story, so that's musicals. And then I realized that I really do like to write stories that interweave community and social justice issues and people. I like the intertwined or familiar, or family things in the community and social justice, and of course historical plays. So just whatever. Whatever struck my fancy, I said, well, let me try to tackle this. I don't know how it'll come out, but I want to do it.

In the *Poetics*, Aristotle defined the major elements of theater as plot, character, thought, diction, melody, and spectacle. Which of these elements are primary or significant as you create a story on the page for the stage?
Often for me, and that's been a little weakness that I had in terms of plot, the characters usually drive me. I have to be interested in the character. I have to care about the character, and then I'll figure out what they'll do—unless it's a historical drama, which is why I love historical dramas because you know the action and the plot and the climax. It's already in there, so all I have to do is just try to weave the characters around the plot. But normally, I think about characters—except in some plays, like with *Camp Logan*, that theme, that subject of the insurrection here in Houston was the driving force, and then I supplied the characters.

What special challenges came with writing and producing your musicals? Do you write your own lyrics?
I wish I did write my lyrics. Now, I have written some lyrics—some very simple lyrics that a real composer can take and shape—but I have had ideas for musicals. And that is a challenge in that I can't write music. I do write the book and the dialogues. I do have plenty of ideas for when I meet a wonderful composer musician that can take my ideas and take what I have and turn it into music. I'm in the process of doing that right now with my play *Over Forty*. I'm interviewing some musicians. There is music that I want to add to it, and I have ideas, but I'm just tone-deaf; I can't sing.

Production History

Shortly after *Sister, Sister*, written in 1978, you wrote one of your most produced plays, *Reunion in Bartersville*, in 1983. What inspired this murder mystery?

I love murder mystery. That's what I cut my teeth on. Sherlock Holmes. I would skip class to go to the library and read Sherlock Holmes mysteries, never thinking that I would write one. But actually, what really inspired me was my dad talking about some kind of event that happened in a little small town in Texas called Bordersville, where somebody got killed. My dad always had stories, was always talking, always sharing different stories. Somebody got murdered in this small town called Bordersville. I thought about what if it was a class reunion where they all gathered. They found out that the wrong classmate had been put in jail with their testimony, and now the classmate comes to the reunion. I don't know where that idea came from, but I knew I wanted to write a murder mystery. I titled my play *Bartersville*, not *Bordersville*. So that's how Bartersville came about.

It was full of fear and suspense and comedy. It was very clear that you had either studied or were very familiar with the murder mystery genre.
Oh, I am. This is my favorite. I still look at murder mysteries every day.

Are there a few interesting production highlights you can share about the murder mystery *Reunion in Bartersville*?
Reunion in Bartersville has been around for thirty years. It was produced in Los Angeles by the Cambridge Players with Esther Rolle. It won the AUDELCO award for best revival of a play in 2019, produced by the Black Spectrum Theatre.

In 1987 you wrote the historical drama chronicling the 1917 military riot at Camp Logan in Houston. What experiences inspired you to develop this historical tragedy?
Camp Logan was a subject that I'd heard about all my life as a youngster in the community. It really evolved out of a piece of oral history. I would hear elders in the community sitting around talking about it, especially when there was some kind of a racial event that happened in the city. They would talk, whisper, and say, "We don't want another Camp Logan." Where was Camp Logan? And I would listen, and I would ask questions, and they would talk to me and tell me. We had a neighbor that lived right across the alley from us who had been involved with one of the men that was in Camp Logan. So I interviewed her and decided that I wanted to try to tell that story because I could hear the actual theatricality in it. I'd heard

it all my life, but I really hadn't paid any attention to it until I started to write. So I interviewed a neighbor across the street and also interviewed my grandfather who was a contemporary of the men that were in Camp Logan. Well, he was not in it, but he was of that same age group, and he had served overseas with them, so he provided context and worldview of that time. And of course, teachers—I had a teacher who had been a very young boy when it happened, Mr. Holland. I interviewed him when I was writing the play. He said he was a four-year-old boy at the time, and he remembered the soldiers just coming through, and he even had a picture with a bullet in it. They had fired into his house while he and his mother hid behind the sofa. So I gathered quite a bit of information orally, and I did gather some information from Texas Southern University library. I did quite a bit of research—oral—at the Texas Southern University library and the Julia Ides section in the Downtown Houston Public Library. I tried to get my hands on the transcripts of the trial, but they were sealed at the time. So I talked to people and interviewed people, and there was the book by Robert Haynes. It is the definitive book on that incident. So I had that as a reference.

What was the role of Mountaintop Productions in producing *Camp Logan* (1983) and several of your plays around the country?
Well, Mountaintop Productions evolved out of wanting to get the play *Camp Logan* out. I originally received a grant from the Carver Cultural Community Center in San Antonio through the efforts of one Mike Kaliski of San Antonio, who is also the coproducer of *Camp Logan*. And out of wanting to get that play out, I realized that I needed to form a company. And so Mountaintop Productions was created to tour *Camp Logan*. I got the title from my mother because she said, "You're going to go to the mountaintop." I created the organization, the company, and began to tour *Camp Logan* with the efforts of the coproducer Mike Kaliski. He'd call around to all the different universities and colleges and military installations. We did quite a few military installations, and it just took on a life of its own, especially during Black History Month. Sometimes we would do enough performances in Black History Month to last the year in terms of funds. But, and so we toured, like I said, all around the country, including the Kennedy Center. We were one of three Texas acts chosen to be represented at the Texas festival at the Kennedy Center in, I think it's 1990, 1991. We toured the Regal Theatre in Chicago, we

toured California, we toured the South. We had a Southern tour and an East Coast tour. Then we did a Texas tour and a midstate tour. So we were out there really for about fifteen years. We were out there so long, some of the actors aged out of their roles.

Mountaintop Productions then went on to produce other plays with the production company after *Camp Logan*.
I did produce a few others. I produced *Brothers, Sisters, Husbands and Wives* with Ella Joyce of *Roc* TV show. I did *Reunion in Bartersville*, that's in Louisiana—and of course, [I worked] with other companies. Other theaters have done the plays many, many times.

You often, with Mountaintop Productions, collaborated with a local theater company.
Sometimes, yes, sometimes I did, depending on what the play was, but the main play I did with it was *Camp Logan*, and now I'm bringing Mountaintop Productions back.

You wrote several additional comedies and historical dramas in the 1980s and 1990s. The historical pageant *Distant Voices* (1997) had you wading through cemetery records and gravestones in a historically Black cemetery in Houston. I understand it was commissioned by the Ensemble Theatre in Houston. What was most interesting or rewarding about this ghostly journey?
That particular piece is one of the adventures of my life. It was one of the highlights for me of my writing career. And it was a finalist in the Susan Smith Blackburn Prize. I think I was the only Texan—the last I checked, that may have changed now—to be a finalist in the international Susan Smith Blackburn Prize. But that play was brought to me by the Ensemble with an idea from the director, Peter Webster. He had been driving through Fourth Ward, and something drew him to this wooded area of town. He was driving, he had to turn around and go back. He didn't know why, and he just walked through the woods, and he discovered a cemetery in the wooded, overgrown, weeded lot. He said, "Oh, this is a story; somebody has to write this story." And he went to the Ensemble. Eileen Morris, bless her heart, said, "Oh, only Celeste can write that." And she pulled me in on it, and I am ever, ever so grateful because it was really a journey. It was really a community effort. It was a combination

of genealogy, history, and writing—the whole community was a part of it. Our genealogist, Shirley—I have to mention her, Shirley Whitmore—she dug through the files, through the census files. I told the story from the headstones, and also once we found a character, a person on a headstone, we would go and see if we could find out a little bit more about their lives other than what was on the tombstone. And that was often in census records or genealogy records, and Shirley Whitmore really helped with that. So it was really, really, really a collaborative effort. The actors, they just brought it all to life. It was just . . . it was a journey.

It's an amazing piece. I really enjoyed the setting and the voices, all the different diverse voices in the piece, and it takes place in a cemetery as well, that was spooky. There are all kinds of people in it—from uneducated to the college educated.
Absolutely, because it covered from 1840 all the way to 1970. People were buried in there from that period of time. That's why I called it *Distant Voices*. There are all different kinds of voices. And one more story I remember about *Distant Voices*: I was at a production performance of the place, sitting in the dark, watching the play unfold, and somebody next to me grabbed my hand and said, "That's my mother's story. Thank you for writing it. Now I have an ending; I have closure." She said her mother had died in the fire. And I tried to capture that with just a few words because we only had a few words. Something from the census said, "Died in fire," or something from the headstone said, "Beloved mother." You just try to put it all together. It was like a forensic exercise in writing. And you just started putting meat on the bones of these characters. I didn't know who the lady was, but the person sitting next to me said, "That was my mother." This is what you live for.

I'm so glad you shared that story. So that brings us right to the Ensemble Theatre. The Ensemble Theatre in Houston began producing your work in the 1980s. What are a few highlights of your ongoing collaboration with the Ensemble?
The Ensemble has just really, really, really been so supportive . . . they just really have opened the doors and given me so many different opportunities. Not only there with the Ensemble, of which I will talk about, but she's so very generous, Eileen tells other theaters about me, so they have really, really, really helped my career to take off. I think through

my very first play, *Sister, Sister* (*Once in a Wifetime*), that's how I met Eileen. Eileen and her husband at the time came with their little four-year-old boy to audition for the role. This was before she became the artistic director. George Hawkins was the artistic director of the theater then, and I remember George Hawkins told me, "There's a place for you; there will always be a place for you here at the Ensemble, Celeste." And this was before they got to Main Street.

From a little shack to a beautiful corner on Main Street.
A whole big corner and a whole destination and their own bus stop.

Yes. They have arrived on Main Street, Central Downtown Houston.
So I've actually been with the Ensemble Theatre since the very beginning. They did *Reunion in Bartersville*; they did *Distant Voices*, *More Than Christmas*, and several others, including *Sassy Mamas*. They've always included me in their good fortune, their grants. *More Than Christmas* came out of the BOLD Theatre Women's Leadership Circle, and Eileen was [part of] one of the five women-led theaters that they chose to receive the grant.

The Ensemble is really a jewel in Houston, and they are nationally known. Eileen is a former president of the Black Theatre Network. She knows people from across the country. It's an award-winning theater; they have won many local awards, and [Eileen] has won national and regional awards as a director. So the connection with them, it just brings together a wonderful talent with a wonderful theater.
 Your creative journey has included several plays focusing on women's issues, starting with *Sister, Sister* in 1978 (changed to *Once in a Wifetime*), but also including works as in *Over Forty* in 1989 and the enduring popular hit *Sassy Mamas* in 2007. What do you see as the through line or relationship between some of these feminist works?
You made me realize that, Sandra, the through line of the women in my plays, starting with *Once in a Wifetime* when I was in my twenties. These women were grappling with two women with one man, and they decided, look, we're going to be friends. We're going to get together on this. And they came together, and there's a trick at the end where the wife actually uses or decides to become a friend in order to hang on to her husband. That was the very first, I think, kind of feminist thread that went through. And then, as you said, *Over Forty*, each one of these plays has the same

characters at different stages and ages in my life. In my twenties, *Once in a Wifetime*—thinking about a man. And then in my forties, these women, like me, in *Over Forty* have had some life under their belts. They're in different situations. One is the divorcee; one is a judge, a very popular judge; she's never been married. Another one has been married, but she's over forty and she hasn't had a child. And then, the other one is a religious person who has been married, raised children, and went the traditional route, then suddenly realizes that, hey, I haven't lived life. So women in their forties, they're at that stage where they are losing their youth, and they realize it, and they're trying to hold that back. Then *Sassy Mamas*, they're the older ones, they're in their fifties, sixties, and seventies maybe, and they have lived life, and they have decided they're going to please themselves. They're at a stage in life when they have pleased family, they have pleased a job, they have pleased the community. Now they are just going to please themselves. And they do so with younger men for different reasons.

I noticed that in each one of these, the women bond—the mother and daughter bond to outsmart the man and the other woman in *Once in a Wifetime*. All three of them at some point come together. And I noticed in *Over Forty*, it's a women's retreat where they are bonding and remembering and sharing and uplifting each other. In *Sassy Mamas*, [there are] three friends, three very different friends, but there's a bond that helps them and strengthens them and nurtures them and gives them courage as they try to pursue their lives after forty.
Women bonding, I see that as a thread. I see that coming from each one of the plays; I see that in all the plays, and that's just very interesting to me. Thank you for throwing that in, Sandra—that is bonding, absolutely, yes.

From coast to coast, several companies have produced *Sassy Mamas*, starting with its premiere in 2007. What are some memorable highlights?
So many special women—all the sassy mamas that have done the play—have just been so very special from the very first production, which, [as] I said, was at the Billie Holiday Theatre, directed by Marjorie Moon. And then, of course, it had a very long run in LA with a company called Sparkling City Entertainment. They put together a very wonderful production, with very wonderful actresses, and really, really, really, really worked so

very hard on it, and really, really helped me develop and see the women because they were such great actresses. So that one—and that one also won the NAACP Image Awards.

Yes. They took it to the National Black Theatre Festival.
There, yes, there you go. And they took it to the National Black Theatre Festival, where it sold out before it even went up, and we had four performances. All four performances sold out before the show even went up. When the people heard about it, it was [the] talk of the town in Winston-Salem. And I mean that literally; it was on the news, people were talking about it in restaurants. It was just really wonderful.

The 2021 staging of the historical tragedy *Greenwood: An American Dream Destroyed* by Tulsa, Oklahoma, Theatre North at the Tulsa Performing Arts Center came at a compelling moment in history, the one hundredth anniversary of the horrific destruction of the prosperous Black community. What led you to write this historical drama, and what influenced your approach to the subject?
What led me to write it was maybe some twenty years ago. It started out as a skit in my church, Miracle Center Church. My pastor at the time was preaching on neighborhood and community economics. I had just gotten some information on that event from a friend in Tulsa who sent me some tapes and letters and everything from some of the survivors. I thought, well, this may be a good little skit to put together to present for the economic seminar that he was having. So that's what he was praying out of, the twenty-minute skit. Then it went on to be produced in New York by Shades of Truth Theatre with Michael Green. He did a very, very wonderful workshop production. Then *Greenwood* went on to have readings with the Essence of Acting Theatre equity group founded by Lynnie Godfrey. And then, of course, it had a very wonderful production workshop reading at Eugene Lee's Black and Latino Playwrights Celebration, which got it ready for the Tulsa production. After the Tulsa production, Karamu House in Cleveland, Ohio, produced a film version that was shown virtually. They've had some fifty thousand views to date.

The amazing Karamu House in Cleveland. They have had a long history and a lot of celebrities involved in their productions. It's such

an honor to have them take up the work. I hope they actually do a live production also at some point in the future.

I do too. They said that they are, so I do too.

Legacy

We've talked about a lot of plays, a lot of productions, a lot of relationships, a lot of success. What are some of your most satisfying accomplishments as a playwright?

I did the best with what I had. There are a lot of them out there I greatly admire who are better and have done more. But I can say this to writers: Take what you have, and do the best with what you have, and you'll notice you grow, and your legacy starts to grow, and things start to grow without really trying. Do what you feel led you to your writing. If you want to write something, write it, and then see what happens. I think when you're young, you do that; you just step out, you just do things. When you get older, you start to wonder, Well, I don't know . . . will there be an audience for this? Or will there be too many actors or will the budget be too high? Then you get to a stage where you know too much. So now I had gotten to that stage. But now, thank God, I've lived long enough, and I'm coming back around full circle. I'm just doing the best with what I have, just getting out there, putting it out there, enjoying the journey as I do it. And like you said, I've met so many different people [and] formed so many different relationships with so many creative generous people. People who generate things. I can't believe it myself.

You've got a lot of life left in you; there's a lot more writing to do.

Well, we will see. I'm going to try to enjoy and work with things that I have already written and try to get them out there. I don't know if it answered the question or not?

You did. If we put it on a tombstone, it would say, "She did her best and it was enough."

Oh, that's a good word. "She did her best and it was enough."

Celeste Bedford Walker, you are just so talented and so prolific, and I'm so happy to have shared this time with you, to have this

conversation with you. Thank you. Do you have anything else you want to say, any final words before we close?

Well, I just want to thank you, Sandra, for all of the work that you have done with me and helping me to gather my legacy and helping with the book; and of course, the Wittliff; and of course, Texas. God told me a few years ago, "Stick with Texas."

Appendix 1

〜〜〜〜〜

Select List of Works by Celeste Bedford Walker

Stage Plays

1. *Once in a Wifetime* (formerly *Sister, Sister*; produced in 1978)
2. *Smokes Bayou* (produced in 1979)
3. *The Wreckin' Ball* (produced in 1980)
4. *Spirits* (written in 1980; produced in 1981)
5. *Adam and Eve, Revisited* (produced in 1981)
6. *Reunion in Bartersville* (produced in 1983)
7. *Camp Logan* (produced in 1987)
8. *Over Forty* (produced in 1989)
9. *Brothers, Sisters, Husbands and Wives* (produced in 1993)
10. *Noble Lofton, Buffalo Soldier* (produced in 1994)
11. *Praise the Lord, and Raise the Roof!* (produced in 1996)
12. *Jack Yates* (produced in 1996)
13. *Distant Voices* (produced in 1997)
14. *The Boule* (produced in 1997)
15. *Blacks in the Methodist Church* (produced in 1998)
16. *The History of Wheeler Baptist Church* (produced in 1998)
17. *The African Talking Drum* (produced in 1999)
18. *Where My Girls At?* (produced in 1999)
19. *Fabulous African Fables* (produced in 2001)
20. *Reparations Day* (produced in 2001)
21. *Freedom Train* (produced in 2002)
22. *Harlem after Hours* (produced in 2003)
23. *Sassafras Girls* (produced in 2003)
24. *Giants in the Land* (produced in 2004)
25. *Hip Hoppin' the Dream* (produced in 2006)
26. *Sassy Mamas* (produced in 2007)
27. *I, Barbara Jordan* (produced in 2008)
28. *Black Spurs* (produced in 2011)

29. *The Red Blood of War* (produced in 2013)
30. *More Than Christmas* (produced in 2019)
31. *Ne Ne* (produced in 2020)
32. *Greenwood: An American Dream Destroyed* (produced in 2021)
33. *Crossing Lake Pontchartrain* (reading 2022)

Films and Videos

1. *Buffalo Soldier Mutiny* (documentary, special thank-you credit for scenes from *Camp Logan* play, Bauhaus Media Group, 2005)
2. *One More River to Cross: The Redemption of Sam Cooke* (film, story editor, 2012)
3. *The Obama Effect* (film, screenwriter, Arc Entertainment, 2012)
4. *A Star Without a Star (Juanita)* (documentary, writer, Cambridge Players, 2022)

Appendix 2

~~~~~~

Production Histories for Plays in This Collection

Camp Logan

1987: Kuumba House, Houston, TX

1990: Carver Community Center, San Antonio, TX

1990–2004: Mountaintop Touring Company, military installations, colleges, and universities

1991: Billie Holiday Theater, Brooklyn, NY

1991: Kennedy Center, Texas Festival, Washington, DC

1992: Ensemble Theatre, Houston, TX

1993: Claremont McKenna College, Claremont, CA

1994: Victoria Five Theatre, New York, NY

1995: University of Southern California, Los Angeles, CA

1999: Enchanted Rock Pictures and Mountaintop Productions, Austin, TX

2008: Shades of Truth Theatre, Kumble Theater for Performing Arts, New York, NY

2019: Texas State University, San Marcos, TX

Distant Voices

1997: Ensemble Theatre, Houston, TX

Greenwood: An American Dream Destroyed

2015–20: Essence of Acting (dramatic readings)
- ArtsQuest, Bethlehem, PA
- Black and Latino Playwright Celebration (dramatic reading via Zoom), Texas State University, San Marcos, TX
- Metropolitan College (dramatic reading), New York, NY
- Sage Russell College, Troy, NY
- University of Delaware, Newark, DE

2021: Theatre North, Tulsa Fine Arts Center, Tulsa, OK

2021: Karamu House (film), Cleveland, OH

Reunion in Bartersville

1983 (premiere): The New Courage Players, the Carillon Theatre, Houston, TX

1985: Cambridge Players, Los Angeles, CA

1987: Billie Holiday Theatre, Brooklyn, NY

1987: Florida A&M University, Charles Winter Wood Theatre, Tallahasse, FL

1989: Ensemble Theatre, Houston, TX

2009: The Next Generation, Los Angeles, CA

2010: White Plains Performing Arts Center (reading), White Plains, NY

2018: Dunbar Repertory Company, Middletown Arts Center, Middletown, NJ

2019: Black Spectrum Theatre, New York, NY

2019: National Black Theatre Festival, Winston-Salem, NC

Sassy Mamas

2007: Billy Holiday Theatre (premiere), New York, NY

2010: Marcus Center for the Performing Arts, Milwaukee, WI

2014: Sparkling City Entertainment, Theatre Theater, and the Robey Theatre Company, Los Angeles, CA

2015: National Black Theatre Festival (Los Angeles production cast), Gerald Freedman Theatre, Winston-Salem, NC

2016: Ensemble Theatre, Houston, TX

2017: Ensemble Theatre, Houston, TX

2017: Hattiloo Theatre, Memphis, TN

2018: Karamu House, Cleveland, OH

2018: Miami's M Ensemble, Miami, FL

2018: New Horizon Theater, Carnegie Library Auditorium, Pittsburgh, PA

2019: Theatre North, Tulsa Fine Arts Center, Tulsa, OK

2020: Black Spectrum Theatre, New York, NY

2020: Karamu House, Cleveland, OH

Appendix 3

~~~~~~~~~~

Awards and Honors for Plays by Celeste Bedford Walker

Camp Logan

NAACP Beverly Hills / Hollywood Theatre Award for best play, 1994

NAACP Beverly Hills / Hollywood Theatre Award for best playwright, 2013

Distant Voices

Susan Smith Blackburn Prize (finalist, best play), Ensemble Theatre, Houston, TX, 1999–2000

Reunion in Bartersville

Five NAACP Image Awards nominations, win for best supporting actor, Legendary Cambridge Players, Los Angeles, CA, 1985

Four AUDELCO award nominations, win for best actress, Billie Holiday Theatre, Brooklyn, NY, 1987

NAACP Award for best producer, Cambridge Players: The Next Generation, Los Angeles, CA, 2009

AUDELCO award for best revival of a play, Black Spectrum Theatre, New York, NY, 2019

Sassy Mamas

AUDELCO award for best ensemble, H.A.D.L.E.Y. Players, NY, 2014

NAACP Awards for best ensemble, best director, best set design, Sparkling Entertainment, Los Angeles, CA, 2016

BroadwayWorld.com, award for best play / best director, Ensemble Theatre, Houston, TX, 2017

Cleveland Scene Theatre Award for best actress, Karamu House, Cleveland, OH, 2018